British Budgets in Peace and War
1932–1945

A

British Budgets
in Peace and War
1932 · 1945

by B. E. V. Sabine

London
GEORGE ALLEN & UNWIN LTD
RUSKIN HOUSE · MUSEUM STREET

PRINTED IN GREAT BRITAIN
in 10 on 12pt. Times roman
BY BILLIING & SONS LTD
GUILDFORD AND LONDON

Foreword

Mr. Sabine has put us all in his debt by extending the famous series of Mallet and George on British Budgets to cover the 1932–45 period. We have here a series of years covering both peacetime depression and wartime inflation: and also one in which there were four strongly contrasting Chancellors (it may suprise some younger readers, unacquainted with Neville Chamberlain's grasp of financial details, to find him described as the strongest of the four). Above all, it was the heyday of the Keynesian fiscal revolution. We have the truly astonishing contrast between the situation in the Budget of 1933 when Keynes' ideas were scorned, rejected and despised and the watershed year of 1941 when Kingsley Wood's Budget not only set out the government accounts against the background of those for the economy as a whole but also incorporated detailed ideas associated with Keynes. 'Blest was it in that dawn to be alive. . . .', and most especially before some of its more unwelcome chickens had come home to roost.

Many readers—economists, historians, students of government and others—will find features of absorbing interest in this account. One which struck me very forcibly was the ability of the Revenue to adopt and absorb PAYE at the height of the war. This immediately prompts the question: why has it been so much more difficult to adjust to Corporation Tax and Capital Gains Tax in recent years? Some future researcher will surely have a ready made topic here. And those who might think that a history of Budgets is inevitably dry-as-dust should be disabused straightaway. There are many light and engaging touches in this account. Future philosophers will surely smile to recollect that in the middle of the greatest war in history, the Mother of Parliaments could solemnly devote a measurable segment of its time to the taxability of the parson's Easter Offering—illustrated with references to the problems of the Rev. A. D. Light and the Rev. O. Howe Boring.

It has been a fashionable pastime in the post-war world to deride the annual Budget as an outworn relic, no longer needed in a world where 'fine tuning' can be practised by the economist-organ builder. Readers of this book will realise why such a view is fallacious and why the Budget is likely to remain a unique economic and political event in each and every year.

April 1970   A. R. PREST
                          Stanley Jevons Professor of Political Economy,
                                       University of Manchester

Introduction

As with my first book, I must begin by thanking the Board of Inland Revenue for permission to write a political history of the peace and war Budgets from 1933 to 1945. I must thank also my colleagues in the Department for their co-operation and for help from the Quarterly Journal of the Association of Inspectors of Taxes and from *Taxes*, the journal of the Inland Revenue Staff Federation.

I am grateful to the libraries of Manchester, Stalybridge and Stockport for their help, and to the Board's Library, especially Miss Williams.

My typist, Miss F. V. Whitehead, must have breathed a sigh of relief after deciphering the last page of manuscript and dealing with the last item on the index. She has throughout been invaluable both in transcription and general assistance.

Finally I must pay a tribute to my long-suffering family who have lived with the book almost as much as I have over the past three years.

May 1967–May 1970   B. E. V. SABINE
Mottram-in-Longdendale, Cheshire

Preface

In 1933 there was published the third of a series of volumes on British Budgets by Sir Bernard Mallet and C. Oswald George, covering the period 1921–22 to 1932–33, that is, ending with Neville Chamberlain's first Budget of 1932. The previous volumes were British Budgets 1887–88 to 1912–13 by Bernard Mallet as he then was, and British Budgets 1913–14 to 1920–21 by the same two authors as the third series. Sir Bernard Mallet, however, died on October 28, 1932, just before the publication of the last volume, and C. Oswald George did not continue them. Since then British Budgets, while they have not gone uncriticized or unremarked by any means, have gone unrecorded.

This is a great pity since they provide valuable raw material for any modern history with a fiscal slant: and very few histories these days have not. The avowed intention of the two collaborators was to give condensed but, as far as possible, readable accounts of each separate budget speech with the discussions which accompanied it and to bring out, by quotations or summaries, the opposing arguments of the main matters at issue in the debates. The balance between direct and indirect taxation is indicated, but more explanation is given of the former as being the more complex. This seems an admirable method and one which any successor should try to follow.

There is one further point. The two earlier volumes of British Budgets are a more searching commentary on the fiscal scene than the last because they were written, although by no means obviously so, with the help of a certain amount of hindsight. As the authors approached contemporary history their judgments became rather more tentative: indeed they gave no considered opinion on the 1932 Budget at all, but simply say 'Here we take leave of a Budget the result of which is still in the future.'[1] It is fair to say, however, that they had become increasingly pessimistic about a fiscal system which, despite its high degree of perfection in the production of revenue, has begun at last 'to show signs of inability to respond to ever-increasing demands'.[2] The theory of 'taxation for revenue

[1] *British Budgets*, Vol. III, p. 424.   [2] *British Budgets*, Vol. III, p. vi.

only' is tacitly lamented and the future is seen as a struggle to find 'some practical compromise between the two seemingly incompatible ideas of capitalism and socialism'.[1] The final prospects were gloomy indeed: they emphasized 'the extreme difficulty under existing conditions of any further increase in the burden of taxation without a fatal reaction in the industrial production of the nation upon which both the national income and the revenue derived from it must ultimately depend'.[2] The authors were not to know that within a decade income tax receipts would top the £1,000 millions mark, well over twice the level they had then considered catastrophic.

For the fascination of fiscal history in the period from 1933 to 1945 lies in the almost melodramatic contrast between the cautious and orthodox budgeting of the limited recovery period from 1931 to 1935, the gradual acceleration of armament expenditure symbolized by one of the taxes which subsidized it, the National Defence Contribution, and the spectacular flowering of all-out taxation in 1941. These three phases merge into one another to some extent, and, looking back, they can be seen as a gradual ascent to the total fiscal effort demanded by total war. But all this was far in the future as Neville Chamberlain, with his 1932 Budget behind him, began that collation of advice from his experts and of suggestions and pressures from outside the House which would in due course emerge as his second Budget.

[1] *British Budgets*, Vol. III, p. viii.   [2] *British Budgets*, Vol. III, p. viii.

Contents

Chapter I

The Finance Bill 1933

THE SHADOW OF SNOWDEN

Time Table:

It was 3.22 p.m. on Tuesday, April 25, 1933, when Neville Chamberlain rose to present the second Budget of his current tenure of office as Chancellor of the Exchequer.[1] There had been no dramatic pre-Budget speculations from the financial experts but the occasion still held its old attraction. The public had swarmed into the galleries as soon as prayers were over and filled them to capacity. The weather was unsettled but mild, which was fortunate as it meant his old enemy, gout, was quiescent. He was wont to say that his father was a man of strongly marked personal characteristics ranging from the wearing of a monocle to a predisposition to gout, and he bequeathed some of these characteristics to his sons. Austen, his half-brother, coming first into the world, had the first pick, choosing the monocle and leaving him with the gout.

Many of the situations and conditions which the Chancellor had had to take into account in framing his statement were both complicated and obscure. The catastrophic events of 1931, the collapse of Continental credit, the May Committee's suggestions for economy and the transfer of financial alarm to this country were still fresh in everyone's mind. The long haul back to recovery, beginning with the puritanical severity of Snowden's Finance (No. 2) Act of 1931, the problem of the unemployed and the shadow of the war debt were the three major factors he had to consider; and the context of the 1933 Budget is a stage in that change in fiscal policy which had begun two years ago with the National Government.

Chamberlain commenced by announcing a Budget deficit of £32 millions; and he proposed 'to follow the example of Lord Snowden' and meet the deficit by borrowing. This deficit had derived principally from a short fall of £12 millions in Customs and Excise receipts and one of £15½ millions in Inland Revenue dues, the latter arising from a drop in arrears caused by 'the patriotic action of the taxpayers in the year before, who had not only paid their taxes with extraordinary punctuality but so greatly facilitated the assessments that there was very little to collect in the year following'.

The Chancellor then turned to 'the other side of the account'. The original estimate for Supply Services augmented by £18 millions extra needed for unemployment benefits and scaled down by a series of minor economies,[2] amounted to £458 millions. The Fixed Debt Charge had been restricted by the Finance Act 1932 to £308 millions.

[1] He had been Chancellor of the Exchequer from August 1923, to January 1924.
[2] H. 25/4/1933, Col. 35.

These two figures totalled in the round £777 millions as against receipts of £745 millions, that is, the deficit as announced of £32 millions. In fact, the Chancellor had been unlucky: the rise in gilts following the War Loan conversion of the previous year had reduced by nearly half the statutory Sinking Fund requirement, and the cost of interest had also been materially reduced by a supplementary operation. The saving here was close on £26 million, but before Christmas 1932 the Government found itself obliged to make provision for the repayment of 90 million dollars to the United States, which was to be met out of Budget revenue.[1] The windfall of £26 million was thereby more than absorbed and recourse was had to borrowing some £2½ million on account of National Savings Certificates interest.[2]

It was now the turn of the Exchange Equalization Fund. This had been announced in the 1932 Budget, when the old Exchange account had been wound up, with initial resources of £150 million. Its main purpose was to give the Government, through the Bank of England, adequate reserves of gold and foreign exchange, both to make the internal monetary system independent of foreign balances and to deal effectively with either the inflow or outflow of capital and gold. Later in his statement[3] the Chancellor claimed justifiably that the new mechanism had 'stood the test of experience in spite of some rather severe financial storms and a great deal of surging to and fro of the waves of capital'. It would be necessary, he went on to say, to make an addition to its resources and in fact these were increased by a further £200 millions. This augmentation was combined 'taking advantage of the present cheapness of money' with a further instalment of conversion. 'Taking leave of the year that has passed I think we may say it is one of substantial achievement.' But what of the future? The Supply Service estimates totalled over £463 millions and the Consolidated Fund Services over £234 millions, making a grand total of nearly £698 millions. This contrasted very favourably with the figure of £785 millions of 1931: not only was it a reduction of £88 millions but a further £25 millions relating to pensions, housing and unemployment grants had been absorbed, making a real saving of £113 millions, nearly half of which was due to the saving on interest. The balance arose from 'economies in other directions'.

[1] H. 14/12/1932.   [2] Authorized by S.29, FA.1928.
[3] H. 25/4/1933, Cols 46/27.

It was just as well the estimates showed a reduction since Chamberlain proceeded to explain he was faced with a contraction in revenue. The Customs and Excise levies, comprising beer duty, spirit duty, liquor licences and import duties were estimated to bring in £281 millions, £7 millions down on the previous year. Receipts from the Inland Revenue, which included income tax, surtax, death duties, stamps and land tax, together with arrears, were also estimated at a diminished yield, including a reduction of £11½ millions for income tax and £10 millions for surtax, at £390 millions. Miscellaneous items, including motor vehicle duties and the Post Office, were reckoned to produce a revenue of close on £42 millions. The total estimated revenue was almost £713 millions.

The Chancellor was now nearly half-way through his speech to the Committee, and it was time to announce the changes in taxation. Minor changes were a steep reduction from £1 per cent to ten shillings in the duty upon the raising of new capital, and a realistic reduction in interest on arrears of death duties and Excess Profits Duty to 3 per cent.[1] The taxation of Co-operative Societies was then briefly touched upon. This was a very sore subject indeed, and in fact discussions on the matter were then in process both with representatives of the Co-operative Societies and of ordinary traders in an attempt to reach some compromise agreement before the introduction of the Finance Bill. This had not proved to be possible and it was not proposed to table a resolution dealing with the matter that day. When, however, suggested legislation was put forward, it was to arouse passion more bitter than from any other single proposal.

But that was all in the future as the Chancellor proceeded to complete his Customs and Excise proposals, a small increase on matches and lighters, the application of the Import Duty Act machinery to the silk and artificial silk industry, and the 'interesting but minor item' of a 6s 0d surtax on British sparkling wines. Two 'taxes on locomotion', to use the old eighteenth-century phrase, were however more significant. The first was in effect a duty of a penny per gallon on heavy hydro-carbon oils which operated by reducing the rebate on these oils, which had been 8d, the full amount of the duty, to 7d. The second was the imposition of substantial increases in the taxation of heavier goods vehicles somewhat on the lines recommended by the Salter Report of 1930.

[1] On death duties the rate had been 4 per cent but on E.P.D. 4½ per cent.

Such were the increases. There was, however, one concession to be made. 'A source of revenue,' as Chamberlain put it, 'which has brought comfort to many of my predecessors has now been seriously undermined.' He was referring to the beer duty which, despite recent increases, had steadily dropped in yield: 'nobody in my position could view that situation without concern'. He had considered the advisability of reducing the duty last year but had decided against it; now he could afford to wait no longer and proposed to take a penny per pint off beer, coupling this with a promise from the Brewers' Society to raise the gravity of their beers by at least two degrees, and to use more home-grown barley.

This concession would cost an estimated £14 millions, or roughly five-sixths of the disposable surplus. It was not to be expected then that there would be any spectacular change in direct taxation unless the Chancellor was willing deliberately to unbalance his Budget. There had been some pressure for him to do this, 'supported by eminent economists, powerful journalists and some Hon. Members of the House'. The reference was to a series of letters to *The Times* initiated by Keynes:[1] the suggestion was that taxation should be relieved by £50 millions more than the estimated revenue, this sum to be recovered over a series of Budgets. Chamberlain was dead against this policy: 'I say at once that I am not prepared to take that course'; and he devoted over four columns of Hansard[2] to 'the reasons which have led me to a decision that the proposal cannot be entertained'.

Briefly these reasons were as follows. He was not dismissing the proposal on account of its unorthodoxy, but he certainly would not presume to forecast what might happen over the next three years: 'If I were to pretend I could lay out a programme under which what I borrowed this year would be met by a surplus at the end of three years, everyone would very soon perceive that I was only resorting to the rather transparent device of making an unbalanced Budget look respectable.' Again he was doubtful whether the stimulus of reduced direct taxation would be as effective as the advocates of unbalancing thought since 'we are not immune from those grim forces that hold the world in their grip . . . world trade shrinking and world prices falling . . .'. Finally, from a traditional viewpoint, no

---

[1] *The Times* 5/4/1933 and 27/4/1933.   [2] H. 25/4/1933, Cols 57/61.

finance minister had ever deliberately unbalanced his budget when he possessed the means of balancing it.

Chamberlain then expounded his credo. 'Look round the world today and you will see that badly unbalanced Budgets are the rule rather than the exception. Everywhere there appear Budget deficits piling up: yet they do not produce those favourable results which it is claimed would happen to us. On the contrary I find that Budget deficits repeated year after year may be accompanied by a deepening depression and a constantly falling price level. Before we embark on so dangerous a course as that, let us reflect upon this indisputable fact. Of all the countries passing through these difficult times. the one that has stood the test with the greatest measure of success is the United Kingdom. Without underrating the hardships of our situation, the long tragedy of the unemployed, the grievous burden of taxation, the arduous and painful struggle of those engaged in trade and industry, at any rate we are free from that fear which besets so many less fortunately placed, the fear that things are going to get worse. We owe our freedom from that fear largely to the fact that we have balanced our Budget. By following a sound financial policy we have been enabled to secure low interest rates for industry and it would be the height of folly to throw away that advantage. If we were to reverse our policy just at the moment when other governments are striving to follow our example and balance their Budgets after experience of the policy we are now asked to adopt we would stultify ourselves in the eyes of the world and forfeit in a moment the respect with which we are regarded today.'

This passage was the highlight of the Chancellor's statement, the last few minutes being something of an anti-climax. He had already mentioned[1] that he was not making any provision for Debt redemption this year and the obligatory Sinking Fund, which stood at roughly £7½ millions, would be borrowed. It only remained to announce the reversion to the old half-yearly system of payment of tax under Schedules B, D and E, instead of taxpayers having to find three-quarters of the tax in January and the balance in July. This postponement of receipt of revenue would cost £12 millions but it would be nearly covered by a Depreciation Fund attached to the 5 per cent War Loan amounting to £10 millions, now no longer required. The final surplus thus became just over £1¼ million. His

[1] H. 25/4/1933, Col. 54.

Budget was, he thought, in conclusion, 'if not a startling or a spectacular Budget, it was at least an honest one'. It had taken some two hours and ten minutes to expound.

The custom had grown up in the past few years before 1933 that the House should adjourn very early after the Budget statement and that Members should not indulge in any survey of the proposals or, still less, in any general consideration of the state of the nation. George Lansbury, however, the Leader of the Labour Party, was not disposed to support this comparatively recent tradition, apart from the customary formal compliments upon the matter and manner of the speech. He launched a bitter attack on the superficial characteristics of the Budget: 'the people who will benefit are those who drink beer and who pay income tax. The unemployed, to whom the Right Hon. Gentleman owes the fact that he has balanced his Budget or that he has brought it so near balancing as he could, are to receive no benefit whatsoever.' This neglect of the unemployed was emphasized by the threat to tax the Co-operative Societies following the report of the Raeburn Committee; and the penny off beer would only benefit those who could afford to drink it.

Sir Herbert Samuel, the Liberal Leader, however, was content to revert to tradition. In twenty years of Budgets he had not heard one to excel this in 'lucidity and conciseness' and although rather pedestrian, a theme he would be prepared to develop later, the conditions of the time did not, he agreed, 'provoke any flights of Pegasus'. An eager back-bencher[1] wound up the formal proceedings for the day.

When the public opened its newspapers on the following day, the general line was seen to be qualified approval. The popular dailies concentrated mainly on the reduction in the beer duty (although it was the *New Statesman* which hit upon 'small beer' as a headline). The reception from the quality dailies was mixed. *The Times*[2] thought a sound and orthodox Budget had been proposed by a sound and orthodox Chancellor, although he had not shown 'the imaginative qualities of a financial genius'. The Chancellor was faced with two seemingly intractable problems—the fall in the yield of direct taxation and the necessity for reducing public expenditure. These two problems interacted upon each other and this was why, in

[1] Hon. R. D. Denman.   [2] 26/4/1933.

the circumstances, Chamberlain had not made up his mind either to apply 'the anodyne of inflation or the virtue of retrenchment'.

The *Manchester Guardian*,[1] looking further below the surface than *The Times*, preferred to find itself surprised that, given his canons of caution, the Chancellor had risked as much as he had since it was by no means an orthodox Budget or, if fiscal canons were pressed hard, a sound Budget; the reference here was clearly to the minor borrowings which had buttressed the small surplus.

The weeklies were critical but not constructive. The *New Statesman* said that audacious new departures in the realm of finance could hardly have been expected; an unbalanced Budget was never on the cards. It commented on the 'remarkable efficiency in tax-gathering' and suggested that the taxation of Co-operative Societies was a mistake. *The Economist* agreed that Chamberlain had done his not very imaginative best with measures that were 'half Draconian, half prodigal', but both expressed fears for the future if the national income did not expand.

Having run its course of criticism in the Press that morning, the Budget endured its first baptism of fire from the House during the afternoon and evening. In all some twenty Members spoke and the debate continued until 11 p.m. when the Financial Secretary, Hore-Belisha, was cut off in full flight.

The two opening speeches were the two set pieces from Attlee, the Labour Party spokesman on finance, and Samuel, the Liberal leader, respectively. Both concerned themselves with the question of whether the Budget was in fact balanced. The former was emphatic that it was not; according to his arithmetic, which tended to blur the distinction between capital and revenue, there was a deficit of some £75 millions;[2] some of the fallacies in his reckoning were, however, later exposed by Samuel[3] in a succeeding speech. But far more serious was his point that the Chancellor's gratification at the high prices of Government stocks and the very low rate of interest ignored the possibility that this was indicative of trade stagnation since it betrayed the existence of a mass of money which could not find profitable investment; and this mass would only be increased by the relief given to income tax payers. It was a hard-hitting speech concluding with 'The Budget is a confession of the bankruptcy of the capitalist system.'

[1] 26/4/1933.   [2] H. 26/4/1933, Cols 107/109.   [3] H. 26/4/1933, Cols 118/119.

Samuel commenced by congratulating Chamberlain on not having listened to 'evil advisers' and unbalanced his Budget; and, as mentioned, he thought Attlee's deficit total of £75 millions was 'fantastic'. But he had two very serious complaints. In particular, the relief which had been given to the beer duty should have gone to the unemployed, for whom nothing had been done. In effect, he said scathingly, 'the Sinking Fund has been suspended in order to reduce the beer duty' or, in other words, with a typical stroke of Samuel's wry humour, 'the fixed charges have been reduced in order to increase the liquid assets'. The second complaint was that in general the hopes of recovery which the Government had confidently held out in the autumn and winter of 1932 had not been fulfilled; and, as a Liberal Leader should, he mentioned that one of the main reasons was the introduction of protection which had neither been a good revenue raiser nor an aid to the recovery of world trade; in fact it had contributed to a general shrinkage of world trade and cost more revenue than it had brought.

After the speeches of the two leaders, the rest of the contributions for the evening tended to be a trifle pedestrian and predictable. Steel-Maitland[1] and Mabane[2] both required a bolder Budget policy to help in the modernization of industry; the present level of profits was too small. The former suggested 'there could be an arrangement which would give relief to industrial reserves', but he remained delightfully vague about the means of achieving this. The latter was far more specific: he maintained the stimulus to industrial development would come from a lightening of direct taxation: 'a straight cut of 6d in the Income Tax' would create the necessary expansion and simultaneously reduce unemployment. Sir William Davison,[3] Chairman of the Income Tax Payers' Society, thought the same. 'The springs of direct taxation,' he declared, 'are drying up,' and there was no chance of a revival of trade with 'the millstone of war taxation tied round the neck of industry'.

There was no denying the fact that even with a shilling on income tax, a 35 per cent increase in surtax and one of 9 per cent on estate duty, there was only the same yield of revenue; the Chancellor had recognized the facts in the case of beer although his suggested decrease had a mixed reception. Cross,[4] in a maiden speech, said

[1] H. 26/4/1933, Cols 136/142.   [2] H. 26/4/1933, Cols 201/209.
[3] H. 26/4/1933, Cols 180/185.   [4] H. 26/4/1933, Cols 142/147.

enthusiastically that 'it was all he had hoped for'; Pike[1] emphasized again that the basic reason for the reduction in duty had been the decline in revenue but rather spoilt the force of his speech by getting mixed up with the price of Chinese eggs and admitting that he was not an expert in financial matters. Rutherford,[2] in another maiden speech, made the same point, but he was all for 2d a pint off, not a mere 1d, a plea echoed by Major Nathan.[3] It was left to Lady Astor[4] to present the case against the reduction; in doing so she inevitably presented the case against drinking beer at all. 'The drink trade is powerful and organized. It fights a horrid fight. I have had to fight it all my life. . . . We are in the midst of a national financial and world crisis, and we have a national Budget which is a Brewers' Budget.'

Beer and unemployment—these two topics recurred again and again during the first day's debate, especially from the Labour benches in speeches which made up in warmth and humanity what they lacked in immediate relevance to the issues in dispute. Kirkwood,[5] for instance, was rebuked from the Chair for being too diffuse, and the contributions of Tinker,[6] Davies[7] and Logan[8] were essentially pieces of special pleading on behalf of the victims of world depression. Davies probably epitomized the sentiments of all four when he said that the Government should try to translate its handiwork into human terms. 'Let me try to picture conditions in a small town in my own division with 6,500 inhabitants where there were once flourishing ironworks, coalpits and some textile factories. For three-and-a-half years not a wheel has turned there. It is as difficult to find in that township today a person who is employed as it was to find a person unemployed during the War. What is there in this Budget for anyone living in such a town? Nothing: no hope.'

Other speakers, such as Nathan,[9] reverted to Samuel's thesis that it was not possible to have an expansionist Budget and tariffs: 'the Chancellor could not have both revenue and trade.' But only one member, Colonel Wedgwood,[10] revealed himself as an out-and-out unbalancer in the interests of what he called 'the Haussemanising of England'. The proposed tax on heavy vehicles was the subject of

[1] H. 26/4/1933, Cols 210/214.
[2] H. 26/4/1933, Cols 157/159.
[3] H. 26/4/1933, Col. 163.
[4] H. 26/4/1933, Cols 167/171.
[5] H. 26/4/1933, Cols 147/157.
[6] H. 26/4/1933, Cols 185/188.
[7] H. 26/4/1933, Cols 194/201.
[8] H. 26/4/1933, Cols 218/225.
[9] H. 26/4/1933, Cols 159/165.
[10] H. 26/4/1933, Cols 171/180.

an attack by Shute[1] who feared its effect on increasing transport costs for Liverpool's dock traffic. And finally there were the ominous signs of a full-scale attack and an equally unrelenting defence in relation to the entrenched position of the Co-operative Societies. Peto[2] claimed their profits were taxable on the law as it then stood. Macquisten[3] made a circumstantial case out concerning bribery and corruption in the Societies. But the real struggle was not to come until the following month.

This summary of the first day's debate shows clearly enough that there was no concerted criticism of any one specific Budget proposal and the Financial Secretary to the Treasury[4] found himself with so little to answer that he must have thought he had even less as he failed to provide himself with enough time to finish his speech before 11 p.m. when the Chairman left the Chair. He was, however, able to claim with some justification that 'within living memory there had never been, in times of peace, a Budget which had evoked so little hostility as this one and to the proposals of which so few alternatives have been forthcoming'.

The debate on the following day was curiously uneven in quality. Of the minor speakers half expressed themselves wholly in favour of the Chancellor's proposals, although not always for the same reason. Gillett[5] congratulated him on not having unbalanced his Budget but was uneasy about the burden of tax on industry. Lord Apsley[6] thought the Chancellor had made the best of a bad job; he had some interesting suggestions to make in the interests of economy including the formation of a super-Cabinet and the reform of the Civil Service, a point which was echoed by Mason.[7] Both Colonel Gretton[8] (understandably) and Boulton[9] praised the reduction in the beer duty and the relief to income tax payers but put in general pleas for economy. These pleas incidentally were no doubt influenced by the fact that the Press had complained in the debate of the day before the word economy was not mentioned. Both these items had been proposed by the Labour Party in 1932, as Stewart[10] pointed out with some satisfaction. Balfour[11] and Rentoul[12] paid their

[1] H. 26/4/1933, Cols 183/185.
[2] H. 26/4/1933, Cols 188/194.
[3] H. 26/4/1933, Cols 225/231.
[4] H. 26–27/4/1933, Cols 231/237, 265/267.
[5] H. 27/4/1933, Cols 307/309.
[6] H. 27/4/1933, Cols 323/331.
[7] H. 27/4/1933, Cols 340/345.
[8] H. 27/4/1933, Cols 333/337.
[9] H. 27/4/1933, Cols 345/351.
[10] H. 27/4/1933, Cols 361/366.
[11] H. 27/4/1933, Cols 370/372.
[12] H. 27/4/1933, Cols 372/376.

'humble tribute' and 'respectful tribute' to the Chancellor respectively; the former had a sensible proposal that an attempt should be made by the Ministry of Labour to halt 'the present uncontrolled and unscientific migration of labour from the North to the South'; the latter was mainly concerned with economies on a substantial scale in public expenditure. Hales[1] summarized the back-bench feeling: 'the Chancellor has successfully avoided the Scylla of Stamp and the Charybdis of Keynes . . . it is a common sense and careful Budget'. Only Stourton[2] was willing to play the part of candid friend: a more expansionist policy was needed; he would suggest a shilling cut in income tax, budgeting for three years, controlled reflation and a stimulus to expenditure on capital goods. 'The longer we follow the disciples of orthodoxy, the deeper we shall sink into the morass of stagnation.'

There were, of course, some more specialized comments. Lambert[3] emphasized the weight of direct taxation and that an increase in rates would mean a drop in absolute receipts. He incorporated in his general pleas for economy a plea for the repeal of the land taxes, a ghostly echo of Snowdenian battles of a few years ago. Leonard[4] fired the first shots in a defence of the Co-operative Societies in reply to Macquisten's attack of the previous day (see p. 21). Boyce[5] found the Chancellor's proposals for increased taxation of commercial vehicles fell very far short of the Salter Committee's recommendations; the sooner this form of transport was on a self-supporting basis the better. There were also two Labour speeches in the classic socialist tradition. Charles Brown[6] gave a fair summary of the two days' debate and asserted that none of the proposals 'would touch what is fundamentally wrong with the society in which we live'. There was declining trade, declining revenue and increasing unemployment; statistical tables proving recovery must be misleading when savings could not receive a profitable outlet and when there was still 'that mass of povery, of want, of despair'. Morgan Jones's[7] speech was complementary: the Chancellor had not faced the problem with which the nation was confronted, namely the question of unemployment. Reduction of taxation was not the way;

[1] H. 27/4/1933, Cols 359/361. [2] H. 27/4/1933, Cols 366/370.
[3] H. 27/4/1933, Cols 289/295. [4] H. 27/4/1933, Cols 295/301.
[5] H. 27/4/1933, Cols 331/333. [6] H. 27/4/1933, Cols 351/359.
[7] H. 27/4/1933, Cols 376/386.

a similar supposed panacea in 1925 had been completely unsuccessful, and this was not the way to change the relative distribution of
wealth between rich and poor; it was a 'bung and bunk' Budget and
showed the statesmanship of the Government as 'utterly bankrupt'.

There three main speeches of the day, however, were from Cripps,
Amery and Bevan. Cripps[1] was in his most belligerent anti-capitalist
mood. 'I suppose it is true that this is probably the dullest and the
gloomiest Budget that this House has debated for years,' he commenced; but this he thought was inevitable as there were 'painfully
few alternatives' under capitalism. 'The brewer, the beer drinker and
the income tax payer are given the preference by that system over
the unemployed and the low-wage earner.' Deflation was simply
resulting in the accumulation of profits and he maintained 'the first
charge on any surplus which appeared in any Budget should go to the
unemployed'.

Amery[2] caught the Chairman's eye immediately after Cripps.
He could not follow the previous speaker's definition of capitalism:
the Co-operative Societies were both capitalistic and competitive; all
the Government was attempting was to secure fair treatment for all
retail traders now that the remissions of early days were no longer
justified. The Budget, he thought, had a dual function. It was an
item in the normal housekeeping of the state, but it was also a vital
factor in the whole economic situation. The country was running
periously near to overtaxation and to destroying the elasticity of
revenue. The unemployment crisis was similar to a military crisis;
borrowing and a certain remission of income tax would stimulate
industry and relieve unemployment. If the Chancellor persisted in
'the kind of fiscal rectitude which was normal in the Gladstonian
period' we might find that 'policies far more desperate and unvirtuous
than anything I have suggested will presently be adopted'.

Bevan,[3] however, was convinced relief of taxation was no panacea:
there was already an abundance of money but industry was not an
attractive investment. Nor was launching into public works subsidized by borrowing, as Amery had suggested, or increased taxation
any solution, although it would at least provide employment; it
would not solve the root problem of a fall in production coupled with
an increase in profits which was producing these unusable surpluses.

[1] H. 27/4/1933, Cols 268/279.   [2] H. 27/4/1933, Cols 279/289.
[3] H. 27/4/1933, Cols 309/323.

He was sorry for the Chancellor: 'his advisers are offering quack remedies'. Not that the speaker could offer any solution given the current economic nexus: 'the whole system of private profits has failed to produce the wealth the Chancellor can tax', and he summarized his conclusions on the proposals with 'as you are making the economic system more intolerable, you have to make the proletariat more drunk'.

Chamberlain[1] was in good form when he rose to reply to the debate at 10.37 p.m. Like his Hon. Friend the Financial Secretary the previous night, he was really embarrassed at having so little to reply to. He repeated that it would not pay the country to have an unbalanced Budget, that the reduction in beer duty would increase the actual revenue and the income tax relief afforded would increase the amount of circulating cash. Import duties were a remedy for unemployment for they would 'transfer work from the foreigner to this country', and tariffs were useful for negotiations with foreign countries 'which had not hitherto paid very much attention to our suggestions'. In less than twenty minutes he had disposed of the Opposition to his own satisfaction and the few members of his own party such as Amery, forlorn in his advocacy of unbalancing, and Stourton ('if there were a last ditch he would be found in it'). He was equally successful when the Resolutions were reported early in May.[2] In reply to Mabane's Resolution[3] amendment to reduce income tax by 6d he said,[4] almost playfully, in the language of *1066 and All That*, a decrease in income tax would be 'a good thing' but 'Chancellors of the Exchequer cannot rely on the forming of a Budget on psychology; they must have finance to go on'.

By May 17th, when the debate on the Seocnd Reading took place, the Opposition had regrouped its small forces for a renewed offensive; but the general line of attack showed little change from those vainly deployed in the exchanges of the previous month.[5]

Morgan Jones[6] moved the amendment: 'no provision had been made for reducing the unjust sacrifices imposed upon the unemployed'; the incidence of taxation generally had swung away from direct to indirect, and there was a failure to deal with fundamental financial and economic issues. These three themes were echoed by

[1] H. 27/4/1933, Cols 386/391
[2] H. 2/5/1933, Cols 681/819.
[3] H. 2/5/1933, Cols 793/797.
[4] H. 2/5/1933, Cols 804/808.
[5] E.g. 27/4/1933.
[6] H. 17/5/1933, Cols 369/380.

subsequent speakers on the Labour benches. Tom Smith[1] maintained that thousands of good men and women were being driven to despair, and both he and Tinker[2] reiterated the socialist virtues of direct as opposed to indirect taxation. Brown[3] summarized: 'the solution of the problem we have to face will never be reached until by some alteration in the general economic system you are able to give back again in ever-increasing volume to those who produce wealth, that wealth which their labours call into existence'. Cripps,[4] in a long speech, the last before the winding up, developed the concept which he was currently disposed to air, that the Budget could not save the capitalist system which was the root cause of the unemployment problem. Surely, he said, a more rapid circulation of money would be achieved by aiding the poor, not the rentier class; but the policy of the Government, instead of public works, which he suggested, was 'to give money to the income tax payers and hope they would do something useful with it'.

The Government supporters contributed their own peculiar brands of financial orthodoxy. Sir A. M. Samuel[5] presented the orthodox back-bench view that the country was now labouring under 'the curse of the type of finance' brought about by Snowden; taxation could be increased no more; the bill since 1918 was already £18,000 millions; and the only remedy was reduction of expenditure. Palmer[6] advocated a complementary cut in taxation with a restoration of the decrease which had been made in the social services; Goodman,[7] however, considered it was not possible to reconcile these two conflicting policies. Three other Government supporters, Harris,[8] Smithers[9] and Allen,[10] maintained that the country would find its salvation through economic recovery, signs of which were already present, although there was still, an echo of the Test Match series of 1932–33, 'body-line bowling to face'.

There was also a considerable amount of informed criticism of the increase in the oil tax, since it would inflate industrial costs and hinder the promising development of the diesel engine as well as the motor transport industry which was already penalized by the

[1] H. 17/5/1933, Cols 393/401. [2] H. 17/5/1933, Cols 426/431.
[3] H. 17/5/1933, Cols 356/463. [4] H. 17/5/1933, Cols 472/483.
[5] H. 17/5/1933, Cols 380/390. [6] H. 17/5/1933, Cols 409/410.
[7] H. 17/5/1933, Cols 431/433. [8] H. 17/5/1933, Cols 390/395.
[9] H. 17/5/1933, Cols 410/417. [10] H. 17/5/1933, Cols 437/443.

proposed increase in duty on goods vehicles. Strickland[1] quoted the case of the vehicle which had carried the rudder of the *Berengaria*, the tax on which would now be £1,367 instead of £66. O'Connor[2] protested that the rudder should have been taken by sea, but was politely informed that as it was forged in Sheffield this would have been a matter of some difficulty. But perhaps the most picturesque reason for criticism was Wise's,[3] who deplored its effect on the travelling showman.

But there was nothing new in any of these arguments and neither Chamberlain[4] nor his Financial Secretary, Hore-Belisha,[5] were troubled. The former intervened at 6.38 p.m. and spoke for half an hour. He had been accused by the Opposition on three counts: failure to redress the inequitable financial sacrifices by the unemployed, laying the heaviest burdens on those least able to bear them, and having no effective policy for the restoration of trade and employment. In reply, he argued that his policy over the beer duty and income tax was correct, and the actual benefit paid to the unemployed had effectively risen because of the increase in the purchasing power or money; although, as McGovern pointed out, 27s 3d for a married man with two children was not a tremendous sum. He was emphatic that 'no policy (for the restoration of trade) which can be effective can be embodied in the Finance Bill, as this country could not be an oasis of prosperity amid world depression'. Hore-Belisha summarized in his winding-up. £697½ millions were needed; £16 millions more than had in fact been found. Direct taxation has reached its limit; even Snowden had admitted this,[6] and indirect taxation was not so inequitable since half of it was imposed on luxuries. Finally, more than half the social expenditure, £244 millions out of £463 millions 'was spent directly on the working classes'.

So far the attitudes taken by the protagonists on either side had been predictable and to that extent the debate had not generated any great heat. But now, as already hinted, tempers were to flare over the issue of taxing Co-operative Societies although it is difficult to appreciate, at this remove, how this issue could have been so explosive.

Up to 1933, Co-operative Societies were liable under Schedules A

[1] H. 17/5/1933, Cols 450/456. [2] H. 17/5/1933, Cols 463/472.
[3] H. 17/5/1933, Cols 448/450. [4] H. 17/5/1933, Cols 417/426.
[5] H. 17/5/1933, Cols 483/490. [6] H. 11/2/1931, Col. 447.

and B only, the umbrella of mutuality covering their trading transactions, and this exemption had enabled the infant societies, fathered
by the Rochdale Pioneers, to grow and prosper. Now their success
seemed to constitute a menace to the ordinary retail trader although
at the same time a tribute to working-class enterprise. Thus any
attempt to tax the Co-operative Societies' profits on equitable
grounds instantly provoked a strong political reaction and very
few members of either side could approach the issue with proper
detachment. This accounts for the fury of the debate on May 22,
1933, which lasted over seven hours, took up 127 columns of Hansard[1] and pulled 22 members to thier feet.

Chamberlain[2] opened in his usual reasonable fashion. The Raeburn Committee, set up in 1932 to enquire into the present position
of Co-operative Societies, had recommended, briefly, that the Societies' profits should be taxed, dividends[3] being allowed as a trade
expense. The Societies, however, were not prepared to accept, although Chamberlain had discussed the matter with them in person
and had been criticized for doing so.[4] Compromise having failed,
he was now preparing the repeal of Section 39(4) of the Income Tax
Act 1918 which had exempted the income of Co-operative Societies
trading with members from taxation.[5] This was not penal legislation; it simply put the Societies in the same position as other
traders.

Cripps[6] opened for the defence: the proposed legislation was penal,
not revenue-producing, and amounted to an attack by private
enterprise on the whole system of mutual trading. In addition he
reminded the House of the Prime Minister's pledge that Co-operative Societies would not be taxed as long as he was a member of the
National Government. MacDonald[7] made a typically muddled
reply which provoked McGovern,[8] although he was having trouble
with his teeth, to complain that Ramsay 'talked a good deal but
said nothing'. The general Labour line ranged from the abusive—
'the Raeburn Committee was rigged'[9] or 'Macquisten has not the
courage of a louse'[10]—to the orthodox, that it was an unfair attack

---

[1] Cols 769/896.
[2] H. 22/5/1933, Cols 769/778.
[3] The dividend, familiarly 'divi', was essentially a discount.
[4] H. 22/5/1933, Col. 773.
[5] See S.33, F.A. 1933.
[6] H. 22/5/1933, Cols 778/789.
[7] H. 22/5/1933, Cols 789/790.
[8] H. 22/5/1933, Cols 854/861.
[9] H. 22/5/1933 (Leonard), Col. 879.
[10] H. 22/5/1933 (Kirkwood), Col. 873.

on the savings of the working class,[1] or the frankly sentimental. 'This great movement,' said George Hall,[2] 'was part of his very being . . . there could be no justification for the tax.'

The general Conservative line played on the long privileged position enjoyed by the Co-operative Societies[3] which was now unjustified considering their current prosperity.[4] They should now come under the ordinary rules of income tax and the negotiations with them had been perfectly fair.[5] Hore-Belisha[6] emphasized this in his summing-up. The Royal Commission of 1920 had stated there was no ground for exempting Co-operative Societies; they should be taxed as any other trading concern and their 'divi' allowed as a trading expense.

This valiant rear-guard action, which was lost by 328 ayes to 109 noes, was not quite the end of the controversy. On the Second Reading of the Clause, Hore-Belisha[7] explained that both interest paid free of tax and 'divi' were deductible, which gave the Societies all they wanted. This did not prevent the Opposition from embarking on a debate, on their part, of monumental silliness, exemplified by Kirkwood's[8] remark, 'I am a co-operator, born and bred, and I compare favourably with the best man in this House, mentally or physically.' It was a losing battle, but Labour members such as Bevan[9] and Cripps[10] were determined to 'carry on the opposition to this Clause as far and as long as possible'. The final phase was fought on the afternoon of June 20, 1933, on a suggestion that sums placed to reserve by the Societies should not be taxed—justifiably, as there was no guarantee that such funds should ever be distributed nor any limit set to amount. This Amendment was defeated. Perhaps Macmillan's[11] judicious comment is a fair retrospective summary of this battle of long ago. 'This subject can very easily be approached with prejudice by either side. . . . I cannot work myself up into a state of moral indignation on the comparatively limited issue before us.'

Limited or not, it was the only issue which was hotly debated in

[1] Cf. H. 22/5/1933, Cols 836/841. [2] H. 22/5/1933 (Cove), Col. 877.
[3] H. 22/5/1933 (O'Connor), Cols 794/799.
[4] H. 22/5/1933 (Eastwood), Cols 819/825.
[5] H. 22/5/1933 (Maitland), Cols 830/833.
[6] H. 22/5/1933, Cols 886/893. [7] H. 31/5/1933, Cols 1895/1896.
[8] H. 31/5/1933, Cols 1906/1908. [9] H. 31/5/1933, Cols 1935/1941.
[10] H. 31/5/1933, Cols 683/696. [11] H. 22/5/1933, Cols 799/805.

the various stages of the Bill. The beer duty decrease, the changes in death duties (S.43) now roused little interest. There were some interesting income tax amendments suggested,[1] including an increase in wear and tear rates and an allowance for depreciation of buildings —a hardy annual this—but although the Chancellor[2] was sympathetic, cost, he maintained, was the real difficulty.

On the whole Chamberlain[3] was justified, when he rose to propose the Third Reading, in claiming that his proposals had had 'a calm and tranquil course'. He could hardly expect, he added drily, to satisfy those who regard a Budget 'primarily as an instrument for levelling out inequalities of income'. But further direct taxation was impossible and for the middle course he had steered he did not expect an 'exhibition of irrepressible enthusiasm'. The Labour members deployed for the last time their criticisms that instead of a policy for the restoration of trade and commerce the Chancellor had simply adopted one of soak the poor. For this standard and, it must be said, unconstructive attack, it was not difficult for the Financial Secretary[4] to deploy the standard defence. More than half the expenditure on pensions, insurance, housing and education directly benefited the working class; and 60 per cent of the revenue raised was from direct taxation to which the working-class contribution was minimal. Indirect taxation was also graded and was higher on luxuries. The voting was a foregone conclusion—290 against 42. The Royal Assent was reported by Mr Speaker on June 28th.

Any judgment on this, the second of Chamberlain's Budgets in the run of five before he became Prime Minister in the spring of 1937, must necessarily be an interim judgment. For although, as he said himself,[5] he opposed the idea of a three years' Budget, it cannot be considered in isolation either from the Budgets which came before and after it or the general economic pattern of the decade from 1929 to 1939.

Considering the provisions generally it was an undistinguished Budget and contemporary accounts say that it was expounded by the Chancellor in a tired and almost apologetic voice which sent Morgan Jones,[6] one of the chief Labour spokesmen on finance, off to sleep. Its only newsworthy feature was the penny off beer;

---

[1] H. 1/6/1933, Cols 2187/2190 (Foot). [2] H. 1/6/1933, Cols 2193/2195.
[3] H. 23/6/1933, Cols 1069/1073. [4] H. 23/6/1933, Cols 1143/1150.
[5] H. 24/4/1933, Col. 59. [6] Member for Caerphilly.

there was no true income tax relief in the way of rates; and the Customs and Excise adjustments were minor only. Yet it had a threefold significance which transcended the tentative nature of its proposals.

In the first place there was Chamberlain's resolute (or obstinate) refusal to unbalance his Budget despite the example of contemporary budgets in the United States and Continental countries which had resorted to large-scale deficit financing. There is no final agreement among economists[1] even now whether a public works policy would have hastened the process of economic recovery; the Liberals had been its strongest advocates in the late twenties, but the Labour experts had come to realize that the expenditure involved showed a very high cost per worker. 'We do not subscribe,' said Aneurin Bevan,[2] 'to the notion that public works schemes will do any other than construct very useful things for the country, and improve our economic and social apparatus enormously but at the end it will leave you faced with precisely the same difficulties.' Public works, therefore, were not a solution but 'some useful durable work would remain as a memento'.[3]

Secondly, the 1933 Budget saw a definite swing away from direct to indirect taxation. This had been sharply criticized by the Opposition although it originated from two very different sources, the Import Duties Bill introduced on the February 4, 1932, and the fall in yield from direct taxation caused by the drop in profits and wages. The proportion of direct to indirect taxation had been four to one at the end of World War I; it fell to three to one in 1932 and by 1933 was approaching level pegging. No wonder that this trend was lighted on the Third Reading by the Labour spokesman who summed up his party's feelings on the matter by saying: 'I much prefer a direct tax upon everybody than indirect taxation so that everyone may know exactly what he pays.'

Finally, as far as the monetary setting is concerned, the policy of cheap money was continued, the Exchange Equalization Fund was operating smoothly in its primary function of ironing out short-term fluctuations in the Exchange rates and, a new development, the shadow of the war debts was at last being lifted. It is true that the Opposition could censure the Government, as they did, morally for

---

[1] See, e.g. U. K. Hicks, *The Finance of British Government 1920–1936*, 193 ff.; H. W. Richardson, *Economic Recovery in Britain 1932–1939*, 212 ff.
[2] H. 27/4/1933, Col. 316.   [3] Hicks, *op. cit.*, p. 202.

their unilateral repudiation and fiscally for failing to provide for their payment; this latter criticism was unjustified, however, since the item was a self-balancing one[1] in that the country collected from her debtors an amount approximately equal to the amount paid out to the United States.

It is easy to criticize the Government's policy as mirrored in the 1933 Budget, but such criticism is largely the product of hindsight, for the Opposition speeches make it clear that they had no constructive policy to substitute. It should be remembered, too, that the Government had been given a 'doctor's mandate' and the crisis was not long over. That crisis was more than anything a crisis of confidence; and a balanced Budget was a traditional symptom of recovery; the danger was that the period of convalescence might be unduly prolonged.

[1] W. A. Morton, *British Finance 1930–1940*, p. 281.

Chapter II

The Finance Bill 1934

THE START OF A MISSION

Time Table

Financial Statement		April 17, 1934
Budget Proposals		
	1st Day	18
	2nd Day	19
Budget Resolutions		
	Reported	26
Finance Bill		
	1st Reading	26
	2nd Reading	May 16
Committee		
	1st Day	June 4
	2nd Day	5
	3rd Day	11
	4th Day	12
Report		18
3rd Reading		22
Royal Assent		July 12

It was 3.44 p.m. on Tuesday, April 17, 1934. The House itself and the galleries were crowded when, the last written answer regarding the provision of tumblers of milk for school-children having been disposed of, Chamberlain opened his Financial Statement for 1934. The atmosphere, in comparison with the two past years, he found distinctly brighter,[1] and he wore an expression, as one reporter put it,

[1] H. 17/4/34, Col. 903.

of tranquil cheerfulness.[1] The air of expectancy among his audience was partly due to the occasion and partly to the optimistic estimates of the surplus which the next two hours would reveal, although *The Times*[2] had sounded a typical note of caution about this.

The Chancellor was, however, able to report in his introduction a rise in wholesale prices, new low records in the rate of short-term interest, a rise in the volume of industrial production, and the achievement of equilibrium in the balance of payments. In fact, 'we have now finished the story of *Bleak House* and are sitting down this afternoon to enjoy the first chapter of *Great Expectations*.[3] But this limited recovery, he warned the House, had come from the expansion of the home and not the export market, which in fact stood much lower than a few years ago: 'the spirit of economic nationalism was blocking the channels of trade'.

He then announced a surplus of £31 millions, thus dashing a number of initially great expectations; it was arguably greater since the saving on debt management was enough to defray out of the Exchequer the statutory Sinking Funds, which amounted to nearly £8 millions, so that the real surplus was about £39 millions, a pleasant contrast to the previous year's deficit of £32 millions. A concise breakdown of how this balance had been struck showed total expenditure of £693 millions, comprising Consolidated Fund Services of nearly £11 millions, Supply Services of £459 millions and the Fixed Debt Charge of £224 millions as against revenue of £724 millions made up of Customs and Excise and other heads of Revenue £319 millions, the General Post Office 'under the vigorous administration of my Right Hon. Friend, the Postmaster General'[4] £13 millions, and the Inland Revenue £392 millions. There had been no exceptional saving on any votes but the decrease in the unemployment figures was reflected in the diminished expenditure on benefits. In terms of direct and indirect taxation, the surplus was £14 millions on the former, of which over £10 millions came from a windfall in the shape of the Ellerman estate, 'the largest payment in the whole history of the death duties',[5] and £17 millions on the latter.

The destination of the surplus was disposed of in one short sentence. 'According to the law [it] mist be devoted to the redemption of debt, and will very nearly make good the £32 millions which I

[1] *Manchester Guardian*, 18/4/34.   [2] 18/4/34.   [3] H. 17/4/34, Col. 903.
[4] Kingsley Wood.   [5] H. 17/4/34, Col. 907.

had to borrow in the year before in order to meet the deficit of that year.' (See p. 12.)[1]

The Chancellor then passed on to make a brief statement to the Committee on the position of the National Debt. He emphasized the 'extraordinary cheapness' of the rate of interest on Treasury Bills which over the year had averaged only 12s 6d per cent. In fact 'the whole amount of Treasury Bills and National Saving Certificates together at their lowest point in the year was over £1,200 millions but interest amounted to a little more than £15 millions, only $1\frac{1}{4}$ per cent on that whole vast total'.[2] With regard to the Exchange Equalization Fund, this had now been augmented by the £200 millions forecast in 1933 (see p. 13) and now stood at £350 millions; it continued to show a profit.[3]

About a third of the statement had now been completed and it was time to turn to prospects for the future. On the expenditure side, the Fixed Debt Charge was to remain at £224 millions, although it was necessary to issue a warning[4] that a larger provision might have to be made in future financial periods to cover the interest on Treasury Bills and Savings Certificates, averaged over a number of years, and also a reserve for a Sinking Fund. The total of all the Consolidated Fund Services was put at £236 millions, and the figures of the Supply Services, already published, stood at £462 millions, the Ministry of Labour Vote showing a welcome decrease of nearly £11 millions. The grand total of estimated expenditure was thus £698 millions. No provision was made for War debt payments to the United States nor for the receipt of War debts as reparations.

On the receipts side he estimated a £9 millions increase in Customs and Excise to bring in a total of £290 millions, although 'we must not expect to have such thirsty weather as we had last year'. The Inland Revenue estimate at £393 millions, or an increase of £3 millions over the previous year, was interesting. The three major items in this total were income tax £240 millions, surtax £50 millions and death duties £76 millions, and in view of the turn in the economic tide these estimates seemed far from sanguine. Chamberlain had to point out that the profits on which tax would be paid in 1934 were those made in 1933, during the first half of which profits were still actually falling;[5] despite this, for the first time since 1929, he was

---

[1] H. 17/4/34, Col. 908. [2] H. 17/4/34, Col. 908. [3] H. 17/4/34, Col. 909.
[4] H. 17/4/34, Col. 910. [5] H. 17/4/34, Col. 913.

able to budget for no fall in the assessments under Schedule D as profits began to rise in the latter half of 1933. With regard to surtax, this lagged one year behind income tax so that the current yield depended upon the course of trade in 1932 when profits were still falling; a further drop had to be provided for here. As for death duties, he had already mentioned (see p. 33) the single very large payment made this year which could not be expected again, so he had held the figure at roughly the same as 1933. Other heads of revenue would produce £44 million including receipts from motor vehicle duty, the Post Office and miscellaneous receipts which this year could not be swollen by the special item of £10 millions from the War Loan Depreciation Fund (see p. 16). To summarize, he had estimated receipts of £727 millions to set against estimated expenditure of £698 millions, giving a balance of £29 millions. This figure, too, would dash 'some of the rather wild guessing which has been going on' but 'the sum of £29 millions, if not dazzling, is at any rate a very substantial surplus. It is the largest for ten years, and it is sufficient to enable me to begin the long-awaited process of relief from the burdens and sacrifices of the last few years.'[1]

But the House was to remain in suspense until Chamberlain had dealt with some minor changes affecting collection of tax on mineral rents and royalties and estate duty: there were some small Customs amendments in addition. There was, however, an alteration in the motor vehicles duty of some importance since it did represent a real attempt to stimulate car exports. The manufacturers had long been complaining that the tax of £1 per horse-power militated against the development of cars suitable for the Continental market. The duty would therefore be reduced to fifteen shillings per horse-power and the cost, after consultation with the Minister of Transport, would fall mainly on the road fund by an ingenious rearrangement[2] of the previous statutory requirements.

It was now past five p.m., the hour which by custom must strike before the chief disclosures are made, and the 'momentous question' was posed: 'What am I to do with our surplus?' He had given a good deal of anxious thought to the question and, he added drily, 'I have formed the impression that a good many other people have been devoting their attention to the same subject. Quite a large proportion have been good enough to give me their advice, frequently coloured,

[1] H. 17/4/34, Col. 915.   [2] H. 17/4/34, Cols 918/9.

as one would expect, by their own experience or their own interest.'[1] All the advice tendered had been fully considered, but in the end he had decided to found his policy on two general principles. The first of these could not be put in better words than those used by 'my predecessor, Lord Snowden'[2] in an article published in December 1933: 'A surplus must now in justice be devoted, as far as it will allow, to relieving those classes who suffered when the crisis was acute.'[3] Chamberlain considered himself precluded from any examination of other claims to relief, however well founded, until the victims of the 1931 depression measures, whom Snowden clearly still had on his conscience, had been compensated. The surplus was not adequate fully to compass this, so the second principle must be to distribute what was available to those who had been forced to endure the increases in taxation on the one hand, and the cuts in the rates of unemployment payment and emoluments on the other.

First he dealt with the reduction which had been made in the pay of state and local government employees: these were to be restored by one half from July 1, 1934. The cost would be £4 millions this year, £5·5 millions in a full year.

But 'whatever may be the sufferings and hardships of those who may have had their income reduced, their position must still be preferable to that of the unemployed with no income at all'.[4] A new clause was therefore being introduced into the Unemployment Bill providing for the full restoration of the unemployment benefit as from July 1, 1934; this would carry with it a corresponding alteration in the maximum rates of transitional payments. The cost was estimated at £3·6 millions, £4·8 millions in a full year. Chamberlain, however, was at pains to point out, although not in the Budget 'strictly concerned with the cost of unemployment benefit', that the new Unemployment Bill[5] would set up a self-balancing unemployment insurance fund, the contributions to which would cover all unemployment relief payments and provide for the debt service incurred during the depression.

Thirdly, there was the question of remission of taxation. The concessions announced thus far had reduced the available surplus

[1] H. 17/4/34, Col. 919.
[2] Cf. the reference to him in the 1933 Budget (p. 12).
[3] H. 17/4/34, Col. 919. [4] H. 17/4/34, Cols 921/922.
[5] Later the Unemployment Act of 1934.

to £21·3 millions. Fortifying himself with a further quotation from the Snowden article (see p. 36) that income tax payers had made by far the largest contribution to meeting the national emergency in 1931,[1] he announced the proposal to remove the 6d imposed on standard rate in 1931 at a cost of £20·5 millions, £24 millions in a full year. The case for remission was overwhelming; the only question was what form it should take. 'I thought I ought to consider the effect of any remission not merely upon the individual taxpayer but upon the country as a whole. Looking at it from that point of view I had no hesitation in coming to the conclusion that the relief which would confer most direct benefits upon the country, which would have the greatest psychological effect and which would impart the most immediate and vigorous stimulus to the expansion of trade and employment, would be a reduction in income tax.'[2]

The three stages of remission had been cheered with increasing enthusiasm. There was silence now as the Chancellor with 'but a very few more words to address to the Committee' moved to his peroration. He emphasized, as he had done in the previous year, the progress of recovery in the British Empire as opposed to the rest of the world; and he 'rejoiced to think' that the sacrifices made in 1931 had led to the relief he was now able to give which would in turn lead to further progress in the coming year. An ovation from a House which included five former Chancellors[3] greeted him as he sat down at 5.23 p.m.

Last year George Lansbury had broken with the usual convention of formal congratulation and engaged, as Samuel put it, 'in a somewhat long criticism of all the proposals'.[4] This year, in his absence, Attlee[5] observed the normal custom of recognizing 'the brevity and businesslike manner of his statement' but it was 'quite the meanest Budget on record'. The unemployed were getting only £3·5 millions and the main relief was to the rentier class; in addition there was a sinister shift from direct to indirect taxation. Sir Herbert Samuel was more charitable;[6] the statement had been 'comprehensive, clear and admirably simple', but although he approved the restora-

---

[1] In fact out of £81·5 millions extra taxation, income tax payers found £57·5 millions.
[2] H. 17/4/34, Cols 923/4.
[3] Baldwin, Horne, Austen Chamberlain, Lloyd George and Churchill.
[4] H. 17/4/34, Col. 928.　　　　　[5] H. 17/4/34, Cols 927/8.
[6] H. 17/4/34, Cols 928/9.

tion of the whole cut to the unemployed and the reduction of standard rate by sixpence, his immediate criticism was that the allowances to smaller taxpayers still remained at the 1931 level.

There were four more brief speeches before the closure at 6 p.m. James Maxton,[1] for the Communist Party, attributed the restoration of the cuts to the moral suasion created by the hunger marchers. Macquisten,[2] as befitted a Highland member, mingled his congratulations with a lament for 'the persecuted industry of distilling'. The industrial sector, in the person of Sir George Gillett,[3] was firmly of the opinion that the interests of trade were better served by a reduction of rate than by a restoration of allowances; and the chairman of the Income Tax Payers' Society, Sir William Davison,[4] traditionally allowed 'a few sentences' following on the Budget statement, stressed that the income tax yield was down £22 millions from the previous year and £59 millions from three years ago. The point of diminishing returns had been reached and the country should now be relieved from a war rate of taxation.

The Wednesday morning headlines, as might be expected, greeted the tangible signs of improvement shown in the reduction of income tax, the reinstatement of unemployment benefit and of half the 1931 salary cuts. Among the heavier papers, The Times[5] was the most enthusiastic. It was a welcome Budget indicating the country was at last on an ascending curve of prosperity and confidence; and although the burden of taxation on larger incomes was still in excess of the highest wartime level, recovery, like the depression, was likely to prove infectious.

The Manchester Guardian,[6] however, was more critical. While praising the simplicity of the Budget 'which could easily be grasped and reduced to a few words', it considered the removal of the stringent economy measures of three years ago rather rough-and-ready, the flaw being the relief given to the larger taxpayers by the sixpence off standard rate rather than to the smaller taxpayers by an upward revision of allowances. A David Low cartoon entitled 'In Different Worlds' summarized the Radical economic opinion. It showed on one side a frustrated worker standing beside some massive but silent machinery labelled 'Power to Produce Plenty', and on the other side

[1] H. 17/4/34, Cols 929/30.   [2] H. 17/4/34, Cols 931/33.
[3] H. 17/4/34, Col. 931.   [4] H. 17/4/34, Cols 930/1.
[5] Leader, 18/4/34.   [6] Leader, 18/4/34.

was the front bench with Chamberlain holding up his meagre dispatch case on which was stencilled 'Economy and Scarcity'.

The weekly journals tended to continue the somewhat more disparaging attitude. The *New Statesmen* agreed with the *Manchester Guardian* that 'those whose need was the least got the most', and under a leader heading of 'Rich Man, Poor Man'[1] commented on the effect of tariffs which had caused a shift in taxation to the poorer classes and concluded, 'Although he has made a show of fairness in distributing his blessings, the fairness dissolves under analysis of the incidence of this new tax system built up on a tariff basis'.

The Economist,[2] too, could give only qualified praise to the Chancellor's measures. His conciseness and his determination to restore the cuts before any redistribution of the national income could be attempted was approved, but, as with the *Manchester Guardian* and the *New Statesman*, it also found the standard rate reduction uneven in its incidence and, although the increasing barriers to international trade were admittedly a limiting factor, it concurred with Low's interpretation in maintaining that 'Chamberlain's policy offers no prospect of a recovery on a full scale which would enable the two million unemployed to work again'.

As a postscript to the reaction of the British Press, it is interesting to note that when Chamberlain contrasted British Budgets with those of the rest of the world, his words were echoed by the *Journal des Débats* which commented that it was a Budget to be envied. Even the United States added its congratulations despite the equivocal position over war debts.

The first day's debate on the Financial Statement brought additional consolation, if indeed it was needed, for academic criticism. There was a quiet opening from Morgan Jones[3] with a speech plainly the outcome of prolonged and painstaking statistical study, but he did cover most of the points which were to recur during the next seven hours or so. After paying tribute to the lucidity of the Chancellor's address, he went on to criticize the Budget proposals under four heads. There was a distinct switch from direct to indirect taxation; the reduction to horse-power tax (see p. 35) came from raiding the Road Fund, 'feeding', as he put it, 'the dog on its own tail'; taxation relief should have been in the form of allowances since there was no evidence that the sixpence off standard rate would encourage

---

[1] *New Statesman*, 21/4/34.   [2] 21/4/34.   [3] H. 18/4/34, Cols 975/989.

a trade revival; and in general he thought the surplus would probably be heavier than anticipated. His solution[1] was an expansionist public works policy; otherwise, turning Chamberlain's Dickensian reference against him, 'the poor, from this great House, can derive only bleak expectations'.

Sir Herbert Samuel,[2] the Liberal spokesman, agreed that the surplus would probably be more and that the money in the Road Fund should properly be used for road works. But there had been no promise that any of the burdens imposed in 1931 had a built-in precedence for relief as Morgan Jones[3] had claimed and as the Chancellor had properly refuted.[4] He suggested the relief of reserves from taxation, a hardy annual, and maintained, as a good free-trader should, that the blocking of the channels of trade was the result of the Government's tariff policy.

Mabane[5] was at pains to contradict two charges laid by the two previous speakers, pointing out that the country, as far as direct and indirect taxation was concerned, was simply moving back to the pre-1914 proportion of 54/46, and that tariff receipts had now become a fundamental contribution to the national accounts. The concessions made could have gone further, as he had suggested last year; and although he disapproved of the principle of surpluses[6] he realized that political tactics demanded something being kept in hand.

The last of the opening set pieces was from Major Nathan,[7] an Independent Liberal, and was the most effectively critical of the four. The admitted industrial and economic stagnation needed more than the stimulus of a mere restoration of the cuts; the surplus was not due to expanding trade but to indirect taxation and the death of one rich man, and it should be applied to a recovery loan, not debt reduction. The depreciation allowances[8] to industry were too low and he advocated relief from taxation for capital spent on re-equipment;[9] and he concluded by charging the Chancellor with having budgeted 'with a view to a surplus'.

There were, of course, a considerable number of diehard speeches such as those of Major Hills[10] or Sir Arthur Samuel,[11] the latter's

[1] H. 18/4/34, Col. 988.   [2] H. 18/4/34, Cols 989/1003.

[3] H. 18/4/34, Col. 987.   [4] H. 18/4/34, Col. 996.

[5] H. 18/4/34, Cols 1009/1016.   [6] H. 18/4/34, Col. 1013.

[7] H. 18/4/34, Cols 1016/1032.   [8] £87 million in 1933.

[9] An anticipation of Investment Allowances and Grants.

[10] H. 18/4/34, Cols 1003/1009.   [11] H. 18/4/34, Cols 1022/1032.

Greek tag provoking a cry of 'Translate!' from his fellow-members but the main controversy was now centering round whether the Chancellor should have restored allowances, and so helped the smaller taxpayer, or, as he did, reduced standard rate for its psychological effect. Amery[1] and Wilmot,[2] for instance, were in direct contradiction on this point.

It was now about 8 p.m. and the House was fairly empty. Half-a-dozen speakers, however, kept the debate going. Sir William Allen[3] suggested incomes below £130 should be exempt and criticized the effect of death duties which were being squandered as income, an opinion repeated by the Hon. J. J. Stourton,[4] who was also in favour of cutting the standard rate by 1s 0d. Both he and J. W. Banfield[5] were in favour of public works, as was W. Boulton,[6] who cited the building of the new Cunarder[7] as an example. The orthodoxy of the Budget presented by 'that good old Gladstonian Radical, the present Chancellor of the Exchequer', was approved by Horobin,[8] but it was left to Mason[9] to emphasize the point which speakers had so far neglected, that foreign trade was languishing and, although local trade was recovering, 'we live by our foreign trade'.

The benches now began to fill again as Bevan[10] rose to launch his expected attack. He saw a complete contradiction between the disposal of the surplus and the Chancellor's implied promises; and 'this surplus has been brought about by the depression' which had created cheap money which in turn had created the surplus.[11] And now £21 millions was going to income tax payers 'who are even now not able to find useful employment for their money'. The decline in exports was permanent; never again would they reach 25 per cent to 30 per cent. Home industry should therefore be fostered but a surplus simply meant the withholding of restoration, In view of the continuation of the Means Test, the replacement of the unemployment cuts which cost nothing was 'cant and hypocrisy'; the whole proposals he summed up as 'a class Budget'.

Hore-Belisha,[12] in his second year of office as Financial Secretary to the Treasury, deplored the change in the tone of the debate 'from

[1] H. 18/4/34, Cols 1039/1044.   [2] H. 18/4/34, Cols 1032/1039.
[3] H. 18/4/34, Cols 1044/1047.   [4] H. 18/4/34, Cols 1068/1074.
[5] H. 18/4/34, Cols 1048/1054.   [6] H. 18/4/34, Cols 1054/1058.
[7] *The Queen Mary.*   [8] H. 18/4/34, Cols 1058/1064.
[9] H. 18/4/34, Cols 1064/1086.   [10] H. 18/4/34, Cols 1074/1081.
[11] H. 18/4/34, Col. 1074.   [12] H. 18/4/34, Cols 1081/1091.

a softer, gentler and more gracious note' to 'that which the Hon. Member has so cacophonously sounded'. Direct and indirect taxation were not two separate categories; the justification for the latter was that, in the current vogue of economic nationalism, it was partly protective; and with regard to the former there is not a constant fund from which direct taxation may be taken, as a higher rate did not necessarily mean a higher yield. He agreed that there was room for a difference of opinion on whether to restore allowances or reduce the standard rate, but 'the burden of income tax is primarily judged by the height of the standard rate'[1] and the lightening of the burden on industry was essential. Over the whole period income tax payers had suffered the longest and, in view of that incontrovertible fact 'the Budget cannot give rise to genuine controversy'. Croom-Johnson[2] made a plea for the small taxpayer who suffered from both deduction of tax at source and the cut in allowances, to close the debate for the day.

The second day's debate on the Financial Statement was opened by David Grenfell,[3] M.P. for Glamorgan. He rather surprisingly accused Chamberlain of throwing the whole responsibility for the cuts on Snowden while claiming personal credit for their restoration; in fact the present surplus showed that 'the country could have carried on quite comfortably without any concession being required from the unemployed'. He then painted a vivid picture of 'the orgy of speculation' which had followed the Budget;[4] he felt very strongly that 'the Budget surplus has not been put to a wise use but has been given as a pretext for unwise and foolish speculation to large numbers of income tax payers who will have money they are not capable of spending';[5] it should have been used to restore allowances to at least the 1931 level; and any residue 'should be spent on the reconstruction of our national life'.

This was a fair statement of the orthodox Labour line; it was followed by an equally illuminating declaration[6] of the standard Tory policy by Sir Robert Horne, himself an ex-Chancellor of the Exchequer.[7] The Budget was a turning point in a critical epoch; he approved the relief to motor taxation, the stimulating power of the

---

[1] H. 18/4/1934, Col. 1090. [2] H. 18/4/1934, Cols 1091/5.
[3] H. 18/4/1934, Cols 1129/41. [4] H. 18/4/1934, Col. 1132.
[5] H. 19/4/1934, Col. 1139. [6] H. 19/4/1934, Cols 1141/56.
[7] He was responsible for the Budgets of 1921 and 1922.

standard rate reduction,[1] and the restoration of the cuts which had stolen the Opposition's thunder. 'From this side of the House, Hon. Members opposite looked like a parterre of roses suddenly nipped by an autumn frost.'[2] But he pointed out that a surtax rate rising to 13s 3d was the highest in the world, that, in his view, the estimates were rather cautious, and that he disagreed with the application of the surplus; its correct destination was the Unemployment Insurance Find, the contributions to which were a direct burden on industry. But for all that, like our taxation, our exports were the highest in the world and the only ones currently on the increase.

'One of the dangers,' said Wardlaw-Milne,[3] 'facing us in this debate is the danger of repetition,' and this was certainly true of the theme of the restoration of allowances as against the reduction in standard rate. Four succeeding Labour speakers—Tinker,[4] T. Smith,[5] Batey,[6] and E. Williams[7]—stressed their feeling, as the last named put it, that 'most of the £24 millions given to income tax payers will not go to assist the country'.[8] Public works were one solution and to close 'the financial year with a balance of £31 millions was not a credit but a crime'.[9]

Tory opinion was just as solid for the reduction in standard rate, Wedgwood,[10] Nall-Cain,[11] and Lord Burghley,[12] the Olympic hurdler, agreeing that the 6d off 'was a great thing for industry'. Indeed, Lord Burghley slyly suggested that if Labour had remained in office 'many of them might be coming to me to ask how to become proficient in a sphere of activity of which I have some experience in order to escape from an angry electorate'. The more right-wing Tories, such as Lord Apsley[13] and Sir H. Croft,[14] deplored the lack of relief to surtax payers; and Mainwaring[15] considered the rate reduction a compensation to income tax payers for losses through conversion operations. Pike[16] produced his usual rather muddled speech but he did bring up the question of death duties: he agreed with

[1] This was his own policy in 1922—see B. E. V. Sabine, *History of Income Tax*, p. 165.

[2] H. 19/4/1934, Col. 1147.

[3] H. 19/4/1934, Cols 1162/1170.

[4] H. 19/4/1934, Cols 1170/1175.

[5] H. 19/4/1934, Cols 1187/1192.

[6] H. 19/4/1934, Cols 1215/1220.

[7] H. 19/4/1934, Cols 1227/1231.

[8] H. 19/4/1934, Col. 1231.

[9] H. 19/4/1934, Col. 1218.

[10] H. 19/4/1934, Cols 1156/1162.

[11] H. 19/4/1934, Cols 1220/1223.

[12] H. 19/4/1934, Cols 1223/1225.

[13] H. 19/4/1934, Cols 1175/1181.

[14] H. 19/4/1934, Cols 1181/1188.

[15] H. 19/4/1934, Cols 1196/1201.

[16] H. 19/4/1934, Cols 1201/1210.

Sir Robert Horne that estimates of this tax were not reliable: and other speakers[1] had criticized their operation as converting capital which produced income into tax which was then spent and lost as a revenue-producing asset. Sir Assheton Pownall[2] probably produced the most sensible survey of the income tax scene, pointing out that payers of direct taxation were receiving back nothing like the increased levies paid since 1929; he reminded the House that the decrease in personal allowances in 1931 had at least been accompanied by an increase in earned income relief; and while admitting the fall in the real value of allowances in the terms of purchasing power, pleaded that this gave the black-coated workers the strongest claim to help as they got nothing from the social services.

Two minor pleas, one by Lovat-Fraser[3] for the reduction of entertainment tax, which he described as a tax on culture, to enable the theatre to combat the cinema,[4] and another by Mallalieu[5] for a decrease in the fuel oil tax which was restricting the development of the diesel engine, gained a sympathetic hearing but no more, despite their eloquence.

The best speeches, before the winding up, came from Sir Arthur Steel-Maitland,[6] late in the evening, and Boothby,[7] somewhat earlier. The latter ascribed the miraculous recovery of the country as being due partly to 'cheap and abundant money' and held that 'the 6d off the standard rate is incomparably the greatest stimulus that could be given to industry';[8] the restoration of allowances might have been immediately better from a humanitarian standpoint, but the increase in employment would create an increase in purchasing power in the long run. He had two criticisms, one against the tax on whisky, 'the most savage imposition of modern times',[9] and the other, following Samuel and Horne, against the 'absolutely useless' appropriation of the surplus for debt redemption: it should have gone to the Unemployment Insurance Fund.[10] Steel-Maitland's

---

[1] E.g. Lord Apsley, Lord Burghley, and Mr Nall-Cain.
[2] H. 19/4/1934, Cols 1192/1196.
[3] H. 19/4/1934, Cols 1225/1227. See also Chamberlain's winding-up H. 19/4/1934, Col. 1260.
[4] Average weekly attendances were about twelve millions.
[5] H. 19/4/1934, Cols 1237/1240.   [6] H. 19/4/1934, Cols 1231/1236.
[7] H. 19/4/1934, Cols 1210/1215.   [8] H. 19/4/1934, Col. 1211.
[9] H. 19/4/1934, Col. 1213.
[10] Hansard for once nods here and has the ironic misprint 'fun'.

analysis was deeper. 'A remission of income tax brings into play a much greater stimulus of investment in enterprises which involve a greater use of capital goods',[1] but precautionary measures must be taken to prevent a boom-slump cycle. He felt very strongly that not enough was known about the mechanism of these movements, including the effect of public works, and suggested the setting up of another Macmillan Commission.[2]

Sir Stafford Cripps, in winding up for the Opposition,[3] took up Steel-Maitland's point at once. Attempts to control the capitalist system, as in the United States, showed conclusively that controlled capitalism was an impossibility. He gave an analysis of the Socialist boom and slump theory,[4] but found it difficult to relate this to the policy of the Government 'even assuming, as I am doing, that the Government has a policy'. The extra spending was going into the wrong pockets; there might be a boom in profits but not in individual prosperity. The Budget was 'the effort of an accountant to bring out a favourable balance, rather than an effort to plan out the economic life of the community[5] . . . it was a Budget in the best traditions of orthodox capitalism'.[6]

To Cripps this was the gravest charge in his speech for the prosecution; to the Chancellor it was one of the main lines of his defence. Starting[7] with a personal statement about Snowden, 'for whom I had and have the greatest respect', he claimed that this year's progress justified last year's Budget. Booms and slumps were, he thought, not susceptible of unilateral control, being to a large extent swayed by the conditions of world trade. He justified his distribution of the surplus 'for those who suffered and made their contributions to the national emergency of 1931'; he justified his cautious budgeting by the fact that he had made no allowance for possible Supplementary Estimates; and he justified his deduction of the surplus from the National Debt on the grounds that he had added almost the same amount to the Debt in 1933.[8] He also reminded the House that his treatment of the Unemployment Fund was that recommended by the Royal Commission.[9] In short he had 'tried to make an honest

---

[1] H. 19/4/1934, Col. 1232.
[2] A reference to the Maxmillian Report, Cmd. 3897 (1931).
[3] H. 19/4/1934, Cols 1240/1250. [4] H. 19/4/1934, Cols 1240/1241.
[5] H. 19/4/1934, Col. 1242. [6] H. 19/4/1934, Col. 1249.
[7] H. 19/4/1934, Cols 1250/1264. [8] H. 19/4/1934, Cols 1257/1259.
[9] And later embodied in the Unemployment Act, 1934.

attempt to distribute the surplus as fairly as possible'; he could not get a 'mathematically correct allocation', but it was more important to secure the maximum employment of taxpayers rather than reduce their income tax by a few pounds, especially as world trade was still tending to contract.

The Report stage, on April 26th, passed off with the usual polite interchange of question and answer, apart from the heat engendered by the Sixth Resolution on the 6d reduction in standard rate which sparked off a repeat of the arguments of the week before. Wilmot,[1] Tinker,[2] Miss Rathbone,[3] and Morgan Jones[4] all delivered variations on the theme that the effect of the Resolution, instead of a restoration of allowances, was to favour large incomes against small, elaborated in Tinker's case by a criticism of the proportion of direct to indirect taxation. Hore-Belisha[5] had no difficulty in making at least an effective debating reply: he exposed the figures used by the Opposition on the proportion of direct to indirect taxation; the former was increased twice in 1931, yet the yield fell; the yield of the latter tended to fall too if increased, which would alter the proportion again; and the reduction in rate, he argued, would relieve the reserves of companies and co-operative societies and assist industry more than a restoration of allowances. And both Cove and Sir Stafford Cripps were pulled up by the Chair[6] for speaking on the Budget rather than the Resolution.

As Braithwaite[7] observed on the Second Reading, in a speech generally complimentary to the Government, 'it happens not infrequently that when a Budget is introduced amidst almost universal approbation, by the time the Resolutions have passed their Report stage and the Finance Bill is introduced, the ardour in favour of the proposals is somewhat cooled . . .'. Certainly the phraseology of the Amendment, moved by Grenfell,[8] with its talk of the 'evils of the maldistribution of purchasing power' and the 'concessions to privileged interests', still demonstrated a singular disenchantment with the current proposals. But there was nothing new in his speech, which dwelt on the twin themes of the proportion of direct to indirect taxation and the iniquity of putting the reduction of standard rate

[1] H. 26/4/1934, Col. 1963.
[2] H. 26/4/1934, Col. 1968.
[3] H. 26/4/1934, Col. 1971.
[4] H. 26/4/1934, Col. 1974.
[5] H. 26/4/1934, Cols 1979/1981.
[6] H. 26/4/1934, Cols 1986/1988.
[7] H. 16/5/1934, Cols 1877/1883.
[8] H. 16/5/1934, Cols 1781/1796.

before the restoration of allowances, apart from his attack on the proposal[1] to repeal the provisions of Part III of the Finance Act 1931 which charged a land value tax.

Now this measure had been a cherished plan of Snowden's which, with the assistance of Cripps and the guillotine procedure, he had steam-rollered through both Houses.[2] The Tories had always bitterly opposed it and, shortly after the 1931 General Election, Neville Chamberlain had raised the question of repeal, succeeding initially in getting the revaluation of land, which was an integral part of the scheme, suspended on the grounds of expense.[3] Now its complete repeal was proposed. Snowden held that Chamberlain 'was evidently ashamed of what he was doing for neither in the Budget Speech, nor on the Second Reading, did he make a word of comment'.[4]

This of course was a Parliamentary windfall which Opposition members exploited to the full. Besides Grenfell, Mallalieu,[5] Wedgwood,[6] Stewart[7] and McLean[8] all spoke of the proposal, as Snowden had done, in terms of the sharpest of practice, the last-named even comparing the Chancellor to the ill-fated financier Clarence Hatry. Of the other Labour speakers, West[9] went back to 1931 when 'the greatest burden had to be borne by the poorest people'; now in 1934 the same thing was happening, the cry of equality of restoration being 'an even more fraudulent mockery'. Charles Brown[10] went back in history, too, but thinking as he did 'the Budget was a trivial incident in the manipulation of state income and expenditure', he labelled the 1931 crisis as a 'faked crisis' designed to perpetuate the maldistribution of wealth in the country; the national income had increased between 1925/26 and 1931/32 but wage-earners had become poorer.

Probably the most reasoned criticism was that of the Liberal Leader, Sir Archibald Sinclair.[11] He agreed the Budget vindicated the 1931 policy of the National Government but it did not reveal 'one single new constructive idea for the relief of the burdens on industry or for the reduction of unemployment'. He suggested a

[1] Ultimately S. 27 F. A. 1934.
[2] Snowden, *Autobiography*, Vol. II, pp. 905/916.
[3] Snowden, *op. cit.*, p. 918.   [4] Snowden, *op. cit.*, p. 919.
[5] H. 16/5/1934, Cols 1837/1844.   [6] H. 16/5/1934, Cols 1847/1856.
[7] H. 16/5/1934, Cols 1874/1877.   [8] H. 16/5/1934, Cols 1890/1898.
[9] H. 16/5/1934, Cols 1821/1826.   [10] H. 16/5/1934, Cols 1859/1867.
[11] H. 16/5/1934, Cols 1796/1814.

reduction in the rate of contributions to the Unemployment insurance Fund, an increase in the wear and tear allowance to industry,[1] and the promotion of public works. He, too, was particularly scathing on the proposed land value tax repeal. 'They did this deed in the dark, and they did it in the dark because they were ashamed of it.'[2]

But, of course, the main phalanx of Tory opinion was solidly behind the Chancellor. There were a few aberrations: Mason,[3] for instance, calling the Budget 'a financial triumph rather than a triumph of finance', suggested a commission of enquiry on monetary policy, and Sir Adrian Baillie[4] making a short plea for the reduction of entertainment duty.[5] There was also some qualified agreement with the Opposition on helping the small income-tax payer[6] and on putting the surplus to the Unemployment Insurance Fund instead of to debt redemption. But Sir George Gillett[7] redeemed himself by praising the reduction in standard rate and its assistance to industry, and Emmott[8] felt the same; his argument was that purchasing power stemmed from industrial activity which was galvanized by a decrease in taxation.

Chamberlain,[9] as usual, intervened half-way through the debate. He reiterated his two main principles that emergency burdens ought to be removed now the emergency was over, and that he had not favoured one class against another; the House should remember that the income-tax payer was still worse off than he had been in 1931. In direct reply to specific criticisms he argued that, in the current economic climate, advocates of free trade were flogging a dead horse, that as far as public works were concerned the unemployment figures were down by over half a million and he had yet to be convinced that prosperity came from the mere spending of large sums of money, and that finally the application of the surplus to the Unemployment Insurance Fund would only reduce the contributions by one farthing. Hore-Belisha[10] had no difficulty in winding up. He would like to go back to first principles. The Budget provided both for revenue and for the revision of fiscal machinery; as revaluation had been put into

---

[1] Cf. also H. 16/5/1934, Col. 1848 (Wedgwood).
[2] H. 16/5/1934, Col. 1810.   [3] H. 16/5/1934, Cols 1883/1889.
[4] H. 16/5/1934, Cols 1889/1890.
[5] Cf. also H. 19/4/1934, Col. 1226 (Lovat-Fraser).
[6] H. 16/5/1934, Cols 1844/1847 (Allen).
[7] H. 16/5/1934, Cols 1814/1821.   [8] H. 16/5/1934, Cols 1867/1874.
[9] H. 16/5/1934, Cols 1826/1837.   [10] H. 16/5/1934, Cols 1898/1904.

abeyance and the tax could not now be levied in the life of the existing Parliament it was practical to remove it; in any case it 'would not be a lucrative source of revenue'.[1] He also wished to point out that the working-class saved as well as spent: small savings[2] had increased by £90 millions in the past three years. Finally the reason why the reduction in income tax did not equally affect the small tax payer was because the effective rate was small. The Amendment was lost by 290 to 55.

The proceedings at Committee Stage were to a very large extent concerned with the cut in standard rate. This was debated in two stages. The discussion on Clause 17,[3] in which nine members took part, was on the best way of utilizing the surplus; Hore-Belisha was not inclined to be dogmatic: 'We made the choice upon what we considered to be the balance of advantage.[4] Wilmot returned to the attack by proposing new clause[5] which attempted to return income tax allowances to their pre-1931 position, and in reply to Hore-Belisha's point about working-class savings[6] he maintained they were due to fear, not to prosperity, and represented an over-restriction of consumption. Allied with this clause was a proposal[7] to allow 'housekeeper'[8] allowance to an unmarried man or woman in place of, briefly, a widow or widower or the head of a family with a widowed mother;[9] the mover thought that this might appeal to the Financial Secretary, being a bachelor himself. Hore-Belisha,[10] though moved by the 'sage and parental advice given', maintained that the purpose of the allowance was to keep the old home together; this clause would import an entirely new principle into the income tax code. The Financial Secretary,[11] in the Chancellor's absence, upon which Cripps[12] sardonically commented, gave the final and definitive reply on the Opposition line. Every direct taxpayer was getting a 10 per cent relief and so generous was the present allowance system that out of eight million incomes within the taxable limit, four and a half million were exempt. The standard rate was only

[1] H. 16/5/1934, Col. 1900.
[2] I.e. Post Office and Trustee Savings Banks and National Savings Certificates.
[3] S. 19/F.A., 1934.
[4] H. 5/6/1934, Col. 813.
[5] H. 11/6/1934, Cols 1377/1387.
[6] H. 16/5/1934, Col. 1902.
[7] H. 11/6 1934, Cols 1423/1425.
[8] The term is not statutory.
[9] See S. 22 F.A., 1924.
[10] H. 11/6/1934, Cols 1426/1427.
[11] H. 11/6/1934, Cols 1401/1403.
[12] H. 11/6/1834, Cols 1403/1404.

effective on incomes of £4,000. In any case the restoration of allowances might be 'within our financial resources of the future'.

The rest of the Committee Stage discussions were somewhat desultory. There were the usual esoteric points raised on death duties,[1] the usual complaints about the surtax rates,[2] and, an echo of last year's Co-operative Societies' controversy, a back-door attempt to get the tax on mutual societies repealed;[3] incidentally this tax had produced 'a little more than anticipated'.[4] There was only token resistance to the abolition of land value tax but it might be noted that S.28 was retained as the Valuation Department found it 'of first importance in saving public money'.[5] One of the most valuable suggestions was on the revision of wear and tear allowances to industry.[6] The Financial Secretary pointed out that the increase in the allowance by one-tenth in Snowden's second Budget in 1931 was to offset the increase in standard rate. This compensatory concession would not, however, now be withdrawn but no further addition could be afforded.[7]

By the time the Third Reading of a Finance Bill is reached there is a strong sense if not of *déjà vu* at least of *déjà dit*. Hore-Belisha must have shared the feeling. He had taken, even for a Financial Secretary, an unusually large share in the Budget discussions, and when on June 22nd he moved[8] the Third Reading of the 1934 Finance Bill, he did so in a three-minute speech. The Budget had brought general and widespread relief: in particular three-and-a-half million taxpayers would retain in the next twelve months £24 millions which previously went in taxes. Both the Opposition in reply and the Government speakers in support, seemed frozen in their original attitudes; Morgan Jones,[9] for example, re-emphasized the inequality of restoration; and Boothby[10] gave almost a repeat performance of his speech on April 19th.[11] Only Wedgwood[12] and Kirkwood[13] made truly individualistic speeches, especially the latter with his biblical phraseology and humanitarian generalizations.

[1] E.g. H. 11/6/1934, Col. 1469. [2] E.g. H. 11/6/1934, Cols 820/824.
[3] H. 18/6/1934, Cols 23/25. [4] H. 22/6/1934, Col. 694.
[5] H. 5/6/1934, Col. 845.
[6] Messrs Foot, Williams and Curry, H. 18/6/1934, Cols 144/149. See also p. 29.
[7] H. 18/6/1934, Cols 149/150. [8] H. 22/6/1934, Cols 601/602.
[9] H. 22/6/1934, Cols 692/702. [10] H. 22/6/1934, Cols 706/722.
[11] H. 19/4/1934, Cols 1210/1215. [12] H. 22/4/1934, Cols 722/726.
[13] H. 22/4/1934, Cols 726/736.

The Chancellor[1] had little trouble in winding up. His tone was almost bantering. The discussions over the past two months had, he thought, been of an 'unusually moderate character'. With regard to the land values tax, Wedgwood was the only person who understood it—'he says so himself'—and he chided the Opposition for its ingratitude for the way the ground had now been cleared for any future Labour legislation on the subject. On the question of the standard rate reduction he had always said 'there was room for a reasonable difference of opinion'. Perhaps 'some dashing young sprigs' might think the Budget showed a certain want of imagination; but he repeated, by implication, Hore-Belisha's hint that the restoration of allowances held a very high priority for his 1935 budgeting. The Royal Assent was reported on July 12th.

The Budget of 1934 marks the half-way stage in the Government's recovery plan and the first move away from the repressive measures associated with the name of the Chancellor's one-time fiscal Svengali, Lord Snowden. Chamberlain had opened his 1933 Statement with an acknowledgment to his predeccessor's policy; a year later he was quoting approvingly his article on the disposal of the surplus (see p. 36), and although he was quick to resent any suggestion that he was blaming the 'iron Chancellor' for the 'unpopular sacrifices' of the depression,[2] his repeal of the land values tax and the priority given to the reduction in the standard rate over the restoration of allowances indicated a radical departure from Snowdenian orthodoxy.

It was a Budget of deceptive simplicity with two side issues, whether the Chancellor had underestimated either by instinct or design and whether he should have applied his surplus to debt redemption, and one main issue. This was, granted the premise, which no one in fact disputed, that a start should be made on repaying the sacrifices of 1931, whether it should be done by restoring allowances or reducing rates.

Whatever his supporters might argue, and some opposed him on all three issues, and however the Labour Party might accuse him of gross inequity on each count, Chamberlain never deviated from the stand he had taken on the afternoon April 17th. On his estimates for the current year he declared 'there is no foundation for any idea

---

[1] H. 22/4/1934, Cols 752/760.   [2] H. 19/4/1934, Col. 1250.

that I have deliberately underestimated the revenue with any sinister intention',[1] and he went on to examine some of the suggestions where he and his critics differed for any 'gross flaw or error' in his calculations; needless to say, he found none. On debt redemption his duty was plain. 'In the year before, we had a deficit of £32 millions which had to be added to the National Debt. It seems to me that if you have a surplus of almost the same amount in the following year you really want a very good reason if you are not to make good to posterity what you put on the year before.[2] And on the major talking-point, neither he nor Hore-Belisha wanted to be dogmatic, but the necessary stimulus to industry as represented by the rate reduction had seemed on balance to be best for the country.

Nathan had said that the Budget reminded him more of *The Old Curiosity Shop* than *Great Expectations*, and the discussions certainly followed a curiously restricted course. The advocates of public works did not press their case with any conviction, possibly because of the half-million drop in the unemployment figures without the deficit budgeting recommended by Keynes.[3] The proportion of direct to indirect taxation was treated almost as a theoretical exercise by both sides; in any case it was fair to argue that tariffs were acting as a crude but necessary form of import control. Finally, the controversy over the land values tax had proved something of a red herring and diverted attention from more valuable topics such as a monetary policy commission which never got further than the suggestion stage.[4]

This narrow range of debate arose from the fact that the 1934 Budget was unique in that it was deliberately devoted to an *ad hoc* purpose 'that the first call upon the surplus must be for those who had suffered and made their contributions to the national emergency in 1931; any question of redistributing according to your political conceptions is ruled out'.[5] Admittedly the standard rate revision was a clumsy panacea, since it affected individuals and companies alike; a more precise instrument, as suggested,[6] would have been an uplift of wear and tear allowances. There might then have been a balance available for the workers still facing what Wedgwood, in a phrase worthy of Profesor Paish, called 'the deadly competition of the unemployed'. But in very general terms there was

---

[1] H. 19/4/1934, Col. 1254.
[3] Letter to *The Times* 5/4/1933.
[5] H. 19/4/1934, Col. 1253.
[2] H. 19/4/1934, Col. 1257.
[4] H. 16/5/1934, Col. 1886 (Mason).
[6] Cf. pp. 40 and 50.

unemployment both in savings and machinery: that was why industrial production had to be stimulated.

This then was the basic justification of Chamberlain's policy in 1934. Perhaps as *The Times*[1] put it, 'It my well appear to him preferable to change the severity of the past two Budgets by stages into beneficence'. A simpler explanation is that extra taxation of £81·5 millions was levied in 1931 of which income tax payers found 70 per cent. The surplus was £29 millions, of which he now proposed to give income tax payers £20 millions or roughly 70 per cent. Fiscal justice could not be dispensed more accurately.

[1] 16/4/1934.

Chapter III

The Finance Bill 1935

MISSION COMPLETED

Time Table:

Financial Statement		April 15, 1935
Budget Proposals		
	1st Day	16
	2nd Day	17
Budget Resolutions		
	Reported	May 1
Finance Bill		
	1st Reading	1
	2nd Reading	21
Committee		
	1st Day	June 18
	2nd Day	19
	3rd Day	24
Report		July 1
Third Reading		5
Royal Assent		10

The latter part of 1934 had been a trying period for Chamberlain: 'I am more and more,' he complained, 'carrying this Government on my back.' A possible move to the Foreign Office, in place of Simon, had been in the air, but this was 'too much to ask'. People, he thought, would suggest that 'I had worked for the change because I saw Budgetary difficulties ahead'.[1] It was with a sense of relief, therefore, that he was able to open his Budget Statement[2] on the April 15,

[1] Keith Feiling, *Neville Chamberlain*, p. 240.   [2] H. 15/4/1935, Col. 1615.

1935, by announcing 'a substantial advance towards recovery'. Manufacturing had set new records, with a new low in trade disputes; the retail sector showed an almost equal expansion. Exports were up by £20 millions and small savings by £50 millions. "I calculate that this year the people of this country sweetened their lives with 80,000 tons of sugar more. They smoked 6,500,000 lbs more tobacco. They spent £2,750,000 more on entertainments and they washed away their troubles with 270,000,000 more pints of beer and 700,000,000 more cups of that beverage which cheers but not inebriates.'[1] It was not without significance, he claimed, that this forward movement had followed upon a series of balanced Budgets.

Turning now in his review of the past year, the Chancellor reminded the House that his estimated surplus had been £796,000 only; but revenue had exceeded the forecasts by nearly £10 millions, and although he had had to finance expenditure on a further £3 millions or so, his surplus was £7·5 millions; indeed, including over £12 millions spent on Debt redemption, the true out-turn was close on £20 millions.

A breakdown of receipts showed Customs and Excise had yielded nearly £290 millions, almost the same as the estimate and a £3·5 millions increase on the previous year. Inland Revenue produced £388·5 millions, £16 millions above the estimate, made up of an excess of £9·377 millions on income tax, of £5·356 millions on death duties and of £1 million on surtax; a better rate of collection had helped for the tax on increased profits was only just beginning to effect the Exchequer.[2] Death duties incidentally benefited twice over from the current increase in the value of securities which not only enhanced the value of estates but brought them into the range of a high level of duties. Only the Post Office had disappointed at £1·75 million below the estimate, but that was attributable to the restoration of the pay cuts.

Then came a short statement about the National Debt.[3] Last April £105 millions of 4 per cent and £11 millions of 3 per cent Treasury Bonds had been repaid by raising £150 millions through the issue of a 3 per cent Funding Loan which had provided a small margin as well for the reduction of floating debt. Last December,

[1] H. 15/4/1935, Col. 1616. [2] See p. 34.
[3] H. 15/4/1935, Col. 1619.

taking advantage of the continued cheapness of money, notice had been given to draw for repayment £44 millions of the remaining 3 per cent bonds. Since then £34 millions had already been purchased and redeemed out of Sinking Fund money so that the redemption of the remainder now could be carried out with no disturbance of the market. He ought to mention gratefully as well the repayment by South Africa of £7·5 millions of War Debt which had been posted to Debt redemption: as a result the National Debt had decreased by £21·75 millions and the annual interest by £1·65 millions. Finally he wished to emphasize that the Exchange Equalization Account was still showing a profit; he was obliged to the Committee 'for their forbearance in not asking for details of the working of the account'.

Turning now to the Fixed Debt Charge, he had already warned the Committee[1] of a prospective increase to cover Debt reduction 'on a more appropriate scale' and the estimated average cost of National Savings Certificates and Treasury Bills interest over a period of years. But there had in fact been no change over the year. Treasury Bills had remained at the extremely low average of 12s 6d per cent and there had been less encashment of National Savings Certificates than anticipated. The Fixed Debt Charge could then be held at £224 millions. Three other smaller items were a charge on the Consolidated Fund, Northern Ireland, at £6·75 millions, miscellaneous Consolidated Fund Services at £3·7 millions and a payment to the Post Office of £1·13 millions, making a grand total of £235·58 millions.

The estimates for the Supply Services were already known to the Committee: they amounted to £490·59 millions. In addition there would be various subsidies requiring, as usual, supplementary estimates which he calculated at £4 millions, giving a final total under this head of £494·59 millions. It was not due, Chamberlain hastened to add, to any relaxation of control but to 'definite decisions approved by Parliament'.[2] £10·5 millions extra had to be provided for the armed forces and £14·5 millions for shipping, agriculture and social services. The Post Office and the Road Fund were self-balancing items and were excluded from the ultimate total of £729·97 millions.

The Chancellor had now been speaking for about half an hour.

[1] See p. 33.   [2] H. 15/4/1935, Col. 1621.

Pausing for a glass of water, he then proceeded to the rhetorical question, 'What revenue can we find to finance this enormous out-lay?', over £30 millions more than 1934. He decided to take the smaller items first, £5 millions from motor duties as fixed last year, £11·85 millions from the Post Office, the drop due to restoration of the cuts and a reduction in telephone charges, and miscellaneous receipts[1] of £26·73 million. This gave a minor receipts total of £43·58 millions.

Then came the larger items.[2] The Inland Revenue amounted to a stupendous £396 millions composed of income tax £237 millions, surtax £51·5 millions, death and stamp duties £105 millions and remaining duties such as Excess Profits Duty and Corporation Profits Tax £2·5 millions. In view of the improvement in trade there should be a gain of £14 millions in income tax over the 1934 yield, after taking into account the increase of £6 millions due to improved collection. Surtax would not be likely to show any improvement, or death duties, but stamp duties should yield more. Customs and Excise should respond to the general expansion of trade and there should be an all-round increase in receipts estimated at £6 millions to bring in a total of £296 millions. Minor items of £43·58 millions, Inland Revenue at £396 millions and Customs and Excise of £296 millions gave an estimated revenue of £735·58 millions against estimated expenditure of £729·97 millions, or an estimated surplus of £5·61 millions.

This was a comparatively modest figure, but happily not the final surplus. Leaving his calculations in the air for the time being, he dealt briefly with the financing of local Loans Funds by 3 per cent Local Loans Stock, indicating a change in conditions for future borrowing.[3] He then passed on to small Customs and Excise changes and a slight estate duty concession, the effect of both on the revenue being negligible. The alteration in heavy oil duty, however, was more important. There were now over seven thousand diesel-engined vehicles on the road and the tax on their fuel oil was a penny per gallon only as compared with eightpence per gallon on petrol. Bearing in mind that a gallon of fuel oil provided nearly twice the mileage of a gallon of petrol he did not think it inequitable to increase the heavy oil duty to eightpence.

[1] H. 15/4/1935, Col. 1622. [2] H. 15/4/1935, Cols 1623/1624.
[3] See Sections 28/31, F.A., 1935.

Then came the turn of the Road Fund which had accumulated a surplus of £4·47 millions. A five-year plan of road construction and improvement was being drawn up with the help of the local authorities, but meantime until 'commitments matured'[1] the surplus was not needed by the Fund. It would, however, fill a 'very pressing need . . . as an addition to my modest surplus to be used for the relief of taxation'. Hore-Belisha, now Minister of Transport,[2] 'expressed some reluctance to assume even temporarily the role of the dying Sir Philip Sidney', despite the fact that the Chancellor promised reconsideration should more money be required for roads, in the next year or so, than the Road Fund could supply. These various additions brought the surplus up to £11·025 millions.

Snowden still rated a mention in Chamberlain's opening remarks on his disposal of the surplus, that the first relief ought to go to those who suffered most. Heading the list was entertainments duty[3] which in 1931 had been extended to admission charges between 2d and 6d besides increasing the scales over 6d. The duty on the seats up to 6d had raised no less than £2·3 millions: these would now be wholly relieved, and there would also be a reduction on the seats over 6d in entertainments given by living performers, costing £400,000.

Next came income tax.[4] 'I want this year,' said the Chancellor, 'to see the small taxpayer have his turn.' He proposed to achieve this by revising reduced rate relief to the first £135 of taxable income at 1s 6d[5] and the next £40 at 4s 6d[6] which would give substantial relief to the small tax-payer with taxable income under £135, this relief gradually dying out as taxable income of £175 was approached. The allowance for a married taxpayer would be raised from £150 to £170, and child allowance would be increased to £50 for each child.[7] There was also to be a proposed new exemption limit of £125 for income whether earned or unearned, together with marginal relief between £125 and £140. The full cost of these amendments would be £10 millions but in the current year £4·5 millions only.

Finally the salary cuts were to be fully restored at a current cost of £4 millions, making a final relief figure of £10·525 millions.

---

[1] H. 15/4/1935, Cols 1628/1629. [2] Since the latter half of 1934.
[3] H. 15/4/1935, Cols 1629/1630. [4] H. 15/4/1935, Cols 1630/1634.
[5] Instead of 2s 3d. [6] Instead of 2s 3d.
[7] Instead of £50 for the first and £40 for each subsequent.

This, deducted from the original surplus of £11·025 millions, left a prospective balance of £·5 millions.

Chamberlain had now spoken for an hour and a half. His summary was brief. The 'solid, continuous and steady improvement' over the past three and a half years had been derived from a combination of tariffs, conversion operations, cheap money, balanced Budgets, remissions of taxation. 'Given peace abroad and a fair measure of unity at home I see no reason why we should not during this current year make a further substantial advance towards prosperity.'[1]

Attlee, on behalf of the Labour Party, indicated formal approval of the Budget[2] in doing belated justice to the smaller taxpayer although it was 'carrying on rather than introducing'. The surplus, however, had been bolstered by the 'Churchillian device' of a raid; and he found sinister overtones in the provision for increased armaments involving the danger of an arms race. Samuel, the Liberal leader, also welcomed[3] the restoration of allowances and of the remaining cuts; and he too thought the raid on the Road Fund 'a departure from the canons of strict finance'.

There were five more speakers before a fairly early adjournment at eleven minutes to six. Maxton,[4] for the Communist Party, added his congratulations but pleaded for the abolition of the Means Test and found the increased expenditure on armaments a matter of regret. Sir William Davison,[5] Chairman of the Income Tax Payers' Society and a traditional post-Budget commentator, ascribed the £7·5 millions surplus to the improved yield of income tax but held that the prosperity of the country would not return until war taxation, which was a drag on industry, disappeared. During this speech the House was almost counted out so that few members heard Sanderson's[6] point on soya beans or Bevan's[7] inability to keep silent over the Chancellor's failure to relieve the Means Test and the distressed areas. It was left to Macquisten[8] to provide a somewhat eccentric conclusion with his attack on the increased heavy-oil duty which he saw as a threat to the development of the diesel-engined aeroplane and on the 'terrible penal taxation of the whisky duty'.

[1] H. 15/4/1935 Col. 1635.   [2] H. 15/4/1935, Cols 1636/1637.
[3] H. 15/4/1935, Cols 1638/1639.   [4] H. 15/4/1935, Cols 1639/1641.
[5] H. 15/4/1935, Cols 1641/1643.   [6] H. 15/4/1935 Col. 1643.
[7] H. 15/4/1935, Cols 1643/1644.   [8] H. 15/4/1935, Cols 1644/1645.

It had been generally expected that the Budget speech would be short and contain no dramatic surprises; this no doubt had accounted for the empty benches and lack of excitement. The reaction of the Press on the following day was predictably lukewarm. The popular papers concentrated on the income tax reliefs but it was the *Manchester Guardian*[1] which pinpointed the reason for this comparative apathy. Under the heading 'A Charted Course' the leader took the view that while Chamberlain was probably correct in assuming that the psychological stimulus of reduced taxation could be relied upon for some time to come and that consistency was a virtue, he had also produced 'a fairly barren Budget'. Since last year's relief to the standard rate taxpayer had intensified the injustice of the Snowden increases to the smaller taxpayer, it was inevitable that the Chancellor should have 'worn his blinkers and kept his eyes on the 1931 course'.

The Times,[2] however, was far more enthusiastic. The Budget was certain to be popular although it was very much as anticipated; and solid approval was expressed of the Government line which had now redeemed its pledge to repeal the austerities of the depression period. There was no mention of the industrialists' realism, reported elsewhere in the paper, that what was needed was a bold Budget not 'a Budget of forty winks from Sleepy Hollow'.[3]

This sentiment was echoed by the *New Statesman*;[4] 'the present discontents cry out for bold measures', but the Budget was unsensational, conservative, fair within limits; however, the social services had been starved for the armaments industry, and while the Chancellor was probably right to bank on the revival of prosperity, what sort of prosperity was it when a restoration of 80 per cent[5] still left $2\frac{1}{4}$ millions unemployed?

The Economist[6] was equally critical: while admitting that with the twin factors of increased expenditure on the Forces and the 6d off standard rate in 1934 the Chancellor had left himself with little room for manoeuvre, this did not wholly excuse him from producing 'the most pedestrian Budget of recent years'. The figures ruled out any general remission so that it was a foregone conclusion who the beneficiaries would be. The following week's leader[7] was en-

---

[1] 16/4/1935.   [2] 16/4/1935.
[3] Sir Keith Joseph, President of the F.B.I.   [4] 20/4/1935.
[5] See p. 63.   [6] 20/4/1935.   [7] 27/4/1935.

titled 'Still Drifting' and accused the Government of lack of planning, quite apart from its reticence on the Supplementary Estimates, unemployment and future defence expenditure. The Budget had become 'a mere discussion of small margins available for disposal in the cash account of the year'. There was one source of satisfaction, the taxation remissions in a world of unstable economics, a point which was commented on by the Press of both France and the United States.

Morgan Jones[1] opened the first day's debate with a fifty-minute set piece on behalf of the Opposition. He challenged the Chancellor's claim to have balanced the Budget: war debts had not been mentioned and there was a negligible decrease in the National Debt. Having disposed of his preamble, he then proceeded to mount a five-pronged attack against the Government. He protested vigorously against the drift away from direct and towards indirect taxation; he accused Chamberlain of excessive caution in his estimates of prospective revenue; he argued that there was nothing for the man below the income tax exemption limit and less than nothing for those subject to the Means Test; he castigated the jaunty air with which the Road Fund had been raided—'it was only a transaction'—and the increase in heavy-oil duty was a tax on 'the travelling poor'. In general he welcomed the growing prosperity of the nation; but in this affluence there were still two million unemployed; there were still the distressed areas.

Samuel, for the Liberal Party, made a speech[2] which complemented that of his Labour colleague. There must be general satisfaction at the certain measure of economic recovery, but the unemployment problem still remained and the increase in exports was marginal only. Nor had anything definite been said about the policy of national development[3] or the distressed areas. Even the ordinary taxpayer was receiving sparse benefits from the more favourable financial out-turn, for although the general choice of recipients for relief was right the small income tax payer was still more hardly pressed than in 1931. As for the raid on the Road Fund, 'Dick Turpin only stole from passengers on the highway: the Chancellor was stealing the highway from the passengers.' This hold-up raised £7 millions

---

[1] H. 16/4/1935, Cols 1687/1700.　　　[2] H. 16/4/1935, Cols 1700/1711.
[3] Chamberlain in fact saw Lloyd George, 17/4/1935, on the subject but nothing came of it.

towards the £10·5 millions cost of the reliefs; where was the cost of £18 millions in a full year to come from? But 'the very worst feature in the accounts and most ominous for the finances of the future was the £10·5 millions needed for armaments'.[1]

Both these speeches are worth study in detail, for between them they incorporate most of the points made during the rest of the day. The Opposition took its cue from Morgan Jones and emphasized the lack of provision for the unemployed. Tinker,[2] Cleary[3] and Batey[4] all took this line, the first two emotionally, the third making the practical suggestion that public works would not solve the problem: 'the Government must set up industries'. Logan[5] linked his plea for the distressed areas with the argument that to give the unemployed more spending power was the best way to stimulate trade.

The general Conservative attitude was equally predictable: there were the usual criticisms of death duties 'that they were taking £80 millions out of the country's capital for use as income'; as Wardlaw-Milne[6] said, 'a curious exception to the general orthodoxy of the Budget'. O'Connor[7] took the same view, linking the danger of converting capital into income with the declining yield of direct taxation and the increase in national, especially social, expenditure. 'You can either economize or expand; and economy having failed, the only other policy is expansion.'[8] This, too, was Stourton's[9] idea in a thoughtful speech in which he not only advocated what he called a 'labour utilization study' in the Civil Service and a 'withdrawal of wasteful subsidies' in the interests of economy, but also a 'selective expansionist policy', for example, in electrification of railway services and modernization of water supplies.

On the whole, however, such was Chamberlain's hold over his policy in the House that the majority of members toed the orthodox mark. The small taxpayers would appreciate the concessions, said Allen,[10] 'the voice from Northern Ireland', and Braithwaite,[11] while Hills[12] declared roundly that sixpence off income tax would be the best cure for unemployment. This opinion was the keystone of

[1] H. 16/4/1935, Col. 1707.
[2] H. 16/4/1935, Cols 1716/1721.
[3] H. 16/4/1935, Cols 1759/1762.
[4] H. 16/4/1935, Cols 1770/1777.
[5] H. 16/4/1935, Cols 1794/1799.
[6] H. 16/4/1935, Cols 1740/1747.
[7] H. 16/4/1935, Cols 1747/1757.
[8] H. 16/4/1935, Col. 1754.
[9] H. 16/4/1935, Cols 1786/1794.
[10] H. 16/4/1935, Cols 1721/1724.
[11] H. 16/4/1935, Cols 1780/1786.
[12] H. 16/4/1935, Cols 1711/1716.

the speeches by Fleming[1] and Waldron Smithers;[2] but for once he was not the most representative Tory voice. This belonged to Sir Isidore Salmon.[3] 'We are not looking,' he declared, 'for a Chancellor to come along with a spectacular Budget or spectacular programmes'. The secret of the Budget's success was its stimulus to confidence. Mabane,[4] as usual, was the spokesman of those who thought the estimates were not 'a reasonable anticipation of the prosperity which is likely to come', an argument he had used in the previous year; and the only other minor criticism was the industrialists' plea for taxation relief on company reserves.[5]

Into the opposing benches, fixed in their familiar attitudes, Wilmot[6] then injected his controlled ferocity, taking upon himself Bevan's usual role. Last year's surplus went to the richest section of taxpayers; but this year the poor were not receiving their promised relief. There was only the appearance of restitution, for the value of the increased child allowance and life assurance relief was vitiated by the change in reduced rate relief; and the principle of extending exemption to investment income was 'vicious'. Examples were provided to drive home his point.[7] The heavy-oil duty increase would destroy the infant diesel-engine industry and the raid on the Road Fund was thoroughly dishonest. 'The Budget was a Budget of tricks and subterfuges'; there was an inherent contradiction between the claim of restoration of 80 per cent prosperity with 2·25 millions unemployed; this the Government seemed to regard as normal, but the electorate would do well to ponder 'the full meaning of that sinister phrase'.

This 'intolerant tirade',[8] the Financial Secretary to the Treasury, Duff Cooper,[9] said correctly in his summary of the speeches, was the only 'violent attack' during the debate. The rest were mainly general criticisms 'which are brought against any Government in order to spend the time which they felt it was their duty, as Members of the Opposition, to devote to the annual Budget'. He continued

[1] H. 16/4/1935, Cols 1777/1780.

[2] H. 16/4/1935, Cols 1764/1770. (and see also his letter to *The Times* 9/4/1935).

[3] H. 16/4/1935, Cols 1799/1803. (Incidentally his speech also advocated decimal coinage.)

[4] H. 16/4/1935, Cols 1724/1732.

[5] Cf. Samuel Col. 1708, or Hills, Col. 1711.

[6] H. 16/4/1935 Cols 1732/1740.   [7] H. 16/4/1935, Cols 1733/1734.

[8] The phrase is O'Connor's.   [9] H. 16/4/1935, Cols 1803/1813.

with an urbanity which befitted the biographer of Talleyrand that he too deplored the defence expenditure, but no one had said it was unnecessary; and in reply to Jones's point on its amount,[1] armament's expenditure was 14 per cent of the total Budget compared with 50 per cent in 1914. It was not the business of the Treasury as a Department to come forward with schemes of social reform but rather to review them when propounded. The real cure for unemployment was a gradual restoration of prosperity; and he must point out that the two millions unemployed did not represent a permanent unemployed figure. He defended the heavy-oil duty and the Road Fund appropriation. There had been no promise of a complete restoration of the pre-1931 position; there was a limited surplus and the Chancellor was not a 'kind of Spring Santa Claus'.

The second day's debate on the Budget proposals often makes more interesting reading than the first because of the additional time for study and reflection. But in the reports of the long hours from 3.38 p.m. to 11 p.m. on April 17, 1935, there would be a vain search for any real originality; indeed, after nearly four hours' discussion the House was hard put to it to find a quorum.

This was partly the Opposition's fault for their four main speakers contented themselves with somewhat general and academic criticisms. Attlee[2] commenced by a satirical account of Chamberlain's ability 'to get away with it' on account of 'his air of supreme respectability and orthodoxy'. But he did not show any grasp of the realities of the situation; he had produced an essentially 'mark time Budget' with no long-term planning. Banfield[3] adopted the same line: it was 'a hand-to-mouth' Budget which did nothing for the unemployed, those on Pensions and the Means Test, or the distressed areas; the final restoration of the cuts and the income tax concessions affected relatively few. West[4] went further: the best stimulus to trade would be the abolition of the Means Test and the increase of pensions. All sorts of reasons were being given for recovery—tariffs, cheap money, taxation reductions and the depreciation of sterling. But in fact the Chancellor was lucky to be in office when world trade was on the upgrade. Griffiths[5] agreed the scope of Budget benefits was a very narrow one; this was in effect a summary of the Opposi-

[1] See p. 61.
[2] H. 17/4/1935, Cols 1859/1866.
[3] H. 17/4/1935, Cols 1886/1893.
[4] H. 17/4/1935, Cols 1910/1917.
[5] H. 17/4/1935, Cols 1936/1942.

tion's case. Mason[1] was the odd man out; he compared the yield of direct taxation with that of indirect in 1934/5 with the figures ten years earlier; the former was down by £35 millions but the latter was up by £52 millions; this was an unhealthy trend and the increase pressed hardest on those least able to bear it.

The main body of Government opinion swung solidly behind the Chancellor for his restoration of reliefs. Pownall[2] and Clarke[3] (in a three-minute speech—the shortest of the day) appreciated the effect on the middle and working classes. Orr-Ewing,[4] too, wished to stress 'the tremendous value of the reliefs' although he was critical of the heavy-oil duty increase. Guy[5] and Somerville,[6] one speech following the other, agreed that the greatest measure of relief had justly gone to those who suffered most in 1931, and that the net result was a material increase in purchasing power. Even Buchanan,[7] Member for the Gorbals, praised this aspect of the proposals and the Chancellor for not giving way to the clamour for reduction of death duties and surtax. Gillett[8] summed up: most of the 1931 cuts had been restored but no one imagined that it would, in the present circumstances, be possible to restore income tax allowances on the old scale. The coming problems, he thought, related to foreign exchange rather than purely domestic difficulties.

Gillett had, however, touched upon an internal fiscal problem 'that we are approaching the level on which taxation is possible'. This saturation theory was the theme of a number of speeches. Samuel[9] thought the law of diminishing returns was beginning to operate and that the resources of the rich were being seriously depleted; the incidence of taxation on smaller investors might have to be increased. Balfour,[10] too, felt that the country was living on a very narrow margin between its maximum taxable capacity and its revenue requirements; there was little hope of any further relief to taxpayers. Loftus[11] was equally concerned with the significance of a diminishing yield of taxation allied to an increase in national expenditure which only a resurgence in world trade could remedy:

[1] H. 17/4/1935, Cols 1866/1876. [2] H. 17/4/1935, Cols 1895/1899.
[3] H. 17/4/1935, Cols 1905/1906. [4] H. 17/4/1935, Cols 1922/1927.
[5] H. 17/4/1935, Cols 1942/1947. [6] H. 17/4/1935, Cols 1947/1949.
[7] H. 17/4/1935, Cols 1899/1905. [8] H. 17/4/1935, Cols 1949/1955.
[9] H. 17/4/1935, Cols 1881/1886 (Marcus Samuel).
[10] H. 17/4/1935, Cols 1893/1895. [11] H. 17/4/1935, Cols 1927/1931.

C

and Evans,[1] who followed him, suggested the dropping of subsidies as one move in the economy campaign.

Some of the right-wing Tories went further: Lindsay[2] demanded that any increase in social services should be opposed and advocated a tripartite pension scheme. Albery[3] suggested using pension and superannuation schemes for withdrawing the older men from the labour market, thus providing more jobs for younger men. Allen[4] considered the revival of industry the best cure for unemployment and advocated the freeing of reserves from taxation when they were used for the purchase of plant or the development of the business. The palm of the evening should, however, be awarded to Doran:[5] 'I am not a financial expert,' he confessed, and then proceeded to make the confession entirely unnecessary by cross-talk with the Opposition whose Socialism he accounted for by the assumption that they had been 'brought up and fed on bilge water'.

The last two speeches of the evening were quite the most significant for they illustrated the contrast between the old and the new fiscal thinking, thus bringing to the debate an authority which it had lacked for most of its course.

Grenfell[6] summed up for the Opposition. He allowed that the Chancellor had attempted to make the largest possible concessions but, apart from that, he did not seem to have any definite plan to his Budget, despite the fact that the total estimate was four times the largest pre-war estimate and represented 20 per cent of the national income as compared with 10 per cent pre-war. What the Chancellor had not realized was that 'this large sum is the result of a much more formidable mechanism than any which existed in pre-war days and has a more direct bearing on the life of the nation. The Chancellor today is a much more important person: he represents the most important officer of the State . . . he is the key to the structure of finance and industry.' The latter was very heavily taxed as was the ordinary man; and this raised the question of the relation of both to the State. The Budget was too static: it dealt neither with this vital problem nor, for example, the co-ordination of transport or the depressed areas.

Chamberlain[7] in his reply commenced predictably by saying that

[1] H. 17/4/1935, Cols 1931/1936. [2] H. 17/4/1935, Cols 1917/1922.
[3] H. 17/4/1935, Cols 1906/1910. [4] H. 17/4/1935, Cols 1876/1881.
[5] H. 17/4/1935, Cols 1955/1961. [6] H. 17/4/1935, Cols 1961/1970.
[7] H. 17/4/1935, Cols 1970/1977.

criticism should be directed against the Budget he had proposed, not one he might have proposed; and it did have a simple and obvious plan—'a fair distribution of the surplus among the 1931 sufferers'. It was always as well to be cautious in estimates of revenue but he was certain the extra cost of the concessions, in reply to Samuel,[1] would be met by the increased yield of taxation from increased profits; he agreed with the opinion already expressed that the rate of direct taxation was too high for a rise in rate to give a rise in receipts.[2] There was nothing directly for the unemployed, but the best service to them would be to render the country more prosperous. He felt, too, that he was justified in ignoring war debts when there were virtually no receipts. Finally, he pointed out that he was concerned to make general points only; 'there would be further opportunities at different stages for discussing particular items in the Budget'.

The debate on the Second Reading[3] was far more interesting than those of the two previous years and repays detailed study. Attention was focused on three main features, the Road Fund, the heavy-oil duty and the standard rate of income tax. On the first, some speakers[4] treated the House to a historical lecture, going back to the Fund's institution in 1909; eleven years later, in Austen Chamberlain's Chancellorship, a specific pledge had been given that it would not be 'diverted to the relief of general taxation'.[5] The basic criticism, however, was that essentially it was a tax on industry, as Harris pointed out.[6] In his reply, Chamberlain[7] dismissed 1909 as irrelevant and took his stand on the old constitutional doctrine that a Minister could not pledge succeeding Parliaments for all time; in addition, he had asked local authorities to submit road work programmes to cover the next five years.

The discussion on the heavy-oil duty produced sound arguments on both sides. It was generally agreed that the Government did not wish to cramp the progress of the diesel engine but the inevitable result would be to handicap road transport unfairly *vis-à-vis* rail transport;[8] and that lighter diesel engines might prove uneconomical to develop was the opinion of a director of A.E.C.[9] Chamberlain's

[1] See p. 61.
[2] H. 17/4/1935, Col. 1976.
[3] H. 21/5/1935, Cols 379/520.
[4] H. 1/5/1935, Cols. 379/385
[5] H. 2/12/1920, Cols 1529/1930.
[6] H. 1/5/1935, Col. 385.
[7] H. 1/5/1935, Cols 500/405.
[8] H. 1/5/1935, Cols 432/439 (Jones).
[9] Moore-Brabazon, H. 1/5/1935, Cols. 439/441.

reply was sweetly reasonable. His sole object in proposing the measure had been to prevent 'a hole in the wall increasing in size'. He admitted, too, that it was Government policy to stop further transfers from road to rail, but his critics should remember that there was still a slight discrimination in favour of diesel oil which was to balance the cost of diesel-engine research. It was, he concluded almost pathetically, 'a defensive measure taken by a hard-pressed Chancellor.[1]

Major Hills[2] had no luck at all with his proposal to reduce the standard rate to 4s 0d; in fact he admitted himself it was a 'forlorn hope'. He was opposed by the official Labour line, as expounded by Tinker,[3] who deplored the increase in indirect taxation, and by Chamberlain himself; the cost, £26 millions, was more than the country could afford. By now it was close on midnight and everyone 'wanted to get away';[4] the latter part of the evening had, however, been enlivened by Duff Cooper's attempts to speak about rice in the husk from a brief hurriedly thrust into his hands by an enterprising Private Secretary in the absence of the Parliamentary Secretary to the Board of Trade. As the Opposition complained, he 'appeared to know nothing at all about it', which was not surprising; and they were by no means mollified when the Parliamentary Secretary did appear and proceed to read exactly the same brief.

The Resolution stage is usually concerned with specific points on the Finance Bill; the Second Reading is traditionally the time for a general, if sometimes discursive, financial review. The Opposition chose to fight over a motion to reject the Bill 'which continues to cast an unfair burden of taxation upon the indirect taxpayer, encourages the limitation of production and embodies no provisions for securing to the people that improvement in the standard of life which the increased productive capacity of the nation has made available'.[5]

The first and last criticisms embodied in this motion were popular features in current Labour dogma and were expounded by Tinker,[6] who deplored any reduction in income tax since it would involve an inevitable increase in indirect taxation, and emphasized that the new prosperity had not yet touched the army of the workless; this point

[1] H. 1/5/1935, Cols 444/448. [2] H. 1/5/1935 Cols 511/513.
[3] H. 1/5/1935, Cols 513/516. [4] H. 1/5/1935, Col. 515.
[5] H. 21/5/1935, Col. 187. [6] H. 21/5/1935, Cols 214/219.

was reinforced by Williams:[1] 'when would it reach the distressed areas?' The novel point, however, was that relating to the limitation of production, an implied stricture on Clause 24[2] which proposed to authorize the deduction from profits of contributions paid to rationalize industry. The Labour complaint was that this provision took no account of workers' redundancy since the operation of the clause would restrict production and thereby reduce employment in productive industries.[3] This view was expressed with great vigour by Batey,[4] who regarded the whole scheme as a capitalist ramp: 'this way of helping the capitalists is just the limit'. This theme was to recur throughout the various stages of the debate.

Conservative comment was more diffuse. There was no lack of sympathy for the unemployed: Hamilton[5] deprecated 'the loss in character and vigour to the nation as a whole'. There was the usual difference of opinion between those who sought prosperity from a reduction in taxation[6] and those who were convinced it could come only from a revival in world trade.[7] There was the routine plea for a reduction in death duties and surtax, and the annual claim from Foot[8] for a revision of wear and tear allowances. But on the whole a good deal of time was spent in mulling over what was not in the Bill rather than what was, so that when Chamberlain[9] made his customary intervention in the middle of the debate he could justifiably claim, as he did in summarizing the speeches to date, that he had been given very little to answer. The three-point Labour charge he summarily dismissed. Import duties had altered the significances of the proportions of direct to indirect taxation: Clause 24 required that any removal of machinery must be in the national interest before any allowance would be due, and in general the present measures were the fairest possible in the circumstances. 'The Bill remains,' he wound up, 'in all the glory of its fresh plumage without having lost a single feather.' No wonder Mason[10] followed by saying he had exhibited 'a complacency unequalled from that bench' and reminded him of the Ciceronian fiscal dictum *Magnum vectigal est parsimonia*.

[1] H. 21/5/1935, Cols 261/266.
[2] Later S. 25, F.A. 1935.
[3] H. 21/5/1935, Cols 187/197 (Paling).
[4] H. 21/5/1935, Cols 268/276.
[5] H. 21/5/1935, Cols 197/202.
[6] H. 21/5/1935, Cols 254/261 (Apsley).
[7] H. 21/5/1935, Cols 197/207 (Hamilton).
[8] H. 21/5/1935, Cols 276/284.
[9] H. 21/5/1935, Cols. 235/244.
[10] H. 21/5/1935, Cols 244/254.

Cripps[1] summarized for the Opposition: apart from his brilliance of presentation and occasional flashes of mordant wit, he was content with a formal attack on the debt policy, the Road Fund raid, the lack of help to the distressed areas and the imbalance of direct and indirect taxation. Only on the now notorious Clause 24 did he rouse himself. 'We shall certainly most strenuously oppose this system of income tax for the purpose of organizing a diminution of productive capacity and the consequent suffering which will come upon men associated with different productive units.' Duff Cooper[2] was therefore in no difficulty with his reply. He stressed the control of the Board of Trade to prevent any possible abuse of Clause 24. In his judgment the burden of taxation had been laid most lightly on those least able to bear it, and the benefits accruing from four years of wise administration had been distributed amongst the largest number.

The Committee stage occupied three days. The Customs and Excise debate[3] was comparatively quiet as usual and the debate on the Inland Revenue clauses the following day opened equally quietly. The first six hours were spent in discussing allowances; but any attempt to propose a decrease in standard rate or an increase in the personal allowances, despite the fact, as Cripps demonstrated,[4] that the 1931 position had not fully been restored, was doomed to failure on the grounds of cost; for example, Chamberlain pointed out in his reply on the proposal to raise the higher personal allowance to its pre-1931 level of £225 that the cost would be £9 millions; and he had already refused to admit to any charge of underestimating. The Liberals, incidentally, were prepared to accept that the economic revival was still not sufficient to underwrite a complete return to taxation before the crisis.[5] The only slight breakthrough was the sympathetic consideration of treating unpaid apprenticeship as full-time education, proposed by Tinker.[6] The formal proposal had in fact been redrafted by Treasury officials, but it was lost in the Report stage on the ground that it would create too many anomalies.[7] Strangely enough a similar proposal had been turned down by Austen Chamberlain fifteen years before.[8]

[1] H. 21/5/1935, Cols 296/305.
[3] H. 18/5/1935.
[5] H. 19/6/1935, Col. 429 (Samuel).
[7] H. 1/7/1935, Cols 1645/1649.

[2] H. 21/5/1935, Cols 305/314.
[4] H. 19/6/1935, Col. 428.
[6] H. 19/6/1935, Cols 444/455.
[8] H. 7/7/1920, Col. 1538.

But again it was Clause 24 which engendered the most heat. Morgan Jones[1] moved an amendment designed to secure the re-employment or compensation of workers displaced by rationalization, and it was strongly supported by Cripps,[2] Attlee[3] and Bevan.[4] All three used the Clause as a stick to beat capitalism, with Cripps throwing in for good measure the advocates' point that if the scheme were in the interests of industry as a whole, why should the industry be compensated? Bevan made the general point that the Government was promulgating measures in a way which did not allow of their proper discussion and thus 'this miserable collection of has-beens' was bringing legislation by discussion into disrepute.

The spirit had evaporated from this stage, however, by the third day, which was concerned mainly with sweeping-up suggestions including a new Clause[5] which effectively gave relief to promoted judges and civil servants, on which all parties agreed.[6]

The Report stages occupied one hundred and thirty-two columns and lasted some seven hours,[7] but apart from a renewed attack on Clause 24, which was assuming a King Charles' head position in Labour's commination, a docile majority saw the new clauses, mainly on points of procedure, safely through. The Third Reading took place four days later, on July 5, 1935.

At eleven a.m. on that day Chamberlain[8] stood at the dispatch box for the fourth time in four years to summarize a debate which had occupied the best part of his time for nearly three months. He was in his usual confident mood. The Budget had commanded 'a generally favourable acceptance'. The Opposition had condemned the Bill on the ground that it consisted of a 'parcel of presents' to the Tories but had tried to show, inconsistently, that each of these presents was worthless. As far as 'the usual applications for the usual concessions' were concerned, acceptance had not been possible usually because resources were limited. But he had come 'very near the completion of one of the aims that I set before myself . . . so to conduct the finances of the country that it would be possible safely to remove those burdens which were imposed in 1931'. It was not an election Budget: 'I am not a believer myself in election Budgets . . .

---

[1] H. 19/6/1935, Cols 455/457. [2] H. 19/6/1935, Col. 470.
[3] H. 19/6/1935, Col. 477. [4] H. 19/6/1935, Col. 482.
[5] S. 26, F.A. 1935. [6] H. 24/6/1935, Cols 893/895.
[7] H. 1/7/1935, Cols 1563/1674. [8] H. 5/7/1935, Cols 2141/2145.

I am profoundly sceptical as to the value of Budgets if they are de-signed purely for the purpose of catching votes.' He concluded by quoting figures on industrial progress generally, which he claimed justified 'the spirit of reasonable optimism' in which the Finance Bill had been framed.

The immediate summary of the Opposition's case was under-taken by Rhys Davies.[1] The poorest section of the community, the unemployed, gained no benefit. The remissions of taxation, despite the Chancellor's remarks, were mere electioneering. Rationaliza-tion might be an industrial pick-me-up but it ignored the human element. If this was the final balance sheet of the Government the certificate should read 'Audited and found totally incorrect'.

Labour support for their opening speaker varied between critic-ism of Chamberlain himself, whom Tinker,[2] for example, found 'full of complacency and satisfaction', and variations on the themes al-ready elaborated over the past months. Brown,[3] for instance, claimed that rationalization would create more unemployment and that the Bill did nothing to readjust 'the maldistribution of wealth', which was hardly surprising in view of Chamberlain's refusal to regard the Budget 'as an instrument for levelling out inequalities of income'.[4] Wilmot,[5] for once, after a gibe at the 'lurid financial melodrama' provided by the Tories, gave a very fair epitome of his party's case. If trade was improved by remission of taxation, then surely it was better to improve the lot of the lowly-paid taxpayer, and thus in-crease consumption, than improve the position of the more highly paid which did not, to the same extent.

The most impartial and reasoned summary, however, of the Chan-cellor's aims and achievements came from Boothby.[6] He praised the results of tariffs and the Exchange Equalization Account and fore-cast an equal success for rationalization. But he also recognized that 'we still have the depressed areas and two million people out of work'. The reason fundamentally was industrial depression all over the world and there was thus no unilateral solution, although something might be done by weeding out inefficient concerns and expanding markets through overseas loans.

[1] H. 5/7/1935, Cols 2145/2153. [2] H. 5/7/1935, Cols 2166/2170.
[3] H. 5/7/1935, Cols 2185/2189. [4] H. 1/6/1933, Col. 1069.
[5] H. 5/7/1935, Cols 2194/2203. [6] H. 5/7/1935, Cols 2173/2185.

Duff Cooper[1] found winding up a comparatively simple task. He contented himself by exposing the cruel dilemma with which the Opposition was faced. If it was accepted that taxation should not be increased, the only way of balancing would be by means of reducing expenditure. But the only possible spheres were national defence and social services. No Opposition member had come out with an unequivocal suggestion that expenditure on either should be curtailed. He agreed there was nothing spectacular about the Bill: it was simply one more step in consolidating British finances in a period of profound economic and political disturbance. There were only eleven Noes; and on July 10th the Royal Assent was reported.

The Finance Act of 1935 for all practical purposes ended an interesting series of Budgets which had started in 1932. What Chamberlain then set out to accomplish, a restoration of the 1931 cuts in allowances and salaries while maintaining a balanced Budget, he had almost finished, although he had still not finally dealt with certain of the social claimants and the smaller income tax payers.

For Snowden's crisis measures fell under three heads—direct taxation, indirect taxation and pay cuts. The first he had increased by £57·5 millions; £35 millions had now been remitted by his successor; but half the reductions in allowances still remained, and the surcharge of 10 per cent on surtax. Indirect taxation had been increased by £24 millions; and although this had now been reinforced by the tariff policy, the cost of living was down by eight and a half points and the beer duty had been cancelled to the extent of £14 millions in theory;[2] in fact it was £10 millions only through the increase in consumption. The pay cuts had been wholly restored. Only the Means Test remained; and that had been considerably modified and its over-all effect cushioned by a general improvement in social services. It was this policy of continuous reinstatement and old-fashioned budgeting laid down by Chamberlain as soon as he took over the seals of office four years previously which had won on the whole unswerving support from his party, and, to an extent, from the Liberals.

It is clear from their speeches that it was not easy for the Labour Party members to mount a consistent assault on the Budget. Even so formidable an opponent as Wilmot[3] was haunted by the ghost of

[1] H. 5/7/1935, Cols 2214/2224. [2] See p. 6.
[3] H. 5/7/1935, Cols 2199/2200.

1931 which Chamberlain had successfully exorcised so that criticism was inhibited both by the achievements of the Chancellor
and the difficulty of finding a constructive line of attack. The virtue
of public works, even when specifically to the needs of a local authority, was regarded as highly problematical; the imbalance between
direct and indirect taxation had become largely an academic debating point which the abandonment of free trade had further confused;
the plight of the unemployed was partly the result of a world contraction in trade and so not susceptible to any unilateral solution; and
the various current measures which had come under fire, such
as the increase in the heavy-oil duty, the Road Fund raid, or the in-
completed restoration of allowances, could all be shuffled off on the
plea of financial stringency.

There were, however, two Members who had seen quite clearly
the basic weakness of the Budget; one, awkwardly enough, was
the Tory, Robert Boothby,[1] in his speech on the Third Reading;
playing the part of the candid friend, he underlined the Chancellor's rigid economic orthodoxy which had been throughout the dis-
tinguishing feature of his policy although he did not, understandably, develop the theme. The other was Grenfell[2] in his speech towards the end of the First Reading; as an Opposition speaker he
was not so inhibited. It was 'a Budget of small items, of small concessions'; he forecast that this was the last of this type of Budget
and that it portended an election and a new Government. He summarized by saying that the Chancellor had been 'juggling again this
year' as he had in the last three or four years, keeping a stream of
duties going. But he had produced a Budget which was too static
and which did not develop the economic power a modern Budget
could and should generate.

These criticisms were justified. Even after four years of retrenchment, economy was still seen as a most desirable fiscal virtue by all
parties, with few exceptions and deficit budgeting as the remedy of
the theoreticians. Chamberlain himself was content to be carried
along by the rising tide of economic prosperity, his contribution
being the restoration of confidence by the balancing of his Budgets;
and certainly, in the two years after 1931, this was no small contribution. He would certainly have wished to reduce taxation even
further but 'it is not a thing we can do without any reference to the

[1] H. 5/7/1935, Cols 2173/2183.   [2] H. 17/4/1935, Cols 1961/1970.

amount of money available for the relief of taxation . . . we shall have to wait until some new Mr Gladstone arises'.[1] The tragedy was that neither the Chancellor nor the Labour Party, who might well have agreed with him, realized the days of Gladstonian economics were gone for ever; 'peace abroad',[2] for which he had hoped in his closing remarks, was just what he was not to be given.

[1] H. 1/5/1935, Col. 517.   [2] See p. 59.

Chapter IV

The Finance Bill 1936

THE PRICE OF DEFENCE

Time Table

Financial Statement		April 21, 1936
Budget Proposals		
	1st Day	22
	2nd Day	23
Budget Resolutions		
	1st Day	27
	2nd Day	28
	Reported	
Finance Bill		
	1st Reading	28
	2nd Reading	May 20
Committee		
	1st Day	June 9
	2nd Day	10
	3rd Day	15
	4th Day	16
	5th Day	17
Report		
	1st Day	30
	2nd Day	July 1
3rd Reading		3
Royal Assent		16

The benches which Chamberlain faced on April 21, 1936, when he rose to open his fifth consecutive Budget, presented a very different appearance from the serried National ranks of the past four years. There had been a somewhat confused General Election the previous November with no clear-cut issues, a situation reflected in the very poor turnout of the electorate. The Labour seats had increased by over one hundred; the Liberals had faded to a mere twenty; but even so there was still a massive National phalanx of four hundred and thirty-two. The limited economic recovery was continuing, restricted by the economic nationalism of the tariff war; but far more ominous was the political nationalism of the Italian and German dictators as they probed the strength of so-called collective security in Abyssinia and the Rhineland. Such was the sombre background to the proposals of 1936.

Nevertheless the Chancellor seemed undaunted either by the current political uncertainties or by the biting north-east wind as he launched out on his customary opening, the review of the past year. He announced a final surplus of nearly £3 millions or £2·5 millions more than expected even after providing for an anticipated £4 millions Supplementary Estimates. These in fact had amounted to no less than £22 millions, largely due to £14 millions more than expected being required for supply services. This surplus demonstrated the buoyancy of the revenue and justified his conservative estimates.

A breakdown of this remarkable achievement, in effect a surplus of £20·5 millions, showed it had come from Customs and Excise, receipts of £303·3 millions giving £8·5 millions over the estimate and Inland Revenue receipts of £404·9 millions, £13·5 millions over the estimate; although these excesses were whittled down somewhat by, for example a disappointing Post Office figure of £11·65 millions, due partly to a full year of pay cuts restoration. The National Debt position was very healthy. There had been a useful consolidation of the short-term debt position by the issue of new loans[1] and 'on balance the National Debt showed a reduction during the year of £51·25 millions'.[2] The Exchange Equalization account still happily continued to show a profit.

Chamberlain then turned to the expenditure for 1936–37. The Fixed Debt Charge would be maintained at £224 millions as in the last three years; the other Consolidated Fund Services would require

[1] H. 21/4/1936, Col. 40.   [2] H. 21/4/1936, Col. 40.

£11·3 millions. Then the usual caveat was entered: "I must say again, as I have said before, that in normal times I would not consider such provision adequate; but times have not been normal during these three years and the past year; and much as I would like to make an increased provision, I do not feel justified in doing so in present circumstances.'[1] To continue, the estimates for supply services, as last year, had already been published; they provided for Civil Departments' spending of £378·7 millions and £158·2 millions on Defence account, and he felt he should provide supplementaries of £5·6 millions for the former and £20 millions for the latter. All this gave a grand total of £797·9 millions.

The quest for this sum, £68 millions more than last year, was a formidable exercise. In view of the growing purchasing power of the community, budgeting for an increased Customs and Excise yield was fully justified: Chamberlain put this at £314 millions. From Inland Revenue duties, too, substantial increases were expected judging from the forecasts, mentioned for the first time, which traders had begun to furnish on request to the Department and taking into account the permeation of trade improvement into the surtax returns; the total here he estimated at £420 millions. The product of such miscellaneous items, amongst others, as Motor Vehicle Duties, Crown Lands and sundry loans, should reach £42·6 millions. The grand total came to £776·6 millions, leaving a deficit of £21·3 millions to set against the estimated expenditure of £797·9 millions.

Chamberlain had developed a form of Budget statement as fixed almost as that of a sonnet; but here he found it 'necessary to turn aside from the main course'[2] and deal with the question of tax avoidance,[3] arising from the burden of direct taxation 'being high enough to attract the attention of ingenious minds and their discoveries and inventions have now proceeded to such a point that it is necessary to ask Parliament to intervene'.[4] Legislation was accordingly proposed against transfer of income abroad in such a way that the transferer still continued to enjoy the income and retain the control; the income arising from property of this kind was now to be taken as the measure of the tax liability.[5] The second proposal dealt with the so-called 'one-man companies' against which legis-

---

[1] H. 21/4/1936, Cols 40/41.   [2] H. 21/4/1936, Col. 45.
[3] See B. E. V. Sabine, *History of Income Tax*, pp. 183/4, 190/1.
[4] H. 21/4/1936, Col. 45.   [5] See S. 18, F.A. 1936, and Second Schedule.

lation had already been directed;[1] now surtax devices relating to control and distribution were put a stop to, the section[2] to operate from 1935–36 since the surtax assessed as payable in the current year was that for the previous year. Finally, there was to be preventive legislation[3] against the abuse of the educational trust so that the liability of parents should not be affected by these instruments; this was to be achieved by aggregating the income of the infant if in any way derived from the parent with that of the parent for all purposes of the Income Tax Acts. Agents and canvassers had been busy hawking about schemes of this kind, one inducement being 'a cheque for 10s 6d in respect of any new client introduced'.

Stopping up these loopholes would produce an estimated saving of some £5 millions. But seeing that the Chancellor also proposed to increase child allowance to £60 and the higher personal ('married') allowance to £180, a rise of £10 in each case, there would be a loss of some £4 millions there. Three other minor changes were mentioned at this stage: parallel legislation was proposed in the Estate Duty field relating to income transferred abroad; an anomaly was removed in the rules for Schedule A rating on a building which housed plant; and there was to be an import duty on lager. More interesting was the experimental suggestion[4] for the setting up of a Special Areas Reconstruction Association Limited with the special function of financing small businesses either existing or to be formed in the special areas. The maximum amount of the loan to any one business was to be fixed at £10,000. The net result of these various amendments was to increase the revenue by £1 million merely, so that the deficit was still an ominous £20·3 millions.

Chamberlain then announced firmly: 'I may say at once that I propose to cover that deficit out of the revenue of the year.' This might have seemed an ordinary remark; but in the circumstances it was extremely significant. Defence expenditure, in the past two years, had risen by £44 millions, and the White Paper on defence of the previous month had indicated the necessity of entering upon the largest programme of arms expenditure ever undertaken by this country in peacetime. It was envisaged that costs would rise swiftly to a peak in a few years and then level out at a figure substantially in excess of the £158 millions provided for in the original estimates

[1] S. 21, F.A. 1922.   [2] S. 19, F.A. 1936.
[3] S. 21, F.A. 1936.   [4] H. 21/4/1936, Cols 51/2.

of the year. Chamberlain felt he could distinguish between what he termed maintenance expenditure and emergency expenditure. The former should be met out of revenue; but to collect the whole of the latter in the same way would 'raise taxation to a level which would seriously cripple the industry of this country'. A part of this emergency expenditure would clearly have to be met out of loan.

The immediate problem, however, was how to meet the current expenditure. Three sources were proposed: the Road Fund was to be tapped to the extent of £5·2 millions; and in passing the Chancellor said that 'this system of feeding the Road Fund by the varying produce of duties specifically assigned to it is an irregularity which ought to be corrected'.[1] Secondly, the standard rate was to be increased to 4s 9d; the additional 3d was estimated to produce £12 millions. Finally the tea duty was to go up by 2d a pound, the anticipated yield being £3·5 millions. The total from these three sources was £20·7 millions which, when set against the deficit of £20·3 millions, left a final, very bare surplus of less than £·5 millions.

Finally the Chancellor looked back at the changes which had taken place in the fiscal scene since had had opened his first Budget in 1932. The recovery of the country had been remarkable;[2] agricultural and industrial output had increased by 14 per cent and 29 per cent respectively; exports were up by £50 millions and unemployment was down; and revenue had expanded to allow the redemption of £70 millions of National Debt, increased expenditure on social services and tax remissions. His financial policy was not the sole agent of recovery; this he had never claimed. But he felt justified in thinking that the 'two main pillars' of his policy, cheap money and tariffs, had made a very considerable contribution.

He had hoped to give in this Budget greater relief to the taxpayer than anything he had been able to afford so far, and it had been a 'bitter disappointment' to find this was not possible. 'But no man hesitates to set his fire-fighting appliances in readiness when already he can feel the heat of the flames on his face. Our safety is more to us than our comfort . . .'. It was all over in just under ninety minutes, the first semi-wartime Budget in the nominally peaceful thirties; he sat down with barely a cheer.

Both Opposition leaders were very brief in their formal replies.

[1] H. 21/4/1936, Col. 55.   [2] H. 21/4/1936, Cols 57/8.

Attlee,[1] in a somewhat tart speech, praised the Chancellor's opening lucidity, which he thought tailed off when he came to discuss armaments expenditure, and he blamed the Government for creating the situation which had led to the position where the benefit from trade revival was being thrown away on rearming. 'It is a Budget,' he concluded, 'which will ultimately lead to war.' Sinclair[2] was equally depressing; a ritual acknowledgment of the 'characteristically clear, compact and revealing statement' was followed by a warning of the economic consequences of arms expenditure which made it a 'Budget of shattered hopes'. Maxton[3] and Gallacher,[4] for the Communist Party, predictably had a field day in contrasting the money poured out on defence against the armed nations of Europe instead of being spent on defence against maternal mortality, malnutrition and the Means Test. There were only two other speeches: one was a typical back bench performance from Allen,[5] who was disappointed with the standard rate increase and the pressure of Estate Duty which converted capital into income; the other was from Tinker,[6] who complained about the House rising early on Budget Day which prevented back bench Members from getting their say: 'during the next few days we shall have the so-called big men pegging out their claims and taking the best part of the time'. Clearly he was determined to get in his say. He was opposed to the tea duty and was in favour of 6d in the standard rate provided the proceeds went to the social services, especially the abolition of the Means Test, which was still not part of the 1931 restorations.

The national papers, almost unanimously, expressed some surprise at the increase in direct and indirect taxation. There had been little prior interest in the Budget, the apathy being due to lack of any great expectations. But on the whole, although it was reasonable to assume that the series of tax remissions would now end, it came as a shock to find that this trend had not only been halted but reversed.

The Times[7] headlined its leader 'An Orthodox Budget', which from its point of view was a justifiable summary. The all-round increase in taxation, covering rich and poor alike, was equitable; and it was

[1] H. 21/4/1936, Cols 59/61. [2] H. 21/4/1936, Cols 61/3.
[3] H. 21/4/1936, Cols 63/6. [4] H. 21/4/1936, Cols 71/3.
[5] H. 21/4/1936, Cols 66/7. [6] H. 21/4/1936, Cols 67/71.
[7] 22/4/1936.

fortunate that the buoyancy of the revenue had kept this rise within bearable limits. The reason for the swelling expenditure on armaments was not challenged: collective resistance required that the armed forces should be adequate to the discharge of the country's obligations 'when dark clouds are backing up on the Continental horizon'. In these circumstances the receipt of £46 conscience money and the first halves of fifteen £1 notes (the balance to follow at some date unspecified) announced in the same edition was not a significant contribution.

The *Manchester Guardian* had been nearer the mark with its forecast of the commencement of 'a new, almost desperate cycle of national finance'[1] and its leader started on the Wednesday morning[2] with the melancholy comment that this should have been the real recovery Budget. The essentials were there; industry on the upgrade, unemployment still falling, revenue above estimates, but the demands of national security must be met. The shape of the Budget was approved with its principle of spreading the load, and the Chancellor's 'courage to begin to make us pay'. But nothing could conceal the fact that it was the first of a series of crisis Budgets.

Of the weeklies, the *New Statesman*[3] was the most apprehensive. The Budget had been received with gloomy resignation even by the Chancellor's partisans in the House; and while the increase in standard rate was a sensible move, the increase in the tea tax was a piece of class legislation and the formation of the Reconstruction Association was simply tinkering with the unemployment problem. In short, 'the Budget is formed in the fear of war'.

The Economist[4] had thought that there would be nothing additional to demand from the taxpayer in view of the considerable expansion of revenue. No wonder, then, its leader[5] bore the banner 'A Bitter Disappointment'. Arms were the villain of the piece, but the decision to meet the deficit out of revenue was undoubtedly the correct one. The 2d on tea and the raid on the Road Fund were both regarded as objectionable. But quite apart from the present position the future outlook was disquieting, for public expenditure in general was increasing and there was every expectation that it would continue to do so.

But Fleet Street was discussing another matter apart from the Budget itself. There were rumours, and more than rumours, of a

[1] 21/4/1936.   [2] 22/4/1936.   [3] 25/4/1936.   [4] 18/4/1936.   [5] 25/4/1936.

Budget leakage. The week before the Chancellor's statement a number of orders had been placed on what was called the 'spec' market at Lloyds insuring against a possible rise in income tax. Such orders were usually handled by one very experienced broker; he noticed that all these orders originated in one Fleet Street office. A judicial enquiry was ordered and the leakage was traced to J. H. Thomas, National Labour, the Colonial Secretary, who resigned before the findings of the enquiry were made public. This meant, besides the disgrace of a once-popular figure, that the National Government now resembled even more a fully Conservative Government.

The regulation two days' debate was opened by Pethick-Lawrence,[1] who had been Parliamentary Secretary to the Treasury in the 1929 Labour Government. The Budget was 'utterly depressing ... and staggering in its future outlook'. This was only the beginning of an accelerating growth of both direct and indirect taxation, not for useful schemes of public works but for defence, the weapons of which had a high obsolescence so that Chamberlain's 'peak' theory, that expenditure would fall off when an adequate state of preparedness had been reached, was fallacious. In addition, profiteering was taking place in the armament industry. This was the direct result of the Government's inadequate foreign policy in failing to resist Japan and Italy: 'the right course is for the Government, at whatever expense, to prove once and for all, that aggression does not pay'.[2] But they had failed to use the League, and Imperial Preference had proved a provocative policy. As for the Budget itself, he approved the attack on evasions, where he noted the silence of the Tories, and the increased allowances. But he opposed the tea tax, the raid on the Road Fund, and he found the projected Distressed Areas scheme too small. In all the Chancellor had caused grave financial disquiet by committing the country to a menacing arms race.

Sinclair,[3] the Liberal leader, shared these gloomy forebodings. The Government had done much to provoke the present foreign situation, if they were not wholly responsible for it, and 'now the Chancellor's economic policy lies in ruins'. He underlined Pethick-Lawrence's objections to Imperial Preference by arguing it would be a better policy to restore overseas trade by co-operation with the

[1] H. 22/4/1936, Cols 157/171. [2] H. 22/4/1936, Col. 165.
[3] H. 22/4/1936, Cols 171/183.

World Economic Conference than to continue the tariff policy which even in terms of yield was not very satisfactory and had proved useless as a bargaining counter. He was not in favour of the increased tea duty or of depriving the Road Fund of its financial independence. The Chancellor had now run off with the whole goose instead of stealing an occasional egg. The Distressed Areas scheme should not be restricted to those areas only; and he wished to remind the House that married allowance had not yet returned to its pre-1931 figure.[1] He concluded that 'the Government's present path leads us to the edge of financial disaster'.

So began a very lively debate based largely on the themes expounded by the two opening speakers. The most frequently recurring topic was, inevitably, that of rearming. The Conservative line was an endorsement of Chamberlain's arguments; as Russell[2] said, although the country would be disappointed by the end of remissions, the rearmament programme must be supported provided strict economy was exercised, and Salmon[3] argued that 'any body of men occupying the Ministry today, of whatever party, would find it essential, having regard to the general affairs of Europe, to increase our armed forces'. Only Beaumont[4] took the really die-hard view that defence expenditure should be paid for by economizing on the social services. The Labour line was not so clear-cut, ranging from the frankly pacifist of Wilson,[5] who reminded the House of the 'message of the Peace Ballot,' to the standard complaint that rearming was starving the social services as expressed by Stephen.[6] Logan[7] even declared approval of the expenditure itself but quarrelled simply with the means of raising it. Banfield[8] was probably the most effective: behind the façade of an apparently humdrum Budget was 'a preparation-for-war Budget' which must be, if only indirectly, an attack on the social services since the cost of rearming would swallow up any increases in revenue.

It was the increase in the tea tax, however, which aroused the most opposition. It has been 'the plaything of every Chancellor', complained Smiles,[9] and the general complaints were based partly on the

---

[1] This was £225 as against the current £180.
[2] H. 22/4/1936, Cols 183/188.   [3] H. 22/4/1936, Cols 251/255.
[4] H. 22/4/1936, Cols 200/207.   [5] H. 22/4/1936, Cols 223/226.
[6] H. 22/4/1936, Cols 207/214.   [7] H. 22/4/1936, Cols 256/260.
[8] H. 22/4/1936, Cols 231/235.   [9] H. 22/4/1936, Cols 244/247.

fact that it increased indirect taxation as Adams[1] argued, and that it directly affected the cost of living especially of the poorer section of the community. The Tories had claimed it was a fiscal virtue to spread the load of increased taxation so that all should participate. After all, it was not a very severe tax; and it is possible to feel a certain sympathy for the Member[2] who suggested, with some justification, that 'it could be avoided by drinking weaker tea'.

It is worth noting that apart from Sinclair's routine advocacy of Free Trade, tariffs had ceased to be a live issue and rated a mention from only two Members. Davison,[3] taking his stand under a banner with the strange device of 'Taxation is not good for the State', proposed tariffs rather than income tax as a revenue-raising mechanism; and Hills[4] felt that defence expenditure should also be met by tariffs rather than increases in internal taxes. So little interest did these arguments arouse that the debate sagged somewhat and the House was nearly counted out.

There was, in fact, little discussion on the general theory of taxation until towards the end. Mabane[5] said, fairly, that the Chancellor had promised a Conservative financial policy when the country needed it, although he had tended to underestimate (the usual Mabane criticism); looking at the Budget as a general picture of the national finances, he had to admit his admiration for the manner in which they had been conducted. Benson,[6] however, argued that high taxation did not endanger industry; it had been higher in the last fifteen years than ever before but, despite this, national prosperity had increased at an unprecedented rate. This thesis was clearly capable of being pushed to absurdity. He was on firmer ground when he discussed the increase in indirect as contrasted with direct taxation, for the latter was being asked to find £2 millions less, but the former the increased sum of £72 millions more.

These two speeches were the preliminaries to the two final set-pieces of the day. The first was from Dalton:[7] he thought this was to be the last balanced Budget in view of Chamberlain's warning about borrowing and he felt that the cheap money era was coming to

---

[1] H. 22/4/1936, Cols 238/244. [2] H. 22/4/1936, Cols 235/238.
[3] H. 22/4/1936, Cols 188/194 (Chairman of the Income Tax Payers' Society).
[4] H. 22/4/1936, Cols 226/231. [5] H. 22/4/1936, Cols 214/223.
[6] H. 22/4/1936, Cols 194/200. [7] H. 22/4/1936, Cols 260/270.

an end which meant increased taxation as well. The Special Areas Reconstruction Association was a promising idea but Billinghams were needed not the stimulation of small businesses merely. He considered, after reading the Board of Inland Revenue's Report for 1935 which showed a marked rise in Surtax and death duties, that the rates of both should be scaled up and that surtax should start at £1,500;[1] and he concluded that it was 'a dreary Budget . . . it lacks life and sources of interest . . . it presents no new expedients . . . and I believe that it will hasten the end of the Government.'

Morrison,[2] Chamberlain's third Financial Secretary in three years, did not find it difficult to reply. There had not been many speeches on the point; perhaps there had been some confusion with a debate on foreign policy. He agreed it was the problem of defence which had given the Budget its peculiar character; and speakers had tended to criticize the Government's foreign policy, which they thought was to blame for the reversal of taxation reliefs. In fact great danger had been averted this year at small cost, due to 'the rising revenues created by the financial policy of my Right Hon. Friend'.

The second day's debate was quiet and there was a comparatively small attendance. It opened with a typically humanitarian appeal from McGovern.[3] Pensions and the social services were being neglected for the sake of arms expenditure. The speaker was totally opposed to this policy: 'nor will we encourage any man in the country to give his life in defence of the investing classes'. This also was the theme of Seaton[4] and of Smith,[5] whose disquisition on foreign policy was mildly rebuked by the Deputy Chairman as hardly relevant to the debate. Price[6] took the most reasonable view for the Opposition; his party was not in favour of unilateral disarmament and he was prepared to vote for arms if the cash were properly spent and used in support of the League of Nations and collective security. Acland[7] blamed the Government for not backing up the League and thus involving the country in an armaments race; but the Conservative Party line was expressed immediately afterwards by Gunston.[8] He praised the Chancellor's frankness; like the Deputy Chairman,

[1] Instead of £2,000.   [2] H. 22/4/1936, Cols 270/280.
[3] H. 23/4/1936, Cols 317/326.   [4] H. 23/4/1936, Cols 392/395.
[5] H. 23/4/1936, Cols 379/385.   [6] H. 23/4/1936, Cols 413/418.
[7] H. 23/4/1936, Cols 354/361.   [8] H. 23/4/1936, Cols 361/367.

he too felt that not enough attention was being paid to the Budget itself; rearming was the inevitable price of protection.

As on the first day, there was a strong body of opinion from both sides of the House opposed to the tea tax increase, the raid on the Road Fund and the inadequacy of the Spcial Areas fund. Naturally the Opposition was more censorious: Morgan Jones,[1] for example, in a lengthy speech, referred to the depressing effect of the measures on the Government benches, too, where 'the Hon. Members looked like a collection of undertaker's mutes'. His main criticism, however, was the alteration between the proportion of direct and indirect tax. Griffiths[2] pointed out how prosperity had not affected the 'other side of the medal' in South Wales. The Special Areas Fund was fiddling while the Special Areas were burning and it was better to keep the old industries then attract new. The back-bench Conservatives, however, while glumly deploring the increases, generally followed the line of Stewart[3] or Smithers[4] in emphasizing the continuing importance of the preservation of credit and confidence for international trade. As Lyons[5] expressed it, 'we are paying our way in a plain straightforward way without any financial trickery' and everyone in the country was rightly bearing their share of the heavier burden of taxation.

Fiscal theory again received scant attention. Hopkin,[6] concerned about diminishing returns from conventional forms of taxation and the disproportion between direct and indirect taxation, suggested the taxation of land values. Wilson,[7] equally worried about diminishing returns, was inclined to blame the Inland Revenue 'in their ruthless endeavour to strain the law and stretch the net'. He thought that avoidance was not only legal, it was proper.

But before the final summaries the high spot of the debate was the intervention by Churchill.[8] He had found the speeches after the Chancellor's opening 'one long dreary drip of disparaging declamation', a typical example of Churchill's alliterative flowers. He had not taken part in a Budget debate for a good number of years but the pattern of debate had not changed. 'All those who have benefited by the Budget naturally remain silent lest worse things should occur;

[1] H. 23/4/1936, Cols 339/351.   [2] H. 23/4/1936, Cols 367/373.
[3] H. 23/4/1936, Cols 373/379.   [4] H. 23/4/1936, Cols 385/392.
[5] H. 23/4/1936, Cols 395/404.   [6] H. 23/4/1936, Cols 404/408.
[7] H. 23/4/1936, Cols 408/413.   [8] H. 23/4/1936, Cols 326/339.

all those who are injured by the Budget are clamant and vociferous.'
He then dealt, half-humorously, half-seriously, with the transformation in the whole structure of British finance since 1929[1] and revealed
himself to a stupefied House as 'the last orthodox Chancellor of the
Victorian era', Snowden, a rival claimant, being merely 'a deplor-
able episode'. He compared, too, economic conditions in 1928–9
with those in 1935–36 and how 'the dark cloud of economic priva-
tion envelopes the once brilliant North'. He could only approve the
expenditure on rearming since he had 'for a long time past made
grave and startling statements on Germany's expenditure on wartime
preparations'. His main criticisms were that with the expansion of
the revenue he felt standard rate could have remained unchanged;
and nothing had been done in the way of a Ministry of Munitions
or to get the co-operation of the unions, which could not be won
without making sure that 'there are not a lot of greedy fingers having
a rake-off'.

Greenwood,[2] concluding for the Labour Party, had found it one
of the dullest Budget discussions he could remember. The Government had committed the country to a vast expenditure arising out
of the futility of their foreign policy, and taking Chamberlain up on
his Dickensian references, the future could only offer 'Bleak Expectations'. He objected in particular to the Road Fund raid, the default-
ing on debt repayment, and the tax on tea, and in general to the increase in indirect taxation. But his severest strictures were reserved
for the arms expenditure which was twisting the economic life of
the nation out of its normal course.

Chamberlain[3] was undismayed. He admitted the Budget was a
defence Budget and he found the Labour Party hypocritical if they
did not agree defence expenditure was necessary when holding that
aggression ought to be curbed. On the other hand he did not agree
with the control over defence industries advocated by Churchill in
peacetime. He had steered a middle course and in his proposals had
spread the load. 'It is much better to have done what I have done,
namely to give the people at once the taxation which I feel is necessary and to express the view that in submitting to that taxation, as far
as the present programme of Defence is concerned, they might hope
to escape any further burden.' So ended the preliminary skirmishes.

[1] H. 23/4/1936, Col. 328.   [2] H. 23/4/1936, Cols 418/427.
[3] H. 23/4/1936, Cols 427/437.

The somewhat formalized discussions on the initial report of the Budget resolutions, a procedure designed simply to give the Government power to draft a clause covering the point in question and to introduce it to the House, did not produce a great deal of controversy except on the increase in the tea tax and the standard rate of income tax. The vocal opposition to the former was wholly from the Labour benches, the humanitarian argument was that it was 'mean and indefensible'[1] (Benson); the fiscal argument was that it increased indirect taxation[2] (Tinker); and the practical solution to taking 'the widow's mite for armaments' was to increase income tax and sur-tax[3] (White). Griffiths concluded with an attack on what he termed the Chancellor's Puritanism: 'whatever is unpleasant is bound to be wholesome.'[4] Conservative sympathy was not expressed in the division on the amendment which was lost.

The Conservative mover and seconder of an amendment to retain standard rate at 4s 6d. landed themselves in a state of some confusion since the former, Mabane,[5] thought, as usual, that the Chancellor had been underestimating while the latter, Adams,[6] spoke on the danger of diminishing returns; in other words, as Morrison[7] pointed out, one was saying if the rate was increased, the Chancellor would get too much the other that he would get too little. The motion was a lost cause in any event since the Labour Party was wholly in favour of this increase in direct taxation; eventually it was withdrawn.

The anti-avoidance measures had won general approval but the Opposition view was that they were not drawn with a wide enough scope. Pritt[8] emphasized how 'the ablest technical brains in the country were arranging these avoidances', but his speech was more suited to the Committee Stage, as Morrison pointed out.[9] He was also called upon to explain the precise intention behind all those measures and at one juncture Chamberlain himself intervened with a stern warning against importing questions of morality into the issue.[10] In fact very good progress was made at this stage of the Bill so that the discussions on the following day were mainly concerned with points arising out of expositions on the draft clauses by Morrison.

---

[1] H. 27/4/1936, Cols 575/577.
[2] H. 27/4/1936, Cols 577/578.
[3] H. 27/4/1936, Cols 578/581.
[4] H. 27/4/1936, Cols 600/602.
[5] H. 27/4/1936, Cols 646/650.
[6] H. 27/4/1936, Cols 650/657.
[7] H. 27/4/1936, Cols 657/659.
[8] H. 27/4/1936, Cols 659/667.
[9] H. 27/4/1936, Col. 668.
[10] H. 27/4/1936, Col. 684.

The Opposition chose to fight the Second Reading on the ground that the Bill did not contain 'sound financial provisions for meeting out of income the large undisclosed expenditure on national armaments' and 'imposes additional burdens on the poorest section of the community'. In fact there was so much more emphasis on the cost of rearming and the reason why this had to be incurred than on the social implications of the Budget that a visitor entering the Strangers' Gallery on that May 20th during the debate might well have thought from the paucity of members[1] and the tone of the speeches that it was a Foreign Office topic.

Lees-Smith[2] set the tone with a powerful party speech. The importance of the Budget was the prospect that it contained for the years to come. The Chancellor could not bank on continued recovery which was due to general world conditions and the building trade, not to cheap money and tariffs. He would not be facing the need to borrow if the Government had followed a consistent policy regarding the Disarmament Conference. All the Labour speakers emphasized in one way or another their conviction that the Government's fiscal dilemma was the direct result of its failure to take a firm line abroad, without being able precisely to define what that firm line should be. Perhaps Pethick-Lawrence[3] came the nearest to outlining a consistent Labour policy: he advocated oil sanctions, and was willing to enforce these by war if necessary, provided the imposition was not unilateral.

Chamberlain[4] rose, with his usual impeccable sense of timing, half-way through the debate. He thanked his supporters and then had no difficulty in dissecting the Amendment and proving the inconsistency of the various parts of it. He was not going into details of the Bill which was the most complicated he had introduced: that was proper to the Committee stage. He took his stand on the proposition that the safety of the country, which concerned everyone in the community, should be contributed to by everyone in the community though not in the same proportion; and he concluded with the warning that high taxation was going to be an unavoidable evil. Morrison,[5] in summing up, gave some useful explanation of the avoidance provisions and ended by saying that these were not the

---

[1] There was barely a quorum at 8 p.m. [2] H. 20/5/1936, Cols 1211/1220.
[3] H. 20/5/1936, Cols 1311/1322. [4] H. 20/5/1936, Cols 1254/1267.
[5] H. 20/5/1936, Cols 1322/1332.

essence of the Budget: its prime virtue was it demonstrated that defence could be paid for 'without any dubious financial expedients' out of the expanding revenue which was the result of 'four or five years' good work in the past'.

But quite the most thoughtful contribution was from Macmillan.[1] He pointed out how the report of the Unemployment Insurance Statutory Committee, under the chairmanship of Beveridge, had made the inevitability of the trade cycle, 'that twentieth-century dogma', respectable. He could not accept this economic Calvinism. He felt it should be possible to maintain an equilibrium between the production of goods and services which he called a functional equilibrium and a similar balance between rate of savings and the rate of investment, or a monetary equilibrium. He therefore reaffirmed his belief in free will.

After the Second Reading, which traditionally covered a wide field, Members tended to find the Committee stage somewhat restricting. The Customs and Excise clauses went through without a great deal of opposition apart from a token resistance over the increased tea duty. Tinker[2] realized he was fighting a forlorn battle since the Chancellor wanted to see everyone paying a little towards the cost of national defence. The general Conservative attitude was that, at an average increase of some 6s 6d on the cost of living, the measure was not unreasonable and, as with the Customs and Excise clauses generally, there was little difference between the Bill and the Act.

This was but the first day of a discussion which was to extend over five days in all. There were two main subjects, the rate of income tax together with allowances and the avoidance clauses. Many suggestions were made for amending or extending allowances; but as far as avoidance was concerned the Opposition was mainly interested in seeing that conditions were stringent enough within the design and intention of the proposals.

Mabane[3] led the last-ditch resistance to the standard rate increase, stressing the importance of reducing direct taxation as a stimulus to industry. Boothby[4] in support argued that it was not clear how the immediate expenditure on armaments justified the extra 3d; his practical suggestion was to finance permanent works such as

---

[1] H. 20/5/1936, Cols 1301/1310.   [2] H. 9/6/1936, Col. 57.
[3] H. 10/6/1936, Cols 248/251.   [4] H. 10/6/1936, Cols 255/256.

aerodromes by loans, taking advantage of cheap money, and recurrent expenditure out of revenue. Chamberlain,[1] in reply, representing himself as 'yielding by nature', was still unconvinced by those critics who 'though showing no increase in numbers deployed the same remarkable tenacity in their views'. On the oft-repeated charge of underestimating he explained how current yield was accurately estimated, 'but the amount which is going to be collected from the past year and the amount which is going to slip through collection in the current year must always be speculative'. The Opposition,[2] of course, supported the increase; although it was serious it was to be preferred to an increase in indirect taxation.

It was the Opposition, too, which took the major share in proposing amendments to allowances with a discouraging lack of success. The allowance for a married man should go back to the 1931 figure of £225; '£180 is not the point at which taxation ought to start for a married couple'. Child allowance should be granted for full-time apprentices. Housekeeper allowance ought to cover the cases of unmarried claimants without children. Dependent relative allowance should be due when such a relative was denied unemployment assistance relief. It was also suggested that earned income allowance should be raised from a fifth to a quarter and that exemption should commence at £150. All these amendments were lost or withdrawn; it was not difficult for the Government to show they were either too costly, too inconvenient administratively or that they would lead to undesirable extensions; and even where the argument was a trifle thin, for example, over full-time apprentices and child allowance, a docile majority always provided sufficient 'Noes'.

One further proposed amendment does deserve mention; Foot's[3] perennial attempt to have wear and tear allowances increased by 10 per cent. The official reply, given by the Chancellor,[4] was that the original 10 per cent increase had been given as compensation for the higher crisis rates in 1931 and had not been rescinded when rates were reduced. It might be a grievance; 'but that does not seem to be a conclusive argument as I hardly know any form of tax which is not regarded by those who pay it as a grievance'.

The discussions over the avoidance sections were curiously uneven

---

[1] H. 10/6 1936 Cols 269/275.
[2] Cf. H. 10/6/1936, Col. 277 (Pethick-Lawrence).
[3] H. 17/6/1936, Cols 1077/1079.   [4] H. 17/6/1936, Cols 1081/1082.

both in quality and in quantity. On the prevention of transfers of income abroad,[1] the main point of controversy was whether a new legal provision was being imported in that the onus of proof was put on the taxpayer; but the proposed legislation made it quite clear that until it was found that a man had made a transfer of assets and was enjoying the product of those assets in a form which did not render him liable at present did the shift of onus take place. There was no debate at all on the clause[2] designed to stop leakage by a closer definition of one-man companies in relation to their control which had led to a loss of surtax; and there was very little comment on the following clause[3] which went with it, which applied the same principles somewhat more stringently to a particular form of one-man company, namely the investment company, the holdings of which consist entirely of securities.

The projected legislation[4] to prevent avoidance by way of transfers of income from parents to children was in a different category from the previous three clauses; there was an element of tax saving but there was also a recognizable element of parental prudence; the existence of these two factors put the House in a highly ambivalent state of mind. It seemed when the clause was first drafted that it was to include irrevocable trusts which, the Opposition thought, were 'a luxury of the rich'; in addition, one particular sub-section[5] was so obscure that it gave rise to complaints of legislation by reference. In fact the proposed legislation excepted pre-Budget irrevocable trusts only, not fresh trusts of that character; and as far as the complaints about sub-Section 5 were concerned, it was in fact a perpetuation of existing machinery.[6] Perhaps it was a lawyer's excuse, but it did possess a definite validity in relation to legislation subject to very technical scrutiny when Morrison[7] commented: 'Clarity is a very desirable thing but certainty of meaning is equally desirable ... it is well to preserve certain phrases which have acquired a definite meaning as terms of art.'

There was, as usual, little during the Report stage June 30th and the day following of more than technical interest; even the avoidance sections were now only provoking drafting amendments. In

---

[1] Section 18, F.A. 1936.   [2] Section 19, F.A. 1936.
[3] Section 20. F.A. 1936.   [4] Section 21, F.A. 1936.
[5] Later S.S. 5.   [6] Section 20, F.A. 1922.
[7] H. 16/6/1936, Col. 848.

fact it was to these that Morrison mainly referred in moving the Third Reading[1] and which he neatly summarized by saying, 'One man's evasion raises another man's standard rate.' Apart from this point he simply stressed that even with national necessity being what it was, additional taxation was only 2d on tea and 3d on income tax.

The Opposition did not find it possible to exploit any new themes in reply. While admitting the need for defence expenditure they could not accept the Government was taking the country into its confidence or contributing its arms to pooled security. There was still the disproportion between direct and indirect taxation and although the nation was more prosperous, that prosperity was not shared. The avoidance provisions were obscure and did not go far enough. Pethick-Lawrence,[2] in his summing up, was more moderate than most of his party's speakers. The Budget was a landmark in proposing expenditure of £800 millions in peacetime; he was not going to divide on it, but he remained critical of its provisions and the policies which had produced it.

Chamberlain[3] wound up by thanking both the House, the Attorney-General[4] and Morrison for their help during the long course of the debate. The Budget had four main points. The increases in taxation were justified by defence exigencies and the House had been given all possible information about them. The increases in allowances showed that the inequity of the 1931 restorations were still in his mind. The avoidance provisions had stopped up all the most profitable loop-holes and in relation to these devices he would not hesitate to introduce retrospective legislation if need be.[5] The abolition of the Road Fund was justified by the principle that earmarking was a bad fiscal canon. He was sensible (with perhaps a backward glance at his Health Ministry days) of the need to watch the welfare of the nation; this depended on the commercial prosperity he was trying to foster.

Grenfell[6] had forecast that the 1935 Budget would be the last of the old mark-time Budgets; and Dalton[7] had followed up the prophecy a year later by classifying the current Budget as the end of the balanced Budgets. If challenged on these two general descriptions of his last two sets of proposals, Chamberlain would have been forced

[1] H. 3/7/1936, Cols 761/765. [2] H. 3/7/1936, Cols 806/814.
[3] H. 3/7/1936, 814/826. [4] Sir Donald B. Somervell.
[5] H. 3/7/1936, Col. 822. [6] See p. 74. [7] See p. 85.

to admit their justice. He had attained a precarious equilibrium by abandoning every canon of Gladstonian finance by reverting to a tariff system, by virtually suspending the sinking fund, by ingenious conversions of the National Debt, by non-payment of the loans from the United States and by such fiscal devices as the raiding of the Road Fund. Now what should have been a happy issue out of all the afflictions of the past five years was being directly menaced by the cost of rearming.

This had become a political issue as early as 1935 with the publication of the 'Statement Relating to Defence'.[1] This stated baldly: 'Hitherto, in spite of many setbacks, public opinion in this country has tended to assume that nothing is required for the maintenance of peace except the existing international political machinery and that the older methods of defence—navies, armies and air force—on which we have hitherto depended for our security in the last resort are no longer required. The force of world events has shown that this assumption is premature.' But neither side of the House could immediately adjust to the realities of the situation; and the electorate in the main blandly ignored it. By 1936, however, with a second White Paper[2] for that year, Chamberlain was compelled, as he himself admitted,[3] to make provision for the cost of the estimated expenditure on reconditioning and modernizing the armed forces.

The Government had now to accept an expenditure on arms which cut directly across their old dogmas of economy and balanced Budgets; and, in general, as their speeches show, while bowing to necessity, their members differed on how this additional revenue was to be raised, whether by taxation, which posed a further problem of direct or indirect, or by loans. There was in any case a certain unreality in the arguments since the cost of rearming was still an unknown; as late as 1935 Chamberlain himself was thinking in terms of £120 millions[4] over the next five years; and only in the course of the current debate had he acknowledged its magnitude and evolved the idea of funding it partly by taxation and partly by loans.

Labour's pronouncements showed them to be even more distracted, between out-and-out pacifism, doctrinaire Marxism and simple opposition to any foreign policy advocated by a Conserva-

[1] Cmd. 4827.   [2] Cmd. 5107.   [3] H. 21/4/1936, Col. 41.
[4] Macleod, *Neville Chamberlain*, p. 182.

tive Government. In addition the party was in a woeful state of ignorance about the country's defences, receiving no confidential information about British armaments until 1939.[1] It was hardly surprising that although they supported collective security they could put forward no practical or unanimous suggestions for making it effective.

Apart from the emphasis on the cost of rearming, the Budget was also notable for a revival of the perennial war against avoidance, and for the way in which it illustrated the differing attitudes towards the Revenue's attempts to get behind the façade of increasingly numerous and complex artificial transactions. Opinions shaded from the frankly censorious to the cynically legalistic, while the Government was on the whole expressing the common morality of the country and, unusually, threatening retrospective legislation.

The Budget of 1936 exercises a three-fold fascination: socially, in the way the debates so faithfully mirror the varying convictions of the various members on such issues as unemployment, the depressed areas or the incidence of taxation; politically, in the ruthless exposure of the lack of any consistent foreign policy of principle on either side of the House; and economically, in that the injection of expenditure on defence was beginning to be needed in order to temper the possible start of a recession. Chamberlain, although he did not know it, but with perhaps instinctive prudence, while inaugurating a defence programme was also covering the economic sector.

[1] A. J. P. Taylor, *English History (1914–1945)*, p. 361.

Chapter V

The Finance Bill 1937

THE MASTER BOWS OUT

Time Table

D

When Chamberlain took his stand at the dispatch box on the afternoon of April 20, 1937, to introduce the Budget for the sixth time in six years, both he and the House knew it was to be his valedictory opening. Baldwin, a tired man when he succeeded MacDonald in 1935, and strained by the constitutional crisis of the Abdication, was only waiting for the Coronation to be able to say: 'I have had my hour; I pass soon into the shade.' Chamberlain, so long the linchpin of the Government, was the recognized Prime Minister apparent; and yet, with political supremacy but a few short weeks away, there was neither in his speech nor in the quiet and precise tone in which he delivered it, any hint of his coming accession except an extremely guarded reference to the fact that he had held the Chancellorship for a number of years and 'it would be presumptuous in me to expect that I could retain it for many more'.[1]

He started with his customary review of the past year, prefacing it with the ominous words: 'The national finances have, and must continue to be, dominated and governed by the vast expenditure on Defence.'[2] This time last year he had anticipated a small surplus, but by the time of the Third Reading[3] the potential deficit was clear. This was disappointing; but for the excess of Defence expenditure over the provision of close on £8 millions he would have had a surplus of £2·25 millions even while providing £13 millions for debt redemption since the Fixed Debt Charge this year had provided a welcome margin over the cost of interest and management.

The revenue for the past year, the Chancellor continued, totalled £797·289 millions, within £·75 million of the estimate. Details revealed a curious coincidence in that Inland Revenue receipts at £429·637 millions were £3·25 millions under the estimate, but Customs and Excise had come up with £320·782 millions or £3·25 millions above the estimate. Post Office at £10·97 millions and other items of £35·9 millions made up the balance. In his review of the 1936/1937 expenditure, Chamberlain did not give full details of the final out-turn but, dealing in differences, Defence expenditure was, as he had said, nearly £8 millions above the estimate while Civil Votes showed a saving of £3·2 millions.[4] This deficiency of £4·8 millions, plus the shortfall in revenue of £·8 millions, made up the final £5·6 millions deficit.

[1] H. 20/4/1937, Col. 1621.   [2] H. 20/4/1937, Col. 1601.
[3] H. 3/7/1936, Col. 819.   [4] H. 20/4/1937, Col. 1604.

There had been more funding of the National Debt during the year but little change in its nominal total since the £13 millions available[1] had been swallowed up including the offset of the deficit. The nominal total, however, was not so significant as the cost of interest and management which had been steadily decreasing since 1931.[2] As for the Exchange Equalization Fund, it was still wrapped in mystery but, he could assure the House, it was still continuing to show a profit.

The House was ready now, the Chancellor hoped, 'to face the new year with all its implications'. But before he dealt with forthcoming expenditure he would like to clear the question of the Fixed Debt Charge. This should be retained for the fifth successive year at £224 millions: "it would be absurd to start a sinking fund for debt redemption while borrowing £80 millions for Defence'.[3] He also wished to claim exemption from the operation of Section 48, Finance Act 1930, which provided in the case of a deficit for any year for the redemption in the next year of a corresponding amount of debt, following the precedents of the Parliamentary years 1931 and 1933.[4]

The comparatively minor items came next. On other Consolidated Fund services he would need £11·5 millions, slightly under last year's total. Roads would take £22·5 millions, this being a new addition to Supply expenditure, but covered by the estimated product of Motor Vehicle Duties. The two major items were £198·3 millions for Defence and £396·6 millions for Civil Votes with a £10 millions margin for Supplementary Estimates. The grand total was £862·9 millions.

Chamberlain now turned to consider the revenue he could expect to receive on the existing basis. Customs and Excise he put at £333 million, £12 million up on last year: he was, although he did not put it quite so bluntly, expecting to cash in on the Coronation festivities.[5] All Inland Revenue Duties he assessed at £452·5 millions, an increase of £32·5 millions; and he wanted to hear no more from his critics who had accused him last year of underestimating and even imposing an unnecessary income tax increase when in fact the yield fell below expectations. Motor Vehicle Duties at £34

---

[1] See preceding paragraph but one.   [2] H. 20/4/1937, Col. 1605.
[3] This was the figure in the Defence estimates.
[4] See S. 27, F.A. 1937.   [5] H. 20/4/1937, Col. 1607.

millions and Miscellaneous Items, including Crown Lands and sundry loans at £28·45 millions, completed the balance of his expected contributions, which aggregated £847·95 millions or a deficit of £14·95 millions when set against the expenditure of £862·9 millions.

Then came a typical Chamberlain hiatus: although he knew members would be anxious to hear how the deficit was to be dealt with, he asked the Committee's indulgence to deal with certain other matters first, which could conveniently be grouped under three headings. Most important was a follow-up to last year's legislation against avoidance. The first proposal[1] concerned 'bond-washing', a technique whereby the owner of securities sells them at a price covering accrued dividend and then buys them back after the dividend has been paid, at a lower price. These transactions, technically of a capital nature, result in the real owner not paying tax on the dividends. The second proposal[2] was a piece of retrospective legislation relating to investment companies which was designed to circumvent some highly artificial arrangements not fully covered by Section 19, Finance Act 1936.[3] Then followed some minor Customs and Excise amendments including the abolition of one of the last remnants of the eighteenth century expenditure taxes, the Male Servants Licence Duty.[4] The final group of proposals concerned the standardization of the so-called 'Mills, Factories Allowance'.[5] a deduction from profits to give some recognition of the depreciation in buildings housing machinery, and the continuation for five years of the increased allowance for repairs under Schedule A.[6]

Then came the major taxation proposals. Another £15 millions was needed, almost the same sum as in the previous year; and although the taxpayer might groan he would find consolation in 'the ever-quickening approach to the goal of safety' combined with the contribution of the Defence Loans Act. There had been suggestions of new and untapped sources including such miscellaneous items as slot machines, cats, cosmetics, loudspeakers, tricycles and antiques. Grateful as he was for these ideas he would have to look elsewhere for his missing revenue for, suddenly becoming serious, a Chancellor 'has to consider first the amount of tax which can be produced;

[1] S. 12, F.A. 1937.   [2] S. 14, F.A. 1937.   [3] See p. 78 and p. 93.
[4] S. 5, F.A. 1937.   [5] S. 15, F.A. 1937.
[6] As this was a relieving provision, no Resolution would be needed.

he has to set against that the cost of its collection and although he can never leave out the social, moral or economic effects or any proposal, he cannot allow personal taste and personal prejudices to govern his procedure'.[1]

He turned therefore to the one source which had never failed Chancellors, namely income tax, and with the encouragement of Hoare and Churchill, ex-Chancellors both, proposed by a further 3d to raise the standard rate to 5s 0d. This would produce £13 millions in the current year.

The House took this quietly enough, for it had been forecast by the fiscal prophets. The Chancellor then sprung his surprise. He did not wish to impose 'a succession of new taxes hitting first in one direction then in another' but rather 'a means of providing at least a major part of the expenditure (on defence) by some device capable of growth in itself but easily adjustable'.[2] Basically he felt he should tax those profits which were not part of the current general expansion of trade but, in so far as they were consequent upon orders placed by the Government, arose directly from the expenditure of the State,[3] and to underline this purpose he proposed to call the tax the National Defence Contribution.

It was to be levied on the growth of profits in industry, trade or business (not professions) where in any accounting period after April 5, 1937, such profits exceeded £2,000. The growth would be measured by comparison with either a profits standard or a capital standard and the rate of charge would be graduated according to the return on capital of liable concerns. There would be allowance for losses and an abatement of profits by a fifth of the difference between those profits and £12,000 when they were less than £12,000.

This complicated measure, even when explained in very general terms, occupied nearly four columns. It was not surprising therefore that Chamberlain found himself forced to confess 'that I can hardly expect Hon. Members to grasp at the first hearing all the implications of the system which I have been endeavouring to describe'; and he went on to recommend study of the relevant White Paper. In answer to one enquiry he could not say how long the tax would continue; its duration was, tentatively, the duration of the rearmament programme.[4] Its yield would be something over £2 millions

---

[1] H. 20/4/1937, Col. 1613.   [2] H. 20/4/1937, Col. 1615.
[3] H. 20/4/1937, Col. 1616.   [4] H. 20/4/1937, Col. 1620.

currently, but he confidently expected £20 to £25 millions in a full year.

It was now time to strike the final balance. Estimated receipts had been £847·95 millions; with the reinforcement from income tax and N.D.C., which he put at £15·15 millions, his resources totalled £863·1 millions to set against estimated expenditure of £862·9 millions, leaving a modest surplus of about £200,000.

Quietly the Chancellor moved towards his conclusion. It was the sixth financial statement he had submitted in succession, and in his brief examination of future prospects he could only testify to the recurrent theme of the pressure of armaments. But it was some comfort to know that this pressure had come at the right time when credit was high and revenue expanding. There were two possible dangers, 'some great world disturbance' or 'too reckless expenditure on objects not vitally necessary'. His apologia for this, his last Budget, came right at the end. 'I have endeavoured to avoid, on the one hand, the tremendous increase in taxation which would have been required if we had attempted to defray without borrowing the full cost of rearmament because I was convinced that the shock of such a sudden and tremendous increase of our burden would have checked, perhaps even have reversed, the process of convalescence. On the other hand, I have increased taxation with a careful choice of method to exercise a decided check upon any development of speculation without impairing the present upward trend of national welfare.'[1]

The House cleared rapidly after the Chancellor had resumed his seat; despite this, the comments went on rather longer than usual and ranged beyond the merely formal of previous years. The Opposition, as represented by Attlee,[2] Maxton[3] and Tinker,[4] suggested successively that the unbalanced Budget openly advertised the complete failure of the Government's policy, that Chamberlain was 'going to get away with it while the going was still good', and that as well as the standard rate increase and N.D.C., the surtax limit should be lowered to £1,500 from £2,000. The Liberal leader, Sinclair,[5] was more moderate: after a sincere tribute to a 'masterly series of Budget statements' he found fault with unbalancing the

[1] H. 20/4/1937, Col. 1622.
[2] H. 20/4/1937, Cols 1623/1625.
[3] H. 20/4/1937, Cols 1627/1629.
[4] H. 20/4/1937, Cols 1632/1635.
[5] H. 20/4/1937, Cols 1625/1627.

Budget and put the pertinent question that if it was necessary to borrow when trade was still favourable what would be the position if depression returned.

These reactions were to a certain extent predictable. The speeches from the Government benches, however, showed an interesting division of opinion, not of course amounting to anything like a real split in the ranks. N.D.C. was given a guarded welcome by Loftus[1] and Somerville[2] as 'a safeguard against profiteering and a comfort to the workers', but Wardlaw-Milne[3] was critical of the tax on top of the 3d increase in standard rate. Exports were still flagging and he was afraid the Budget would put a damper on the rate at which prosperity was growing. Boothby[4] echoed Sinclair: it would be a catastrophe if a deflationary spiral commenced; and he argued that what he called 'economic disarmament' must precede physical disarmament. Samuel[5] followed the Labour line to an extent: prosperity was not prosperity when there was still unemployment and the depressed areas; he did not approve of subsidies, but he suggested the promotion of export trades in such regions as South Wales.

Only one morning paper of any size attacked the Budget as going too far in the direction of 'soaking the rich'. *The Times*[6] had devoted its eve-of-Budget leader to a summary of Chamberlain's career as Chancellor, paying a tribute to his 'capable, business-like administration'. Its leader after the Budget,[7] in common with most other papers, headlined the need to pay for defence and commented generally that it was a characteristic Chamberlain Budget and one which could have been anticipated, apart perhaps from the imposition of N.D.C.

The *Manchester Guardian*,[8] however, was more analytical. Chamberlain had resisted the temptation to tide over his last short period as Chancellor but had done something positive to allay the social unrest which comes from the sight of high profits made out of a country's need. The form of the new tax might need modification; some of the provisions were somewhat obscure; but it would serve a dual purpose of a check on profiteering and a brake on the boom.

The *New Statesman*[9] was at its most censorious. It disagreed flatly with the *Guardian's* theories and argued that N.D.C. was inflationary

[1] H. 20/4/1937, Cols 1640/1642.   [2] H. 20/4/1937, Cols 1643/1644.
[3] H. 20/4/1937, Cols 1629/1632.   [4] H. 20/4/1937, Cols 1635/1640.
[5] 20 H./4/1937, Cols 1644/1647.   [6] 19/4/1937.   [7] 21/4/1937.
[8] 21/4/1937.   [9] 25/4/1937.

and would lead to evasion rather than act as a boom tax. It was by no means against a tax to cream off the profits from defence contracts but the objection was a technical one to N.D.C. in its proposed form; it failed to see how important the principle was of suggesting profits should be limited.

The Economist[1] opened by commenting that the Chancellor had followed his expected course, that the present level of taxation was not far short of wartime, and that there was little hope of any expansion in the social services. This was fairly routine; but there followed a long discussion on N.D.C. It was clear that a workable compromise would have to be effected between a pure tax on growing profits and a tax on high business profits, and that a tax both on prosperity and on the trade cycle was desirable. The tax, however, in its present form, was difficult to administer as, for example, in the necessity for assessing all capital; although even this, and other glaring technical defects, did not justify some of the Opposition's hysterical comments. This was the beginning of a campaign against N.D.C. which was to be intensified over the months to come, an attack based not on politics but sheer fiscal expediency.

The debate, which occupied April, 21st and 22nd had occasional flashes of interest and of economic insight, but in general it was undistinguished. There was a small attendance almost throughout, one of the notable absentees for the greater part of the time being the Chancellor himself. The reason was probably the concentration by most of the thirty-four speakers on N.D.C. which did not make for breadth of discussion or variety of treatment.

The Opposition did, however, try to make its usual political capital out of the wider issues raised by the Budget. For the Labour Party, Pethick-Lawrence[2] had heard the Chancellor's speech 'with a sensation of sadness': the amount to be spent on defence was three times the 1932/33 figure and he doubted very much whether the even spread of borrowing over five years would grapple with the anticipated steep rise in rearmament costs. As for N.D.C. it was 'E.P.D. resurrected from its grave and decked in new clothes'. The whole tendency of the proposals was to increase 'the hidden taxation of the poor'. Cripps[3] attributed the current boom to expenditure on arma-

---

[1] 25/4/1937.   [2] H. 21/4/1937, Cols 1769/1782.
[3] H. 21/4/1937, Cols 1814/1820.

ments which he regarded as wholly artificial with an inevitable slump to follow. Alexander[1] took the orthodox Socialist line. The Budget was a very mundane affair: an unbiased summary of the financial position showed that the Budget was really unbalanced on account of borrowing, despite the highest standard rate of tax in peacetime and the pressure from indirect taxation which had risen from £245 millions in 1931 to the present estimate of £333 millions. Wages were falling; the cost of living was rising; and there was even a slight deficit on the balance of trade. Morgan Jones[2] summed up for Labour just before the Chancellor rose to reply. He analysed the causes of the boom described by Cripps as the departure from the gold standard, the change in tariff policy, the lack of provision for both the Sinking Fund and the American debts, and the reduced interest charges; but he warned that some of these factors would not recur and, for all the apparent affluence, there still remained a solid core of a million and a half unemployed.

The Liberal case as presented by Sinclair[3] stressed the increase in the cost of living which had overtaken increases in wages and the dangers of high taxation; he thought the arms industry alone should bear the weight of increased rates. Davies[4] expounded the classic Radical theories: 'the single tax is the fair tax' and the revenue needed should have been raised from increased income tax.

The Tory experts were quick to rally in defence. Horne,[5] an ex-Chancellor himself, considered Chamberlain had pursued a course of 'undeviating resolution and rectitude' which had resulted in increasing employment and productivity, although he was afraid that if taxation were kept at concert-pitch there would be no margin or reserve for war and he suggested a co-ordination of defence to prevent the present scramble between Departments. Mabane,[6] too, found the Budget 'a remarkable conclusion to a remarkable series' and suggested the Chancellor had made a prudent anticipation of inevitably increasing expenditure. The back-benchers were less critical: Benn[7] had never heard, out of twenty-two Budget speeches, one presented 'with greater mastery of the material or clarity of expression'. Adams[8] emphasized the success of the Government in

---

[1] H. 22/4/1937, Cols 1940/1954. [2] H. 22/4/1937, Cols 2029/2037.
[3] H. 21/4/1937, Cols 1806/1810. [4] H. 22/4/1937, Cols 1954/1963.
[5] H. 21/4/1937, Cols 1782/1806. [6] H. 21/4/1937, Cols 1820/1834.
[7] H. 21/4/1937, Cols 1862/1871. [8] H. 22/4/1937, Cols 1993/1997.

reducing unemployment, and[1] Mellor thought the Government could claim due credit for national prosperity.

Pure economic theory received only scant attention in the debate, the main issue being the balance between direct and indirect taxation. Direct taxation was still the ark of the Labour covenant, 'the only honest way of raising revenue'.[2] Jack Jones,[3] the fiery member for Silvertown, made an impassioned plea for more direct taxation and suggested a Committee to look into the whole question. Bellenger[4] devoted his speech to the same theme: 'direct taxation is probably the fairest form of taxation in order to distribute the wealth of the country'. This concept was anathema to Tories such as Rankin,[5] who criticized the use of the 'capital resources' of death duties to liquidate revenue expenditure and, in a plea for economy, 'a word last mentioned in the House in 1931', reminded Members that the yield from income tax and surtax indicated the possibility of diminishing returns. Price[6] summarized the incidence and effect of the increase in indirect taxation claiming that this increase had largely financed the improved social services so that the wage earner and small-business man was, over-all, no better off. Colville,[7] the Financial Secretary to the Treasury, was at some pains to refute the use of taxation as a leveller. 'They (the Opposition) held that a higher rate of income tax is one of the best methods of redistributing wealth and as such a good thing in itself. We on this side of the House cannot share that point of view.'

The best speech of the two days came from the Independent Member for Oxford University, Sir Arthur Salter.[8] He defined indirect taxes as 'a kind of income tax graduated the wrong way round'; it was not realized how far these indirect taxes had subsidized the great extension in social services, and he welcomed the Chancellor's proposals which were 'stopping and to some extent correcting this development'. He joined issue with Chamberlain, however, in the inference to be drawn from his statement that 'our situation would have been much more difficult had our credit been weakened by large expenditure on public works during a depression'; he felt it was extremely useful that expenditure on public works should ex-

[1] H. 22/4/1937, Cols 2021/2024. [2] H. 21/4/1937, Col. 1840 (Quibell).
[3] H. 21/4/1937, Cols 1848/1852. [4] H. 22/4/1937, Cols 1988/1993.
[5] H. 22/4/1937, Cols 1986/1988. [6] H. 22/4/1937, Cols 1997/2005.
[7] H. 21/4/1937, Cols 1871/1883. [8] H. 22/4/1937, Cols 1972/1978.

pand at times of depression and be restricted at times of prosperity. He also argued that a modification of protection was needed to help in re-establishing international trade.

Most of the participators in the first two days' debate, however, devoted the major part of their time to a discussion of the Chancellor's new tax, the National Defence Contribution; and there were almost as many opinions of it as there were speakers, shading from out-and-out objections for a variety of reasons to enthusiastic welcome. sometimes from motives its proposer could hardly have approved of. Common ground was, of course, its complexity which Chamberlain had warned his hearers of[1] in his Budget introduction; but its details are a matter of academic interest only since the Sections which appeared on the Statute Book were very different from those put forward by the original White Paper.[2] It is interesting to note that Colville had some difficulty with its exposition of which he had to repeat part; and it was by no means clear whether he followed his own explanation.[3]

The earlier speakers on the first day had all given qualified approval. Horne[4] considered it should have been limited purely to the armaments industry. Sinclair[5] agreed, adding for good measure that such taxes had always led to extravagance in business expenditure, both capital and revenue. Anderson,[6] for the City, followed by conceding that some such measure as N.D.C. was necessary but it was 'full of difficulties and dangers'. Cripps,[7] at his most Marxist, had hailed the tax as a device for getting rid of capitalism, but Croft,[8] in contrast, held it was a patriotic duty to co-operate in paying it.

The three opposers based their objections on the argument that income tax was easier to collect, and that there was a danger of inflated expenses.[9] Allen[10] was willing to suspend judgment but he warned the Chancellor of the anomalies created after World War I by Excess Profits Duty.[11] Finally there was a Labour polemic from Ellis Smith;[12] N.D.C. should have been imposed earlier to pay for

[1] See p. 128.

[2] For a full description of N.D.C. Mark I, see Hicks, Hicks and Rostas, *The Taxation of War Wealth*, pp. 90/91.

[3] H. 21/4/1937, Cols 1873/1875. [4] H. 21/4/1937, Cols 1782/1896.

[5] H. 21/4/1937, Cols 1806/1810. [6] H. 21/4/1937, Cols 1810/1814.

[7] H. 21/4/1937, Cols 1814/1820. [8] H. 21/4/1937, Cols 1834/1840.

[9] H. 21/4/1937, Cols 1840/1842 (Quibell).

[10] H. 21/4/1937, Cols 1842/1848 (Hills).

[11] H. 21/4/1937, Cols 1852/1855. [12] H. 21/4/1937, Col. 1855/1862.

the social services; profits had risen but wages had remained static; industry should therefore pay more or 'the common people will be paying for rearmament'.

Criticism of the tax on the second day, however, was far more severe, sparked off perhaps by the strictures of *The Financial Times*.[1] The Chancellor's surprise at the reaction to N.D.C. was, it wrote, 'not only unpleasant but extremely regrettable. He has succeeded in courting a little easy popularity. As the price of that he has done a great deal of fundamental harm'. The attack was taken up from both sides of the House. Alexander[2] argued that it was an entirely wrong principle to let profiteers make profits in the first place and then tax those profits later. Owen[3] saw, as Cripps did, the significance of N.D.C.'s discrimination and called it 'communism without bloodshed'. Morrison[4] thought the prospective yield of the tax was not worth all the furore it had caused; and the chairman of the Income Tax Payers' Society, Sir William Davison,[5] feared its effect would be 'to cripple private trading and to discourage individual enterprise'. It was Clement Davies,[6] the Liberal second-in-command, who mounted the most ferocious attack. The Budget was virtually balanced before the imposition of N.D.C. so that there was 'no possible justification for upsetting trade in this way'. The money should have been raised from income tax, and the exemption for the professional classes and the small traders from the new impost was a piece of political gerrymandering for 'their voices were large and their votes numerous'. Using a bridge metaphor, he described some of the liable companies as vulnerable and some non-vulnerable; the shares of the former had dropped 3 per cent on the Exchange. The tax was ill-conceived, it would impose an unnecessary burden on the Revenue staff and there was a danger it would be permanent instead of, as promised, temporary. The most charitable assumption was that the Chancellor had not thought it out before presenting it; it was a bad tax fundamentally; he would speak and vote against it.

The Government could still muster loyal back-benchers such as McCorquodale[7] who thought N.D.C. was 'sound and just' or Mel-

---

[1] 22/4/1937, its Editor then was Brendan Bracken.
[2] H. 22/4/1937, Cols 1940/1954.   [3] H. 22/4/1937, Cols 1963/1965.
[4] H. 22/4/1937, Cols 1965/1972.   [5] H. 22/4/1937, Cols 1978/1981.
[6] H. 22/4/1937, Cols 1954/1963.   [7] H. 22/4/1937, Cols 2006/2008.

lor[1] who approved it as a 'prosperity tax'; but most of the support came from the Opposition. Adams[2] approved because it was selective and semi-Socialist in effect; he hoped this fiscal principle would be continued. Garro Jones[3] took the same view: a separate levy on industry was entirely justified and it should be made permanent. Mabane[4] had said at the opening of the debate that the proposal of a national defence contribution 'put everything in the present Budget in the shade'. By the end of the debate speakers were saying that nearly every aspect of it had been discussed in the speeches from one side of the Committee or the other and it had been dissected almost *ad nauseam*.[5]

Chamberlain picked up the major themes of the speeches and incorporated them in his usual skilful summary.[6] In reply to earlier points he stressed that tariffs were now being used as a bargaining counter, and with regard to the Exchange Equalization Account he would of course be making a statement to the Public Account Committee, although general secrecy was still necessary. He vindicated the imposition of N.D.C. by reminding Members that his deficit was only £2 millions because he had borrowed £80 millions. He could, as Clement Davies[7] had suggested, have ignored this small deficit and 'gone on my way rejoicing . . . but it was necessary to look beyond this single year'. It was fairer to tax industry than the smaller taxpayer to raise the additional revenue required, although 'I do not believe that there is any considerable amount of profiteering'.[8] He agreed that the tax in its present form gave rise to anomalies and difficulties, and he asked to 'be allowed in the interval which must now elapse before the Finance Bill to make such enquiries as are open to me'. But he did wish to emphasize that, whatever form the tax might take in the future, it was intended to be a levy on increased profits only.

The report of the Resolutions on April 27th recorded dealing with the first eleven Resolutions in less than an hour with very little discussion apart from some sensible remarks by Boothby[9] on the dangers of a falling yield in direct taxation and how the real problem

[1] H. 22/4/1937, Cols 2021/2024.   [2] H. 22/4/1937, Cols 2008/2013.
[3] H. 22/4/1937, Cols 2024/2029.   [4] See p. 105.
[5] H. 22/4/1937, Cols 2029/2037 (Morgan Jones).
[6] H. 22/4/1937, Cols 2037/2048.   [7] See p. 108.
[8] A view confirmed by the Select Committee on Estimates, March 1937.
[9] H. 27/4/1937, Cols 225/228.

was to stimulate international trade. It seemed that the House wished to get to grips with N.D.C. again, which was in fact the subject of the rest of the evening's debate.

Alexander's[1] speech pinpointed the Labour dilemma. N.D.C. had given equities their worst beating since 1931. The consequent disturbance to industry was unjustified, the danger of extravagant expenditure had not been faced, and the scheme itself had not been properly thought out or explained. But, and here was the rub, 'we do not want it so whittled down that it gives practically no yield . . . we want the Chancellor to reconsider the matter from the point of view of taking effective control of those conditions which lead to rising prices and heavier profits at the expense of the country in time of need, and we think that if he moves to alternative forms of taxation he should do so upon the well-known and tried lines of direct taxation.'[2]

Chamberlain[3] was moved to intervene much earlier than he had intended. He was surprised at the estimates of the potential damage to industry; an impost of the order of £20 millions to £25 millions was hardly 'an intolerable burden'; and he still maintained 'we can see the end of this exceptional expenditure'. He gave further explanations: he was prepared to consider amendments to which end he was 'getting in touch with people and bodies from whom to take advice', but, with regard to withdrawing the scheme and trying something else, 'I do not think the time has come for that'.

Subsequent speakers from both sides of the House, reinforced by economists such as Keynes,[4] stressed the justifiable uncertainty created in the business world by the varying interpretation of the proposals. This was common to the objections of Horne[5] for the Conservatives, Davies[6] for the Liberals, who said the Chancellor's recent speech had left confusion worse confounded, and Pethick-Lawrence[7] for the Labour Party. But he objected to 'big business laying down the law' and agreed with Ede[8] in smelling 'a retreat which will develop into a rout'. Peat,[9] in a most reasonable speech, suggested there was no quarrel over taxing any increase of profits

[1] H. 27/4/1937, Cols 236/241. [2] H. 27/4/1937, Col. 241.
[3] H. 27/4/1937, Cols 241/250. [4] Cf. his letter to *The Times*, 24/4/1937.
[5] H. 27/4/1937, Cols 250/257. [6] H. 27/4/1937, Cols 271/276.
[7] H. 27/4/1937, Cols 294/303. [8] H. 27/4/1937, Cols 259/264.
[9] H. 27/4/1937, Cols 278/282.

over the normal level—this would also serve to iron out booms and slumps—but the current tax, as put forward, was too complex.

Only Willie Gallacher[1] was wholly in favour: 'I am all for the tax and for increasing the tax,' adding, 'when profits are at issue patriotism fades away.' Both Boothby[2] and Baxter[3] saw its possible implications which Cripps had originally welcomed; the former feared its use 'as a wrecking instrument for smashing the capitalist system', and the latter revealed he had talked to many heads of industry and 'they have said they would gladly accept a percentage tax on profits', clearly a less dangerous alternative.

This was in fact what N.D.C. finally became. After the initial and subsequent reaction to it, Chamberlain had kept open house and listened to allcomers. When he kissed hands in May 1937 as Prime Minister, his finance committee was still urging him to drop the tax.[4] The new Chancellor, Sir John Simon, 'largely out of loyalty to its author',[5] proposed a revised version on May 31st.[6] It had no better reception than its predecessor. The fiscal experts from Dalton, Davies, Wardlaw-Milne, Boothby to Morrison,[7] whatever their party affiliations, united in a mass attack on the basic complications of the scheme. But it was Churchill who, on the following day, in a devastating speech,[8] applied the *coup de grace*. The tax was unworkable; it had set up a costly reaction in the commercial world; all parties were radically against it; and finally it would now, as amended, produce only £11 millions. 'I hope,' he concluded, 'that we shall not have a draggle-tailed, tattered tax passed through sulky Lobbies.' The culminating weight of argument was too much for the new Prime Minister;[9] at the end of the day's debate he announced that the oringal conception of the tax would be dropped for a simpler version provided a £25 million yield was guaranteed.

On June, 21st therefore, Simon proposed this simplified version, a 5 per cent on the profits of companies,[10] claiming, with some gratification, 'Trade and industry itself in unduly generous terms has

---

[1] H. 27/4/1937, Cols 284/287.   [2] H. 27/4/1937, Cols 287/292.

[3] H. 27/4/1937, Cols 292/294.

[4] K. Feiling, *Neville Chamberlain*, p. 293.

[5] *Retrospect; The Memoirs of Sir John Simon*, p. 227.

[6] H. 31/5/1937, Cols 695/712.

[7] See their speeches *passim* in the debate, H. 31/5/1937, Cols 695/820.

[8] H. 1/6/1937, Cols 880/985.   [9] H. 1/6/1937, Cols 914/926.

[10] For a fuller account see B. E. V. Sabine, *History of Income Tax*, p. 192 and Cmd. 5485.

offered assurances that if the form of the tax was simplified and charged on profits . . . it would be cheerfully accepted.'[1] As Pethick-Lawrence[2] remarked, there were no mourners to N.D.C. Mark I 'except the Prime Minister and the solitary member of the Communist Party'. In general the new scheme was accepted with relief and enthusiasm. Only Colonel Wedgwood,[3] a fiscal maverick by disposition, objected that it was bad in principle because it taxed productive industry and would enter into prices. The truly basic difference was that all pretence of taxing excess profits only had been dropped; now all profits were liable; and it also meant that income received as salary gained over income received as profits. Finally, it was the first time for many years that a principal tax in a Budget scheme had been so fundamentally changed by the will of the House.

The controversy over N.D.C., which incidentally survived the Committee stage without any significant amendments, completely overshadowed the discussions on the remaining provisions of the Finance Bill; in fact, although its yield was only estimated to be one-fortieth of the national requirements, it had occupied about three-quarters of the debating time. For, looking at the Budget as a whole, it was surprising that proposals to raise the enormous sum of £863 millions should have evoked so little notice from the country at large and have been subjected to so little truly critical analysis from the floor of the House.

The charge of income tax, for instance, which at 5s 0d was recognized as 'an unprecedented sum outside war or immediate post-war years',[4] did not even receive the courtesy of an amendment to the clause proposing it on the Order Paper, and Simon[5] was able to sum up after two speeches only. Tinker[6] suggested the lowering of the surtax limit to £1,500; and although the proposal was negatived it is interesting to note in this connection that there were now 90,000 surtax payers as opposed to 83,000 in 1933, a telling illustration of the scale of industrial recovery.

But in general the June and July Committee debates and the Report stage later in the second month raised issues which were either hardy annuals where no new arguments need be deployed on either side and the discussion had almost become ritual, such as the plea for

[1] H. 21/6/1937, Cols 855/869.
[2] H. 21/6/1937, Cols 869/881.
[3] H. 21/6/1937, Cols 902/906.
[4] H. 9/6/1937, Col. 1885 (Boothby).
[5] H. 9/6/1937, Cols 1890/1892.
[6] H. 9/6/1937, Cols 1892/1894.

child allowance for children undergoing training;[1] or which were clearly too expensive to succeed, for example the proposal to restore the pre-1931 married man's allowance which had then been £225.[2] And finally there were phantoms of battles long ago embodied in the plea to have Co-operative Societies declared exempt from N.D.C.[3]

So when Colville came to open the Third Reading on July 16th[4] he was able to present a comparatively amiable summary of the four months' discussions. He emphasized the time spent on N.D.C. but held that both the imposition of the tax and the increase in standard rate had secured general acceptance; and he reminded the House that allowances had been left intact. The National Defence loan policy was inevitable; but despite this, social services expenditure had been maintained.

This somewhat complacent attitude was rudely shattered by Latham's accusation[5] that the net result of the Budget was to penalize the poor to the advantage of the rich. It was a 'golden calf Budget, tender to a degree to vested interests'. In the face of such ritualistic attitudes it was useless for Boothby[6] to put in a plea that the limits of productive direct taxation were being reached and that to finance defence any further from income would be severely deflationary. The discussion continued with a good deal of desultory sniping of this sort in a thin House which at one point was nearly counted out. The only real debating point scored was by Barnes,[7] who claimed with some justification that N.D.C. Mark II 'abandoned all pretence to recover any proportion of excessive profits . . . and became a tax which could be passed on to a very large extent. Observe the celerity with which the Government were prepared to accept the withdrawal of their first tax because it did not meet with the approval of the City. . . .'

Simon's conclusion[8] was a typical piece of advocacy. The Budget provided for three broad bands of expenditure. £219 millions was being spent on the social services as compared with a 1931 figure of £171 millions; £224 millions was the National Debt's portion as against a figure of £282·5 millions in 1931; and the comparative figure for defence, currently £198 millions for a figure of £110 millions

[1] H. 1/7/1937, Col. 2242 et seq.   [2] H. 1/7/1937, Col. 1335 et seq.
[3] H. 15/7/1937, Col. 1660 et seq.   [4] H. 16/7/1937, Cols 1673/1682.
[5] H. 16/7/1937, Cols 1682/1691.   [6] H. 16/7/1937, Col. 1716.
[7] H. 16/7/1937, Col. 1743.   [8] H. 16/7/1937, Cols 1747/1758.

in 1931, was remarkable in view of the national emergency. The current prosperity, he maintained, came from a real revival of trade and not from the artificial stimulus of an armaments boom. The Bill was passed with the usual heavy majority and the Royal Assent was given a fortnight later.

The Great Divide for this century so far occurred during the thirties; the date could justifiably be put at 1936 with the collapse of sanctions and the machinery of the League of Nations. The complex apportionment of guilt for this tragedy is not relevant here but the fact is undeniable; and its effect on the development of British fiscal policy during the period 1932–37 and after was to cause an equally significant split.

The crisis of 1929–31 was the result of two basic processes. The first was the increasingly unsuccessful attempt to defend the inconsistent gold-based exchange rates which had been settled in the currency stabilisations of the twenties; the second was the world-wide fall in the prices of raw materials and foodstuffs which made it more difficult for the developing nations to buy capital equipment from the manufacturing nations and to service the loan interest which frequently financed their purchases. The final collapse, when it came, spread with dramatic rapidity from Vienna, the home of speculative deposits, to Berlin, and then to London; and the ultimate fall of sterling in September 1931 seems in retrospect unavoidable.

This collapse, and the May Committee's recommendations, provide the context for Snowden's last Budgets of 1931 and Chamberlain's first of 1932, which imposed and retained severe increases in direct taxation. There was then a year's breathing space with faint signs of recovery and a reduction in the adverse trade balance; but this did not influence Chamberlain in his notable refusal to unbalance the Budget deliberately in 1933. To an extent this may have been a short-sighted policy; certainly Keynes thought so, for it is from this year he began to advocate with 'dogged pertinacity' the policy of large-scale works on public loan as a cure for unemployment.[1] But the prime need, as Chamberlain saw it, was a general restoration of confidence, and the initial stage of recovery needed as much a psychological as an economic impetus. For the gold standard had been regarded as sacrosanct, the very Ark of the

---

[1] R. F. Harrod, *The Life of John Maynard Keynes*, p. 441.

Covenant; the 1931 devaluation had been a brutal shock to the nation
and time to recover was essential.

Chamberlain's third and fourth Budgets were, to a large extent,
complementary: the Chancellor's avowed intention was to relieve
those who had suffered by the 1931 cuts and clearly, in view of the slow,
if distinct economic revival showing rises in both prices and output,
it would not be possible, according to the canons of orthodox finance,
to dispense fiscal justice to all sections of the community in one Budget
when the country did not possess adequate financial resources for
such an exercise; it would have to be done by instalments.

In 1934, therefore, Chamberlain was faced with a choice of
priorities, whether to reduce the standard rate or whether to
increase allowances. The debate showed that to the Government the
overriding consideration finally was the encouragement of trade and
the promotion of exports which was best secured by the sixpence off
standard rate; the Opposition contented itself simply by making
the two party points that this would benefit the rich and accentuate
the increasing imbalance between direct and indirect taxation to the
disadvantage of the poor; but even this routine reaction was to an
extent invalidated by the very clear hints dropped on the Third
Reading[1] that it would be the turn of allowances in 1935, as indeed it
proved to be.

On the whole the 1934 and 1935 Budgets were Chamberlain's most
successful. He had declared his intentions plainly enough when he
quoted Snowden[2] in his Budget speech of 1934 and within two years
he had succeeded in restoring, with a few minor exceptions, the direct
tax structure which had existed before the crisis; not only his timing
but his method had been right. The real criticism of Chamberlain's
policy in these two years should not have been focused, as it quite
clearly was, on his programme as such but on its tragically limited
objectives. The Opposition would have served the country better
had it accepted Chamberlain's reforms for what they were, a much-
needed corrective to Snowden's fanatical economic orthodoxy, and
then tried to push them further in the direction of a far more
expansionist outlook.

That was the Opposition's last chance ever to influence the
financial conservatism and traditional 'sound money' policy of the
National Government. For that Government was, like all coalitions,

[1] See p. 51.   [2] See p. 36.

essentially a government of the moderates; and opposition to it tended to extremism, not only in the shape of Fascism, although that expression of despair or dissatisfaction was worrying enough, but also in the semi-Marxist pronouncements of Stafford Cripps and his adherents. There had not been enough constructive criticism; and the handful of Members who had tried to advocate the Keynesian doctrine of public works on a massive scale, budget deficits involving credit creation to increase liquidity and lower interest rates as well as staged remissions of taxation, too often confused themselves by humanitarian considerations or fear of a return to 1931. Only Keynes himself, after praising Chamberlain's conversion operation,[1] remained stubbornly hostile to the Chancellor's rigid adherence to orthodox finance.

By 1936, of course, Chamberlain had another answer to the critics who demanded expansionist policies in order to accelerate the increasing prosperity of the country. In the first three years of his régime he had pleaded the necessity of cutting down expenditure and balancing Budgets to effect a restoration of commercial confidence; a feeling shared by Snowden when, with the shadow of doom already on him, he declared, 'I am convinced an essential factor in ameliorating unemployment is a restoration of confidence in industry and commerce'.

But now the plan was changed; now it was quite simply the exigencies of national defence. And even at this juncture Chamberlain could not see that the rearmament programme was to a somewhat limited and erratic extent a substitute for public works; not a very good substitute, it is true, on account of the high obsolescence of such capital expenditure. He simply feared that the defence loans were going to cause inflation and he grumbled privately that 'four years of fruitful finance were to be undone'.[2]

The beginning of a series of Budgets concerned in ever-increasing measure with arms expenditure marked the end of an era which had witnessed a revolution in the fiscal scene. The days of the Exchequer under Churchill were the days of Free Trade, of taxation for revenue only, of high interest rates, of the Gold Standard, of strict adherence to the imperatives of the Sinking Fund and repayment of World War I debts. The next decade saw Protection, the beginning of budgeting

[1] *Economic Journal*, September 1932.
[2] Iain Macleod, *Neville Chamberlain*, p. 191.

as an economic instrument, cheap money, a managed currency, the suspension of the Sinking Fund and the virtual cessation of any further liquidation of the American loans. It was Chamberlain who had been the architect of this almost complete transformation which he had accomplished in a period when the financial probity of nations had sunk to mediaeval standards.

Two final questions arise in reviewing Chamberlain's financial policy; how far was it a significant element in promoting recovery in Britain between 1932 and 1937 and to what extent that policy could have been improved. The general answer to the first question seems to be that the economic revival of the thirties was partly due to cheap money, certain reductions in taxation and tariffs; equally powerful factors at least were the housing boom and the fact that real consumption expenditure remained at least stable.[1] The surge of commercial confidence, of which Chamberlain prided himself as being the author, arose from a combination of both governmental and economic pressures.

Chamberlain was not short of critics during the period; what he was short of was workable solutions, particularly to the unemployment problem. Indeed, the main charge against Chamberlain is that he accepted the inevitability of ten years of massive unemployment, and that he could see no validity in the proposals of Keynes, whose influence has been paramount in banishing the grim misery of the twenties and thirties from the lives of ordinary working people. But it is not enough to have a good idea: the practical problem of implementing it must be thought out. So the final question to be asked, therefore, is whether Keynesianism might have transformed Chamberlain's compromise of a limited parochial success into a spectacular triumph or a dismal administrative failure.

[1] H. W. Richardson, *Economic Recovery in Britain* 1932–1939, pp. 313/316.

Chapter VI

The Finance Bill 1938

SIMON—A TANNER

Time Table

Financial Statement		April 26, 1938
Budget Proposals		
	1st Day	27
	2nd Day	28
Budget Resolutions		
	Reported	May 4
Finance Bill		
	1st Reading	4
	2nd Reading	26
Committee		
	1st Day	June 22
	2nd Day	23
	3rd Day	27
	4th Day	28
	5th Day	30
Report		
	1st Day	July 11
	2nd Day	12
3rd Reading		15
Royal Assent		29

For the first time in over six years there was a new presence to play the leading role on Budget Day, April 26, 1938; not that Sir John Simon was lacking in experience, having been Chancellor since the previous

May and responsible for piloting the 1937 Budget through all its stages from the Second Reading; no longer could he plead, as when he received the seals of office, that he 'had no special knowledge of national finance', which Chamberlain had assured him was 'not a bad qualification to start with'.[1] Apart from the absence of Chamberlain's familiar figure—although like Churchill, another ex-Chancellor, the Prime Minister was in the Chamber—the setting was that usual for a Budget Day, crowded galleries in one of which the Governor of the Bank of England was sitting, and an equally crowded House full of the buzz of nervous conversation. Simon himself, however, seemed calm and almost casual in manner as he spoke the opening lines of 'our annual problem play presented in three acts'.[2]

The first act was the traditional review of the past financial year.[3] In 1937/38 total revenue at £872·58 millions was £48 millions above 1936/37, £9·5 millions above the estimate and, as an interesting comparison, almost precisely five times the 1913/14 receipts; that comparison was also ironic. To come to details, Customs and Excise had yielded £335·261 millions, an excess over estimate of £2·25 millions, and Inland Revenue £471·346 millions, an excess of £3·75 millions. This net figure was an amalgam of some significant out-turns. N.D.C. was £·5 million down and stamp duties, reflecting the drop in Stock Exchange transactions, a dramatic short-fall of £5 millions; but the buoyancy of income tax, with a welcome £10 millions[4] excess, had more than redressed the balance. Admittedly there had been more payments of tax than usual before January 1st, so there would be smaller arrears in the coming year; but surtax, currently £1million down, would be up in the coming year since its assessment was twelve months later than income tax. The Post Office contributed £11·295 millions and continued to show an expansion in revenue although expenditure was rising on account of the development of the telephone system. Miscellaneous items, showing an increase of £2·5 millions over estimates, of £20·08 millons completed the total, along with motor vehicle duties of £34·5 millions. There was, however, one general trend which would need

---

[1] *Retrospect: The Memoirs of Viscount Simon*, p. 227. This is not unlike Derby's reassuring remark to Disraeli in 1852, when the latter first became Chancellor, 'You know as much as Mr Canning did; they give you the figures.'

[2] H. 26/4/1938, Cols 43/67.   [3] H. 26/4/1938, Cols 44/48.

[4] H. 26/4/1938, Col. 44.

watching: the first six months of the financial year had been more prosperous than the second.[1]

The Chancellor then passed on to scene two of the first act, the expenditure actually incurred in 1937/38. The Fixed Debt Charge of £224 millions last year not only covered management and interest but provided £7·767 millions to the statutory Sinking Funds. The remaining charge for this fund, £2·777 millions, was also met from revenue.[2] There were no surprises in the minor payments next dealt with, Northern Ireland £8·887 millions as against £8 millions budgeted for, and Miscellaneous Consolidated Fund services almost as estimated at £3·115 millions. Supply services, however, showed a very large saving of £22·333 millions on various Civil Votes including the welcome charge of £8·5 millions less on unemployment assistance.[3] The Defence estimate of £198 millions had all been used up but only £65 millions out of the £80 millions loan authorized. The total expenditure met from revenue had been £843·794 millions against an estimate of £862·9 millions.[4] The Committee would see that revenue exceeded expenditure by £28·8 millions, broadly because the national income was up, unemployment assistance was down and supplementary demands for ordinary expenditure were less than forecast.

With regard to the National Debt, in passing, the average rate of interest on Treasury Bills was only 11s 2d per cent, a new low record. There had been an issue of £100 millions 2½ per cent National Defence Bonds which, as already reported, had been used for advances under the Defence Loan Act to the extent of £65 millions, the balance for the time being going to reduce the Floating Debt. £10·5 millions had been applied to the statutory Sinking Fund, giving a net increase in the Debt of £257·75 millions, £203 millions of which was covered by assets in the Exchange Equalization Fund.[5] That fund was still making a profit and would be subject to a confidential review by the Public Accounts Committee.[6]

Simon now moved on to the second act, expenditure for 1939/39. The Fixed Debt Charge had remained at £224 millions for the first five years, estimated to cover interest, management and a con-

---

[1] H. 26/4/1938, Col. 46.   [2] H. 26/4/1938, Col. 46.
[3] H. 26/4/1938, Col. 47.   [4] See p. 125.
[5] This has been increased by £200 millions in July 1937.
[6] H. 26/4/1938, Col. 48.

tribution to the statutory Sinking Funds the total this year had, for these three items, reached £227 millions. He had therefore estimated the charge at £230 millions; there would probably be a margin but he had taken the precaution of getting authority to borrow;[1] in view of the necessity of providing for accrued interest as well as capital liabilities. Other minor payments would be to Northern Ireland £8·9 millions and miscellaneous Consolidated Fund Services £3·2 millions; no provision was estimated to be needed for the Post Office; the total under this head was £242·1 millions.

The Committee was already aware that the Supply Services totalled £692·298 millions, made up of Defence £253·248 millions and Civil Votes (including £3·5 millions for A.R.P.) £439·05 millions, an increase respectively of £55 and £20 millions over last year. On top of this was a further £90 millions borrowed for Defence.[2] He also made public for the first time that the Government had been buying up supplies of wheat, whale oil and sugar sufficient for a few months, but 'absolute secrecy was essential to prevent prices from being raised by the knowledge that the Government was coming into the market'. [3]Essential raw materials had already been stockpiled but more might be needed; in addition, further A.R.P. expenditure was likely. Simon decided on that account he ought to provide a further £10 millions for Civil Supplementary Estimates. The total to be met had now mounted to £944·4 millions.

Before the third act, the means of raising this vast sum, the Chancellor found it necessary to make 'an excursion into the winding and secluded backwaters of the law', particularly in relation to tax avoidance which he defined as 'the adoption of ingenious methods for reducing liability which are within the law but none the less defeat the intentions upon which the tax is founded'.[4] He admitted the subject was very complex, difficult and technical, but he thought the Committee ought to have a brief description of the new proposals.

Four of these concerned settlements.[5] The first proposed that in the case of all trusts and settlements the income arising should be treated as the income of the settler for both income tax and surtax purposes if the terms of the settlement provided any forms of revocation by the exercise of which the settler might become entitled

---

[1] H. 26/4/1938, Col. 49.   [2] H. 26/4/1938, Col. 50.
[3] H. 26/4/1938, Col. 51.   [4] H. 26/4/1938, Col. 52.
[5] See now S. 38/41, FA. 1938, *seriatim*.

to the beneficial enjoyment of the income. Secondly, if in the terms of any settlement (apart from a marriage settlement) were such that the funds might revert to the settler in the future on any contingency, the income of the settlement accumulated by the trustees should be treated as the income of the settler. These two proposals ensured that if income was within the power of an individual to enjoy it should be treated as his income for all purposes and, as the Chancellor had warned last year,[1] had retrospective effect for 1937/38 surtax. The third proposal was that loans from the undistributed income of a settlement should be treated as the income of the settler, for tax purposes; this was to apply to past and future settlements but only to loans after the beginning of the current year. Fourthly, it was proposed that in computing an individual's total income for surtax purposes, no deduction should be allowed for any annual payment which he might make under the terms of the settlement if the income represented by that annual payment was not paid out by the trustees but accumulated in their hands.

There was one more proposal dealing with loopholes which was in effect a strengthening of Section 18, F.A. 1936; this had dealt with the avoidance of tax by forming one-man companies abroad in such a way that although the income was receivable by some person abroad the individual at home retained the power to enjoy it. In such a case the income of the person abroad was treated as the income of the person at home. But a proviso to the Section stated it should not apply if the individual could show that the transfer abroad was effected mainly for some purpose other than the purpose of avoidance. The Chancellor remarked caustically that he had been 'very much struck with some of the excuses that have been offered to prove that avoidance of taxation is not the main purpose of such transfers',[2] and now proposed to delete the word 'mainly' which had been so construed as to widen the exceptions beyond the intentions of Parliament.

There were some other 'amendments of income tax law which are necessary to complete the system in places where it has been found to be deficient'.[3] These included some technical amendments relating to the administration of estates where income tax and surtax had been avoided,[4] some redefinition of the law regarding the cashing of

---

[1] On the Third Reading, H. 16/7/1937 (July).   [2] H. 26/4/1938, Col. 54.
[3] H. 26/4/1938, Col. 55.   [4] Part III, F.A. 1938.

coupons,[1] and a proposed tightening of the existing provisions concerning the profit arising on the disposal of stock when a business had been discontinued. These, and other minor matters, would be explained in full when the Finance Bill was introduced.

The Chancellor now came to this third act, the source of the revenue which would be needed to compass the prodigious total of over £944 millions. The preliminary arithmetic was a straightforward if rather depressing exercise in simple addition.[2] Customs and Excise should produce £336 millions with increases expected in beer ('Shame' from Viscountess Astor), tobacco and oil duties. Inland Revenue dues were estimated at £514·25 millions, the yield of income tax and surtax anticipated at £21 millions and £5 millions higher than last year to balance an expected fall in death duties through a drop in the price level of securities. Motor vehicle duties of £36 millions, the Post Office contribution of £11 millions, and various miscellaneous items went to a total of £914 millions only, or a deficit of £30 millions.

'The all-important question,' continued Simon, 'is whether the gap is to be closed by resorting to fresh taxation or by resorting to further borrowing.'[3] The deficit was certainly due to the rearmament programme, originally estimated to cost £1,500 millions, but which was now clearly an underestimate; and he reminded Committee that the Defence Loans Act of 1938 had authorized the borrowing of £400 millions, of which £100 millions had been borrowed already; but such borrowing must be very carefully timed and spread.

In answering this question he had been guided by three main considerations. The gap was really £120 millions since £90 millions had already been filled by borrowing; arms expenditure was accelerating and he was afraid supplementaries might be required later in the year; and thirdly, the Defence White Paper[4] had given a clear warning of the increasing cost of defence. He had decided, therefore, that the deficit must be covered by taxation; there was a heavy enough burden on loans already.

The taxation he proposed was partly direct and partly indirect, but mainly the former; the principal contributor would be income tax with an increase, and at this a gasp went up, of 6d. There would, however, be two concessions: reduced rate relief was to stay at 1s 8d

[1] S. 21, F.A. 1938.
[2] H. 26/4/1938, Cols 58/59.
[3] H. 26/4/1938, Col. 60.
[4] March 1938.

although it was traditionally one-third of standard rate; this would mean no change in the income tax of some two million small payers; and the increase in basic wear and tear rates on plant and machinery by one-tenth was doubled to become one-fifth. This proposal would produce £26·5 millions in a full year. An increase in oil duties, to bring an extra £5 millions, and 2d on tea so that 'the humblest homes could take a share in the defence outlay', to bring in £3·25 millions, completed the indirect tax contributions. This would bring in £30·35 millions, leaving a small surplus of under £400,000. He would like to have reduced taxation but, in view of social services, preservation of financial strength and defence, he could not. An active peace policy was being promoted; meanwhile 'the load which we have to bear will be carried with the dogged determination and dauntless courage of the British race'.

There was a rather more prolonged discussion than usual when the Chancellor had sat down, and the House did not rise until nearly 7.30 p.m. instead of the more usual 6 p.m. The two leaders of the Opposition parties spoke first: Attlee[1] opened lightly enough by saying 'the sport had gone out of Budget-making now a balance could be achieved by loans'; but he concluded with a bitter condemnation of a 'foreign policy both wicked and foolish' which had made this immense expenditure necessary. Sinclair[2] was more moderate: apart from deploring the tea duty as 'a burden on the poorest of the poor', his main complaint was that expenditure was getting out of control.

The House emptied rapidly after these two formal protests so that the back-benchers were able to enjoy a little limelight and to indicate some of the lines of argument which Members would develop over the coming months. For the Conservatives, Williams[3] expressed the orthodox view that the increased standard rate would have an adverse effect on industry, and Tasker[4] blamed the archaic techniques of the Treasury for financial maladministration. For Labour, Ellis Smith[5] took the doctrinaire line that the increase in national wealth stemmed from the workers but they had not been adequately recompensed by a proportionate improvement in social services. Tinker[6] suggested a drop in the surtax limit to £1,500

[1] H. 26/4/1938, Cols 67/70.   [2] H. 26/4/1938, Cols 70/73.
[3] H. 26/4/1938, Cols 79/85.   [4] H. 26/4/1938, Cols 95/97.
[5] H. 26/4/1938, Cols 74/79.   [6] H. 26/4/1938, Cols 92/95.

instead of the increased tea duty, but it was left to McEntee[1] to level the gravest charge that 'we have settled down to the belief that there shall be roughly one-and-a-half million men and women permanently unemployed'. Already the attitudes were beginning to harden despite the increasing pressure of impending danger of war.

The usual flood of pre-Budget guesses in the national press had been a mere trickle in 1938 and consisted of the usual gentle hints that it would be kind of the Chancellor to spare the country this year and make posterity pay. Even *The Economist* in its Budget horoscope[2] thought Simon would be surprising the prophets if he altered standard rate, arguing that a minor increase in miscellaneous taxes would be enought to balance. When Simon had made his proposals, however, although they were regarded as grim, the journal did admit[3] that the 'straight and narrow path of increased taxation' was unquestionably the right course.

This was the view taken also by the *Manchester Guardian* and *The Times*. The former was the more enthusiastic:[4] it was wise to put on now as much as could be borne; the avoidance clauses were admirable; the increased taxation on oil would be easy to raise; only the justification for the tax on tea seemed a little strained. The latter, under the leading article heading of 'Facing the Cost', stressed the Chancellor's awkward dilemma of further borrowing or increased taxation but was not sure whether he had made the right decision, although he would certainly claim the virtue of courage; and it was clear the severity of the measures had made a deep impression abroad among both friends and foes.

The *New Statesman*, however, in a Keynesian exposition,[5] declared implacable hostility to the proposals. There was no quarrel with the decision to tax, although the acquisition of food stocks could justifiably have been covered by loans, but it would have been more equitable to put 10 per cent on estate duty and to lower the surtax limit. 'The Budget was frigid in its severity, risks damage to the sources of the main tax receipts, and takes no pains to lay the increased burdens on shoulders best able to bear it.' Even the plans for checking avoidances were brushed off as 'not impressive'.[6] It was a piece of fiscal masochism proving only that the country could stand up to the economic endurance test.

[1] H. 26/4/1938, Cols 97/98.   [2] 23/4/1938.   [3] 30/4/1938.   [4] 27/4/1938.
[5] 30/4/1938.   [6] It was true the estimated saving was only £1 million.

As last year, Pethick-Lawrence,[1] one of Labour's experts in this field, opened the two days' debate on the Budget proposals; and as usual he fairly epitomized the basic party criticisms. He launched a general attack on government expenditure, its fiscal thinking, being especially severe on the proposed tea duty increase, and the policies which were now culminating in the present crisis situation. A future of crushing taxation faced the country, none of which was earmarked for the omissions which still existed in the social services. For this was a Budget 'based on a prepossession with war'; in fact the real issue before the nation was one of war or peace; beside this the Budget sank into insignificance. It must therefore be judged as a war Budget although there was scant evidence that the lessons of faulty finance in the Great War had been learned; the avoidance provisions were inadequate and the question of a capital levy should be studied. He concluded with a bitter criticism of the Government's foreign policy so that for the first, but by no means the last, time in the discussions they took on the atmosphere of a foreign affairs rather than a financial debate.

His colleagues were quick to follow his lead. It was a simple Budget by Simple Simon, commented Morrison.[2] The Chancellor had turned to the 'good old taxes' and marshalled his figures in a 'cold-blooded and unimaginative way' as if rearmament were the only consideration; certainly the additional duty on tea was a gross psychological error. Benson[3] concentrated on avoidance and suggested that instead of passing legislation which was perpetually one move behind the avoider there should be a comprehensive enactment to enable the Board of Inland Revenue 'to look at reality and not at mere form'.[4] But there was a grudging admission that it was right to bridge the deficit by taxation rather than by further borrowing. 'I can never regard income tax as a burden,' said Ridley, 'no matter what the range as long as you have left the payer with an income sufficient to enjoy a tolerable existence.'[5]

This was certainly the majority opinion on all sides of the House. But there were exceptions: Davison,[6] Chairman of the Income Tax Payer's Society, for instance, reverted to the old-fashioned conception of income tax as 'an emergency tax, a war tax'; by using it as a

[1] H. 27/4/1938, Cols 137/146.   [2] H. 27/4/1938, Cols 164/169.
[3] H. 27/4/1938, Cols 196/205.   [4] H. 27/4/1938, Col. 199.
[5] H. 27/4/1938, Col. 210.   [6] H. 27/4/1938, Cols 190/196.

balancing mechanism, the Chancellor was 'undermining the national reserve.' Loftus,[1] too, was against additional taxation but for a different reason: he felt borrowing would be a hedge against possible deflation.

Sinclair,[2] for the Liberals, put forward a sixpoint programme, namely increases in both surtax and death duties, the taxation of land values, the revival of overseas trade coupled with a positive peace policy; and, especially, economy with the elimination of waste and profiteering in the arms industry. It was this last point which was pursued by his party members with the greatest enthusiasm on the following day. Both Owen[3] and White[4] suggested the setting up of a form of Public Accounts Committee to investigate armaments expenditure, as had been done in 1917 when a considerable number of recommendations by such a Committee had been accepted.

But strictures on the tea duty or pleas for economy had a limited appeal against the orthodox and easily-expounded Conservative line that the amount spent on defence in recent years had been subnormal, that the position must be corrected but that the Chancellor must, as Mellor argued,[5] seriously consider the desirability of being prepared 'to borrow rather more liberally and to tax rather more leniently'. This was the furthest any Government supporter would go in the direction of criticizing Simon's avowed choice of taxation rather than borrowing; or as Anderson,[6] one of the great pundits of the City expressed it, 'income tax must come down as soon as the crisis is over'. The majority endorsed the choice and applauded Mabane[7] when he said: 'There is a deficit of £30 millions and it has to be met. I have read and heard many criticisms of the taxes proposed by the Chancellor but I have not heard a single alternative proposal that appeals to me any more than these proposals for producing the necessary revenue.'

Mabane was a veteran speaker in Budget debates, but he confessed that seeing the essence of correct budgeting, as he understood it, was stability of conditions which certainly did not prevail at the present, he could only suggest as an alternative to a drastic reduction in expenditure 'the assumption by the state of a far wider control of

[1] H. 27/4/1938, Cols 214/222. [2] H. 27/4/1938, Cols 146/158.
[3] H. 28/4/1938, Cols 343/350. [4] H. 28/4/1938, Cols 417/427.
[5] H. 27/4/1938, Cols 206/209. [6] H. 27/4/1938, Cols 180/184.
[7] H. 27/4/1938, Cols 169/175.

economic processes'.[1] The new conditions, however, proved a challenge to a new generation of fiscal experts in the House. One of these was Hely-Hutchinson[2] who, in a brilliant maiden speech, warned the Committee of the frightening total of expenditure in prospect with economies possibly only in administration: 'The present Budget,' he concluded, 'is a warning Budget.' Equally useful was the practical suggestion of Stokes,[3] the chairman of a great engineering firm, that auditors should be used to certify the amount of profit on arms contracts, and the theoretical analysis of Nathan[4] that a general decline in revenue might be imminent and that cyclical budgeting would be called for. But the most pentrating analysis was that of Harold Macmillan.[5] The figures could not be juggled with as some speakers had attempted to do: they must be faced; and this was the first Budget which had confronted the country with any serious attempt to finance defence, for up to 1938 the abandonment of gold and the adoption of protection had increased the national income which had automatically increased the yield of tax. But now 'the State has a duty as well as a right to demand effective organization of commerce and industry from which it may secure its revenue'; the basic criticism of current economic processes was 1·75 millions unemployed and idle plant.

Adams[6] and Jones,[7] for the Opposition, both suggested the taxation of land values, and both objected to the increased rates of wear and tear allowances, although Stokes[8] had made a reasonable proposition that the allowance should be conditional on use for improvement in plant and machinery. This was the Opposition's last attack on the first day; and when Colville[9] came to sum up at 10.30 p.m. he could fairly claim there had been little real criticism on the fundamental issue of taxation as against borrowing; he could point to a definite swing away from indirect taxation; and as for the tea duty, mentioned by half the speakers from both sides of the House, its cost to the average household would be 1s 6d a year only.

The second day's debate began with a swingeing debating speech from Dalton,[10] newly returned from Australia, which amounted to a wholesale condemnation of the Budget proposals. Air-raid pre-

[1] H. 27/4/1938, Cols 173/174.   [2] H. 27/4/1938, Cols 158/164.
[3] H. 27/4/1938, Cols 175/180.   [4] H. 27/4/1938, Cols 184/191.
[5] H. 27/4/1938, Cols 239/247.   [6] H. 27/4/1938, Cols 234/239.
[7] H. 27/4/1938, Cols 247/256.   [8] H. 27/4/1938, Cols 178/179.
[9] H. 27/4/1938, Cols 256/265.   [10] H. 28/4/1938, Cols 327/337.

cautions were inadequate in scale, scope and timing; the saving on
unemployment insurance would be negligible, as the numbers of
unemployed were falling very slowly; the increased tea duty was
iniquitous and evasion had been tackled in a half-hearted fashion.
The £30 million deficit should indeed be met from taxation, but not
by penalizing the middle-class to the extent of 6d in the pound but
by increases in surtax, death duties and N.D.C. He rubbed in the
fiscal truism that the richer the taxpayer the smaller the amount of
his percentaged increase in tax. Companies' profits were up if they
were connected with armaments; and in any case they could contrive
to lower their tax bill by buying new plant. In all, there was no
equality of sacrifice.

These were sound party points backed by a good deal of economic
acumen. But more searching was the analysis of Sir Arthur Salter,[1]
speaking as an Independent. He approved the decision to tax rather
than borrow, reminding the Committee that £90 millions was already
borrowed: 'those Hon. Members who rather like an unbalanced
Budget might well be content with what we are going to get'. Turning
to the detailed proposals, he thought the additional 6d on income
tax came at an unfortunate stage of the trade cycle; the increases in
indirect taxation had been rather lightly dealt with, 'for indirect
taxation is an inversely graduated income tax'; and he hoped, but
it was only a hope, that anti-evasion legislation would lead to a rise in
surtax. The cost of food stores, he felt strongly, was a capital matter
and should not be a charge on current revenue.[2] But in general 'it is
impossible to look back upon those years from 1931 onwards without
feeling they were years of lost opportunities'.

The rest of the debate was curiously uneven in quality: apart from
the Liberal plea for an economy committee already mentioned,[3]
which was elaborated by Graham White[4] in his summing-up for the
party, the speakers were mainly the back-benchers of the two main
parties or those with a particular point to put, somewhat off the
orthodox line of either side.

For the Conservatives the speeches of O'Neill[5] and Smithers[6]
were typical. After approving Simon's proposals generally, apart from

[1] H. 28/4/1938, Cols 372/382.
[2] Cf. the comments of the *New Statesman*, p. 125.
[3] See p. 115.   [4] H. 28/4/1938, Cols 417/422.
[5] H. 28/4/1938, Cols 337/343.   [6] H. 28/4/1938, Cols 401/409.

taking a side-swipe at estate duty, 'a tax on capital used for revenue which is a very undesirable object and result', the former's main theme was the confidence which the policy of successive Conservative Chancellors had engendered in the country and the world at large. The latter developed the same text. 'A balanced Budget, produced on sound and orthodox lines, is vital in this country. It has been said that the Chancellor was unimaginative but I am sure the Budget he has produced is a good, sound Treasury Budget. The new taxes will be easy of collection and no new bureaucrats will have to be invented. A balanced Budget is vital in order that we may maintain our credit and the purchasing power of the £ sterling.'[1]

Whether against taxation for defence on the first day or for continuing confidence on the second day, the orthodox Labour attack could make little headway. Sexton,[2] for instance, had to approve the standard rate increase and the anti-evasion proposals: his criticism was confined to the tea duty, where he did give some telling figures of old-age pensioner's budgets and to a suggestion which could well have been a plank in the party programme, that the rate of N.D.C. should have been increased. Pearson[3] had to be called to order for using the occasion for criticism of the Special Areas Act. And Lees-Smith,[4] in his conclusion for his party, accused the Government of using the political situation as an excuse for its economic policy which had now shattered every canon of finance it was formed to maintain: 'but it was far easier for the Government earlier on to have influenced the European political situation than it was for any Government to influence a world economic blizzard'.

Some Members had not been convinced by Simon's case for a mainly standard rate increase to bridge his £30 millions gap. Albery[5] considered the £15 millions not taken up of last year's borrowing powers,[6] plus the contribution under the Irish agreement, would have sufficed; he also made the prescient suggestion of a form of tax reserve certificate.[7] Boothby's[8] argument was that the natural buoyancy of revenue would have produced the amount required; but if the country must anticipate Budgets of £1,000 millions and more in the near future trade must expand. Wardlaw-Milne,[9] the

[1] H. 28/4/1938, Cols 405/406.
[2] H. 28/4/1938, Cols 389/393.
[3] H. 28/4/1938, Cols 399/401.
[4] H. 28/4/1938, Cols 423/433.
[5] H. 28/4/1938, Cols 383/389.
[6] See p. 120.
[7] H. 28/4/1938, Cols 386/387.
[8] H. 28/4/1938, Cols 350/357.
[9] H. 28/4/1938, Cols 367/372.

next speaker, agreed; only Pethick-Lawrence[1] had commented on the current adverse balance of trade. Certainly it was increasingly difficult to trade with some European States, but trade with others who were well-disposed and with the Empire ought to be actively encouraged; perhaps 'some kind of enquiry should be set up'. A final suggestion for avoiding the increase in direct taxation deserves a mention, Higg's[2] scheme, long before its time, for a levy on football pools.[3]

It had been a quiet debate: the House was nearly counted out on both days and Simon, when he rose to wind up, could justifiably claim that he had received general consent to his proposal for covering the deficit by taxation; this comparative unanimity was probably the reason why, in Sir Arthur Salter's phrase, there were so many 'empty places and silent voices'.

In addition he had not expected a wildly enthusiastic reception, especially as he had given warning that although 'it is a very convenient and perhaps necessary thing to have an annual Budget, it is certainly true that we must look beyond the year . . .'. This was the last generality he permitted himself; for the rest of his speech he stuck very firmly to his brief, which was in fact a detailed justification of his various proposals, which he claimed were receiving a measure of support which was a great encouragement to him.

The debate on the report of the Budget Resolutions on May 4th was a field day for the experts on the avoidance provisions which would occupy some seven clauses and nine pages of the Bill. The rest of the Resolutions, from the rate of tax at the beginning through the stock valuation amendment, the Estate Duty avoidance sections, and finally to the technical changes required in the original N.D.C. legislation, gained general assent after the careful and lucid explanations of the Attorney-General, the Solicitor-General or the Financial Secretary.

These three Government spokesmen also had a comparatively easy passage in the first exchanges of the debate over coupon dealing,[4] but the discussion became much more animated when the four avoidance provisions came under fire which had been incorporated in Resolution 11. As the Solicitor-General explained, it was

[1] See p. 126.   [2] H. 28/4/1938, Cols 393/399.
[3] Their turnover even in 1938 was some £40 to £50 millions.
[4] S. 24, F.A., 1938.

the 'bare bones which will have to be clothed in flesh in the Finance Bill';[1] he summarized the type of avoidance which the Chancellor had in mind,[2] but said it was not possible to give an estimate of the current scale of avoidance as practised, nor the potential saving. This did not satisfy the Opposition: Pethick-Lawrence insisted that some estimate of the leakage, 'however conjectural',[3] should be made; Benson accused the Government of 'limping tardily along';[4] he had raised these matters in 1936; and Ede[5] wondered whether the ultimate results would justify the inclusion in the Finance Bill of complicated clauses and the monopolizing of so much of the House's time.

But amid the interchange of technicalities two interesting general points emerged. The art of avoidance, even a generation ago, was a growth industry, and both sides of the House expressed fears that as fast as one bolt-hole was stopped, others were being diligently burrowed. There was one solution, as Benson put it: 'Until the Government are prepared to take powers of a general character to look at the reality and not the mere form, we shall have an unending spate of tax evasion legislation'.[6] Adams supported him.[7] The Solicitor-General could not accept this. 'It is for Parliament to put down, in terms, what is the law and as long as the subject carries out the law he ought not to be subjected to inquisition.'[8] Salter suggested a compromise 'that the law should be so framed as to give the Courts the right to quash particular arrangements on the ground that they were clearly designed to evade taxation',[9] and the Solicitor-General thereupon invited his co-operation in drafting a clause 'which would get through this House'.[10]

The other minor point concerned an ingenious justification for retrospective legislation. It had been discovered that the N.D.C. enactments held a flaw which permitted a double allowance for losses in the case of principal and subsidiary companies. The amending clause was made retrospective because, N.D.C. being imposed for a specific period of five years, 'it is important that it should be levied upon the same lines over the whole period'.[11]

The terms of the debate on the Second Reading[12] agreed by the

[1] H. 4/5/1938, Col. 927.   [2] H. 4/5/1938, Cols 928/932.
[3] H. 4/5/1938, Col. 934.   [4] H. 4/5/1938, Col. 935.
[5] H. 4/5/1938, Col. 939.   [6] H. 4/5/1938, Col. 937.
[7] H. 4/5/1938, Col. 942.   [8] H. 4/5/1938, Col. 945.
[9] H. 4/5/1938, Col. 945.   [10] H. 4/5/1938, Col. 945.
[11] H. 4/5/1938, Col. 967.   [12] H. 26/5/1938, Cols 1425/1548.

Labour Party were that 'the House regards with concern the continuing policy of unbalanced Budgets and cannot assent to the Second Reading of a Bill which, while permitting excessive profits on rearmament and subsidies to private industry, penalizes road transport and adds to the already heavy burdens of people of small means instead of raising the necessary revenue from the taxation of great wealth'. Alexander[1] introduced it. He could not separate the dangerous international situation from the financial problems which the country had to face; and he thought it rough justice that Simon should have to shoulder the burden as Chancellor, since his policy as Foreign Secretary had produced the current difficulties. White,[2] for the Liberal party, in supporting the amendment was in substantial agreement with it.

The Chancellor's[3] intervention was much earlier than usual and was a skilful piece of special pleading. 'Soaking the rich' was no solution: the 100,000 surtax payers' combined contributions to death duties, surtax and income tax more than covered the cost of the Defence charge for the year.[4] Only £90 millions of this total Defence cost of some £340 millions had been borrowed; this borrowing was justified on strict accountancy principles when it was expended on capital projects such as shadow factories. There was no proof of arms profiteering against which the Government had already taken precautions. It was right to take the middle course and make a modified use of borrowing and taxation: 'and as I expected this course is criticized by two sets of people from opposite points of view'.[5]

After Simon's statement, the debate changed direction somewhat in that there was a large measure of agreement on both sides of the House in relation to economy and the inflow of revenue. Boothby suggested a Ministry of Supply would be necessary[6] and that to maintain a high tax national income must also be at as high a level as possible. This was echoed by Amery[7] and, from the Opposition, by Pethick-Lawrence,[8] who, although he advocated 'the greater taxation of greater wealth', emphasized the necessity of a vast increase in national income: the problem was not one of production but of

[1] H. 26/5/1938, Cols 1425/1440.   [2] H. 26/5/1938, Cols 1440/1542.
[3] H. 26/5/1938, Cols 1466/1480.
[4] Death duties £69 million; surtax £62 million; income tax £134 million.
[5] H. 26/5/1938, Col. 1471.   [6] H. 26/5/1938, Col. 1513.
[7] H. 26/5/1938, Cols 1523/1524.   [8] H. 26/5/1938, Cols 1527/1537.

distribution and sale. The Financial Secretary[1] summed up: he replied
to the amendment point by point, and it was a fair general argument
to say that 'if we wished to achieve a reduction of expenditure on a
scale which would bring considerable relief, we shall have to make
fundamental alterations of a kind no party in the House is
proposing'.

The Committee stage of the Finance Bill opened on June 22nd
soberly enough with the Customs and Excise proposals which aroused
no significant questions of principle. It was accepted that the balance
between direct and indirect taxation was now coming down in favour
of the former, a general point which the Opposition had been ham-
mering for a number of years.

The next two days, June 23rd and 27th, were almost wholly
devoted to the technicalities of the avoidance sections with displays
of fiscal erudition from both sides of the House. The importance of
these discussions lay in the fact that the legal officers of the Government were forced to make their intentions clear, or as clear in the
circumstances as possible. Even this did not always satisfy the Chairman of the Income Tax Payers' Society,[2] who complained bitterly
about the obscurity of the Sections. 'Parliament should not be asked
to pass further Bills dealing with income tax until the Treasury
find words and phrases which will make the taxes understandable
by the people.' Bellenger[3] had a simple explanation: 'The reason
why we have clauses which are so unintelligible to the man in the
street is the ingenuity of the so-called man in the street and those
who aid and abet them.'[4] Simon[5] went into more detail. His summary
was: 'Taxation is a complicated thing and complicated things have
to be expressed in complicated ways'; and again there was the refusal to assume general powers: 'It is possible to imagine taxing legislation applied to the citizens of this country not according to the
exact words of a Statute and then left for its application to some
organ of the executive. . . . We have never done that.'[6]

The final days, June 28th and 30th, were largely occupied with
the ritual of amendments withdrawn by Members and amendments
accepted when Government-sponsored. Amongst the former should

[1] H. 26/5/1938, Cols 1537/1545. Since 16/5/1938 this had been D. Euan Wallace.
[2] Sir William Davison.   [3] H. 27/6/1938, Col. 1585.
[4] H. 27/6/1938, Col. 1585.   [5] H. 27/6/1938, Col. 1589.
[6] H. 27/6/1938, Cols 1584/1585.

be mentioned Tinker's valiant and annual attempt[1] to secure child allowance for apprentices, now to get sympathetic treatment, and the proposal to secure the exemption from N.D.C. of Co-operative Societies which was roughly handled.[2] Nor could Simon, in all justice, allow expenses to Ministers.[3]

The Report stage on July 11th and 12th was notable for two new clauses: one proposed a deduction for children over sixteen undergoing training,[4] thus fulfilling Tinker's long-cherished dream; the other proposed an allowance in certain cases for dependent relatives denied unemployment assistance.[5] Apart from these reforms, long overdue on humanitarian grounds, some more controversies over the more technical sections and the usual failure to secure an increase in earned income relief which would have cost £8·5 millions, the debate was enlivened only by a curiously Luddite attempt by Batey[6] to amend the increase in wear and tear rates on the ground that it would encourage the installation of new plant and lead to the dismissal of workers. Simon was quick to point out that to increase income tax and not wear and tear would endanger 'those big basic trades, trades which give a good deal of employment and which would be seriously handicapped if we debarred them from their essential development'.[7] And finally into the whole field of discussion, fiscal, technical or economic, filtered increasingly the significant theme of air raid precautions.

The Third Reading, or, to return to Simon's opening theatrical metaphor, the epilogue possibly, took place on July 15th. The attendance was sparse when Captain Euan Wallace[8] moved the Bill's acceptance. The Budget was chiefly remarkable for its size and severity; but despite this, the lot of the smaller taxpayer had been improved. The avoidance provisions had won support from both sides and the whole of the proposals had secured general acceptance. Certainly, apart from some arguments on technicalities and on retro-

---

[1] H. 28/6/1938, Col. 1769 et seq.　　[2] H. 28/6/1938, Col. 1788 et seq.

[3] H. 28/6/1938, Cols 1825/1835. This was rather an odd point. Members were entitled to expenses but Ministers were not, since as soon as they became Ministers they ceased to be Members in receipt of a salary and could no longer claim the usual Members' expenses. In fact the Ministers of the Crown Bill of 1937 had adjusted Ministers' salaries on that account; and Simon himself had piloted the Bill through the Commons.

[4] Sec. 20, F.A. 1938.　　　　　　　[5] Sec. 21, F.A. 1938.
[6] H. 12/7/1938, Cols 1150/1152.　　[7] H. 12/7/1938, Col. 1158.
[8] H. 15/7/1938, Cols 1701/1706.

spection, the avoidance legislation put forward had commanded almost universal approval; and the Financial Secretary was largely justified in his second claim of widespread assent to the other terms of the Bill.

There were, of course, some dissentient voices. Conservative critics such as Hely-Hutchinson[1] thought that 'on the expenditure side the horses are running away; on the revenue side taxation is reaching its effective limit'. The only remedy was increased production. This view coincided with that of Boothby[2] who suggested the stimulation of trade by export credits and further co-operation with the United States. White[3] expounded the Liberal line that economy was still possible and that 'taxation must not weaken the economic fabric of the country'. Labour, not for the first time, spoke with two voices: the Right and Centre harked back to the argument that the Government's financial policy was the direct result of their international policy; and the only possible virtue of the arms expenditure was that it might ease the unemployment problem ;this had not in fact happened, a situation entirely overlooked by the Budget.[4] The Left went much further: while agreeing that proper regard had not been paid to 'the causes of poverty, the causes of unemployment and the effect of low purchasing power among the masses', there was a round condemnation of 'this vast expenditure on arms, the worst kind of imbecility and madness'.[5]

Simon,[6] with that air of finality which was part of his forensic technique, had no difficulty in winding up. The Budget proposals had been generally accepted by the House and the country at large, and so had the advance planning implicit in such items as the Defence Loans Act for 'we cannot scientifically handle our financial problems if we limit ourselves to a single twelve-month'. He took no pride in his £1,000 million Budget, but he was comforted by the courage with which the taxpayer shouldered the load. The Royal Assent came precisely a fortnight later.

Because of its manifest dualism, the Budget of 1938 has a deceptive simplicity about it. It was, in the first place, an anti-avoidance Budget not only in its sweeping amendments in the law affecting

---

[1] H. 15/7/1938, Cols 1710/1712.   [2] H. 15/7/1938, Cols 1724/1732.
[3] H. 15/7/1938, Cols 1712/1717.
[4] Cf. Bellenger, H. 15/7/1938, Cols 1734/1737, or Barnes, Cols 1762/1769.
[5] Davies, H. 15/7/1938, Cols 1756/1758.   [6] H. 15/7/1938, Cols 1769/1780.

settlements[1] but in other enactments, such as the value of trading stock on cessation,[2] the restriction on transferring income to persons abroad[3] or the rectification of the carry-forward position of losses for N.D.C.[4] which were not debated so exhaustively as the four essentially technical sections. Secondly, it had to be tailored to subsidize the rearmament programme which was achieved with a remarkable degree of fiscal justice, apart from the increase in tea duty, a merely token sacrifice. For the smaller taxpayer was actually better off, although standard rate was 6d greater than in the 1931 Budget; this was due to the holding of reduced rate at 1s 8d, the increases in personal allowances, and the current concessions for apprentices[5] and dependent relatives denied unemployment assistance.[6]

But the avoidance legislation and the debates on it have a significance beyond the abuses they were designed to check, now in any case a matter of history. Three major points of principle emerged. First, Parliament agreed that any general legislation against avoidance was undesirable. Secondly, qualified assent was given to the principle of retrospective legislation, the qualification being that such legislation was only justified when it altered the law to what everyone had assumed it to be before a test case had shown up a technical flaw in the legislation as it stood.[7] Thirdly, the Budget had been prefaced by a good deal of discussion of the moral and legal aspects of tax avoidance; the consensus seemed to be that the good citizen feels that he has a duty to the State to pay his share of the taxes, but he is not bound to pay the largest possible share nor is he prevented from arranging his affairs to that end. In proposing the current round of corrective legislation, therefore, Parliament was again expressing the common morality of the country. None of these features was really a party issue; neither was a final factor, which indeed hardly emerged as a talking point at all, although it surely must have been considered by the Chancellor and the Treasury, namely that the legislation might provide an additional source of income when Members were crying that taxation limits had been

[1] Pt IV, SS. 38/41, F.A. 1938.   [2] S. 26, F.A. 1938.
[3] S. 28, F.A. 1938.   [4] S. 43, F.A. 1938.
[5] S. 20 F.A. 1938.   [6] S. 21 F.A. 1938.
[7] H. 23/7/1938, Cols 1333/1342 (Hely-Hutchinson, Spens and the Attorney-General.

reached. The main difficulty was no accurate estimate could be made of the yield.[1]

If the Budget is considered solely as a revenue-raising mechanism, two complementary characteristics should be noted. As Simon said in his opening speech: 'We have to look beyond the present year . . . we hold these financial inquests in the month of April . . . but there is nothing to justify our confining ourselves rigidly to a period of twelve month's[2]—a sentiment repeated in his closing speech. Although he did not like the words 'cyclical finance' which left a 'slightly confusing, disturbing, kaleidoscopic impression', he did subscribe to the view that 'we must not work out our financial problems as it were in blinkers so that you can see nothing before April 5th this year and nothing beyond April 5th next year'.[3] This was a turning point in the history of post-war finance. And again the Budget did try to prevent the standard rate increase militating against industry by providing the cushion of the increased capital allowances.[4] This was one of the earliest attempts to use taxation as an instrument of economic policy, in this case to encourage industry to embark on capital expenditure.

The 1938 Budget, therefore, was significant equally for what it actually achieved and for the principles which were implicit in that achievement. What should have given the country pause was not the present measures nor even the conceptions which underlay them, but the outlook at home and abroad which they portended.

---

[1] H. 4/5/1938, Cols 928/932.   [2] H. 26/4/1938, Col. 61.
[3] H. 15/7/1938, Col. 1771.   [4] S. 22, F.A. 1938.

Chapter VII

The Finance Bills of 1939

UNDERTONES OF WAR

Time Table

Financial Statement		April 25, 1939
Budget Proposals		
	1st Day	25
	2nd Day	26
	3rd Day	May 1
Budget Resolutions		
	Reported	3
	Introduced	June 26
	Reported	27
Finance Bill		
	1st Reading	May 3
	2nd Reading	25
Committee		
	1st Day	June 22
	2nd Day	27
	3rd Day	28
	4th Day	29
	5th Day	July 3
	6th Day	11
Report		
	1st Day	11
	2nd Day	12
Third Reading		13
Royal Assent		28

Sir John Simon rose to present his second Budget[1] on April 25, 1939, six weeks after the dismemberment of Czecho-Slovakia, already weakened and diminished by the Munich agreement of the previous autumn. It was an occasion, as always, but the House had perhaps had its fill of occasions in the last few months so that the usual air of expectancy was dulled, and speculation was tinged with fears for the account to be rendered, the principal debit being the inexorable if still gentle build-up of the cost of rearmament.

The analysis of the 1938/1939 out-turn was not as detailed as in previous years; Committee had, of course, the figures before them in the Blue Print. Total receipts had been £927·25 millions, a shortfall of £17·5 millions over the estimated £944·75 millions. This deficiency was mitigated by an overestimate of expenditure of £4·4 millions, £940 millions actual against the £944·4 estimated. He wished to draw especial attention to Defence Expenditure which 'governed and conditioned' the whole of contemporary public finance. The grand total was £400 millions, composed of £254·5 millions from revenue, £90 millions from authorized borrowings, Supplementary Estimates (also borrowed) of £38 millions and the balance expended on food storage and A.R.P.

A breakdown of the 1938/1939 revenue disclosed a short-fall of £3·5 millions in Customs and Excise, and of £16·25 millions in Inland Revenue dues, at £340·5 millions and £520·25 millions respectively. The most serious deficiencies were in death duties, no less than £10·5 millions, and income tax, £5·25 millions. Surtax was up by £·5 million, however, and N.D.C. £2 millions. With other receipts £2·3 millions over, the total overestimate was, as mentioned, £17·5 millions.

Turning now to the 1938/1939 expenditure, he commented first on the Fixed Debt Charge. This had been raised last year to £230 millions which had covered interest, the management charge and even left a small surplus of £2·3 millions for debt reduction. The estimates for the Consolidated Fund had been exceeded by the actual payments to the extent of £2·1 millions; but the Civil Supply Services, estimated at £449 millions including a £10 millions provision for food storage and A.R.P., had shown an eventual saving of £7·75 millions, with an encouraging drop of £5·7 millions in the payments relating to Unemployment Assistance. Almost as an aside,

[1] H. 25/4/1939, Cols 975/997.

he mentioned that with the current addition of £137 millions to the National Debt, of which £128 millions related to issues under the Defence Loans Act, this had now reached the staggering total of £8,163 millions despite the application of some £20 millions to redemption. As a consolatory coda, the Exchange Equalization Fund still continued profitable.

The Chancellor now turned to the future. He proposed to leave the Fixed Debt Charge at £230 millions; other Consolidated Fund Services included £10 millions to Northern Ireland and a balance of £7·2 millions of miscellaneous payments. The Post Office should have been contributing its usual £10·75 millions[1] but its surplus was not sufficient even to be made up by an allowance from the Post Office Fund, depleted by calls in the previous three years. The position would have to be reviewed.[2] The total for Supply Services would be some £675·25 millions, Civil Supply Services accounting for £447·5 millions and Defence £227·75 millions without Supplementaries. On the Civil figure he commented that 'Defence expenditure has not meant and does not mean that our social services must be reduced'.

'Now comes the question,' the Chancellor continued, 'whether, on the existing basis of taxation, I can count on an equal revenue this year.' Customs and Excise receipts he estimated at £327 millions, a drop of £2·5 millions to reflect the doubtful trade prospects. The Inland Revenue should yield £517·25 millions, although income tax would be down, again owing to adverse trading conditions, by some £9 millions. Surtax would be up, since covering the more favourable conditions of 1937, by £3·5 millions. Miscellaneous receipts should reach just over £63 millions, giving a grand total of £918·33 millions.

He then made an unusual approach: 'Let us take the main heads of expenditure for the present year and see how far a revenue of £918 millions will enable us to meet that expenditure.' He must deduct the Fixed Debt Charge of £247 millions and the Civil Vote of £447·5 millions; this left a balance of only £223·5 millions available for Defence. Now the White Paper of February 1939 had given an estimated defence expenditure figure of £580 millions; and when moving the Money Resolution later that month, on which the Defence Loans

[1] Under a statutory obligation for the seven years to 1939/1940.
[2] H. 25/4/1939, Cols 981/982.

Act was based, he had stated how he intended to split this vast sum between borrowing and tax revenue, namely £350 millions to the former and £230 millions to the latter, in round figures. The actual figure to be found in the Estimates was £227·75 millions; and to meet this £223·5 millions was available, which seemed a reasonably satisfactory position.

Unhappily the £580 millions 'was no longer a correct and valid figure'. Such measures as doubling the Territorial Army, for example, meant that £630 millions was now required.[1] This additional £50 millions could, of course, simply be added to the suggested loan allocation, increasing it to £400 millions. 'I do not consider that this simple solution would be justified. If there is a limit to what can be conveniently or tolerably raised by taxation, there is also a definite limit to what can be wisely or successfully raised by borrowing.'[2] £20 millions of this additional £50 millions ought to come out of taxation so that the amount now required was this £20 million plus £4 millions, the difference between the Estimates figure, £227 millions, and the amount available, £225 millions. The final revenue now needed was the £918 millions which should be received from the present system of taxes on their current scale plus the additional £24 millions needed from revenue for Defence, a total of £942 millions.

There were, however, some minor points to be disposed of before the Chancellor could reveal how he proposed to raise the taxation necessary. One of these was the repeal of the archaic[3] medicine stamp duties and another was a reduction in entertainments duty to help the theatre with a corresponding increase in the duty on blank and picture films to compensate. There was also a postscript to last year's avoidance provisions in the shape of further measures relating to surtax and estate duty; the legislation would be retrospective because the devices were 'so flagrant'.

And so, finally, came the proposals for the filling of the gap. There was to be no increase in income tax for 'we ought to avoid any measures which would have a depressing effect on industry'. Indirect taxation would take the major strain. The tax on cars would

[1] As compared with £400 millions in 1938 and £265·5 millions in 1937.

[2] H. 25/4/1939, Col. 988.

[3] One exemption dated from Charles II and applied to all drugs named in the book of rates of Sir Harbottle Grimston, (Bart.)—a record for the endurance of vested interests. Final repeal came in 1941. See p. 185.

go up by 10s 0d to £1 5s 0d per horse-power; this would yield £6·25 millions; £7 millions was expected from a 2s 0d increase in tobacco duty per pound and £4 millions from a rise in sugar duty by 2s 4d per hundredweight. A 5 per cent increase in surtax rates up to incomes of £8,000 and a 10 per cent increase thereafter should bring in £4 millions; a 10 per cent increase in estate duty on estates over £50,000 would bring in £3 millions. The total was a neat £24·5 millions, just covering the £24 millions target. To find even that small portion of the extra money from even such trusty sources had been 'difficult and painful', for he must emphasize again that 'the shape and content of our finances today are determined inevitably by our Defence needs'. It had all been a quieter occasion than usual with a House full but not overflowing; and although some tension was generated during his speech, Simon broke it very sharply at the end.

Attlee[1] rose just after 5 p.m. to put the formal case for the Labour Party. The Chancellor had not faced the problem squarely but was passing it on; and he repeated last year's criticism that interest in the Budget was vitiated since all question of trying to balance had been abandoned. There was no real national planning and 'sooner or later we shall have to come down to the taxation of accumulated wealth'. Lack of planning also was Sinclair's[2] basic criticism for the Liberals: there was no long-term loan policy nor any sign of conscripting productive power.

The ritual comments by the Opposition leaders usually marked the virtual end of the Budget Day's debate. But on this occasion, although the Opposition at times could only muster half-a-dozen Members, discussion continued until well after midnight; in fact the Speaker had to intervene for the formal reading of the Resolutions. Not that the Government was lacking support, ranging from Samuel's[3] tepid 'It is an equitable Budget, likely to cause the least possible disturbance' to Loftus's.[4] 'It will be as little unpopular as any Budget could be which had to raise that amount of money', although to some extent both sides found common ground in arguing that it was time luxury consumption was restricted, especially when it impinged on the exigencies of national defence.[5]

[1] H. 25/4/1939, Cols 997/1000.   [2] H. 25/4/1939, Cols 1000/1004.
[3] H. 25/4/1939, Cols 1042/1047.   [4] H. 25/4/1939, Cols 1065/1072.
[5] Cf. H. 25/4/1939, Cols 1047/1049 (Mellor).

Away from the main stream of the debate was Ellis Smith's practical suggestion of a 1 per cent levy on 'individual fortunes'[1] and the proposal of a betting tax, reckoned to bring in £20 millions annually, from A. P. Herbert.[2] There were also the somewhat wilder representations of the left wing. McGovern's[3] summary that Simon 'has handed down to posterity the right to tax themselves to the limit in order to pay back the money-lending fraternity' was followed by Gallacher's[4] demand that tax-dodgers should be put in gaol. But in general the Government took refuge in the excuse that the disarmament policy of the thirties was the reason for rearming at the current frantic rate; apart from this plea, little enthusiasm for the proposed measures was shown in the Lobbies: Liberal and Labour combined to advocate a policy of more luxury taxes and the heavier taxation of war profits; and overshadowing the debate, too, was the news of Morgan Jones's[5] death, Chairman of the Public Accounts Committee, and a consistent speaker on financial affairs.

Despite its utility as an exercise in astronomical arithmetic the Budget had almost lost its place as news and probably had less column-space expended on it than any Budget of the period apart from its immediate successor. The *Manchester Guardian* and *The Times*[6] both agreed the Chancellor had done a workmanlike job, singling the increase in the horse-power tax for especial praise not only as a revenue-raising mechanism but also as a check on luxury and a deterrent to the expansion of the car industry's civil production. The former, however, went on to say that 'there was no satisfaction to be had out of the background to the Budget'. No longer was there any mention of peak years or of decline in expenditure; the statement of accounts had become largely of formal interest.

The weekly political magazines, apart from *The Economist*, were distracted from the Budget by the imposition of conscription on the following day and a long-awaited but typically equivocal speech from Hitler later in the week. The *New Statesman*,[7] for example, contented itself with the conventional Opposition line that the Chancellor did not appreciate the need for planning and that he showed a marked reluctance to interfere with profit-making enterprise. *The Economist*[8] was far more comprehensive in its treatment.

---

[1] H. 25/4/1939, Cols 1009/1019.   [2] H. 25/4/1939, Cols 1022/1027.
[3] H. 25/4/1939, Cols 1058/1065.   [4] H. 25/4/1939, Cols 1082/1087.
[5] M.P. for Caerphilly.   [6] 26/4/1939.   [7] 29/4/1939.   [8] 29/4/1939.

The Budget contained a reasonable *ad hoc* set of proposals, although it would have been better to tax the sale of new cars than simply the use of large cars; and indirect taxation might have been spread instead of being confined to sugar and tobacco. The major criticism of the Budget, however, was the lack of any basic borrowing policy; the previously-declared principle, expounded by Chamberlain, of meeting recurrent costs from taxation and non-recurrent from borrowing, had gone by the board.

The debate on April 26th and May 1st was overshadowed by the unprecedented proposal of peacetime conscription by the Prime Minister which preceded it and which possibly accounted for the remarkably thin attendance on both days. There were sixteen speakers on each day; but whereas Labour and Liberal deployed their economic experts, the Government was content to put up the Financial Secretary on the first day and the Chancellor to wind up on the second day, leaving conventional support to the backbenchers. This gave the discussions a highly critical atmosphere which the consensus of opinion in the House did not warrant.

The general Labour viewpoint was probably best put by Lees-Smith[1] at the end of the first day. The brutal issue was this: 'Is armament going to be paid for by the wealthy out of taxation or by the poor by curtailment of social services?' He reinforced the proposal of a defence tax on wealth, which Pethick-Lawrence[2] had opened with, which was to be imposed annually. Taxation, he complained, was weighted against earned income, but 'you can without any danger put special taxation on incomes derived from passive sources or from wealth itself'; and if this policy led to a redistribution of wealth in the country, so much the better.

Indeed the current Opposition catch-phrase was 'equality of sacrifice', and Dalton set the tone of the second day in a highly critical speech,[3] the longest in the whole debate. There should be a five-point plan to secure the necessaries of life and adequate defence, to 'ensure no cake until all have bread and the nation arms', to make work available for all willing to work, to secure 'social justice in carrying great burdens', and finally to impose the general mobilization of 'men, money and materials'. The current government policy had no such clear issues in view: labour was being wasted and huge

[1] H. 26/4/1939, Cols 1263/1269.   [2] H. 26/4/1939, Cols 1175/1188.
[3] H. 1/5/1939, Cols 1517/1532.

profits were being made. The rich were not being taxed as highly as they should be; the estimated increase in surtax and estate duty was 'a miserable little nibble'.[1] He too favoured an annual capital levy estimated to bring in between £80 and £100 millions, and although he was not so extreme in his conclusion as Sexton, who had proposed a 100 per cent levy on all incomes above the Old-Age Pension scale, he strongly favoured if war should come 'every member of the community would be given an allowance from the Government and all the apparatus of dividends, rent, interest and profits would be liquidated'.[2]

Stokes,[3] the industrialist, however, and Alexander,[4] a senior party Member, were far more moderate. The former's basic thesis was that there was no particular merit in the Budget. 'It is certainly larger than any other but it does not seem to be any better or any worse than any previous Budget of recent times. They have all been bad and have been getting further into the mire.' In particular he stressed the question of transfers the prospective dislocation of industry would cause. The latter summarized. The Chancellor had not really produced a comprehensive survey of the financial problems to be met; nor had the questions of social justice and indirect taxation been adequately dealt with. He felt that not only must there be reorganization now for the emergency, but, looking far beyond that, planning for reconstruction after a possible world war was equally vital.

The Liberals, for whom White[5] was the principal spokesman, hammered at three main points. They urged the setting up of a Ministry of Supply,[6] the necessity for economy in view of the vast all-over expenditure, and went back to their traditional advocacy of the taxation of land values which also had Labour's support.[7] Objection was raised as well to the increase in indirect taxation, always a Liberal Aunt Sally; and it was fair comment to contrast the yield from the increase in tea and tobacco duty of £12·5 millions with the total yield of N.D.C. which at £25 millions was only twice that amount, a paltry sum compared with the money spent on arms and the profits made.

The standard speech for the Government was in general praise

[1] £7 millions currently and £10 millions in a full year.
[2] H. 1/5/1939, Col. 1531.   [3] H. 26/4/1939, Cols 1252/1258.
[4] H. 1/5/1939, Cols 1614/1630.   [5] H. 26/4/1939, Cols 1188/1196.
[6] There was a draft Bill for that purpose awaiting debate.
[7] Cf. H. 26/4/1939, Cols 1240/1247 (Adams).

of the Budget particularly, as Higgs[1] said, because of its retention of standard rate at the previous year's level, and a predictable opposition to any form of capital levy. The more thoughtful Conservative speakers were inclined to agree with Labour that it was necessary to make a full survey of our resources to create a co-ordinated national effort; but an all-out effort, Schuster[2] argued, was not yet required. The country was not yet at war and 'it was sensible to keep appreciable reserves in the background'.

Macmillan,[3] however, did not agree. 'We are today,' he commenced, 'discussing a war Budget'; and he was most anxious that the errors of World War I should not be repeated. Germany was already spending 25 per cent of her resources on war preparations against this country's 8 per cent. There was the further danger of what he called 'a lop-sided boom', a fear he shared with Price[4] from the Opposition benches. Hely-Hutchinson[5] went even further. In his urbane manner he almost discounted the Budget altogether: It was merely an interim statement and 'we are expecting more later on'. The proposals, he agreed, did reflect a certain determination; that determination was to maintain current standards of living, social services and defence at the expense of posterity. Income tax had certainly lost its virginity;[6] but the capital levy was no solution; quite apart from the problems of valuation, realization and evasion, the tax would be an insidious chipping-away of an income-producing asset.

The Financial Secretary to the Treasury, Captain Crookshank, wound up on the first day. He argued that wealth was already conscripted with income tax and surtax reaching 14s 6d in the £. The export market must be maintained which put any standard rate increase out of court, and on the questions of economy and supervision relating to the massive expenditure budgeted for, he thought the supervision of the Treasury and the forthcoming debate on the Ministry of Supply would provide adequate safeguards. Simon[7] was equally severe when he came to wind up on the second day. He

[1] H. 26/4/1939, Cols 1247/1252.   [2] H. 26/4/1939, Cols 1196/1205.
[3] H. 26/4/1939, Cols 1219/1228.   [4] H. 1/5/1939, Cols 1544/1551.
[5] H. 1/5/1939, Cols 1539/1544.
[6] This was a reference to Disraeli's remark 'There is no fleet and no army which gives England such power and influence in the councils of Europe as the consciousness that our income tax is in a virgin state.'
[7] H. 1/5/1939, Cols 1630/1643.

claimed, with some justification, that his proposals had been widely accepted. There had been two main criticisms of his Budget speech, that he had not taken a sufficiently comprehensive survey and that he could not accept a capital levy. As for the first point, he had had to produce a Budget of expediency: 'It is not possible with great confidence to prophesy exactly what will be the future either of borrowing or taxation.' As for a capital levy, 'which had a natural attraction for the Opposition', there was a possible justification for a once for all impost but certainly not for an annual event. This would lead to the 'disturbing of confidence and would be bound to produce that atmosphere of confiscation which destroys every incentive to save'. It was not possible to have such a levy and preserve the present system of taxation. Taxation of profits and income could be made without reducing capital and estate duty was a form, and a much more convenient form, of capital levy.

The consideration of the sixteenth and subsequent Resolutions on May 3rd[1] was mainly remarkable for a disquisition by the Attorney-General, Sir Donald Somervell, on some anti-avoidance proposals which amounted to a strengthening of the definition of control begun by Section 21, Finance Act 1922. His explanations were, as he confessed, 'not entirely lucid', which moved Pethick-Lawrence to a parallel acknowledgement that 'he could not pass an examination on the proposals', and Albery[2] to suggest that since so many schemes of evasion were connected with private companies they should be licensed annually, the licence to be revoked if they were engaged in tax avoidance.

The terms of the debate on the Second Reading were that 'this House cannot assent to a Bill which continues a series of unbalanced Budgets, shelves all the major financial problems, adds nearly £400 millions to the national debt, fails to exact from wealth an adequate special contribution to meet the emergency, and, under the pretext of spreading the burden equally among all classes, imposes additional taxes, some of which will press severely on the very poor'. With such a motion, the debate was doomed from the start; it was clearly bound to resolve itself into an attack by doctrinaire Socialism on the severely practical proposals of the Government.

Pethick-Lawrence[3] launched a general polemic against Conser-

[1] H. 3/5/1939, Cols 1905/1921.   [2] H. 3/5/1939, Col. 1912.
[3] H. 25/5/1939, Cols 2559/2568.

vative fiscal policy although he was careful to avoid any specific discussion of the Finance Bill. His most interesting suggestion was that for an annual wealth tax at a rate of 2 per cent which could off-set, partially at least, the vast new debts being created. Liberal critic-ism, as expressed by Clement Davies,[1] was equally general: he com-plained that the time had come for a wholesale review of the financial position which the Chancellor seemed unwilling to under-take. White[2] assumed, somewhat rashly, that the idea of an emer-gency tax had been generally accepted; this should be coupled with an economy drive.

It was left to Mabane[3] to bring the debate down to earth. There were two ways, he considered, of looking at the Budget: 'We might concentrate on the question whether, within the limits of the tax revenue, the methods proposed are best, or we might concentrate our attention on whether the allocation of expenditure between loan and tax is justified.' The best way of increasing the yield of taxation was to contrive the increase of total taxable wealth. A capital levy, especially if exacted annually, would be economically disastrous as well as difficult both to assess and collect.

The Chancellor[4] himself made a strategic intervention at this stage. He, too, emphasized the practical difficulties of any sort of capital levy: one of the most important items in his fiscal credo was that a tax should be 'devised in such a way that it can be adminis-tered without inflicting on people an incredible amount of trouble and inconvenience'. In addition there was always the danger of re-ducing a tax-producing asset. And as for the general review, this was a luxury in the context of immediately pressing problems and the need to maintain public confidence.

That marked virtually the end of the debate. Only two of the re-maining speakers showed any sort of orginality, Ellis Smith who put forward the idea of an excess income tax[5] and Boothby who hailed the expenditure on rearming as the begetter of the current upswing in the trade cycle. 'This is a very significant fact which I think will be pondered over for many generations to come; and it may mark a turn in the economic development of the world.'[6] In fact he was expounding the pure Keynesian doctrine that there was no danger

[1] H. 25/5/1939, Cols 2568/2577.
[2] H. 25/5/1939, Cols 2577/2585.
[3] H. 25/5/1939, Cols 2585/2593.
[4] H. 25/5/1939, Cols 2593/2606.
[5] H. 25/5/1939, Col. 2640.
[6] H. 25/5/1939, Col. 2647.

of inflation until the slack in unemployment had been taken up. Crookshank therefore had a comparatively simple task in winding up: his principal point was that the whole aim of the Government[1] had been to raise the vast sums needed with as little harm to industry as possible.

The Committee stage was reached on June 26th and opened with a proposal which had originally been forecast in Chamberlain's conscription speech,[2] namely for an armaments profits duty.[3] This was a charge to be laid on all concerns with a turnover of £200,000 or more directly derived from the rearming programme; the rate was to be 60 per cent and the duration would be three years. The standard was to be purely a profits standard: there was no alternative, as in the old Excess Profits Duty of World War I, of a capital standard. The Chancellor left the House soon after introducing it and did not return.

It was perhaps just as well, since the new tax was assailed from both sides of the House. Pethick-Lawrence[4] claimed it was a political rather than a revenue tax; and he had some justification for this comment since it had not formed part of the budgetary provisions and there was no estimate of its potential yield. Wedgwood,[5] from the Government benches, claimed its selectivity was contrary to the canons of sound taxation, and Macmillan[6] argued it was better to control prices and profits at the start than to siphon off excess profits.

The discussions dragged on throughout the Committee stage despite lack of interest. Two more talking points emerged. Profiteering in food should be included in view of the plum and apple scandals of the last war;[7] and if food, why not beer, was the inevitable comment of Lady Astor.[8] These comments did reflect the wider issue of the extreme difficulty of defining armaments profits. The second discussion was over the standard profits; the Opposition argued that 1937 was too late a year to select since the arms programme and the arms spending were by then well under way.[9] The only real counter was to claim that Armaments Profits Duty was only a secon-

---

[1] H. 25/5/1939, Cols 2662/2663. [2] H. 26/4/1939, Col. 1154.
[3] Cmd. 6046. [4] H. 26/6/1939, Col. 74.
[5] H. 26/6/1939, Col. 97. [6] H. 26/6/1939, Cols 113/118.
[7] H. 29/6/1939, Col. 688. [8] H. 29/6/1939, Col. 696.
[9] H. 29/6/1939, Col. 723.

dary mechanism for creaming off profits; the basic device was the granting of properly-supervised and costed contracts.[1]

It was inevitable that this new tax should monopolize a good deal of the time of the House, so much so that it had little time for some of its favourite hardy annuals such as the increases in dependent relative[2] and the higher personal allowances,[3] as well as earned income relief.[4] There was detailed discussion of the avoidance clauses on June 27th and 28th which did not materially affect the original proposals.

But the clause in the Finance Bill, when it was published, which excited more public attention and more Press criticism was Clause 19[5] which obliged employers to make a return of expenses paid to employees above £15. This was the first attempt to check the abuse of the law on expenses under Schedule E; there had been cases of employees, including directors, taking minimal remuneration and having very large amounts allowed annually as expenses. Basically, however, the clause imposed no new liability nor altered in any way the principle of Schedule E liability.

When the Financial Secretary rose for the twenty-fourth time in the debate to open the Third Reading as was customary, the strange lack of interest, except among the pundits, which had dogged its progress, followed it to the end. The speaker must have been affected by the small attendance; he admitted[6] in his general review there was 'nothing new or original' he could say, and he fully lived up to his promise. The Opposition confined themselves mainly to deploring the ineffectiveness of Armaments Profits Duty, 'a sheep in wolf's clothing', as Pethick-Lawrence[7] termed it.

Simon[8] made no real attempt to reply to the debate, but this was due neither to inability nor discourtesy. The fact was that the whole of his careful arithmetic of three months ago had been overtaken by events. The Supplementary Estimates involved additional expenditure of £150 millions so that the original Defence costs, estimated at £580 millions, which he had warned the House might be £630 millions, had turned out finally to be £730 millions. This additional expenditure would be substantially covered by an issue of Treasury

[1] H. 29/6/1939, Col. 718.
[2] H. 29/6/1939, Col. 780.
[3] H. 29/6/1939, Col. 792.
[4] H. 11/7/1939, Col. 2088.
[5] S. 19, F.A. 1939.
[6] H. 13/7/1939, Col. 2461.
[7] H. 13/7/1939, Col. 2494.
[8] H. 13/7/1939, Cols 2500/2510.

Bills; but the real way to look at the Budget was to realize that out of a gigantic £1,400 millions needed, over £900 millions was coming from current taxation; for a peacetime Budget this was an unanswerable argument.

It is easy to criticize the first of Simon's 1939 Budgets in retrospect. In the first place, it was hardly coincidental that a figure which he had arrived at by *a priori* reasoning appeared to match the amount which he could tolerably raise without recourse to an increase in the direct taxation of industry. This reluctance to increase income tax or N.D.C. must have played a decisive part in formulating the amount to be raised from fresh taxation. Secondly, he was slow to realize the economic consequences of the mounting loan expenditure which now exceeded New Deal proportions; and this posed a third problem. For while the injection of borrowed money was beginning to create employment, there was no deliberate effort to bring men and jobs together.

Simon saw his task as steering a middle course between those prepossessed with vague ideas on the morality or economic necessity of a conscription of wealth and those who advocated the unqualified virtues of unlimited expenditure out of borrowing. Admittedly Armaments Profits Duty was not a very effective revenue weapon; but it was no more doctrinaire than the suggested capital levy. In general, he had kept direct taxation at about half of the revenue; but over three-quarters of the additional revenue required for rearmament was direct. In particular, the car tax was a brave attempt to check both demand and luxury spending, and avoidance was now being restricted to a limited number of incorrigibles who are always one lap ahead of legislation. There was, as yet, no glimmer of a national plan; but that could hardly be expected and was hardly suggested in practical terms from either side; and by the time the Royal Assent was given on July 28th a sinister twilight between peace and war had fallen and Simon with his Treasury advisers realized their sums would have to be done all over again.

THE FINANCE (NO. 2) BILL 1939

Time Table

Financial Statement		September 27, 1939
Budget Proposals		
	1st Day	27
	2nd Day	28
Budget Resolutions		
	Reported	29
Finance Bill		
	1st Reading	29
	2nd Reading	October 2
Committee		
	1st Day	4
	2nd Day	5
Report		10
3rd Reading		10
Royal Assent		12

Historians have not yet been able to agree on the causes of World War II and perhaps they never will. The train of events which led to its immediate outbreak is however fairly well established. It was really the Commons which imposed its will on a reluctant Government, and one of the prime movers behind the scenes in applying this pressure was Simon himself.[1] He was now called upon to prepare an Emergency Budget with, as can be seen, a greatly curtailed time table, for his measures of spring were, as he admitted, 'far short of what had to be done to finance the war'.[2]

The Chancellor, then, opened the first war Budget[3] in effect by continuing his speech on the Third Reading of the Finance (No. 1) Bill.[4] He reminded the House that they had authorized the borrowing of £592 millions when they rose in August, and that when war came on September 3rd a Vote of Credit for a further £500 millions was promptly proposed and adopted. Now even these two vast

---

[1] A. J. P. Taylor, *English History, 1914/1945*, p. 452.
[2] Viscount Simon, *Retrospect*. p. 232.
[3] H. 27/9/1939, Cols 1362/1380.　　[4] H. 13/7/1939, Cols 2500/2510.

sums would not necessarily fulfil the national needs up to March 31st next especially when the estimates of revenue from existing taxes would have to be scaled down from £942 millions to £890 millions. It was within this framework that the current budgetary proposals had to be fitted.

Under the slogan of 'Finance is the Fourth Arm of Defence', Simon expounded the wartime fiscal problem as he saw it. He was faced with the complementary difficulties of consumption of resources and distortion of tax yield; he had to weigh the balance of both gigantic loans and heavily increased taxation, and he must combine the curtailing of civilian demand with the continued promotion of the export trade.

But this was all theorizing: the business of the day was to propose additional taxation for 'the possibility of a three-years' war'. He wanted to put forward a whole scheme although some of it could not be completely applied until next year. First, there were increases in rates: standard rate would rise to 7s 0d and to 7s 6d in a full year and surtax rates to 1s 3d at the bottom of the range to 9s 6d at the top. The corollary was reductions in allowances: reduced rate relief became 2s 4d, the usual one-third of standard rate, but next year it was to be one-half of standard rate,[1] but to cushion the blow, on the first £165 of taxable income instead of the first £135. Earned income relief would fall from one-fifth to one-sixth, and married and children's allowance would be scaled down by £10 each. The Inland Revenue was already coping with an increase of 10 per cent in estate duty on all estates over £50,000; now this 10 per cent increase was raised to 20 per cent and the 10 per cent made applicable to estates between £10,000 and £50,000. Then came the increases in indirect taxation—1d a pint on beer, a rise of 1s 3d per bottle of whisky, 1½d an ounce on tobacco and,for those who neither smoked, drank, nor paid income tax, 1d a pound on sugar. Fourthly, a new business tax was imposed based on the abortive Armaments Profits Duty,[2] entitled Excess Profits Tax[3] imposed at 60 per cent on any excess of the trade or business profits over a variable pre-war standard.

[1] Cf. Snowden in 1931.

[2] See F.A. 1939, Part III, Ss. 20/28. It was repealed by S.20 F. (No. 2). A. 1939 before any assessments were made. It was based largely on the Excess Profits Duty of World War I. See also Board's Report, year ending March 31, 1940, p. 46, para. 58.

[3] F. (No. 2), A. 1939, Pt III, Ss. 12/22.

These new measures would produce £107 millions this year and £226·5 millions next year.

In addition, 'It was,' said the Chancellor, 'a duty to search out for means to avoid wasteful outlay,' and this should apply to both the public and private sector. There was also to be a 'shorn lamb' clause giving relief to any individual whose actual earned income for 1939/40 had, owing to circumstances connected with the war, fallen 'substantially' short of his earned income as assessed.[1] Finally, he did admit the possibility of a post-war capital levy but he felt that 'in wartime, taxation of income is the practical and effective method of proceeding'.[2]

As in the April Budget debate, the discussion continued long after the formal comments of the Labour and Liberal leaders. Attlee[3] attacked the cuts in earned income and child allowance and stressed the need for a levy on wealth at the end of the war. Sinclair[4] emphasized the importance of interest rates, a subject the Chancellor had not touched upon. Both approved the raising of money by taxation rather than by borrowing.

The House did not rise until nearly 10 p.m. but most of the thirteen speakers showed little disposition to stray from their respective party lines. Pleas for economy and endorsement of the heavier taxation were common to both sides. Labour diverged in its criticism of the increased sugar duty[5] and the practicality of a post-war capital levy.[6] The Conservative right wing was concerned about the level of direct taxation. 'The Chancellor,' said Samuel,[7] 'has gone as far as he can without endangering the economic fabric.' Another speaker[8] warned of the threat to the creation of reserves. Gallacher[9] regarded the whole exercise as a piece of fiscal hypocrisy: 'At the end of the war the wealthy will be wealthier than they are today, and the poor, poorer.'

The *Manchester Guardian*[10] reflected the general opinion of the Press when it argued that taxpayers had been 'broken in too gently' in World War 1. Now there was a severity already beyond that of

[1] F. (No. 2) A. 1939, S. 11. [2] H. 27/9/1939, Col. 1378.
[3] H. 27/9/1939, Cols 1382/1386. [4] H. 27/9/1939, Cols 1386/1403.
[5] H. 27/9/1939, Cols 1404/1407 (Tinker).
[6] H. 27/9/1939, Cols 1433/1437 (Lipson).
[7] H. 27/9/1939, Cols 1442/1444.
[8] H. 27/9/1939, Cols 1449/1454 (Gibson).
[9] H. 27/9/1939, Cols 1428/1433. [10] 28/9/1939.

1918. Equally, there was general agreement that to tax was the right course and that borrowing should be kept to a minimum. The political journals accepted the Chancellor's proposals as dictated by stern necessity, although the *New Statesman*[1] thought the moderate increases in surtax and estate duty seemed unfair to the smaller taxpayers who were in any case traditional victims of indirect taxation increases.

The Economist[2] however, was decidedly uneasy. Although the Budget was 'drastic, soundly conceived and equitably distributed', it was a shock to the House, the City and the general public. But even so, in the last analysis, the Chancellor could be charged with shuffling off real economic sacrifices and thereby producing an inflationary situation which was the least satisfactory way of financing a war. A week later[3] a leader appeared entitled 'Wanted—an Economic Policy', pointing out that the Government would soon be responsible for anything up to two-thirds of the economic activity of the country; but there seemed to be no clear indication of adequate or indeed any preparations to mobilize national resources for the war effort.

Budget day itself had aroused little excitement: the side galleries had for once never filled up. Nor was there any sign on the second day that Parliamentary critics on either side would advance far from their prepared positions. Even Pethick-Lawrence,[4] who usually followed his arguments to their logical conclusion and not where doctrinaire Socialism would have liked them to lead, opened the debate in a very minor key, emphasizing mainly the importance of the rate of interest on Government borrowing and the need for a levy on war increases in wealth and capital. White,[5] for the Liberals, followed his Labour colleague on the interest point but maintained that any sort of capital levy in the prevailing circumstances was administratively inconvenient. On the other hand, in common with most Opposition speakers, he was opposed to the decrease in child allowance and the increase in sugar duty.

Extremes of opinion were expressed by Schuster,[6] who advocated the need for maintaining the profit motive, and Stephen,[7] the I.L.P. member, who attacked what he termed 'the current system of robbery and extortion' which had led the country into war. In general,

---

[1] 30/9/1939. [2] 30/9/1939. [3] 7/10/1939.
[4] H. 28/9/1939, Cols 1529/1535. [5] H. 28/9/1939, Cols 1535/1541.
[6] H. 28/9/1939, Cols 1549/1557. [7] H. 28/9/1939, Cols 1566/1570.

however, there were the same demands for economy and approval of taxation as the one valid alternative to inflation which had marked the first day. Not so much was heard of a capital levy, but some suggestions of a land values tax were made,[1] and the sugar duty again was a popular target. The main Conservative line was probably most clearly expressed by Wardlaw-Milne.[2] Labour's delusion was that one can make the poor richer by making the rich poorer. In fact, direct taxation was as heavy as possible now without upsetting the source of most of the country's income and thus the source of the anticipated tax yield. Simon[3] summed up adequately enough. He had taken special measures in the direction of economy and to avoid waste; he had noted the anxiety about interest but did not propose to announce the Government's borrowing plans until the Budget was through, and specific points would be answered as the Bill progressed.

Of the increases in indirect taxation the penny a pound on sugar was the most fiercely assailed because its price had been rising in any event and it entered into the cost of many other commodities. The Opposition, however, failed to secure an amendment on the Resolutions Reported[4] stage. Apart from that slight flurry, it was a very quiet day.

The Committee Stage on October 4th and 5th passed equally quietly. The Opposition pressed to a division only the increase in the sugar tax and the decreases in earned income relief and child allowance; Conservative sympathy for the last of these was not maintained in the lobbies and all three amendments were lost. The second day was devoted to a discussion of Excess Profits Tax but a full debate was promised in the spring. Incomes and professions were not to be included: surtax was regarded as being adequate for Case II of Schedule D. A general warning was sounded on the dangers of such a tax if it was not associated with measures for the prevention of wasteful expenditure.[5]

The Third Reading found Labour still plugging the inquitable distribution of the tax burden. 'The decrease in allowances affected the little man';[6] there was a comparative increase in indirect taxa-

[1] H. 28/9/1939, Cols 1584/1590 (Macdonald).
[2] H. 28/9/1939, Cols 1541/1546.　　　　[3] H. 28/9/1939, Cols 1599/1609.
[4] 29/9/1939.
[5] H. 5/10/1939, Col. 2149 (Benson); Col. 2156 (Hely-Hutchinson).
[6] H. 10/10/1939, Cols 212/219 (Griffiths).

tion; and as for E.P.T., 'We would take the lot: we would stop excess profits being made.'[1] In face of these charges, the Conservative back-benchers' reply consisted mainly of downright opposition to E.P.T., in general as with Sanderson,[2] specifically over reserves as with Schuster,[3] or on the grounds of unfair standards as with Fildes.[4] But at long last one or two Members were beginning to look beyond merely party criticisms. White[5] pleaded for a strong and centrally controlled economic policy, succeeding Finance Bills would have to be more drastic as the net result of the tax increases was comparatively small and represented nothing like a maximum effort.[6] Hely-Hutchinson followed shortly afterwards with an emphatic 'I do not think it is a brave enough Bill'.[7] Implicit in some speeches was an uneasy feeling that, as Cazalet[8] put it, 'A great deal of the old order will have to go', although the mechanism of change was as yet imperfectly grasped. Crookshank[9] summed up in the absence of Simon through the 'exigencies of war'. He was mainly concerned in promoting E.P.T. as the most convincing proof of the Government's resolution to pay its way. The Royal Assent was given only sixteen days after the Budget had been opened.

The second Budget of 1939 had two primary objectives. The first had been expressed by Chamberlain as early as April 27, 1939:[10] 'We intend,' he said, 'that a system shall be introduced to deal with all profits arising out of war and not merely with profits arising out of armaments,' or, briefly, to take the profit out of war. This was to be accomplished by an excess profits tax imposed at 60 per cent. Criticisms of this duty by the Opposition were based largely on the argument that the rate was not high enough; criticisms by the Conservative industrialists reflected a genuine fear that production would be threatened by the inability to plough back adequate profits and that the market value of securities would be depressed by the necessity of passing dividends. Nowhere was there any real discussion of the basic merits or demerits of the tax.

The second objective was a marked upswing in taxation, not only

---

[1] *Ibid.*　　　　　　　　　　　　　　　[2] H. 10/10/1939, Cols 236/238.
[3] H. 10/10/1939, Cols. 222/226.　　　[4] H. 10/10/1939, Cols 231/233.
[5] H. 10/10/1939, Cols 219/222.
[6] The total exacted by the Bill was in fact less than 17 per cent of current total income.
[7] H. 10/10/1939, Cols 228/231.　　　[8] H. 10/10/1939, Cols 238/241.
[9] H. 10/10/1939, Cols 249/253.　　　[10] H. Cols 1350/1351.

to warn the country of the gravity of the times but also to preserve a proper balance between the raising of revenue by taxation against the mechanism of loans. Contrasted with split opinion on the E.P.T. proposals, there was general agreement that the sharp increases in taxation were fully justified, the accepted reason being that it was desirable to minimize what might be a crippling post-war burden of debt; although, as Sayers[1] points out, 'this burden was in turn only imperfectly understood'.

There was a third tentative objective which again had originated in Chamberlain's speech of April 27, 1939,[2] when he suggested that 'permanent changes in the values (of property) . . . could best be grappled with by a levy on wartime increases in wealth'. Simon was content when opening the Budget merely 'to reaffirm the Prime Minister's statement of our intention', and in the early stages of the debate there was a good deal of pressure from the Labour benches for an immediate capital levy, although there was no unanimity on the precise form it should take. But the Board of Inland Revenue had already expressed itself forcibly on the administrative difficulties both of assessment and collection, and although Dalton[3] pressed the matter not only as a justification for the reduction in earned income relief but also as a revenue-raising technique, he received only the discouraging reply that, although investigation was still going on, 'It is a far more difficult thing than would be imagined at first sight.'[4]

But there were two disappointing features of the Bill. It was debated by a 'disgracefully small House',[5] and the net result was to add only some £52 millions to the aggregate of the April estimate, 'mere chicken feed', as Keynes put it, 'to the dragons of war', for neither side saw the danger of the ponderous acceleration of Government expenditure. Perhaps it was as well that really heavy impositions of taxation should be delayed so as to secure the necessary element of consent and to cover the potential loss of yield if the anticipated bombing raids materialized. Historically speaking, this was the first wartime Budget and at best represented only a tentative step in the right direction; from the standpoint of fiscal innovation and sacrifice, however, it was the last Budget but one of a phony peace.

---

[1] R. S. Sayers, *Financial Policy—1939–1945*, p. 28 (History of the Second World War Series).
[2] H. Col. 1351. [3] H. 2/10/1939, Cols 1676/1681.
[4] H. 2/10/1939, Col. 1785 (Simon). [5] H. 2/10/1939, Col. 1770 (Edwards).

Chapter VIII

The two Finance Bills of 1940 : The Foundations are laid

THE FINANCE BILL 1940

Time Table

Financial Statement		April 23, 1940
Budget Proposals		
	1st Day	23
	2nd Day	24
	3rd Day	25
Budget Resolutions		
	Reported	May 1
	(Increase in E.P.T. rate) Reported	6
Finance Bill		
	1st Reading	1
	2nd Reading	29
	Committee	June 6
	Report	19
	3rd Reading	19
Royal Assent		27

Simon's fourth and last Budget was presented in his longest opening speech,[1] lasting just over two hours. The House was full when he rose but not so full when he resumed his seat; indeed, the Government Chief Whip slept through the greater part, and the course of the Bill through its various stages attracted only thin attendances.

[1] H. 23/4/1940, Cols 51/89.

The Chancellor did not deviate from the classical formula of presentation which had served him on his past three occasions, apart from a brief prelude to announce that the September Vote of Credit of £500 millions had been underspent by £71·5 millions; he hastened to add that this did not indicate 'a delay on the part of the services, engaged in the war effort, in carrying through their programme'.

The same significant feature rated first mention when he commenced the traditional review of the previous year, the estimated expenditure of £1,933 million emerging at £1,817 million only, a saving of nearly £117 millions. Estimates of revenue had been exceeded by £54 million, including £5 millions from Inland Revenue, £28 millions from Customs and Excise and £12 millions from motor vehicle duties, income tax and surtax, at £390 millions and £70 millions[1] respectively, were a record not only in amount but in promptitude of settlement. Only the Post Office disappointed at half its fixed contribution of £10·75 millions. To summarize, total revenue was £1,049 millions, total expenditure £1,817 millions, the balance of £768 millions being borrowed. As he had thought he might have to borrow up to £938 millions it was possible to take comfort from last year as consolation for the grave problems of the coming year.

The National Debt had increased by the £768 millions borrowed to £8,931 millions. New savings in National Savings Certificates and Defence Bonds totalled £122 millions against only £13 millions repaid, a net gain of £109 millions; and a conversion operation of $4\frac{1}{2}$ per cent Conversion Loan to 2 per cent combined with a balance received from the 3 per cent Loan had left him with nearly £100 millions net in hand. This would not, however, affect the debt figures for 1939/40.[2]

With regard to the estimated expenditure for the new year, he must admit at once that a large part of the usual material was not available. For security reasons the Committee could only examine large Votes of Credit instead of the usual detailed Consolidated Fund Services statistics. In round figures, then, the first Vote of Credit had been for £700 millions to cover rather more than four months of war. In the first seven months of war, expenditure had reached £905 millions but that could not simply be scaled up for

[1] A comparison with the 1914 figs shows £59 and £10 millions respectively.
[2] H. 23/4/1940, Cols 55/56.

F

twelve months because the pace of war expansion should increase. He was therefore going to assume that £2,000 millions would be needed up to March 1941. A White Paper would be issued giving details of the expenditure of all Departments not affected by official secrecy. The Fixed Debt Charge could remain at £230 millions with an additional £9·5 millions for Northern Ireland and £7·5 millions for other services; the total here was £247 millions. Civil Supply Services he put at £420 millions, making a grand total of £2,667 millions. 'Every effort,' he added, 'is really being made to reduce waste'; the means was a Select Committee under Wardlaw-Milne.[1]

He must now turn to the estimated revenue for 1940/41 which posed three questions: how much could be raised from existing taxes; how much could be raised from additional taxation including new forms; and how could the balance be found. From the Inland Revenue he hoped for £658 millions, comprising income tax £408 millions, surtax £75 millions with death and stamp duties and the combined yield of E.P.T. and N.D.C. (at £70 millions) making up the balance. Although consumption was down, employment was up. Customs and Excise should approach £420 millions. Motor vehicle duties were put at £35 millions, and some £20 millions should come from miscellaneous items including the G.P.O. whose revenue was now being included. The total was £1,133 millions. There was a long way to go.

He then dealt briefly with the proposed changes in legislation. E.P.T. was still in a fluid state and various amendments were required. Precautions were needed to prevent double allowance for children.[2] There was to be statutory limitation of dividends and a prohibition placed on the issue of bonus shares; further steps were to be taken against estate duty avoidance, and there were minor Customs and Excise points. The most interesting suggestion was for the imposition of liability to tax under Schedule D[3] on rents received under short leases to the extent that they were not adequately taxed under Schedule A, or on 'excess rents' as they were popularly called.

Returning to 'the main stream of his discourse' the Chancellor then announced the changes in taxation. Standard rate would become 7s 6d, although relief for diminution of income would be continued.[4] Surtax would now run up to 17s 0d and the ceiling would be lowered from £2,000 to £1,500. This should produce £42·5 millions currently. From Customs and Excise he was looking for £46 millions with 1d per pint on beer, 1s 9d per bottle on whisky, 3d per ounce on tobacco and ½d per box on matches. There were also to be stiff increases in Post Office charges which for the first time embraced a fiscal element as well as a commercial charge. Letters became 2½d, postcards 2d and the printed paper and foreign rate increased by ½d. These, plus increased poundage and telephone charges, were estimated to bring in £12·5 millions. Then came the surprise introduction of a purchase tax, involving the immediate registration of wholesale traders at which stage the duty would be levied. It had a three-fold purpose:[1] to restrict internal spending, to avoid the difficulty of assessing selected luxury articles, and to raise revenue; for although, on the last point, the Chancellor could not offer any immediate estimate, 'this form of taxation, if boldly applied, is capable of producing a larger additional sum towards our revenue than from any other immediately practicable form of tax'. Inland Revenue, Customs and Excise plus the Post Office combined to give a total of £101 millions additional inflow, but there was still £1,423 millions to find.

To bridge this gap there was first the £100 millions,[2] remaining proceeds of the 3 per cent War Loan exercise. Then he could credit the saving produced by using gold reserves for purchases abroad. For the rest, he felt confident he could rely on voluntary saving which had produced £132 millions in twenty-one weeks.[3] He was totally opposed to the Keynesian suggestion of 'compulsory savings'. 'I am far from convinced,' he summarized, 'that such a scheme has all the virtues which in some quarters are claimed for it.' He was convinced it would do untold harm to the National Savings Campaign.

In general, he concluded, the Government was aiming in the economic sphere at maintaining a level in which incomes, prices and profits were regulated to secure a steady flow of goods for civil consumption while ensuring an absolute priority for war materials by an elaborate system of controls. But he must emphasize again that even with £1,234 millions coming from taxation, saving must be intensified to secure the balance required.

---

[1] H. 23/4/1940, Cols 77/78. [2] See p. 161.
[3] H. 23/4/1940, Col. 80.

Attlee[1] made the formal comments for the Labour Party. The general problem was the proportion between loans and taxes; apart from that central theme he summarized his party's attitude by criticizing the under-use of manpower, approving the increases in both direct and indirect taxation, but expressing the fear that purchase tax was 'not a really sound tax'. It was Sinclair,[2] however, who voiced an opinion of which very much more was to be heard inside and outside the House in the ensuing weeks. 'I am not satisfied,' he said, 'with the size of the target at which he is aiming.' The initial comments tailed off early in the evening with the usual criticisms of waste and a reiteration of the dangerous myth that the country's economic position was stronger than Germany's. Fears, however, were again expressed before the closure that the Chancellor had not taken a sufficiently long view.

The *Manchester Guardian*[3] had already been taking a pessimistic view of the Budget prospects before the Chancellor rose. It was afraid that the Government would fall short in action; and the fact that the Vote of Credit had been unspent was not a sign of grace but an indication that it had been slack in its efforts and dilatory in fulfilling its programme. The Budget must become a much sharper weapon and, while protecting the wage-earner, must abandon the pretence that the taxation of the higher ranges of income had reached the bearable limit.

This theme was continued on the following day,[4] and while most of the popular press was congratulating the Chancellor on his realism, the paper again, under the leader heading of 'Too Little Courage', criticized the assumption of too slow a speeding-up of the nation's war effort, and could not see that the proposals passed the acid test of reducing civilian consumption and diverting the purchasing power thus released into the service of the State.

The attitude of *The Times* was interesting. Under the unexceptionable headline of 'A War Budget'[5] it commented on the details and summarized complacently enough that it would 'divert from the pockets of our citizens as much as is conceivably tolerable' as the limit of rates had been nearly reached. The only criticism was that these all-round taxation increases should have been undertaken earlier.

[1] H. 23/4/1940, Cols 89/93.   [2] H. 23/4/1940, Cols 93/95.
[3] 23/4/1940.   [4] 24/4/1940.   [5] 24/4/1940.

By the end of the week, however, *The Times* was urging a bolder policy[1]—the Chancellor's proposals could not be regarded as adequate. This change of line was partly due to the influence of Keynes whose letter the paper published[2] on the Wednesday following Budget day. The Chancellor, he complained, had grossly underestimated the capacity of the nation for sacrifice and had rashly assumed that the failure of the Civilian Departments to increase war output would protect him from the full severity of the financial problem.

The Economist had been highly critical of the September 1939 Budget.[3] Now it declared roundly that Simon had missed his opportunity:[4] an estimate of £2,000 millions only[5] was a spending rate which would lose the war; and no opportunity had been afforded the people (a repetition of Keynes's point) to show their passionate desire to serve their country. The detailed provisions of the Budget were not severely handled, but the total to be raised was alarmingly inadequate. The only hope was that by autumn realism would have supplanted the current unjustified optimism.

Lobby opinion on the Tuesday evening had been, on the whole, favourable and the opening Opposition speech by Pethick-Lawrence[6] was muted and conventional. The Chancellor had not yet succeeded in turning a peace into a war economy: there were still more than one million unemployed; and the new measures bore hardest proportionately on those of moderate means. He was opposed to the increased G.P.O. charges, purchase tax and the Keynes proposals, and he was still pressing strongly for a capital levy.

White,[7] for the Liberals, was at once more critical and more general. 'I am not by any means convinced,' he began, 'that the proposed outlay of the Budget is such as will achieve the essential purpose which we must face at the present time.' He approved the luxury imposts and purchase tax, but these were no safeguard against inflation. In short 'our effort so far only produces inconveniences'.

But it was Amery,[8] and to a lesser extent, Hely-Hutchinson[9] who

[1] 26/4/1940.   [2] 25/4/1940.   [3] See p. 156.
[4] 27/4/1940.   [5] See p. 162.
[6] H. 24/4/1940, Cols 229/239.   [7] H. 24/4/1940, Cols 239/245.
[8] H. 24/4/1940, Cols 245/255.   [9] H. 24/4/1940, Cols 269/274.

followed him, whose contributions really changed the tone of the debate. The principles of steep taxation and voluntary borrowing, said the former, had been applied in too limited a manner and gave no hint of a firm programme for the duration. He was the first but not the last speaker to contrast the efforts of Germany, which had had a flying start, and France, with that of Britain: 'We cannot afford to hide from the nation the sacrifices that are wanted.' Increased taxation must be paralleled with curtailed consumption; the Chancellor had failed to face the scale of effort required. Hely-Hutchinson said the vital decision was to find half the war finance from borrowing. This must mean inflation unless taxation was increased still further. He too felt that the precise suggestions of Keynes should not be adopted but they had performed a great service in highlighting the need for restriction of spending. The Chancellor had not met this problem squarely. It was not surprising that, listening to this basic criticism from Government supporters, Loftus[1] summarized by confessing, 'As I listened I felt that it was a gigantic, severe and decidedly drastic Budget, but on reflection I think opinions have changed and I wonder now whether it is severe enough.'

The tempo of criticism mounted on the following day when, as the *Manchester Guardian* put it, 'Attlee's purr turned to Dalton's roar'. 'Some of the more favourable first impressions,' he commenced 'have faded,' and he then proceeded to demolish, to his own marked satisfaction, the remainder, in the longest speech of the debate.[2] Its theme was equality of sacrifice, but he met the usual difficulties in trying to translate this ideal into fiscal terms: the details of the Budget proposals he found satisfactory enough apart from ignoring the obvious solution of 'a graduated impost averaging 2 per cent on the capital value when that exceeded £10,000'. In addition there should be a general capital levy after the war to liquidate the National Debt. In general the war effort of the country was gravely insufficient.

Crookshank[3] was put up to reply in his role of Treasury trouble-shooter. He made a fair point when he argued that little had been said about the actual taxes imposed and few specific suggestions had been put forward on the lines of orthodox finance; but he spoilt the effect

---

[1] H. 24/4/1940, Cols 290/295. [2] H. 25/4/1940, Cols 397/412.
[3] H. 25/4/1940, Cols 412/420.

by declaring that 'you cannot measure the war effort of the allies with the war effort of Germany on a pound for pound basis: we have a great many imponderables . . . the rightness of our cause, the un-dragooned beliefs of our own people . . . the support of the Empire . . .'.

Clement Davies[1] then interposed for the Liberals in a speech as outstanding as Amery's had been on the previous day.[2] The logic of the Financial Secretary to the Treasury's remarks, he suggested gently, was that we were so right we need not fight. But then the hammer-blows began to fall. The country's efforts were not sufficient nor commensurate with our revenues as could be seen at once by a careful comparison of them with the German war effort: if figures were needed, £3,200 millions was being spent by Germany as against Britain's £2,000 millions out of a £5,000 millions income in each case. It was not a war Budget at all, and time, as the Government so complacently thought, was not on our side when much of the £2,000 millions was going, not to war weapons directly, but to factories and machine tools to produce those weapons. There was a dual campaign needed against our enemies and against a *laissez-faire* which assumed voluntary savings would top £700 millions annually when they were currently at the rate of £300 millions annually at most.

Two other interventions should be mentioned. One was by Bevan,[3] his first for many years, which started with a reasoned analysis of the Budget as 'more a mirror of activities than a sum in arithmetic'. He ranged himself on the side of those Members who had pointed out that the money asked for indicated a gloomy view of the way the nation's resources were being organized, especially with regard to manpower. Then came the typically ferocious climax. This was a common fault of capitalism and a Tory Government, the name of whose Prime Minister was anathema and whose Chancellor of the Exchequer is a 'special pleader with all the superficial gifts of legal casuistry but despised throughout the world'.

The other intervention, by Schuster,[4] was quite the best defence of the Budget, not excepting its author's. Starting with the valid comment that it was easy to criticize without any responsibility for execution, he proceeded to develop two lines of argument. The £2,000 millions budgeted for war purposes was not a maximum but

[1] H. 25/4/1940, Cols 420/431.   [2] See p. 219.
[3] H. 25/4/1940, Cols 460/468.   [4] H. 25/4/1940, Cols 431/440.

a minimum, it was not a final and decisive act 'but a stroke which he thinks it right to play now'. He agreed, in the second place, that voluntary loans might not suffice, but what other alternative had the Chancellor when the union leaders were not prepared to support any other principle? In the circumstances a degree of inflation was inevitable. Simon[1] wound up by pleading the success of his proposals in view of the fact that the main complaint was that they should have been more severe. He must repeat that it was administrative difficulties which had stifled the tax on capital. The critics might be right in saying the country should be spending more: but although expenditure might go up, taxes did not necessarily multiply at the same rate. It was his constant endeavour to keep the proportion of taxes as high as possible but there was no talisman for determining how high this proportion could be in the constantly shifting conditions of financial pressures.

The First Reading of the Bill was on May Day 1940, and this was followed by a brief debate which dealt among other matters with a flaw in the wording of Section II Finance (No. 2) Act 1939[2] and the general principles behind the proposed anti-avoidance clauses relating to estate duty.[3] But academic Parliamentary exercises, whether fiscal or political, were rudely shattered by the outcome of the ill-fated and ill-conceived Norwegian expedition which, ironically enough,[4] swept Churchill into power and Chamberlain out of it. Simon at last achieved the Woolsack; and he was succeeded by Sir Kingsley Wood,[5] by profession a solicitor and an insurance expert. His spells of office as Postmaster General, Minister of Health and Secretary for Air had marked him out for further promotion; and behind his somewhat prim exterior lay a logical mind which led him to propose unhesitatingly the most ruthless taxation when convinced of its need.

A new Chancellor, then, opened the Second Reading. In a business-like speech[6] he summed up the current position on E.P.T., avoidances of estate duty, which he suggested could best be dealt with at the Committee stage, and the new liability to tax under Schedule D of 'excess rents', and, the corollary, rents under long

---

[1] H. 25/4/1940, Cols 498/510.   [2] The 'Diminution of Income' section'.
[3] Now enshrined in Pt IV, F.A. 1940.
[4] A. J. P. Taylor, *History of England 1914–1945*, p. 472.
[5] On May 11, 1940.   [6] H. 29/5/1940, Cols 563/572.

leases. Emphasis was laid on the function of the Board of Referees in assessing E.P.T. standards; but the dramatic announcement was the increase of rate to 100 per cent. Other taxation would also need to be increased; 'but the advance has been so rapid that I think it is essential to afford some short period during which the country can adjust itself to the considerable burdens already placed upon it'.[1]

The new man and the new approach won instant approval from both sides of the House. Pethick-Lawrence[2] sensed 'a new policy, a new drive, a new alertness and a new gravity'. The country was prepared for any increase in taxation provided there was no waste, there were no extra burdens imposed on the poor and that rates of interest were kept down. White agreed for the Liberals with his Labour colleague; he welcomed 100 per cent E.P.T. and suggested the Chancellor might consider an excess income tax.

There were two main streams of criticism and both were probably best expressed by Hely-Hutchinson.[3] He was still convinced the scope of taxation was not broad enough and not sufficiently directed to the restriction of spending and he was very much afraid that the fact of 100 per cent E.P.T. giving 100 per cent relief for all expenditure claimed would be abused and exploited. Lewis[4] took up the first point: the large amount of purchasing power going into the hands of those exempt from tax meant inflation and something on Keynesian lines was needed. The second point was developed by more than one speaker,[5] and it was left to Crookshank when he summed up the day's discussion[6] to point out that the lessons of the E.P.D. days of 1914 to 1918 had been well learnt, that a careful check would be kept on expenses of all kinds and that the House should also bear in mind how necessary it was to have flexible standards when imposing such a penal rate of tax. Above all, the spirit of the times was very different from that of World War I. This was certainly true, for while this debate was taking place so was Operation Dynamo, the evacuation from Dunkirk. This ensured in effect the passing of the Bill with the minimum of delay.

On June 5th,[7] the Chancellor introduced the 100 per cent E.P.T. and promised to inhibit undue spending by legislation; he also

[1] H. 29/5/1940, Col. 571. [2] H. 29/5/1940, Cols 572/579.
[3] H. 29/5/1940, Cols 584/587. [4] H. 29/5/1940, Cols 602/604.
[5] E.g. H. 29/5/1940, Cols 609/614 (Spens).
[6] H. 29/5/1940, Cols 621/626. [7] H. 5/6/1940, Cols 949/953.

emphasized the fact that the labour to indulge in luxury equipment, services and repairs was, quite simply, not now available, and he announced a concession for deferred repairs. Pethick-Lawrence[1] was worried about the basic problem that the motive of private enterprise is profit; E.P.T. might check, if not halt altogether, enterprise and initiative. Perhaps the national emergency would induce capitalism to produce for use and not for profit, as Hely-Hutchinson[2] put it. The rest of the speakers felt they must support the increased rate, however uneasy they might feel, in view of the present crisis.

The debate which took place on the following day was something of an anti-climax with a small attendance apart from the faithful experts. The Case VI clauses were first disposed of, 'the most complicated branch of an exceedingly complicated subject', as the Solicitor-General, Sir William Jowett,[3] expressed it. Then followed a somewhat esoteric discussion on possible amendments to the E.P.T. legislation which culminated in a robust argument on the problem of checking the danger of extravagance and waste resulting from a rate of 100 per cent. Compared with this, the comments on the return of the Post Office receipts to the Exchequer were most amicable apart from Pethick-Lawrence's sly suggestion that the current increases in postal rates would produce a handsome profit.

The Third Reading was one of the shortest on record, occupying nine columns of Hansard only,[4] and it was only the feeling that a Third Reading could not be passed *sub silentio* which brought the principal Opposition leaders on finance to their feet; and it was simply to pledge full support for any sacrifice to help 'this beleaguered fortress', financial or otherwise. Kingsley Wood wound up briefly.[5] He had been in doubt whether to proceed with the whole of the clauses in view of the catastrophic change in the situation between April this year and the present. He knew E.P.T. was unscientific in its application and it must be as fair as possible in its incidence. But further burdens and further revisions would have to

---

[1] H. 5/6/1940, Cols 953/956. [2] H. 5/6/1940, Col. 956.
[3] H. 5/6/1940, Col. 1041.
[4] H. 19/4/1940, Cols 205/213. See now Ss. 13–18, F.A. 1940, and above. The genesis of C. VI was the Salisbury Estates Ltd *v.* Fry Case 15 T.C., p. 266, which Jowett himself had argued two years before and which had held that the profitable rentals of an office block were covered by the Schedule A assessment.
[5] H. 19/6/1940, Cols 210/213.

await a second Budget, and that soon. These were interim measures only.

The immediate judgment on Simon's last Budget is an endorsement of Press and Parliamentary opinion which both, after some initial wavering, criticized the general effect of the proposals as bad because not bad enough, and contrasted Britain's war effort very unfavourably with the statistics available from France and Germany.

This, as Sayers demonstrates,[1] is unfair to the Chancellor. The Budget, it must be remembered, had been prepared in the phony war days and a draconian increase in tax burdens was hardly to be expected. Yet despite this the Chancellor had grasped the basic problem of the need to secure the correct balance between compulsion and voluntarism; and the main reason why the Budget was not more anti-inflationary was the failure by Simon and his advisers to apply the yardstick of the amount of spendable income left after taxation rather than the academic measure of the revenue actually abstracted by taxation.

But this was not all the story. If the Budget is regarded both as the supreme test of the Government's financial policy and of its whole economic policy, the Chancellor was carrying too much responsibility as the only Cabinet member who represented the economic aspects of the war effort. The balance between borrowing and taxation, which had so concerned the House, might cause misery if wrongly struck, but it was secondary to the problem of raising the right amount of money, and this was not necessarily the maximum amount. Gross expenditure was not what mattered but the proper application of economic effort. The plain fact was that Britain was not yet geared for total war: there was no direction of manpower; and planning was mainly concerned with the final not the intermediate stages of production which the Ministry of Munitions in 1914 had discovered were equally important. Now the Ministry of Supply was faced with the same problem. Finance in wartime must be a camp-follower of production.

The Chancellor could have turned to Keynes; but it was quite clear that the country was not receptive enough yet to his proposals. As he said himself, 'the general public are not in favour of any plan'.[2] In addition they were strongly opposed by the Labour Party. That in turn had no positive suggestions; the policy document 'Paying

[1] *Op. cit.*, pp. 42/44.   [2] Sayers, *op. cit.*, p. 33.

for the War' by Douglas Jay merely discussed the problem in terms of class. In the circumstances it was not surprising that he should, not without misgiving, fall back on the principle of voluntary saving[1] which he defended as skilfully and as tenderly as any client in the Courts.

Simon has been badly treated by historians as well as in the debates on his Budgets when the Opposition never let him forget his part in the policy of appeasement. Criticism of his limited target was to an extent justified, but to assess his proposals as ignoring the long view is to disregard the amount of fiscal imagination shown by him and his advisers. His last Budget was notable for three achievements.

In the first place it legislated for the taxation of excess rents.[2] There should have been a Schedule A revaluation in 1939/1940 which the war had postponed. The rise of annual values due to inflation would have led to a considerable loss of tax had it not been for the charging of, in effect, the difference between a Schedule A assessment based on the current rent and the existing Schedule A assessment, under Case VI of Schedule D. Statistics of the yield were not immediately available but this new source of revenue was both productive and easy to administer.

Secondly, it provided for the introduction of purchase tax with the double object of limiting civilian consumption and providing a new source of revenue. The original scheme for the impost envisaged the name of 'sales tax', but Simon did not like the name and the Deputy Chairman of the Department suggested 'purchase tax' as an alternative. The Chancellor accepted this, remarking that he did not want to stop people selling; what he wanted to do was to stop them buying.[3]

Finally, he had been responsible for the introduction of E.P.T., which had its roots in the old E.P.D. of World War I, although it was more complex in view of the more complex types of concerns it was designed to assess. An addition to income tax, it was levied on trades and businesses only, and was allowed as a deduction against the Case I profit. It was an alternative charge to N.D.C., which was the effective charge only when the liability to E.P.T. exceeded that tax, which was rarely the case.

The computation of the E.P.T. profit was very much on the

---

[1] See p. 163.   [2] See I.T.A. 1952, Ss. 175/176.
[3] Sir James Crombie, *Her Majesty's Customs & Excise*, p. 131.

lines of N.D.C. which itself might not differ greatly from the income tax profit.[1] The tax was then payable on the amount by which this profit, arising in the twelve months' chargeable accounting period, exceeded the standard profit. But here complications began. There was first of all a minimum standard of £1,000 below which no liability arose; where, however, a company was director-controlled, the standard was £1,500 for one 'working proprietor', £3,000 for two, and so on; and these standards could be augmented if inadequate in relation to the business capital. More elaborate was the working out of a profits standard where the taxpayer was given various options in his choice of a standard period's profits which were then adjusted to reflect variations in the business capital between the standard and the chargeable accounting period.

The tax became exceedingly complicated and perhaps overloaded with options, reliefs and special *ad hoc* provisions. But Boothby's[2] prophecy that it would become a major source of income was amply fulfilled, for its yield reached £508 millions in 1945.

In fact, therefore, Simon's approach to wartime finance was far from tentative, and it is arguable that the later severity of taxation, which did not follow his transition to the Woolsack immediately, would not have been accepted so readily without his speeches to the jury. In addition it is a classical economic axiom 'that in the early stages of a war it is wise to leave a good deal of scope to the economic incentive: later it may be necessary to circumscribe it more severely'.[3] Simon was the prisoner of the slow momentum of war production which was not within his jurisdiction. That being the case, the question was whether he would have been wise to try and raise a greater revenue than he did at the time; but the long-term success of his 1940 proposals is not in doubt.

---

[1] A good summary to 1941 is in Hicks, Hicks and Rostas, *op. cit.*, pp. 93–117. Tolly has a useful rapid reference compendium covering 1939–1946. The legislation is spread over the Finance Acts from 1939 to 1953.

[2] H. 2/10/1939.   [3] Hicks, Hicks and Rostas, *op. cit.*, p. 7.

THE FINANCE (NO. 2) BILL 1940

Time Table

Financial Statement		July 23, 1940
Budget Proposals		
	1st Day	23
	2nd Day	24
	3rd Day	25
Budget Resolutions		
	Reported	31
Finance Bill		
	1st Reading	31
	2nd Reading	August 6
Committee		
	1st Day	8
	2nd Day	13
Report		15
Third Reading		15
Royal Assent		22

When Sir Kingsley Wood rose at 4.19 p.m. on July 23, 1940, to present the first Budget for which he was wholly responsible, his careful reading[1] from his manuscript gave no hint of the dissensions over purchase tax, principally from the Labour Party, which had preceded it.[2] Ostensibly the reason for another interim Budget was the mounting cost of the war, and there was bound to be increased taxation—the question was simply how much, and, less simply, of what type. There was not a very full House and Members began to leave before the exposition was over. This was also the first Budget of the Coalition Government which had been formed in May 1940, and the party polemics which usually characterise financial debates were not to be expected except in a very modified degree.

He opened, therefore, with a reminder of the position in the previous April. War expenditure was then running at the rate of £2,000 millions annually; the addition of Debt and Supply services, £667 millions, gave a total of £2,667 millions. Revenue had

---

[1] H. 23/7/1940, Cols 635/666.   [2] See Sayers, *op. cit.*, pp. 48/49.

proved buoyant at £1,234 millions, leaving a deficit to be covered by savings or other means, of £1,433 millions. War expenditure was now consuming £57 millions per week, an annual rate of £2,800 millions, thus converting the deficit to a potential £4,233 millions. This he found 'not so alarming as at first sight might appear'. Overseas expenditure could be met by gold, sales of securities and overseas loans. In addition, industry could not spend to much on capital re-equipment, thus saving more to lend to the State.

The economic problem of fundamental importance was the danger of inflation as wages and employment increased and as the supply of commodities decreased. It was equally essential to preserve and extend the export market. The mechanism must be a diversion of excess income by taxation or by saving; it was no use trying to finance the war by simply taxing the wealthy; all sections of the community must contribute.

Direct taxation was first dealt with. The standard rate for the whole year was to be 8s 6d, and reduced rate, normally one-half of standard rate, was pegged at 5s 0d, an ominous hint. The surtax range was lifted to 2s 0d above £2,000 income to a massive 9s 6d on income above £20,000; these increases would bring £95 millions in a full year, and a further £6 millions was expected from a 10 per cent uplift in estate duty where the value exceeded £10,000. To this £101 millions should be added the increases in the April Budget estimated at £62 millions and the 100 per cent E.P.T. which had netted £40 millions, thus producing a total for direct taxation of £203 millions. A minor amendment was to restrict Life Assurance relief by reference to an assumed standard rate of 7s 0d.[1] Finally, employers were required to deduct tax from salaries and wages assessable under Schedule E.[2]

Turning now to indirect taxation, he first concentrated on the Revenue's best payers, beer and tobacco, despite dire warnings of falling consumption which fortunately he did not heed; the former was to be 6d a pint dearer and the latter 1½d an ounce. These increases should produce £22 millions in a full year, and, with a further £6 millions expected from revisions of wine and entertainments duty, this section of dues should yield a total of £28 millions.

Pausing briefly to dismiss land and capital taxes as arbitrary and inconvenient ('what I need is cash and cash out of current income'),

[1] S. 9, F. (2) A. 1940. [2] S. 11, F.(2) A. 1940.

the Chancellor then unveiled his revised scheme for purchase tax. Its purpose was twofold, to limit civilian consumption and to provide a new source of revenue. It was a much more sophisticated instrument than the somewhat blunt weapon proposed by Simon. Some items would be exempt such as food, services, goods already carrying a high rate of duty, and special articles such as children's clothing, medicine and industrial wear. Otherwise there were two sharply differentiated rates,[1] one of one-third on the wholesale value on luxury articles and the other of one-sixth on 'more necessary articles' such as furniture; but care had been taken to consider the cost of living. A new resolution would be necessary[2] and he was expecting some £110 millions in a full year, although the restrictive effect of the tax was even more important than the yield.

Currently, therefore, he was imposing additional taxation of £239 millions, £101 millions from direct levies, £28 millions from the old indirect taxes and £110 millions from the new. If the additional taxation of April, £168 millions,[3] was taken into account, the grand total was £407 millions. 'I think,' he said, 'that this sum is all I can reasonably ask for by way of taxation at the present time.'

He did not refer again to the size of the gap, but gave the latest news of saving,[4] although the figures he quoted, totalling some £688 millions since the outbreak of war, only underlined his plea that 'the efforts to save must be redoubled'. His reception showed the House did not altogether share his optimism. The practice of continuing the debate after the Chancellor's Statement was now well established, and although the revision of purchase tax[5] and the embryo Pay As You Earn scheme[6] were warmly welcomed, there was a general fear that the size of the gap would cause severe inflation despite the potential source of saving.[7] Severe criticism ranged from pleas for further economy (Harris),[8] suggestions for a reconsideration of Keynes's deferred pay plan[9] (Lipson), a root and branch proposal from Tinker[10] for giving each family basic living expenses and con-

[1] H. 23/7/1940, Cols 588/590.   [2] H. 23/7/1940, Col. 652.
[3] Direct and indirect, £128 millions; E.P.T., £40 millions.
[4] H. 23/7/1940, Col. 653.
[5] E.g. H. 23/7/1940, Cols 666/669 (Lees-Smith).
[6] Reed called it 'One of the greatest reforms introduced within my memory with regard to income tax' (H. 23/7/1940, Col. 697).
[7] Cf. H. 23/7/1940, Cols 673/680 (Wardlaw-Milne).
[8] H. 23/7/1940, Cols 669/673.   [9] H. 23/7/1940, Cols 686/691.
[10] H. 23/7/1940, Cols 683/686.

fiscating the balance of its income, to Gallacher's[1] voice crying in the wilderness for the full conscription of wealth and a 'people's Budget'.

Simon's last Budget, four months previously, might have had a mixed reception; his successor's first effort met with universal criticism. The *New Statesman* found it 'incredible if it were not Sir Kingsley Wood's'; the *Daily Telegraph* labelled it 'an anti-climax', the *News Chronicle* 'half-hearted', *The Financial Times* 'inflation by the front door', and the *Spectator* 'half-hearted'. The three most consistent critics of Government finance had a field-day: all paid tribute to his admirable grasp of war finance, but there the compliments stopped. *The Times*, under the leader heading of 'Shirking the Issue',[2] accused the Chancellor 'of a timidity which is afraid to trust the nation's capacity for self-sacrifice'. *The Economist*[3] declared that he had failed to act on his own diagnosis of what was needed and to introduce any major modification of the fiscal system. The *Manchester Guardian*[4] summarized the general feeling of the Press with its comment that the measures would hardly have filled the bill in April. It was to be hoped that when the Chancellor had noted the 'unprecedented apathy'[5] of the House and the fact that the Budget had been given 'the most tepid reception of any for a generation',[6] he would be a sadder and wiser man. Again, as with Simon's Budget of April 1940, the charge was not against any particular proposal but the woefully limited scope.

It was Molson who remarked at the end of the Second Reading that 'never was a Budget so little opposed and so much criticized'.[7] The primary reason for lack of any general opposition was the conviction throughout the House that the basic aim of the Budget, namely the raising of the amount of money necessary for the successful prosecution of the war, was not a matter for argument. A subsidiary reason was the change in the traditional format of the Budget itself; it had largely lost its resemblance to a balance sheet or even a profit and loss account and was now a very guarded statement of estimated revenue and expenditure very difficult to attack. The only vulnerable points were the gap between these two items and the method of controlling inflation when there was a margin which could not be met by borrowing or taxation.

[1] H. 23/7/1940, Cols 691/697.   [2] 25/7/1940.   [3] 27/7/1940.
[4] 24/7/1940.   [5] *The Times*, 24/7/1940.
[6] *Manchester Guardian*, 24/7/1940.   [7] H. 6/8/1940, Col. 172.

This gap proved to be the main general target. Some Members contented themselves with criticising the Chancellor's optimism in thinking it could be bridged by voluntary loans; this was a fairly consistent Labour line following the lead of Pethick-Lawrence.[1] Other Members went further, basing their objections on the statistical fact that only 39 per cent of expenditure was now being met by taxation as against 46 per cent at the April Budget;[2] they argued that this proportion must be increased. But there was a considerable and sharp diversity of opinion on how this should be achieved ranging from straightforward increases in the conventional taxes (one Member made a prescient forecast of 10s 0d in the £)[3] to proposals that the whole mechanism of direct taxation should be recast and linked with a system of family allowances.[4] The old arguments of the proportion of direct to indirect taxation were heard again, a nostalgic re-echo of the early thirties. And there were a few imaginative suggestions somewhat before their time of premium bonds[5] and the charging of interest on arrears of tax.[6]

The main specific target was, of course, the re-jigged purchase tax, although the differentiation between the rates on luxuries and necessaries, and the exemptions, had removed two major sources of grievance which had been well ventilated in the April Budget debates.[7] But there was a considerble overspill of opposition into the current discussions. Time and again[8] the Government had to point out that it was no use attacking purchase tax as such, as the principle had been accepted by the House; but even so Labour Members could not keep their dislike of the whole tax out of their advocacy of their various amendments.

Pethick-Lawrence dealt with the first two objections. He asked[9] what measures were being taken to prevent forestalling and, more important, whether the Resolution imposing the tax did not trespass on the authority of the House in that it gave the Treasury power to vary the basic rates and alter the categories. Crookshank[10] an-

---

[1] H. 24/7/1940, Cols 904/915.   [2] H. 24/7/1940, Cols 915/922 (White).
[3] H. 24/3/1940, Col. 922 (Tasker).
[4] H. 24/7/1940, Cols 915/922 (White), or H. 6/8/1940, Cols 83/91 (Wardlaw-Milne).
[5] H. 6/8/1940, Col. 90.   [6] H. 24/7/1940, Col. 912.
[7] E.g. H. 24/4/1940, Cols 229/239 (Pethick-Lawrence).
[8] See the debate H. 13/8/1940—Customs only.
[9] H. 24/7/1940, Cols 909/910.   [10] H. 25/7/1940, Col. 1057.

swered the first point by referring to Clause 24 of the Purchase Tax
Bill which made provision against deliberate forestalling, and the
Chancellor covered the second by altering the Bill so that the rates
'can no longer be changed by Treasury Order followed by confirma-
tion of this House, but alteration must be made by substantive
legislation'.[1]

The party criticism, most fully developed by Barnes,[2] that the tax
represented unfair pressure on the poorer classes, could only be
met by the reply that the tax was meant to mop up surplus purchasing
power from both rich and poor alike, and that equity had been
served by exempting many items which entered the cost-of-living
index. Finally, there were the inevitable pieces of special pleading
from Members for constituencies where the staple product was
menaced either by being placed in the higher category or by being
subject to the tax at all. The Chancellor here excelled in the soft
answer even if at times logic had to be sacrificed to the need of raising
revenue and reducing consumption.[3] The most spectacular victory
for an exceptional case was the plea for exempting books and newspapers, which nearly brought the Government down and was the
subject of a special statement.[4]

The Conservatives had their points of criticism too, including 100
per cent E.P.T. which was a 'great mistake',[5] the somewhat thread-
bare argument that direct taxation had reached its maximum and
would now produce diminishing returns, and the fear that the
powers of the General Commissioners were being eroded by the
legislation proposed for deducting Schedule E tax from wages. In
general, however, the Conservative attitude was more than usually
muted and dispassionate.

But despite the criticism from the Press, from both sides of the
House, and at least one Department,[6] Kingsley Wood pursued his
bland, almost complacent course, deploying virtually the same
arguments, from his opening address through the Second Reading[7]
to his final remarks on the Third.[8] Briefly his theme on each occasion
was that the entire financial arrangements of the country were under
continuous review: very substantial burdens had been imposed in

[1] H. 6/8/1940, Col. 71. [2] H. 25/7/1940. Cols 1023/1030.
[3] See for example H. 13/8/1940, Col. 682. [4] H. 13/8/1940, Cols 747/751.
[5] H. 6/8/1940, Col. 167 (Craven-Ellis).
[6] The Board of Trade: Sayers, *op. cit.*, p. 51, footnote 4.
[7] H. 6/8/1940, Cols 65/74. [8] H. 15/8/1940, Cols 1076/1095.

the last ten months increasing the taxation yield from £888 millions to £1,500 millions 'not without hardship and distortion'. Before further taxation was imposed, 'as some now advocate, it is right and just that adequate time should be given', or, in his colloquial paraphrase, 'it is no good smashing people'. He ended by promising 'an evolving economic policy'; 'if savings and lending do not contribute enough, taxation will have to be increased'. His only sign of impatience was an administrative one in trying to force the closure of the Second Reading well before time.[1]

These arguments were reasonable enough in theory, but with the advice which the Chancellor now had available,[2] including that of Maynard Keynes, it was astonishing that his admitted grasp of the fiscal problems produced measures so comparatively inadequate and unimaginative. The explanation may well be that a major section of the Budget proposals was axed at the last minute; and that section, as the *New Statesman*[3] hinted, must surely have been taxation on the under £250 income group, a glaring omission commented on by two Conservative back-benchers, although not taken up as party policy and to which there was marked Labour opposition.[4] If a Coalition Cabinet was to accept the increased indirect taxation represented by purchase tax, it was too much to expect the newly co-opted Labour Members to swallow an extension of income tax to lowly-paid workers at the same time.

The saving grace of the second Budget of 1940 was purchase tax and the pilot Pay as You Earn scheme. Otherwise, as Price commented, 'it was just another turn of the screw all round'.[5] Essentially it was a Budget of a newly-formed Coalition Government still to find corporate identity; and the tentative nature of the measures was due not to fiscal ignorance but political expediency.

[1] H. 6/8/1940, Cols 157/158.   [2] Sayers, *op. cit.*, p. 45.
[3] 26/8/1940.
[4] Fraser (H. 24/7/1940, Col 933) argued that workers should make their contribution as wages increased; Wolmer (H. 25/7/1940, Col. 1045) emphasized the need of taxing the 'well-paid artisan.' Richards (H. 24/7/1940, Col. 938) stressed the hardship caused by even small deductions from middle-range incomes.
[5] H. 15/8/1940, Col. 1068.

Chapter IX
The Finance Bill 1941

KINGSLEY, KINDERSLEY AND KEYNES

Time Table

Financial Statement		April 7, 1941
Budget Proposals		
	1st Day	7
	2nd Day	8
	3rd Day	9
Budget Resolutions		
	Reported	23
	Introduced	June 17
	Reported	18
Finance Bill		
	1st Reading	April 23
	2nd Reading	May 22
Committee		
	1st Day	June 17
	2nd Day	18
	3rd Day	July 1
Report		1
Third Reading		1
Royal Assent		22

In 1941 the country lay under siege. The Battle of Britain had been won, but night bombing quickly succeeded it, the target being civilian morale. Less spectacular, although far more dangerous, was the Battle of the Atlantic, which was just being joined. In the Mediterranean and the Middle East the advantage of early, although limited, successes was soon to be cancelled out by the loss of Greece and Cyrenaica.

It was a subdued and not very crowded House therefore which assembled on the April 7, 1941, to hear Kingsley Wood's second Budget, as the thin spring sunshine came through the windows of 'another place', for the bombing of the second chamber had forced the Commons to sit in the House of Lords.[1] Simon was in the Press Gallery and Keynes in the upper gallery. Very unusually, the Prime Minister was missing, being absent abroad, although the Chancellor must have been uneasily aware of Churchill's feelings about high rates of tax 'as a deadly blow to good housekeeping and good management'.[2] But there was no sign of nervousness as Sir Kingsley rose to present what was generally anticipated would be the most massive Budget Statement ever submitted to the Committee of Ways and Means.

He began quietly enough,[3] without the usual flurry of figures, for detailed statistics were already available in the first National Income White Paper. It would be a greater service to take a wider survey, and his first thesis was that 'the financial front since the beginning of the war has stood firm and strong'. Current efforts in all directions had gone far beyond anything attempted in World War I and inevitably so since the sophistication of the weapons of modern warfare had made them infinitely more expensive. Here the Lease and Lend Act would be making a vital contribution.[4] The Government loan policy, under the guidance of Lord Kennet's Capital Issues Committee, had held the rate at less than 2 per cent.[5] Nor was anyone able to make a fortune out of the war. He must emphasize, however, that the problems of total war economy could not be settled by financial means only; there were in addition such important measures as rationing, price control, wage restraint and the concentration of industry. But the financial front was paramount not only to temper the increase of debt but for its contribution to the war effort, an adequate export trade, and to the struggle against inflation.

[1] The Peers sat in Church House, Westminster.
[2] R. S. Sayers, *Financial Policy 1939–1945*, p. 557.
[3] H. 7/4/1941. Cols 1299/1334.   [4] This began in March 1941.
[5] Compared, for instance, with a general minimum of 5 per cent in 1916.

After these preliminary observations, he proceeded to a rapid review of 1940/41. The expenditure out of the vote of credit had greatly exceeded the £2,800 millions assumed in the Budget of July 1940; it had amounted in fact to £3,220 millions against the £3,330 millions actually voted; the total expenditure for the year had been £3,884 millions. The estimated revenue for the year of £1,234 millions, scaled up by the July Budget to £1,360 millions, had in fact been exceeded by £49 millions.

A breakdown of this surplus showed that Inland Revenue duties at £792 millions had provided nearly half the excess, namely £22 millions. Income tax and N.D.C./E.P.T. had proved especially buoyant at plus figures of £13 millions and £26 millions respectively, minus figures on estate duty and stamps, however, had whittled this down. Customs and Excise showed the same sort of picture: the traditional best payers, beer and tobacco, were up by £25·5 millions and £15·5 millions respectively, but other duties were down, especially those relating to imports, so that the net surplus was only £6 millions. Purchase tax was working smoothly and had yielded £26 millions. Other sources had given an over-all excess of £20 millions, including £3 millions on motor vehicles account and £13 millions from free gifts. In arriving at the over-all total of £1,409 millions, he would like to pay tribute to the co-operation of the public in the payment of all taxes and especially to the help from employers in launching the embryo Pay as You Earn procedure. Towards the total expenditure of £3,884 millions, already mentioned, he had a tax contribution of £1,409 millions, leaving a deficiency of £2,475 millions.

This last figure inevitably led to consideration of the National Debt, and, in addition to covering this deficit, £104 millions had had to be borrowed to pay off holders of the 4½ per cent Conversion Loan who did not wish to convert, £100 millions to repay the 1 per cent Treasury Bonds and £17 millions as the Sinking Fund contribution. The Chancellor then listed the borrowings, which had taken 'a variety of forms'[1] from war savings of various sorts to the proceeds of Ulster Savings Certificates.

But he was conscious that this summary did not give a complete picture of the position and the financial policy generally. This involved an assessment of what was popularly called the gap, which,

[1] H. 7/4/1941, Cols 1305/1306.

expressed in its crudest form, was the difference between revenue and the budgetary total of expenditure. He felt, however, that confusion had arisen in analysing the exact relationship between this comparison and the danger of inflation. For instance, purchases abroad, although part of the gap, did not affect inflation. Then the measure of the gap was not even the difference between domestic expenditure and the produce of taxation, for 'borrowing as such is neither necessarily nor normally inflationary', and he proceeded to illustrate this from the statistics of the first eighteen months of the war, which showed that the national accounts would always balance and it was only in so far as they were balanced otherwise than by the result of taxation, plus other Exchequer aids and resources, plus genuine savings, that the danger of inflation would arise. He was confident that the gap had not so far introduced inflationary perils into the economy and he would be publishing statistical evidence of this as a White Paper.

It was now time to turn to the prospects for 1941/42, exclusive of any Lease/Lend receipts and of any payments to be made in the United States. He was asking for a Vote of Credit amounting to £3,500 millions, on the assumption that there would be no increase in domestic costs for reasons he would give later. Known expenditure was the Civil Supply Services at £435 millions, the Fixed Debt Charge at £255 millions, and other Consolidated Fund services at £17 millions, making the total of £4,207 millions which would be found in the White Paper. Domestic expenditure he put at a total of £3,700 millions as compared with an annual rate of £2,055 millions for the first year of the war and of £3,190 millions based on the first half of the second year of the war, 'tangible evidence of the continued expansion of our war effort'. The campaign against waste was unremitting, and in this context he paid tribute to the vigilance of the Select Committee.[1]

Kingsley Wood was now just about at the half-way mark. Without any pause he plunged into his estimates for the coming year. Inland Revenue duties he put at £992 millions, assuming an increase of £81 millions in income tax from a full year of the current rise in wages and the effect of Finance (No. 2) Act, 1940, and assuming N.D.C./E.P.T. would show a threefold yield under the full force of the 100 per cent rate with a spectacular estimate of £210 millions

[1] Under the Chairmanship of Wardlaw-Milne.

as against £70 millions last year. Indirect taxation would inevitably be affected by restrictions: Customs and Excise, for instance, at £578 millions was a modest £49 millions over last year's estimate, and the estimate for purchase tax, £70 millions, was equally conservative. He did not propose to go into the remainder of the items in any great detail, having drawn attention to the most significant. The grand total he hoped to raise came to £1,636 millions.

The House was now becoming a little impatient, for the Chancellor announced there were some minor matters he wished to dispose of before dealing with the major financial problems of the year. The medicine stamp duties, that museum-piece of administrative complexities, were to be repealed. Farmers whose lands exceeded £300 in value were to be assessed under Schedule D[1] which would mean the production of annual accounts. There was to be an allowance for 1939/40 and subsequent years for income tax in respect of exceptional depreciation, due to the war, of buildings, machinery or plant similar to that already provided for N.D.C./E.P.T.[2] The relief authorized for 1939/40 and 1940/41 in cases of diminution of earned income owing to the war circumstances was to be continued.[3] There was to be no allowance for income tax purposes of payments by traders, by way of insurance or otherwise in respect of death or injury of employees from enemy action;[4] private schemes were not to be financed at the State's expense. Traders affected by concentration schemes were not to be penalized.[5] And, finally, estate duty was not to be levied on gifts to the State.[6]

E.P.T. merited a short section to itself. He was aware of the criticism of the 100 per cent rate and its motives, but the House was well aware that the reason for this rate was not purely fiscal but 'was directed primarily to take the profit out of war'.[7] But such concessions as could be made would be made. He was proposing to include borrowed money in capital, although the interest paid on it would of course be no longer allowable.[8] There were to be scaled allowances to concerns engaged in developing wasting assets to compensate for the loss of future profits entailed in the using up of these

---

[1] F.A. 1941, S. 10. [2] F.A. 1941, S. 19. [3] F.A. 1941, S. 8.
[4] F.A. 1941, S. 14. [5] F.A. 1941, S. 18. [6] F.A. 1941, S. 36.
[7] H. 7/4/1941, Col. 1317.
[8] The rate allowed on increase of capital for addition to the standard for E.P.T. purposes was 8 per cent, so the lender gained to the extent of this rate over the rate of interest paid.

assets in the present national emergency. Thirdly, and most important, at the end of the war, subject to conditions to be laid down by Parliament, 20 per cent of the net 100 per cent E.P.T. should be refunded as a reserve for purposes of reconstruction.

The Chancellor had already made the assumption that there would be no increase in domestic costs. This was because he was prepared to extend the principle of subsidizing foodstuffs, already running at the rate of £100 millions annually, to all essential goods and services[1] in 'an endeavour to prevent any further rise in the cost-of-living index number'.

This attempt to peg the cost of living was highly relevant to the question of the gap and its effect on inflation. He was now prepared to estimate its extent; with revenue of £1,637 millions and saving of £1,600 millions, a total in round figures of £3,200 millions to set against domestic expenditure of £3,700, it was of the order of £500 millions. How was this inflationary gap to be filled?

An analysis of the progress of the Savings Campaign,[2] during which he paid a well-deserved tribute to Lord Kindersley, showed that the average savings of a year ago, £21 millions per week, had now increased to over £30 millions. He felt entitled to assume, therefore, that personal savings would continue to rise and produce a further £200 to £300 millions. 'A considerable gap remains: it cannot wisely be put at less than a sum between £200 and £300 millions.'

He had considered a number of taxation curiosa including an excess income tax and a services tax, but he had decided they would be riddled with 'exemptions and exceptions' if they were to work fairly. The old war-horse of direct taxation would therefore be called upon both to raise the money and restrict consumption. The changes in reliefs and allowances proposed were to charge the first £165 of taxable income at 6s 6d, to reduce earned income and age allowance from one-sixth to one-tenth with a maximum of £150, to reduce single allowance to £80 (from £100) and married allowance to £140 (from £170) and to reduce the exemption limit to £110. The standard rate was raised to 10s 0d and the highest surtax rate would be 19s 6d. This would bring in some two million new taxpayers,[3] and raise £150 millions currently, rising to £250 millions in a full year. But there was to be a relief parallel to that proposed

---

[1] H. 7/4/1941, Cols 1321/1324.   [2] H. 7/4/1941, Cols 1324/1327.
[3] In the event it was nearly four millions.

for E.P.T. For every year of assessment for which these reductions operated, the extra tax ultimately borne by any individual because of these reductions should be recorded and notified to him, and credited to him after the war, at a date to be fixed by the Treasury,[1] thus creating 'a substantial nest-egg'. In short he was raising £500 millions more than last year and almost £1,000 millions more than in the last pre-war financial year, and of the net expenditure to be financed from domestic loans and taxation almost a half was by the latter. He had spoken for over two hours without even a sip of water.

The speeches which followed were notable for a comparative failure to appreciate what the Chancellor was trying to do both in the new format of his speech and in his general approach. Lees-Smith,[2] for example, simply contented himself with agreeing that inflation, the central problem of the Budget, was not yet dangerously large and that rationing and price-control were the major restraints, and Barnes[3] summarized the general feeling when he declared that 'this is the first Budget which begins to reflect some understanding of the financial consequence of a totalitarian war'. The more left-wing Labour opinion maintained hostility to both purchase tax and E.P.T. post-war refund.[4] But it was left to Willie Gallacher,[5] the Communist Member, to interpret the measures of reconstruction earmarked for after the war as 'the same old Tory measures of the same old system of society'. His attack rose to a crescendo in a diatribe against the 'damned scandal' of taxing wages, for which phrase he was called to order by the Chairman for using unparliamentary language.

The Tory line was one of qualified approval, with an emphasis on the importance of saving[6] and the prevention of waste.[7] The complaints against the rate of E.P.T. had been met to an extent by the post-war refund provisions. Even the transfer of farming to Schedule D was welcomed, although Adams[8] was possibly a trifle over-optimistic when he said that farmers 'had felt a deep shame for their industry to know that it was paying altogether less than it should'.

For once the Press was wholly in favour of the Budget, although enthusiasm was in some cases tempered. *The Times*[9] led off in a dra-

[1] F.A. 1941, S. 7.   [2] H. 7/4/1941, Cols 1337/1342.
[3] H. 7/4/1941, Cols 1362/1367.   [4] H. 7/4/1941, Cols 1375/1379 (Tinker).
[5] H. 7/4/1941, Cols 1379/1384.   [6] H. 7/4/1941, Cols 1342/1345 (Harris).
[7] H. 7/4/1941, Cols 1345/1349 (Smithers).   [8] H. 7/4/1941, Cols 1272/1275.
[9] 8/4/1941.

matic leader by declaring: 'Nothing more drastic could be imagined than proposals which will add two millions to taxpayers, raise taxation to 19s 6d and produce £1,860 millions in a single year.' It correctly pinpointed the anti-inflationary motive and underscored the current Conservative line that 'waste in face of these proposals is more than ever a crime'.

The *Manchester Guardian*[1] was somewhat more critical. While recognizing that the Chancellor had faced the essential problem by cutting down on civilian expenditure as much as possible without losing sight of the need for a fair distribution of essentials through rationing and pegged prices, he had perhaps unwisely segregated expenditure abroad and had ignored the problem of estimating total expenditure ahead. In some ways, as the City page comment expressed it, the Budget was only 'half-revealed': the total deficit figure was not made available and for the first time in history Treasury calculations had to be taken at their face value. But the enforced savings scheme did represent a revolution in British taxation, and the simplicity of the measures in form and purpose was admirable.

The weeklies had seen the Budget grow in popularity over the week. *The Economist*[2] epitomized the general feeling by hailing it as 'the first war Budget' ('a real war Budget' was the *Spectator's*[3] contribution). It commended the survey of the financial problems of the war as a whole, pointed out that the purely budgetary part of the speech was very short, the changes simple, and the most interesting section the post-war rebates. It was most impressed by the innovation of the White Paper[4] and on the whole agreed with the Chancellor's estimate of the gap, apart from a little wholesome scepticism about the quantitative details.

The *New Statesman*[5] paid tribute to Kingsley Wood's attempt 'to frame for the duration the principle of fiscal strategy applied to totalitarian war', which was a remarkable concession as the Chancellor had never been one of its favourite politicians. Still, however, advocating strongly a 'siege economic system', it naturally was guarded in its approval of post-war credits.

The Coalition Government had been under way now for nearly a year so that the second and third days' debate on the Budget proposals cannot be analysed on the usual party lines. Not that these

[1] 8/4/1941. [2] 12/4/1941. [3] 11/4/1941.
[4] Cmd. 6261. There was a separate article on this. [5] 12/4/1941.

were still not discernible. But the period of co-operation had begun to blur the once rigid demarcations; and in any case the object of the proposals was not merely fiscal logic but national security.

There was only a restricted time at the speakers' disposal, but of the twenty[1] who caught the Chairman's eye over the two days, none wholly opposed, only one was mainly so, three had some basic criticisms and the rest displayed considerable enthusiasm modified only in some cases by regret at the Chancellor's misguided failure to accept a favourite panacea. Common was a genuine attempt to be constructive, and one bout of long-windedness was met by the implied rebuke of a Member who donned a gas-mask in self-defence.[2]

Typical of the spirit of the debate was the first speech, also probably the best, delivered by Pethick-Lawrence,[3] the doyen of Labour's fiscal caucus. The Budget should be subject to three tests, whether it faced up to the facts, whether it delivered the goods, and whether it was fair. The first criterion was satisfied, especially in view of the praiseworthy publication of the White Paper; the second criterion involved financing without inflation, that he agreed would be satisfied if the Vote of Credit did not exceed £3,500 millions, which was a calculated risk, if the new taxes came up to expectations, which was more than likely, and if savings increased as anticipated, a justifiable assumption. The third question was the most important and needed examination in depth, but on balance he thought the post-war refund and credit systems,[4] provided they were properly used and not bogged down in administrative detail, and the fact that there was no increase in indirect taxation or any 'fancy taxes', had secured a fair sharing of the tax burden; although he would still like to see a capital levy, a point taken up by Edwards[5] shortly afterwards.

The most critical speech came from Stokes.[6] After referring caustically to the Chancellor's 'two-hour economic lecture', he summed up his proposals as 'a paper bridge which will collapse sooner or later',

---

[1] There were in fact twenty-two speakers, including Crookshank and Kingsley Wood.

[2] H. 8/4/1941, Col. 1483. [3] H. 8/4/1941, 1438/1447.

[4] Post-war refund refers to the promised 'repayment after the war of certain excess profits tax'. (S. 28, F.A. 1941); post-war credit refers to the 'crediting of certain amounts of income tax'. (S. 7, F.A. 1941).

[5] H. 8/4/1941, Cols 1471/1479. [6] H. 9/4/1941, Cols 1642/1650.

and although he praised some aspects, notably post-war refund and the use of taxation to prevent inflation, the fundamental weakness was the failure to deal decisively with the National Debt and the land question. In a typically telling over-simplification, he concluded: 'The total paid to landlords every year is £500 millions . . . and the total to be paid to the money-lenders when the war is over, £600 millions annually . . . £1,100 millions going to the biggest sets of parasites in the country.' Wedgwood[1] was even more dogmatic on the land point, claiming: 'The perfect tax would be a tax on land values.'

There was still a slight hang-over from the criticism of the last three Budgets that taxation was still not high enough. Thomas[2] maintained 'We should continue to tax and tax' because of the possible deficiency in the savings programme, and Lipson,[3] in advocating more taxation of luxuries, wondered whether war expenditure was adequate even now. But complaints were starting that taxation was too high. Loftus[4] emphasized the danger of the small business being undermined by E.P.T. Hely-Hutchinson[5] pointed out the possible adverse effect on savings of the present high rate of direct taxation. Craven-Ellis[6] thought the limit of what could be taken out in taxation had been reached, and Henderson[7] went even further in maintaining the increase was premature and created a taxation which was penal not fiscal.

The basic justification for the taxation changes was of course the post-war credit principle and for retaining E.P.T. at 100 per cent the post-war refund mechanism. The latter was mentioned specifically by over half the speakers: Sir P. Bennett,[8] for instance, answered Loftus by arguing that the small firms (and there were 77 per cent in the country with twenty-five employees or less) would benefit from the refunds for replacement of plant and for industrial development generally. Post-war credit was little mentioned, to Crookshank's[9] surprise; when it was, White's[10] speech was an example; the

[1] H. 8/4/1941, Cols 1504/1509.   [2] H. 8/4/1941, Cols 1447/1455.
[3] H. 9/4/1941, Cols 1636/1642.
[4] H. 8/4/1941 and 9/4/1941, Cols 1522/1523, and 1606/1617.
[5] H. 8/4/1941, Cols 1461/1471.   [6] H. 9/4/1941, Cols 1631/1636.
[7] H. 9/4/1941, Cols 1627/1631.
[8] H. 8/4/1941, Cols 1479/1485. He incidentally had succeeded to Chamberlain's old constituency.
[9] H. 8/4/1941, Cols 1513/1522.   [10] H. 8/4/1941, Cols 1455/1461.

general tendency was to propose that it should be linked with family allowances. Braithwaite[1] introduced the one sour note. He thought all was far from well on the financial front; wages and expenses were being inflated; 'once a man is put in Government service he becomes taxi-minded'; and he challenged the Government to declare whether in fact the whole post-war credit system was a 'hard promise'.

There were, however, Members whose comments were still primarily party inspired. Schuster[2] praised the Chancellor for his courage in extending income tax liability downwards and for the post-war refund proposal since 'underlying industry must be in a sound financial situation'. He then went on to develop a theory that the question of amounts possibly disallowed by the Inland Revenue distorted the original tax reserves and that it would be better to bring in both capital losses and gains. Finally, the Government's subsidy policy should be balanced by a wages policy.

Benson[3] followed immediately after and took up the previous speaker's point at once. 'If we are to have taxation of capital let us have proper taxation of capital and not merely the proposal, so frequently put forward, that certain expenses which the Board of Inland Revenue refused to allow as current expenses shall be allowed.' He doubted whether the enormous volume of saving would come about unless prices were pegged and the savings campaign better organized.

The Chancellor had already examined and rejected the suggestion of an excess income tax[4] which might have been used as a means of limiting the high wages in war industries as well as a source of revenue. But there was a surprising amount of support for such a scheme despite the Chancellor's turn-down. Wardlaw-Milne[5] argued that if 'it is right to tax companies to take the profit out of war it is equally right we should tax individuals for the same purpose'. Loftus[6] found the idea more equitable than the proposed flat rate increase in income tax, and Albery[7] tied his support to a general complaint that no bigger burden was being imposed on those profiting from the war and no real effort was being made to mitigate the burden on those suffering from it. In fact none of its sup-

[1] H. 9/4/1941, Cols 1620/1625.
[2] H. 8/4 1941, Cols 1485/1493.
[3] H. 8/4/1941, Cols 1493/1501.
[4] H. 7/4/1941, Cols 1327/1328.
[5] H. 8/4/1941, Cols 1501/1503.
[6] H. 8/4/1941 and 9/4/1941, Cols 1522/1523 and 1606/1617.
[7] H. 8/4/1941, Cols 1509/1513.

porters saw that the basic virtue of an excess income tax is to cream off those salaries paid to managerial and executive staff to avoid an excess profits tax.[1]

Other suggestions were concerned either with the need for economy and for avoiding waste, which Gledhill[2] linked with the suggestion of a pruning of Civil Service manpower and the occasional hint of a capital levy. And finally, on the lunatic fringe, there was Elliston's[3] prophecy of 'an orgy of self-medication' from the abolition of the medicine stamp duties with threepenny and sixpenny packets of drugs pouring out of slot-machines and covering the counters of chain-stores.

Kingsley Wood had good reason to feel pleased with himself when he rose to make his over-all reply.[4] He stressed the effect British determination, as represented by the Budget, had produced abroad and especially in the United States. Regarding the doubts which had been voiced on the needed increase of savings, he reminded the House that the heavier rates of taxation only began to bite for salaries in November and, for weekly wages, not until January 1942. He emphasized again the underlying purpose of his proposals which was to cut purchasing power, if possible, by up to £500 millions, and in arriving at this figure he had taken the effect of subsidies into account. The 100 per cent E.P.T., he continued, would be substantially mitigated by the post-war refund which would be repaid net of income tax.[5] No more concessions could be made in the direction of allowing capital expenditure; he had already gone as far as he thought prudent with the scheme for exceptional depreciation,[6] he 'could not have the tax revenue at the mercy of every Board of Directors'. He concluded with a tribute to 'the advantage of advice from many people outside the Treasury' not only in relation to immediate matters but with an eye to the position when the war was over.

The debate[7] when the Resolutions were reported was brief but

[1] See Hicks, Hicks and Rostus, *Taxation of War Wealth*, pp. 65/70.
[2] H. 9/4/1941, Cols 1625/1627.   [3] H. 9/4/1941, Cols 1650/1654.
[4] H. 9/4/1941, Cols 1654/1663.
[5] Because, of course, the original 100 per cent E.P.T. had been allowed as a deduction in computing the Case I profit. This procedure seemed to puzzle a number of Members when the Chancellor reached the point. See his explanation at H. 9/4/1941, Cols 1559/1560.
[6] S. 19, F.A. 1941.   [7] H. 23/4/1941, Cols 185/224.

well-informed and cut right across party lines. The main talking-point was the increase in the incidence of income tax. The necessity of these 'savage provisions', as Davies[1] called them, was freely admitted, but speaker after speaker stressed the perils inherent in this almost confiscatory rate. For Woodburn[2] the destruction of incentive represented the greatest danger, and Hammersley[3] maintained it constituted almost a capital levy since if a heavy surtax payer had inescapable obligations he might have to 'disinvest' himself to satisfy both these and his tax bill. Even Benson,[4] one of the principal Labour speakers on finance, had to admit that 'we are possibly reaching a limit where on certain ranges of income we shall get a diminishing return' due to the lack of incentive. But there was a more sinister reason: there must be a certain amount of evasion since the growth of total taxable income of the country was much greater in proportion than the growth of surtaxable incomes. Reliance on 'steady patriotism' was not enough with, including War Damage Contribution[5] of 2s 0d in the £, a possible rate of over 20s 0d in the £; he personally did not regard this as anomalous but safeguards ought to be introduced.[6]

The most fruitful suggestion, however, was that put forward by Mainwaring,[7] that if the £200-a-year man was to be brought within the taxation net he ought to be given some concession for travelling expenses arising out of war circumstances. Pethick-Lawrence[8] referred specifically to this point when summarizing the speeches, and Kingsley Wood,[9] in his concluding remarks, dealt at length with the same question, which he promised to look into. On the problem of evasion, 'People do,' he admitted, 'sometimes have a run but the Inland Revenue, the Finance Act and the House generally overtake them . . . and provision has been made retrospective.'

The third main issue was that of E.P.T. It was Woodburn's[10] turn again, as a member of the Select Committee on National Expenditure, to complain about unjustifiable waste by companies which the 100 per cent rate encouraged, and the manipulation of accounts which disguised capital expenditure as revenue in order to

---

[1] H. 23/4/1941, Cols 188/190.
[2] H. 23/4/1941, Cols 185/188.
[3] H. 23/4/1941, Cols 191/192.
[4] H. 23/4/1941, Cols 192/196.
[5] S. 36, War Damage Act 1941.
[6] H. 23/4/1941, Col. 196.
[7] H. 23/4/1941, Cols 196/189.
[8] H. 23/4/1941, Cols 200/202.
[9] H. 23/4/1941, Col. 205.
[10] H. 23/4/1941, Cols 212/216.

build up a favourable post-war position. Tinker,[1] following, repeated his criticism of post-war refund which he had initiated after the Budget opening,[2] with caustic comments on 'these patriots who feel they should not be paying 100 per cent E.P.T.'.

It was a month before time could be found for the Second Reading.[3] By then Kingsley Wood had accumulated enough evidence to cover his claim, as he opened,[4] that he had secured a very general agreement with the Budget proposals and the conceptions on which they had been founded which were that the dual purposes of raising revenue and restricting purchasing power must be served. War production was now getting into its full stride, but heavy taxation[5] and increased saving were vital; the progress of the latter was most encouraging.

Equally vital was the need for avoiding waste and extravagance.[6] But there were some more specific points which he ought to mention. The first was Clause 26 which contained far-reaching powers to counteract transactions designed to avoid E.P.T. liability and, in passing, he had seriously considered whether he ought not to extend such general powers to income tax and surtax avoidance schemes. He also mentioned the relief of the first £5,000 from death duties in the case of death due to the operations of war. Finally he had under review the question of free-of-tax payments which were seriously affected by the massive rate of taxation; and he concluded with a tribute to aid from the Empire, which was a welcome adjunct to the efforts of the mother country as exemplified by the Budget.

As usual with the Second Reading, the debate gave Members the chance of indulging in generalities before applying themselves to the detail demanded at Committee stages. Pethick-Lawrence,[7] for instance, contrasted the current financial position favourably with that which had prevailed in World War I, and he felt that the genuine savings required would be forthcoming. He wondered, however, how the Government envisaged the future and whether his cherished plan of a total capital levy, not merely one on increased war wealth, would ever be adopted. If not, he feared after the war

---

[1] H. 23/4/1941, Col. 216.　　　[2] See p. 249.　　　[3] 22/5/1941.
[4] H. 22/5/1941, Cols 1607/1614.
[5] There were now 7·8 millions income tax payers.
[6] The Ministries of Supply and Aircraft Production the War Office and Air Ministry had all recently appointed Directors of Economy.
[7] H. 22/5/1941, Cols 1614/1621.

Labour would be the victim of 'the stranglehold of vested interests'.

Clement Davies,[1] for the Liberals, was far more critical of contemporary efforts. On a simple arithmetical basis the total revenue to be raised was £4,200 millions. £850 millions was going in ordinary expenditure, including subsidies, leaving a balance of £3,350 millions for war purposes; this, he maintained, was inadequate. Secondly, the proposals would not prevent inflation. Thirdly, taxation was at a level which was killing individual enterprise and destroying any sensible plan for post-war reconstruction. His remedies,[2] however, were somewhat disappointing, involving amongst other suggestions complete rationing of all articles.

Wardlaw-Milne[3] made his usual thoughtful contribution. He agreed with the previous speaker that inflation was taking place, although tolerably controlled. The White Paper had made it clear that the largest increases in free income[4] had been to the wage-earners and this called either for a wages policy or increased taxation. He was still very much afraid that although the country was '100 per cent behind the war psychologically ... in regard to working for victory it is not yet a 100 per cent effort'.

The rest of the speeches were mainly concerned with dangers of the effect of taxation generally on industry,[5] especially E.P.T. at 100 per cent which prevented capital outlay[6] and stimulated extravagance. In this last connection, Denman[7] confessed he had only been able to understand the avoidance Clause 26 with partial success; he was not the only one to be confused before the debate was over.

The Left was in agreement with the extravagance point and even with the Chancellor's point that the problem was one of savings of which the source must be the middle- and working-classes,[8] and that it was necessary to secure by those means, or taxation, as much as possible of the increased income created by the activities of the

[1] H. 22/5/1941, Cols 1621/1628. [2] H. 22/5/1941, Cols 1626/1627.
[3] H. 22/5/1941, Cols 1628/1635.
[4] The speaker was basing his argument on the fact that the national income had increased by some £1,100 millions between 1938 and 1940. Profits and interest accounted for £336 millions and wages for £663 millions.
[5] H. 22/5/1941, Cols 1655/1660 (Spens).
[6] H. 22/5/1941, Cols 1646/1651 (Sanderson).
[7] H. 22/5/1941, Cols 1641/1646.
[8] H. 22/5/1941, Cols 1635/1641 (Benson).

State. There was, however, uneasiness regarding the long view of the nation's finances.

Crookshank[1] wound up. He admitted it was not easy 'to gather the threads of the debate into an artistic whole'. The problems were partly financial and partly economic, but, as he saw it, one of the most important factors was the Government's success in keeping the interest rates low. He made a considered reply to Davies's[2] criticisms, and with regard to Clause 26 he argued that 'we simply cannot afford on many grounds to let abuses creep in and have a run of six months or nine months or whatever it may be, until the next Finance Bill'. Finally, he presented figures[3] to the House which gave grounds for qualified optimism about savings, 'the real test of my Right Hon. Friend's Budget'.

The problem of free-of-tax payments which Kingsley Wood had mentioned when opening the Second Reading[4] was introduced in three new clauses,[5] the purpose of which was to provide a remedy for the inequity resulting from carrying out, at the current rates of tax, of arrangements entered into before the war to make payments free of tax; annuities were an obvious example. The preliminary discussion centred round whether the proposals should apply to pre-war contracts only[6] or whether it should be illegal for such contracts to be made at all.[7] The Chair ruled that detailed discussion was out of order at this stage, but the Attorney-General did explain[8] that the beginning of the war had been taken because then it was plain that increased war taxation was something outside the contemplation of those who entered into transactions before 1939.

This was the view taken by the Solicitor-General when the proposals were again discussed on the following day.[9] Free-of-tax dividends were, however, not included; it was clearly undesirable to vary legal contractual obligations except in cases of great hardship.[10] The broad effect of the legislation ultimately passed was, therefore, that the person under an obligation prior to September 3, 1939, to make a 'free-of-tax' payment was able to meet his liability out of

---

[1] H. 22/5/1941, Cols 1668/1678.   [2] See p. 195.
[3] H. 22/5/1941, Col. 1675.   [4] See p. 194.
[5] See now Ss. 20/22, F.A. 1941.
[6] H. 17/6/1941, Cols 510/513 (Pethick-Lawrence).
[7] H. 17/6/1941, Cols 513/515 (Albery).
[8] H. 17/6/1941, Cols 522/536.   [9] H. 17/6/1941, Cols 701/805.
[10] See the comments in *The Times* and the *Manchester Guardian*, 18/6/1941.

the same amount of gross income before tax as would have sufficed before the war, and that the recipient of the 'free-of-tax' payment was required to bear the war increase of taxation.

The Committee stage of a Finance Bill usually has three distinct ingredients. First, there are the attempts to amend the proposed legislation usually by scaling down—the official reply is normally that the suggested concession would be too costly.[1] Secondly, there are the attempts to introduce new clauses which were generally negatived on the grounds of administrative inconvenience.[2] Thirdly, there are the new clauses introduced by the Government which, in the case of the current Finance Bill, have already been dealt with.[3]

Apart from the invariable arguments about rates and allowances, the most significant controversies were over E.P.T. post-war refund and the avoidance legislation. It was argued on the first issue,[4] with a certain injection of political venom, that industrialists did not place a great deal of value on this promise; what they wanted was the elimination of waste and the reduction of E.P.T. to 80 per cent. Tinker,[5] however, regarded even the post-war refund promise as unfair to the workers: 'We are taking a very wrong step.' The Chancellor himself replied that the refund 'was not to be repaid for any selfish reasons . . . if properly administered, and under proper conditions, [it] will be of considerable value to workers as well'.[6]

But far more interesting was the discussion on Clause 26. The original wording was: 'Where the Commissioners are of opinion that the purposes, or one of the purposes, for which any transaction was or were effected . . . was the avoidance or reduction of liability to excess profits tax, they may direct that such adjustments shall be made . . . so as to counteract the avoidance or reduction of liability. . . .'[7] The debate on the first day[8] revolved round the insertion of the word 'improperly' for the guidance of the Commissioners. The Solicitor-General agreed that the difficulty was to find a proper form of words and the Chancellor then undertook to improve it: 'I desire to see the clause in some better form.'

The debate was resumed in the following month over the insertion of 'main' before 'purposes' so that the proposal would relate to 'the

[1] Cf. the discussions on allowances, H. 17/6/1941, Cols 529/543.
[2] Cf. Gallacher's attempt to get overtime tax free.
[3] See p. 194.   [4] H. 17/6/1941, Cols 573/591.
[5] H. 17/6/1941, Cols 582/584.   [6] H. 17/6/1941, Col. 585.
[7] Bill 24, p. 26, S. 26 (i).   [8] H. 17/6/1941, Cols 602/613.

purpose or one of the main purposes'. This sparked off a short, sharp engagement.[1] Benson[2] saw in the suggestion not the key to the difficulty but the key to the stable door. His warning went unheeded; the Chancellor[3] held that the Commissioners were not likely to apply the avoidance powers to innocent trading transactions; they were equally not likely to allow to pass unchallenged any case in which avoidance, not genuine business, was the governing motive. Both the law officers had accepted this view and the Amendment.

Two new clauses were also accepted. One extended to professions and vocations[4] the provision for the set-off of losses against profits where a person carried on two or more distinct trades, and the other arose from the Chancellor's favourable reaction to the suggestion of some relief for additional travelling expenses which was an obvious corollary to the taxation of lowly-paid workers. In the event the section[5] only gave relief of £10 to manual wage-earners whose place of work or residence had changed owing to the war. One of its sponsors regarded it as 'paltry', which moved the Chancellor, as it was costing £4 millions, to say resignedly 'how little gratitude there is in the world'.[6]

The Third Reading,[7] however, was tranquility itself. Crookshank[8] briefly drew attention to the clauses which he thought had been the most interesting, dealing with post-war credits, the transfer of farming to Schedule D, tax-free payments, the inclusion of borrowed money in computing capital for E.P.T. purposes,[9] the main benefit section and, finally, the limited relief from death duties in cases of deaths due to operations of war.[10] It was the most enormous burden of taxation ever placed upon the country; to illustrate, it was £1,000 millions more than the last pre-war Budget, but there was not a single criticism of this colossal weight. Benson[11] spoke for most of the House when he declared: 'The Chancellor has handled the Finance Bill well from beginning to end,' although he had reservations about the size of the burden being relevant; its adequacy was surely the salient factor. Only Wardlaw-Milne[12] decided to play Cassandra. 'I fear the task of my Right Hon. Friend is only begin-

[1] H. 1/7/1941, Cols 1274/1279.
[2] H. 1/7/1941, Cols 1276/1277.
[3] H. 1/7/1941, Cols 1278/1279.
[4] S. 20, F.A. 1941.
[5] S. 23, F.A. 1941.
[6] H. 1/7/1941, Col. 1243.
[7] H. 1/7/1941, Cols 1281/1303.
[8] H. 1/7/1941, Cols 1281/1284.
[9] S. 29, F.A. 1941.
[10] S. 46, F.A. 1941.
[11] H. 1/7/1941, Cols 1284/1288.
[12] H. 1/7/1941, Cols 1291/1295.

ning.' Incentives, wages and prices policies, and a post-war financial plan were needed. Kingsley Wood[1] accepted the compliments with natural modesty. The Budget was in a sense not a financial Budget but an integral feature of the Government's economic policy which found expression in many other directions, but finance was a vital factor in the war effort.

There was a curious equivocation inherent in the Budget of 1941. It was, as Sayers[2] points out, 'the fruit of longer and more exhaustive discussions in the Treasury than had preceded any other of the war Budgets'. The advice of eminent outside authorities on finance and economics was continually available and readily adopted. The peril in which the country stood had sharpened the national appetite for sacrifice and convinced the Chancellor that the half-hearted measures of the September Budget of 1940 must be replaced by redeeming the promise[3] of an evolving economic policy and by withholding a major part of the surplus purchasing power through the instrument of taxation.

And yet, ostensibly, the Budget appeared a comparatively simple affair, the product, it would seem, almost of a Philip Snowden redivivus. There was no change in indirect taxation. There was no pursuit of fiscal novelties such as excess income tax or a flat rate war tax on all incomes, both of which the Board of Inland Revenue claimed would be administratively inconvenient. Instead the whole weight of the increases fell on direct taxation with allowances reduced, rates stepped up, four million new taxpayers and the estimated yield swollen by some £250 millions. It is not known how Kingsley Wood converted the Prime Minister and his War Cabinet to a standard rate of ten shillings; but one factor must have been that it was a reasonable *quid pro quo* for the extension of income tax so far down the earnings scale.

If this had been all, even the impact of the heaviest standard rate in British fiscal history would not have saved the Chancellor from further doses of the criticism which he had had to undergo in the previous September. Fortunately it was not, for allied to the tax proposals was a consciously new Budget presentation of the financial facts of life which owed a good deal to Keynes. In the first place the Chancellor explained in simple terms his theory of inflationary

[1] H. 1/7/1941, Cols 1301/1303.   [2] *Financial Policy 1939–1945*, p. 58.
[3] See p. 194.

finance which was based to an extent on *How to Pay for the War*.[1] In the second place he recast his Budget arithmetic by taking the national income first, determining its war potential and then the amount of taxation required, instead of basing taxation simply on what was estimated to be a tolerable burden. This was how he had presented his case to the House by comparing domestic expenditure of £3,700 millions with revenue of £1,637 millions and various savings of £1,600 millions, creating a gap 'of the order of £500 millions'. This had to be closed by additional taxation and savings or the result would be inflation.[2]

In addition the opportunity was taken to make two important modifications to E.P.T. The inclusion of borrowed money in capital[3] was a wise move, for a company stood little chance of financing any expansion of its business from its own profits under E.P.T. conditions, and to allow no return on borrowed capital apart from the interest payable would have checked expansion almost completely, save where Government support was available. The second modification was the provision for preventing avoidance,[4] already discussed. This was drawn in very wide terms, its only weakness being due to the amendment introduced at Committee Stage inserting 'main' before 'purpose'. In practice it was found very difficult to identify the 'main' purpose when a taxpayer could produce a variety of reasons for a transaction open to challenge. The amendment was not surprising: Parliament had always fought shy of wide powers which savoured of government by *Diktat*, but the Board of Inland Revenue was equally reluctant to guarantee immunity from the operation of the avoidance sections in hypothetical cases.

But, of course, the truly novel measure in the 1941 Budget was the Keynesian conception of enforced saving as applied to both income tax and E.P.T.[5] The E.P.T. post-war refund, despite initial doubts whether it would in fact be paid and, if it were, whether it would be hedged with administrative restrictions, was a comparative success; and, since repaid shortly after the end of the war, was not overtaken by inflation. But the post-war credits arising from the taxation at

---

[1] This was the book published in 1940 based on Keynes's *The Times* articles of November 1939.

[2] H. 7/4/1941, Cols 1321/1322.   [3] S. 29, F.A. 1941.   [4] S. 35, F.A. 1941.

[5] The idea was first put forward by the Committee on Financial Risks in 1918 and revived by a group of Manchester economists in 1941 (Hicks, Hicks and Rostas, *The Taxation of War Wealth*).

individuals from 1941/42 to 1945/46, originally intended to be credited to Post Office Savings Bank accounts, and later notified in the form of a certificate, did not become repayable eventually until the holders were fifty-five for women or sixty for men; and the steady fall in the value of money continues to erode their original value despite the compensation of $2\frac{1}{2}$ per cent compound interest from September 1, 1959; moreover they will not all be repaid until the late eighties or even beyond. It may be that the idea was only an interesting experiment; but it was only a truncated version of Keynes's original grand design which embraced family allowances and a capital levy, and which had certainly aroused some Labour opposition.[1]

The 1941 Budget is generally regarded as the watershed in the war Budgets. Kingsley Wood always referred to it as his 'stabilization Budget', and Spens[2] was echoing the thoughts of many Members on both sides of the House when he referred to it as 'the greatest financial revolution we have ever gone through'. This revolution is perhaps not so dramatic viewed in perspective. The recasting of Budget arithmetic to highlight the gap was certainly a valuable innovation even if the calculation was somewhat rough and ready and even if inflation was controlled rather than avoided; the E.P.T. reforms were practical although the avoidance section was sadly watered down; and the enforced savings for both companies and individuals formed a useful immediate palliative for the crippling rates of tax.

But as far as the actual proposals, which became law July 22, 1941, were concerned, they showed not a spectacular break with previous measures but a logical and orderly extension of them. There had already been in 1940 suggestions from Members and hints from the Press[3] that the next section of the public scheduled for direct taxation must be the lowly-paid workers. This policy was dictated in the first place by the need for revenue; it was underlined by the White Paper which clearly showed that the largest increase in income was in the direct wage sector; it tied in therefore with the need to control inflation; and it was made effective by the P.A.Y.E. system (Mark I). In short, the fiscal mechanism for raising revenue and controlling inflation was ready to hand; the real change was the more exact definition of the target.

[1] *The Keynes Plan—its Danger to the Workers*, Labour Research Dept (1940).
[2] H. 22/5/1941, Col. 1660. [3] See p. 180.

Chapter X

The Finance Bill 1942

RETURN TO ORTHODOXY

Time Table

Financial Statement		April 14, 1942
Budget Proposals		
	1st Day	14
	2nd Day	15
	3rd Day	16
Budget Resolutions		
	Reported	22
Finance Bill		
	1st Reading	22
	2nd Reading	May 5
Committee		
	1st Day	13
	2nd Day	14
Report		June 9
3rd Reading		9
Royal Assent		24

Germany's invasion of Russia gave the country a certain respite; and Churchill's first meeting with Roosevelt in August 1941, two months later, together with a comparative success in the Middle East, although with overstretched lines of communication, even generated a cautious optimism, despite the loss of the *Ark Royal* and the *Barham*. These events proved to be a false dawn, a prelude to disaster. The German campaign against Russia was moving fast; in the Far East, Japan was set for war in the Pacific, and the ten weeks or so from December 1941 to mid-February, 1942 saw Pearl Harbour, the sinking of the *Repulse* and the *Prince of Wales*, defeat in Libya and the loss of Singapore. The political discontents aroused had not fully abated by the time of the Budget.

Kingsley Wood had gained confidence, and although he was still capable of plastering his speeches with the most jejune of observations, his capacity for concise and penetrating financial analysis had improved with expert tutelage and constant practice. Now he was quite the master of his material as he rose to present his third Budget on April 14, 1942.[1] He was cheered by a crowded House when he arrived; and, which was more important, he was cheered when he sat down, although there had in fact been little anticipation or excitement in the Press.

As in 1941, he began with a wider and more general survey of the economic front, giving pride of place to the first twelve months' operation of Lease-Lend: £650 millions had been provided, the major part of which was given to this country; in addition Canada had contributed 1,000 millions dollars. At home the menace was still inflation: 'the supply of goods is much curtailed; on the other hand money incomes of the community as a whole are much increased'.

The attack on inflation had been mounted from many angles. Rationing not only decreased consumption but ensured a fairer distribution; this was especially true of clothing, which accounted for nearly one-fifth of personal expenditure. Taxation and savings had siphoned off a good deal of excess purchasing power. Food, rents and travelling had all been controlled, and the price level of the main staple foodstuffs had actually been reduced. All this had cost £125 millions and the requisite sum in 1942 would be higher.

One of the most important results of this all-round stabilization was the holding of a reasonable wages level, especially where automatic increases were linked to the cost-of-living figure; the rise had been 6 per cent only in the year from March 1941 to March 1942. A parallel control had been exercised in the technical financial sphere. Borrowing policy had been at low interest rates and marked by the 'diversity of its appeal' to both large and small investors. This had been rendered possible by the continued use of tap issues for both medium- and long-term borrowing,[2] and mention

[1] H. 14/4/1942, Cols 101/139.   [2] H. 14/4/1942, Col. 106.

should also be made of the Tax Reserve Certificate, a method of paying tax in advance yielding 2½ per cent interest free of tax. All these items the Chancellor put forward as evidence of 'the maintenance of our financial front on safe and sound lines'.

He then dealt briefly with the charges of waste and extravagance which were often the subject of Members' specific complaints, reminding the House that not only was the Select Committee on National Expenditure, chaired by Wardlaw-Milne, in frequent session, but that the spending departments had designated officers especially for supervising economy in revenue and capital outlay. At this stage, too, he wanted to pay a special tribute to his financial advisers, especially Catto, Keynes and Henderson.[1]

It was now time to deal with the main budgetary figures for 1941/42. Expenditure apart from the Vote of Credit, estimated at £707 million, had come out at £691 millions; expenditure out of the Vote of Credit, estimated at £3,500 millions, had come out at £4,085 millions, but as £300 millions had been provided by the United States the excess over estimate was some £285 millions, representing higher expenditure partly at home and partly abroad.

Revenue had exceeded expectations. Inland Revenue duties were £75 millions above estimate, the bulk being an excess of £60 millions from E.P.T./N.D.C. Customs and Excise showed an excess of £127 millions of which purchase tax, representing the mounting purchasing power in consumers' hands, accounted for £28 millions. In sum there was a total of £2,074 millions, £288 millions above the estimate against a total expenditure of £4,776 millions.[2]

What really mattered in the battle against inflation, a theme Kingsley Wood returned to time and again, was the total expenditure requiring domestic funding. He had continued last year's innovation of publishing a White Paper to enable comparisons to be made between the forecast and the out-turn. It did not, however, cover his forecast for the trend of events up to March 1942, when he had estimated a net £1,900 millions[3] would have to be met from other sources. This figure had turned out to be a net £2,000 millions, so that he had achieved a fair level of accuracy.

[1] H. 14/4/1942, Cols 107/108.
[2] That is, the sum of the Vote of Credit expenditure, £4,085 millions, plus the £691 millions outside the Vote.
[3] H. 14/4/1942, Cols 111/112.

The crucial question was to what extent personal savings had helped to deal with the problem. He had said that savings between £200 millions and £300 millions ought to be possible, which had in fact proved to be the case.[1] After taking account of this and various other known sources shown in detail in the White Paper, the gap narrowed to some £500 millions which, he maintained, 'had been largely met out of that part of the depreciation and sinking funds of companies and institutions which they have not been able to employ on repairs and renewals . . . and the running down of private stocks of goods'.[2]

Last year's innovation was the White Paper; this year, instead of appreciating the prospects of the coming year, balancing expenditure against existing revenue, and then interposing the proposed statutory amendments, together with a general commentary, which was the traditional progression, he intended to deal immediately with his suggested miscellaneous amendments in the law.

There were two minor Customs and Excise points: the present margins of preference for sugar and tobacco were to be continued and the purchase tax on dutiable stationery was to be levelled out. The proposals affecting the Inland Revenue were, however, more significant. The £10 allowance for additional travelling expenses granted in 1941 to manual wage earners was extended[3] to cover all Schedule E; the rate of land tax[4] and its redemption terms were to be stabilized; N.D.C., which had been imposed for five years in 1937, was now renewable from year to year subject to the will of Parliament; and for farming the proposal was to lower the dividing line between Schedule B and Schedule D to £100 in place of last year's £300 annual value, and where the annual value was less than £100, the assessment would be on three times the annual value of the actual profits whichever was the less.

He was worried, however, about wage earners. No doubt they appreciated the tax they paid was an essential contribution, but there were complaints about the method of collection.[5] Deductions lagged too far behind the related wages which caused difficulties when these varied. Ideally tax should be deducted from current earnings if the

---

[1] Table D in the Preamble to the new Statistical White Paper shows gross personal savings of £640 millions in 1940 and £909 millions in 1941, an increase of £269 millions in 'genuine personal savings'.

[2] H. 14/4/1942, Col. 113.   [3] S. 26, F.A. 1942.

[4] An archaic tax, perpetual but redeemable.

[5] In 1941/42 5½ million taxpayers paid £125 millions.

problem of end-of-year adjustments could be overcome. Both the T.U.C. and the British Employers Federation agreed with the current basis in theory but no practicable and equitable scheme had yet been formulated. The best he could do was introduce a higher wages minimum below which deductions must not be made and make some concession for seasonal employment.[1] He was also proposing to increase the so-called wife's earned income relief from £45 to £80,[2] and to introduce a simplified return form. With regard to post-war credit, as no assessments had yet been made no documents of entitlement could be issued. The same was true of E.P.T. post-war refunds, which would also accrue by statutory right, but he was careful to point out that this was only one of the many concessions which mitigated the force of the 100 per cent E.P.T.[3]

This led on to the importance of tackling post-war problems 'with foresight and energy'. The release of pent-up demand would create steady employment, but the restoration of exports would be a primary requisite; the country had a vital interest in the prosperity of other nations. Precautions must be taken to prevent an inflationary boom which would be a natural reaction against wartime restrictions.

It was now time to discuss the statistical position for 1942/43. The estimated total expenditure was £5,286 millions, comprising £444 millions for Civil Supply Services, £325 millions for the Fixed Debt Charges, £17 millions for other Consolidated Fund Services and a massive £4,500 millions for the Vote of Credit. This total included provision for any payments in the United States not covered by Lease-Lend and for the generous arrangements made by the Canadian Government.[4] It also included £254 millions for Social Services, the price of stabilizing the cost of living and improved pay for the Fighting Services.

When he came to examine available resources, he put foreign disinvestment and Commonwealth aid at £786 millions, leaving a round £4,500 to find. From extra-budgetary funds, including savings, he reckoned to raise some £2,100 millions; but there was still a solid requirement of £2,400 which must come from taxation.

From Inland Revenue duties he anticipated a grand total of £1,524 millions, the two major sources being £915 millions from income tax and £425 millions from E.P.T./N.D.C., and from Customs and

---

[1] S. 24, F.A. 1942. [2] S. 23, F.A. 1942. [3] H. 14/4/1942, Cols 124/125.
[4] Resulting in fact in a credit of £225 millions.

Excise £645 millions. To those totals should be added £75 millions of miscellaneous revenue, making a gross domestic revenue figure of £2,244 millions against the £2,400 millions needed, or some £150 millions below the target. He had no alternative therefore 'but to look to the taxpayer for further and substantial contributions'.

Before mentioning his proposals he emphasized again the imperative need for stabilization which he underlined by announcing the new scheme for utility clothing subject to price control at all stages and exempt from purchase tax; this was a comparatively expensive concession, a drain of £15 millions in a full year.

Reverting to the £150 millions needed, he was 'quite clear that on this occasion direct taxation cannot be looked to'; it was now nearly £1,000 millions as against £400 millions in the last full financial pre-war year, and the recent widening and deepening of the area of direct taxation was too recent to contemplate any immediate extension. Nor could there be any further taxation of the rich as Table F in the Preamble to the Statistical White Paper showed; these home-truths[1] were not to the liking of the Left and the Chairman had to call interrupters to order.

He had therefore to fall back upon the old faithfuls of Customs and Excise. Twopence a pint on beer should raise £48 millions and 4s 8d on whisky £15 millions. Six shillings a gallon on wine gave a mere £2 millions, but ten shillings a pound on tobacco would yield a massive £90 millions; the forces would have the privilege of pre-Budget rates. Entertainment tax was to be doubled and the purchase tax on luxuries, giving another £24 millions. The total yield currently, less the purchase tax concession on utility clothing, would be £158 millions This, added to the previous gross domestic revenue figure of £2,244 millions, amounted to a final total of £2,402 millions, just exceeding his target, and attaining 53 per cent of the £4,500 millions he was budgeting for. The balance should come from savings, a reasonable assumption in view of the increase in national income from Government expenditure. His proposals, he concluded, after over two-and-a-quarter hours without refreshment, would maintain financial stability and social security.

As Williams[2] pointed out, it used to be the practice on Budget day for the Committee to adjourn after a few complimentary remarks, but now it provided a chance for back-bench Members to express

[1] H. 14/4/1942, Col. 134.   [2] H. 14/4/1942, Cols 156/165.

their views, although the Financial Secretary 'looked a little distressed' when he saw the numbers anxious to speak, of whom eleven managed to catch the Chairman's eye.

Half the speeches were congratulatory and made the acceptable point that the Chancellor had adequately sensed the mood of the country [1] Others put forward tentative suggestions for taxing cider and cyclists, and increasing the rates levied on dogs and on armorial crests.[2] The main target of criticism was the working of P.A.Y.E. and the need for converting it to a current basis,[3] which Kingsley Wood had in fact touched upon.

Tinker and Gallacher, however, were wholly critical in their speeches. The former[4] replied to the bromide that confiscation of all incomes above £2,000 would only produce £30 millions by arguing that a question of equality was involved, not simply one of fiscal yield; he felt that all goods and prices should be Government controlled. The latter[5] took up the Chancellor on his review of the post-war period; there was no sign of foresight and energy now, so he had no faith in a possible display of these virtues at a later date. To say the wealthy were really poor was 'all a fake'; and he resented the fact that there was no allowance for reduced tax on overtime although there was exceptional depreciation for plant and machinery; evidently there was more consideration for machines than men.

The reception from the Press was as varied as the immediate reaction of the House. The popular dailies were on the whole in favour, although the Left and Liberal opinion still felt impelled to express their traditional opposition in principle to indirect taxation. The *Manchester Guardian*[6] took as its theme 'Austerity by Tax', emphasizing the dual purpose of the measures both as a source of revenue and a brake on consumption. The City Page editor referred to 'a compromise Budget', for there were few constructive changes, and despite a slight mitigation of the severity of Schedule E there were no real incentives.

The Times[7] leader, under the heading 'Taxing the Consumer', reached the same conclusions as the *Manchester Guardian*, and both concluded by raising a tentative query as to the basis of future war

---

[1] Cf. Shakespeare, H. 14/4/1942, Cols 152/153.

[2] H. 14/4/1942, Col 154 (Wayland); col. 169 (Tinker).

[3] H. 14/4/1942, Col. 177 (Collindridge).   [4] H. 14/4/1942, Cols 166/159.

[5] H. 14/4/1942, Cols 172/175.   [6] 15/4/1942.   [7] 15/4/1942.

taxation and whether the proposed increases would sterilize enough of the increased spending power. Incidentally, *The Times* misreported the Chancellor as having said that 'farmers should be treated like other traitors' when his actual term was 'traders'; a hasty apology was published on the following day and an inspired fourth leader.

Of the weeklies, the *Spectator*[1] alone was wholly approving. The Budget was realistic in singling out as the essential problem ensuring that the right proportion of national expenditure should go into the war effort; therefore it was correct to use consumption taxes to check inessential spending. The *New Statesman*[2] and *The Economist*[3] were far more critical. The former agreed that the Chancellor had rightly directed his attention to restricting real expenditure but summed the proposals up as being neither bad nor very good: 'It was out of the question to close the gap except by methods which would have so seriously upset the class system that the present Government would be clearly incapable of standing for them.' The latter had anticipated a decrease in surtax, an increase in purchase tax and possibly more deferred pay, and found the proposals guilty of the old sin of under-estimation, of failing to undertake much-needed taxation reforms, and of a lack of imaginative planning for putting finance at the service of production. On the whole, however, there was qualified praise for a commonsense othodoxy.

The speeches throughout the initial two days' debate after the Budget were somewhat subdued. In the first place, there was very little objection to the principles behind the Chancellor's proposals; in the second place, the urgency of discussing such matters as rates of interest, post-war credits and taxation generally was almost misplaced when set against the background of the loss of the *Dorsetshire* and the *Hermes* and of the penetration of the Japanese fleet into the Indian Ocean. Nevertheless, the solemn ritual of Parliament had to be played out; there might even have been some solace to be found in the traditional and familiar procedure.

Pethick-Lawrence[4] was clearly determined to preserve the usual routine as far as possible with a wholly orthodox opening speech. He complained about the way the deduction scheme operated; its faults would be mitigated merely by such proposed concessions as the increase in the allowance for the earnings of married women. With

---

[1] 17/4/1942.　　[2] 18/4/1942.　　[3] 11/4/1942 and 18/4/1942.
[4] H. 15/4/1942, Cols 223/236.

regard to purchase tax, he had agreed reluctantly to its original imposition before income tax had touched the lower ranges of remuneration; now it was a serious burden on the lowly-paid worker despite the new utility scheme for clothing. The increased rates on tobacco and alcohol also imposed further loads on the working- and middle-classes. On the wider issues he felt that equality of sacrifices was not yet being realized; and when the war was over the three most serious problems would be the reorganizing of industry, the removal of vested interests and the securing of workers' participation in management.

Pethick-Lawrence's criticism of the Schedule E deduction scheme touched upon a theme which was to recur constantly during the debate: of the two dozen or so speakers, at least half elaborated on his discussion of the subject and most were equally critical. Two main objections had developed: after a comparatively successful start, the continued growth in the number of wage-earners had delayed the start of the deductions due in January 1942. This had in turn increased the deductions due for the remaining months of the half-year to June 1942, which, in some cases, created certain hardships.[1] To this administrative and transitional difficulty was added a more basic flaw. Since deductions lagged behind the earnings relating to them, there were justifiable protests from workers with seasonal earnings at having to pay large amounts of tax on their summer wages in the lean winter months, which had, said White,[2] almost provoked a taxpayers' strike. As Webbe[3] pointed out, they were 'not grumbling about the tax but the method by which it was assessed and collected'. Wilmot[4] thought there should be a complete reform of the whole conception of collection and suggested a simplified version which amounted to a wages tax of 'a penny or more per shilling per week as earned, deducted at the time of payment'. Other speakers, for example Elliot[5] and Magnay,[6] suggested the setting up of a Committee on the subject.

The Government was well aware of the increasing sense of grievance felt by the increasing number of taxpayers. Before the Budget there had been a campaign of factory visits and an explanatory booklet[7]

[1] Cf. H. 15/4/1942, Cols 236/240 (Spens).   [2] H. 15/4/1942, Cols 267/272.
[3] H. 15/4/1942, Cols 289/295.   [4] H. 15/4/1942, Cols 283/289.
[5] H. 16/4/1942, Cols 380/386.   [6] H. 16/4/1942, Cols 396/399.
[7] *Income Tax Quiz for Wage Earners.*

combined with a simplified return. A formal explanation of the existing arrangements was contained in the White Paper, 'The Taxation of Weekly Wage Earners',[1] which had in effect been paraphrased by the Chancellor in his Budget speech when he stressed the complications of the end-of-year adjustments and the fact that neither the Trade Union Council nor the Employers' Federation had produced an acceptable solution of the problem of deducting taxes on a current earnings basis.[2] Members admitted that the Chancellor had gone a long way in meeting complaints; some, like Schuster,[3] remained unconvinced, but others, Hammersley[4] for example, agreed with the view put forward in the White Paper—he thought that the one month's break suggested by the Chancellor,[5] on which few Members had commented, would enable arrears to be overcome. 'I am convinced,' he concluded, 'that the Chancellor is right in sticking to the existing, though modified, system even if it has to be altered in the light of future experience.'

The second main stream of disapproval was directed against E.P.T. This had always been a favourite target, but the critical emphasis was beginning to shift from complaints about the direct burden of the tax on the insidiousness of its effect on industrial reserves. Spens[6] emphasized that both plant and land were being overworked with inadequate recompense for depreciation. Schuster[7] lent him strong support. 'As regards killing the goose that lays the golden eggs,' he declared, 'the Chancellor knows my views on the methods of excess profits tax. He knows that I do not object to the burden as a sacrifice to be borne by individuals. But what I have asked is that he should have an impartial enquiry into the effect of the present methods of taxation on the financial structure of business in general.' Wilmot[8] took the view that E.P.T. encouraged waste and extravagance: 'We all know that a very large amount of luxury expenditure in restaurants and places of entertainment is coming out of E.P.T.' Hammersley[9] summarized the current fiscal thinking of the Right. 'I do not want to raise a plea for the alteration of the rate . . . but I do say the fixation of the standard might well be reviewed.'

Benson,[10] on the other hand, claimed that to argue E.P.T. would

[1] Cmd. 6348.　　　　[2] See pp. 205/6 and H. 14/4/1942, Cols 117/120.
[3] H. 15/4/1942, Cols 272/283.　　　[4] H. 16/4/1942, Cols 423/429.
[5] H. 14/4/1942, Col. 121.　　　　[6] H. 15/4/1942, Cols 236/240.
[7] H. 15/4/1942, Cols 272/283.　　　[8] H. 15/4/1942, Cols 283/289.
[9] H. 16/4/1942, Cols 423/429.　　　[10] H. 16/4/1942, Cols 417/423.

result in grave industrial difficulties on a large scale was an unfounded exaggeration. Certainly the national balance-sheet value of real assets had increased considerably since 1939. Surprisingly enough, he agreed with Schuster's suggestion for a committee, although not for the same reason: he thought there were hardship cases which individually needed investigation, but the over-all relief of E.P.R. post-war refund mainly helped wealthy firms who did not really need it; for such it was 'a mere bagatelle'.

Apart from these main lines of attack, there was some criticism of the Government's failure to produce a coherent wages policy which had kept alive interest in the idea of an excess wages tax.[1] It was felt, too, that not enough ruthlessness was shown in dealing with both men and management.[2] But the general opinion, despite the vagaries of the current P.A.Y.E. system and E.P.T., which after all were not strictly relevant to the proposals currently at issue, was, as Woodburn[3] put it, 'The Chancellor has found a business-like method of taxing the country and financing the war'.

There was only one real fighting speech, that of Stephen,[4] a member of the I.L.P. He thought the whole Budget was 'fundamentally bad'. It had three aims, to finance the war, to prevent inflation and to see that the rich continued to enjoy their privileges after the war. He could approve the first aim but not all of the methods; with regard to inflation, he compared Kingsley Wood to Canute; and he hoped earnestly the third aim, of the prolonged exploitation of the people, would fail. It was still true that 2 per cent of the population owned all estates over £5,000.[5] The income tax imposed on the workers was unfair in view of the immense increase in capital as represented by loans, property, and industrial assets. To declare, as the Chancellor had, that the rich could pay no more was 'cynical audacity'.

Orthodox Labour, however, as represented by Barnes,[6] was far more co-operative and appreciative. No great division of opinion, he admitted, had developed between the Committee and himself over the Budget. He agreed with the suggestions that further experiments should be carried out to try and make the tax deductions more

[1] Cf. Braithwaite, H. 15/4/1942 Cols 251/256.
[2] Cf. Cobb, H. 16/4/1942, Cols 261/267.
[3] H. 15/4/1942, Cols 240/251.   [4] H. 15/4/1942, Cols 256/261.
[5] This was Professor Clay's figure. He was the economic adviser to the Bank of England.
[6] H. 16/4/1942, Cols 435/442.

equitable; but he did not 'join in the general approval of the Chancellor for raising the whole of his extra revenue from indirect taxation'. If the tax deductions scheme could be worked more fairly, this was the ideal revenue-raising mechanism. The increase in indirect taxation pressed heavily upon some members of the community, and he felt the concessions given to the Forces should be extended to old age pensioners. Purchase tax was also a serious burden, only mitigated by the utility scheme. But he finally 'joined with all those other Members who have expressed their gratification at the strength of our financial system'.

Kingsley Wood[1] had an easy task when he came to wind up. A graceful reference to the country's 'instant and willing response', a convincing claim that P.A.Y.E. complaints had been exaggerated (he had had none, although he represented an industrial constituency), a repetition of the excuse that the T.U.C. and the employers had failed to produce a better scheme than that currently in use—and he was well on the way to his conclusion in which he justified his reliance on indirect taxation by pointing out, in reply to the previous speaker, that pensioners and those on fixed incomes could obtain supplementary benefits and that the general policy of stabilization gave all-round help.

The original report of the Budget Resolutions[2] was quickly disposed of. The main point of principle at issue was the effect of the proposed increases in indirect taxation on what Pethick-Lawrence referred to as the 'poorer section of the population' and the possibility of relieving the burden on them. Silverman[3] was more critical. As the purpose of the Chancellor was the limiting of consumption, 'I should have thought that a Government which had full powers to control production and consumption did not need a financial instrument to do so and that where it had such full powers the tax instrument was an inappropriate one to use'. This was an argument which would recur before the final stage of the Bill was reached.

Kingsley Wood[4] opened the Second Reading with marked confidence—in fact he even repeated the words from his 1941 speech, which Silverman had criticized, that his avowed intention was not taxation for taxation's sake but for restriction's sake.[5] He did not think

[1] H. 16/4/1942, Cols 442/452.   [2] H. 22/4/1942, Cols 640/679.
[3] H. 22/4/1942, Cols 647/649.   [4] H. 5/5/1942, Cols 1236/1245.
[5] H. 7/4/1941, Col. 1328.

it necessary to make any exhaustive review of the general financial position since he felt his policy had been generally accepted. Inflation, however, was not dead: it was still necessary to guard against its possibility and to continue saving.

With these broad observations, he now turned to some points of the Bill on which he wished to comment. With regard to the Customs and Excise proposals, the House would note some minor administrative amendments to Clause 6 affecting entertainments duty and to the charge of liquor licence duty.[1] He had also decided to advance the exemption from purchase tax for utility clothing and footwear so that it would take effect as soon as these goods appeared in the shops.

On the Inland Revenue duties he had a good deal more to say. The criticism of the tax deduction scheme was still rankling, for on Clause 23, which granted the concession to seasonal employees, he quoted at length[2] from a broadcast by the Chairman of the T.U.C. which admitted the difficulties in finding equitable reforms of the system. Passing briefly over two details relating to repairs under Schedule A[3] and stamp duty,[4] he proceeded to Clause 38 which redeemed the Government's promise to convert the post-war refund for E.P.T. into a statutory right.[5] Another equally important development was the proposed simplification of the assessing and collecting machinery[6] which included the appointment by the Board[7] of all collectors in Scotland and Northern Ireland in future.

But the three clauses he spent the most time on were Clauses 32 to 34,[8] which were designed to strengthen the hands of the Inland Revenue in dealing with evasion. The effect of these proposals was to enable assessments to be made without time limit in the case of fraud or wilful default; to provide for the admissibility in evidence in criminal or penalty proceedings when fraud or wilful default was involved, of information supplied by the taxpayer; and to empower the Commissioners of Inland Revenue where necessary to require a trader to deliver to the inspector copies of his accounts and to make his original books available for examination. The section dealing with admissible evidence stemmed from the Board's practice of

---

[1] Clauses 10/15.   [2] H. 5/4/1942, Col. 1240.   [3] Clause 36.
[4] Clause 43.   [5] S. 40, F.A. 1942.   [6] S. 42, F.A. 1942, 10th Schedule.
[7] The City of London General Commissioners still retained the right to appoint their own collectors (but see p. 287). Their appointment in England and Wales was already vested in the Board (S. 37, F.A. 1931).
[8] Ss. 33/35, F.A. 1942.

promising immunity from prosecution when full disclosure had been undertaken by the taxpayer; if in such a case full disclosure was withheld, the result had been successful prosecution. But recently the Court of Criminal Appeal had held that the evidence which consisted of books and documents was inadmissible as evidence since part of a confession.[1] The proposed legislation would make this newly-discovered deficiency good.

The Chancellor concluded with a brief survey of post-war prospects. In many ways the economic problem might be even more intractable than those of the present period, and certainly the mistake ought not to be made, as it was in 1918, of sweeping away controls too rapidly.

As usual with the Second Reading, most of the compulsive speakers in the Budget debates preferred to reserve themselves for the Committee stage. This gave room for the amateurs or those with some particular hobby-horse to deploy their opinions, always provided they could manage to catch the Chairman's eye. The debate began at a rather late hour so that many members had to be disappointed; this accounts for the somewhat uneven balance in the subjects discussed, some being very wide-ranging and some just as specific.

Pethick-Lawrence,[2] however, opened formally enough. He agreed that the proposals had aroused 'no opposition and hardly any grumbling', but he was not convinced that this enormous burden of taxation had been adjusted fairly, particularly as it affected the elderly and the pensioners. He thought also there ought to be some relaxation of the rules of postponement for post-war credits for old people who might not live to enjoy the benefit of them, and there should be further extensions of the utility principle.

As in the debate of the previous month, the criticisms of the deduction scheme and of E.P.T. continued unabated without any visible suggestion for improving the former or much hope of obtaining any concessions in the latter. There were admitted anomalies arising from the operation of the standard principle, and the mitigation of the E.P.T. provisions, as far as businesses dealing in wasting assets were concerned, did not give as much relief as was intended. 'If income tax was the foundation of our financial system,' said White,[3] 'E.P.T. was the crazy paving.' Summers,[4] incidentally, was the first to use the phrase 'Pay as you earn'; he felt the difficulties of

[1] H. 5/4/1942, Col. 1242.
[2] H. 5/4/1942, Cols 1245/1251.
[3] H. 5/4/1942, Cols 1258/1264.
[4] H. 5/4/1942, Cols 1251/1258.

simplification had been exaggerated as did the Inland Revenue Staff Federation.[1]

Further specific complaints ranged from requests to ease the burden of tax on lower incomes,[2] checking wasteful use of manpower and extravagance generally,[3] looking into tax avoidance practised by some charities,[4] to pleas for the surtax payer[5] and the taxing of capital profits.[6] No wonder, when the Financial Secretary intervened not very long before the closure was applied, he paid tribute to the 'varied topics' which had been introduced, although expressing a mild surprise that no one had mentioned the stupendous size of the Budget itself.[7] He agreed the necessity of spreading the burden fairly, but it was posing an impossible dilemma to ask for an easing of direct taxation while expressing a doctrinaire dislike of indirect taxation. With regard to the evasion clauses on which some Members had intended to speak, he could assure the House that there was no need for anxiety as books would not be called for as a general practice. The current period was prolific of suggestions for improving E.P.T. and any proposals both from inside and outside the House would be carefully considered. And finally, with regard to the taxation of wage-earners, like the Chancellor he had had no personal complaints and he reckoned he was 'a pretty good target'.

The Committee stage got off to a good start, Clauses 1 to 9, relating to Customs and Excise duties, being accepted without discussion as part of the Bill. The first brush came with Mrs Tate's[8] attempt to introduce a feminine income tax rate of 6s 8d in the pound. She gained so much support that Crookshank[9] had to take the proposal more seriously than perhaps the original intention warranted, which had been in fact to draw attention to the unequal payments of compensation to men as compared with women in the case of air-raid injuries. This stone-walling set the pattern of the debate: for when Pethick-Lawrence[10] repeated his complaints of the Second Reading that the aged were being neglected, the Chancellor himself replied that there was no need (very unusually for Hansard, in italics)

[1] H. 5/4/1942, Col. 1307 (Price).   [2] H. 5/4/1942, Cols 1271/1276 (Woods).
[3] H. 5/4/1942, Cols 1276/1281 (Lipson).
[4] H. 5/4/1942, Cols 1281/1285 (McEntee).
[5] H. 5/4/1942, Cols 1288/1292 (Savory).
[6] H. 5/4/1942, Cols 1292/1297 (Edwards).   [7] H. 5/4/1942, Cols 1297/1305.
[8] H. 13/5/1942, Cols 1775/1777.   [9] H. 13/5/1942, Cols 1781/1782.
[10] H. 13/5/1942, Cols 1784/1785.

for anyone to suffer hardship since the tax was on the luxuries of alcohol and tobacco, and everyone had benefited from the stabilization of prices and the utility scheme.

Clause 22, the increase in the allowance against a wife's earned income, was next attacked by Savory.[1] £25 was too much to give away in such a cause: it was more than a third of the surtax yield. He felt, too, that the food subsidies of £125 millions and the failure to tax the cheapest cinema seats were both pandering to the old Roman vice of *panem et circenses*, a somewhat strained use of classical erudition in a speech which began with Juvenal and ended with Ovid.

The most prolonged discussion, however, was on Clauses 32 to 34, which dealt with fraud and evasion. Spens[2] said he would not challenge the first two clauses which were concerned with out-and-out fraud, but he confessed he was uneasy about Clause 34 which was not confined to that but dealt with the power to call for books and similar documents where returns had either not been received or were unsatisfactory. This power had never previously been given by the House and he was not clear who should do the inspecting and what should be inspected. Benson[3] was strongly opposed to any alteration. The Inspector of Taxes himself must have the right to scrutinize the records: the General Commissioners would not have the expertise to make the necessary investigation. 'This clause is required,' he concluded, 'not because farmers jot down their transactions in a notebook, but because there are a large number of very clever and unscrupulous people who dodge taxes by keeping two sets of books or possibly by failing to enter important transactions and whose machinations can only be traced by a very careful and expert examination of the whole books of account.'

The Attorney-General[4] agreed it was a fair question to ask why these powers were now necessary when in general the taxing authorities had relied on the honesty of the great bulk of taxpayers and the power of assessing on estimated figures when necessary. The fact was that current procedures had been proved vulnerable, but he would like to emphasize that the right to require production of books was vested in the Commissioners of Inland Revenue, not the local inspector, although it was essential that he should have the

[1] H. 13/5/1942, Cols 1789/1790.   [2] H. 13/5/1942, Cols 1795/1798.
[3] H. 13/5/1942, Cols 1799/1801.   [4] H. 13/5/1942, Cols 1801/1806.

power of examining them. All the three clauses were eventually carried as drafted.

There followed a series of suggestions for new clauses which, although abortive, did indicate trends in current fiscal thinking whether from proposing Members or an opposing official side. For instance, there was a long discussion on the possibility of extending the so-called 'housekeeper'[1] allowance to single taxpayers, from which it emerged that, as expected, not only would it be a 'costly undertaking', but that the whole thinking behind the allowance was to consider it in relation to care of children.[2] The Chancellor himself intervened here to proffer the cold comfort that while he could not extend the scope of the allowance, he had at least not reduced it.

Inevitably the complaints about E.P.T. continued, but they were concerned more with particular cases[3] than general principles and the Chancellor was justified in arguing that the legislation was sufficiently complex without further exceptional provisions. One of the most interesting arguments turned on a claim for sums put to reserve for export schemes. Kingsley Wood[4] admitted the cause was a deserving one, but he could not depart from the traditional defence that on strict income tax principles such a reserve was not allowable since not actually expended and not an ascertained liability; in addition, to give such a concession now would be at the expense of E.P.T. receipts.

The debate ended as it had begun, this time with Benson[5] grumbling again, as he had done half-way through, about the failure of the Government to curb the powers of the Clerks to Commissioners, who, he maintained had been nothing like as helpful as the Chancellor had respresented. Checked by the Chair here, he returned to the charge over the Tenth Schedule which dealt with revised procedures for the assessment and collection of tax. He was especially critical of the retention of the General Commissioners' power to appoint Collectors in the City of London; many of these officials were aged gentlemen simply enjoying lucrative sinecures.[6]

All this clearly rankled, for when the discussion on the Finance

---

[1] The description is non-statutory.   [2] H. 13/5/1942, Cols 1835/1837.
[3] Cf. H. 13/5/1942, Col. 1820 (Crookshank), on home-grown timber.
[4] H. 14/5/1942, Col. 1924.   [5] H. 13/5/1942, Col. 41.
[6] H. 14/5/1942, Col. 1981 pp. 221 and 287.

Bill as amended shaded without pause into the Third Reading, Benson was scheduled to deliver a general tribute to the Chancellor. He said[1] he could quite sincerely praise the proposed measures, apart of course from the undue consideration given to the Clerks to Commissioners. With that parting shot, he was succeeded by Pethick-Lawrence[2] returning to his basic theme of the flaws in the deduction scheme. With that, he said, 'I take my farewell of a Bill of which I do not think anybody is particularly enamoured.' Schuster[3] and Brooke[4] both affirmed their belief that the contemporary structure of taxation could do grave harm to industry and that a Committee should sit on this and allied matters.

Kingsley Wood[5] brought the proceedings to an end in his customary quiet and decorous manner. He thanked the House for its co-operation in getting the Bill through its allotted time-table. Speaking generally, there was still more scope for reducing civil expenditure and increasing savings, and referring specifically to the two main sources of complaint he hoped that the deduction scheme, with its current amendments, would now work more smoothly; with regard to E.P.T., he had to agree it provided 'no cushion against rough edges', although from his experience real inequities were few. He could promise the palliative, in each case, that Post-war Credit Certificates would be issued later in the year. Finally, to return to generalities he had tried to produce practical solutions for practical difficulties; a formal committee was not the answer in wartime, but he would undertake to keep a close watch on criticisms.

This had been the fifth war Budget and quite clearly a natural corollary of the fourth. There is a tendency to dismiss the later war Budgets briefly as making little contribution towards the progress of fiscal policy or principles, for example, Sayers considers they 'did little more than consolidate the ground and polish the rough edges'.[6] This opinion has some justification if the Budgets are considered simply and solely as war Budgets; but they must also be looked at in the context of general budgetary development.

The struggle against inflation had to be won by the restriction of consumption. The method adopted in 1941 for achieving this had

---

[1] H. 9/6/1942, Col. 977.   [2] H. 9/6/1942, Col. 878.
[3] H. 9/6/1942, Cols 985/987.   [4] H. 9/6/1942, Cols 998/1001.
[5] H. 9/6/1942, Cols 1001/1010.
[6] Sayers, *Financial Policy 1939–1945*, p. 94.

been increases in direct taxation. Now, as the Chancellor said, it was the turn of indirect taxation. As a principle, this was generally accepted, apart from the almost routine complaints from the traditional defenders of the lowly-paid and the pensioners who, in the last analysis, were not being taxed on necessaries. A second reason for falling back on Customs and Excise which was not widely debated was the solid fact that revenue from this source had been steadily declining and it would have been necessary to restore the balance, at least to some extent. Thirdly, a motive implied rather than expressed, taxing the consumer was a policy which ensured that exemption from income tax was no talisman against suffering the increased rates on alcohol and tobacco—only complete abstinence could guarantee that.

But the results of this general acceptance of Kingsley Wood's basic premise that direct taxation could not be looked to this year and that indirect would have to bear the brunt meant that Members had more time to devote to ancillary matters once having paid suitable tribute to the Chancellor's official principle. In fact far more Parliamentary time was spent on the problems arising from E.P.T. and the Schedule E tax deduction arrangements than on the actual provisions of the Finance Bill.

The main complaint against E.P.T., although not always openly made, was its rate, and it should be noted at this time that the promised post-war refund embodied in the 1942 Finance Act did not at first remove the extreme scepticism with which the proposals had been greeted. This factor and the examples of hard cases quoted were the two main reasons why criticisms were often pressed to a division; the anomalies and inequities would not have been felt so hardly had the rate of duty been lower.

One of the difficulties arose from the fact that the profit for the purpose of taxation is not the same as the ordinary commercial profit. Certain items which a company would regard as revenue expenditure to be met out of profits over a number of years are not admissible deductions in computing profits assessable to tax. The commercial lobby in the House, supported by the accountancy profession, instanced such matters as the amortization of wasting assets, discrepancies between rates of depreciation allowed by the Revenue and the commercial rates, losses on scrappings not re-placed and contributions under the 1941 War Damage Act. The official explanations were always reasonable, but the economic effect of these discrepancies still remained in the shape of lower liquid resources.

The charges levelled against the Schedule E deduction scheme were purely administrative. The plain fact was that to exact deductions from wages in a succeeding half-year based on the wages received in the previous half-year could and did produce hardship, but so far all attempts to create a system whereby current tax could be deducted from current wages had failed.[1] This was a serious matter since a weekly wage-earner naturally budgeted on a weekly basis and would therefore prefer to pay approximately the right amount of tax according to the size of his weekly pay packet. The only consolation was that, as with E.P.T., the Chancellor had promised to keep its incidence under constant review, although he had refused to consider the appointment of a Committee.[2]

The controversies surrounding E.P.T. and the embryonic P.A.Y.E. schemes were essentially forwardlooking. But the Budget was also notable for a start on removing some of the archaic machinery which was retarding the efficient operating of the taxing Acts. But the process needed both tact and circumspection. The Chancellor had been careful to see that his reforms did not encroach on the privileges of the City of London, and "Ware bureaucracy' could still be a rallying-cry, as the debate on the merely marginal extension to the inspector's powers in fraud, or suspected fraud cases, showed. It was in fact the first Budget since 1935 which proposed no specific anti-avoidance legislation.

But the simplest explanation of the principle underlying the Budget of 1942 was buried in *An Analysis of the Sources of War Finance*[3] which revealed that 85 per cent of the national income belonged to taxpayers with incomes of £500 or less. If the Chancellor was to accomplish his dual purpose of restricting consumption and

[1] There was an interesting sidelight on the attempts to revise the Schedule E deduction scheme. The Association of Inspectors of Taxes and the Inland Revenue Staff Federation submitted their ideas on a revised system to the Chancellor and the Board of Inland Revenue. This was referred to by Sir Peter Bennett in the House on the June 9, 1942, and the Chancellor in his winding-up speech on the same day was somewhat embarrassed by the attempt of the Revenue staff to form a pressure group. Certainly the White Paper on the taxation of weekly wage-earners (Cmd. 6348) was largely a deliberate rejection of the various procedures which had been suggested.

[2] See p. 298.   [3] Cmd. 6347.

increasing revenue he had no option but to use the weapon of indirect taxation as the only way of reaching the vast majority of the people, short of an impossibly drastic reaching down of direct taxation.

Chapter XI

The Finance Bill 1943

£16 MILLIONS A DAY

Time Table

Financial Statement	April 12, 1943
Budget Proposals	
1st Day	12
2nd Day	13
3rd Day	14
Budget Resolutions	
Reported	21
Finance Bill	
1st Reading	21
2nd Reading	May 18
Committee	
1st Day	June 2
2nd Day	3
Recommittal	29
Report	29
3rd Reading	July 7
Royal Assent	22

The twelve months from April 1942 saw the beginning of co-operation, however uneasy at times, between Great Britain, the United States and Soviet Russia, and in retrospect the beginning of the final stages of the war. But there was till a long way to go: convoy losses did not begin to diminish until the early part of 1943; the bombing campaign did more good to civilian morale than harm to German output. On the credit side, success in North Africa had given the public new hope and a new hero; discussions on a second front were becoming more realistic; and inevitably, as the immense build-up of men and materials accelerated, leadership of the crusade against Fascism both in the West and East moved away from Great Britain to the United States.

Perhaps it was this realization that the country must perforce play a secondary role to her more powerful partner which accounted for the thinness of the House which greeted the Chancellor on the afternoon of the April 12, 1943, when he rose to present his fourth war Budget.[1] Alternatively, perhaps it was because Members felt, correctly as it turned out, that the proposals could hold few surprises. Or perhaps it was for the more mundane reason that Kingsley Wood had announced that he would be speaking for just over two hours; and as the more interesting details are usually in the latter part of a Budget speech, Members might not miss a great deal by coming in towards its end, as in fact many did. Churchill, however, set a good example, being in his place at the start and showing a minimum degree of restlessness except when the change in tobacco duty was proposed.

He began by dealing immediately with the external costs of the war. These were normally met by the profits of exports, and this in fact was how the war had been financed for its past two years. Exports had now fallen to one-quarter of their pre-war level, but Lease-Lend had taken their place, and the major part of supplies received under those terms was now munitions rather than food.

He must emphasize that this was not a one-way traffic. £170 millions of war materials had been sent to Russia, convoyed in conditions which were not measurable in cash. China was being helped in a similar fashion. But the largest proportion of aid was to the United States: already, for example, £150 millions had been spent on buildings for American forces in this country. In fact 'large though the help from the United States is, it is no greater than the help we ourselves are affording to all our Allies without charge',[2] quite apart from paying the costs of war in the Middle and Far East; 'we are borrowing between £400 millions and £500 millions from the countries concerned; no one but ourselves plays any part in

[1] H. 12/4/1943, Cols 936/971.   [2] H. 12/4/1943, Col. 940.

shouldering this debt'.[1] This was why he felt he had to emphasize to the Committee the problem of the post-war balance of payments.

On the domestic front the outstanding point again must be the growing cost of the war, the corresponding increases in both the sums raised in taxation towards it and the amounts borrowed to balance. To illustrate, the war had cost £13,000 millions to date, the total of all expenditure being £15,600 millions. But even so the amount expended on social services had risen from £160 millions in 1938 to a present £219 millions. The most significant figure, however, was the daily cost of the war, which had trebled from £5 millions at the time of his first Budget[2] to £15 millions at the present time. To anticipate any possible queries, he could assure the Committee that a careful check was being kept on any possible extravagance.

To meet this vast expenditure, war taxation had garnered this year the unprecedented sum of £2,483 millions including income tax for the first time in excess of £1,000 millions. Current domestic revenue had met 44 per cent[3] of all expenditure since 1939, a far better record than in the 1914–18 war. A sensible balance had been achieved between direct and indirect taxation: 83 per cent of the latter consisted of what he was pleased to all 'optional forms of expenditure', that is liquor, tobacco and entertainment. He thought the current deduction scheme was working well, factory visits by revenue officials had proved helpful, and he had still got the possibility of a true pay as you earn plan in mind.

War borrowing now totalled £8,667 millions over the period of hostilities, at an astonishingly low rate of interest. This was due partly to the system of controls which had reserved the capital market primarily for war purposes and partly to the variety of sources tapped. Details of private savings[4] totalled nearly £5,000 millions or 55 per cent of the total borrowings.

The Chancellor then gave his own comments on the statistical White Paper, which showed in effect how the large increase in personal incomes had been disposed of.[5] The rise in savings was noted, but equally significant was the rise in expenditure which should

---

[1] H. 12/4/1943, Col. 942.   [2] July 23, 1940.
[3] This percentage was 36 in 1940, rising to 46 currently.
[4] H. 12/4/1943, Col. 947.   [5] H. 12/4/1943, Col. 948.

H

be curtailed. He was in fact considering the publication of 'a national balance sheet', although he could hardly be expected to do this in wartime, but preparatory work could be done in readiness for peace. With regard to post-war financial policy in general, he had already referred to cheap interest rates; he proposed to retain these after the war. Similarly it would be necessary to continue the checks on inflation and to keep up the level of saving.

The current danger of inflation had been held at bay at some cost[1] but it had been possible to peg the price-level at less than 30 per cent above the pre-war level,[2] apart of course from non-necessaries— it was not a bad thing that they should rise. Stabilization was also intended to secure an adequate supply of essential articles to all members of the community. But it must be coupled with a wages policy; there was danger inherent in a rise in wages greater than the rise in the cost of living. Restraint in this sector was an essential pre-requisite for industrial peace and progress. If he could summarize at this stage, half-way through his speech, the Chancellor claimed he had created sound economic conditions for war production; he proposed the continuance of the measures which had combated inflation; and in his present policies he was ever mindful of post-war developments.

Kingsley Wood now turned to taxation matters of general interest since he proposed to review 1942 and 1943 together in a later part of his speech. The first three concessions he announced sprang from humanitarian considerations. He proposed to exempt all utility cloth from purchase tax; and on the Inland Revenue side, he proposed, a point strongly pressed in 1942, to widen the scope of the housekeeper allowance to any taxpayer entitled to child allowance who employed or maintained a resident housekeeper.[3] This would cost £2 millions. He also proposed to increase the dependent relative allowance to £50[4] but so that if the relative had an income of £30 or more the allowance should be adjusted to such a way that the total of income and allowance together would mount to £80 This would cost £7 millions.

The incidence of taxation on industry had been the subject of a series of discussions at which representatives of the principal com-

---

[1] £180 millions.
[2] In World War I prices rose to nearly 100 per cent above pre-war.
[3] S.15, F.A. 1943.   [4] S. 16, F.A. 1943.

mercial and industrial bodies and of the accountancy profession had consulted with the Board of Inland Revenue.[1] Considerable progress had been made and the Chancellor was able to give an assurance that, amongst other matters, there would be an allowance for E.P.T. for repairs deferred until after the end of the war, for costs in connection with the lay-out of factories including the restoration of dispersed units and for scrapping as well as loss of value in the case of plant. An allowance for the fall in value of stock[2] was under consideration, as were other general points. But he could say here and now that he was prepared to extend the relief to concerns operating wasting assets[3] to those which dealt with sand and gravel.

It was now time to review the past year. He had estimated that £4,500 millions would require domestic finance: £2,400 millions should come from revenue so that he would require to borrow £2,100 millions. In the event the Vote of Credit expenditure was £4,840 millions or £340 millions over the estimate. The reason for this was partly war damage payments and partly the growing tempo of war operations and aid to allies: 'The Committee will, I believe, regard the increase as satisfactory rather than otherwise.'

Fortunately, both Inland Revenue and Customs and Excise duties had proved remarkably buoyant. The former had produced an excess of £47 millions composed of a surplus of £94 millions of income tax but a deficiency of £47 millions on E.P.T., probably the effect of prepayments through tax reserve certificates. The latter had turned in a 'handsome surplus' of £80 millions, including tobacco £30 millions, beer £14 millions and purchase tax £30 millions. In total there was an excess of nearly £200 millions. Against this revenue of nearly £2,600 millions, that is the estimate of £2,400 millions plus the surplus of £200 millions, domestic finance required some £4,800 millions. The balance, say £2,200 millions, would be met by domestic borrowing; it was clear from the figures in Table A of the White Paper that this was a reasonable proposition although £200 million above the 1941 figure.

It was in the context of these figures that the Chancellor turned to the prospects for 1943, his calculations in the first place being designed to work down to 'the residue'. Gross expenditure of £5,756

[1] H. 12/4/1943, Col. 959.   [2] As for E.P.D. in World War I.
[3] S. 31, F.A. 1943.

millions comprised Fixed Debt Charge £375 millions, an increase of £64 millions owing to mounting interest and management charges; Consolidated Fund Services which were held at £17 millions; the total of Civil Votes which was increased by £20 millions to £464 millions to cover the cost of supplementary pensions; and Vote of Credit expenditure which, at £4,900 millions, would have been larger but for the help of the Canadian Government.

The source of financing this vast sum were overseas disinvestment £600 millions, £425 millions from extra-budgetary funds, £350 millions from undistributed profits and £1,300 millions from private saving. These items totalled £2,675 millions, leaving a balance of say £3,080 millions of the £5,756 millions needed originally. Taxation he put at £2,900 millions, leaving a 'residue' of £180 millions, a figure satisfactorily on the same scale as that of 1941 and 1942.

How was he to raise this £2,900 millions? From Inland Revenue he expected £1,873 millions, budgeting for £168 millions more from income tax through increased wages and £122 millions more from E.P.T. from increased war production. Customs and Excise would be down somewhat, partly through the utility scheme; he put the figure at £873 millions. Miscellaneous receipts, including the G.P.O., would yield £59 millions. The total was £2,805 millions. Where was he to find the missing £100 millions?

The House was not kept waiting long. The answer was again indirect taxation and, as anticipated, on 'drinks, smokes and shows'. Beer would cost 1d a pint more, whisky 2s 4d a bottle more; tobacco would be up 5d an ounce, cigarettes 2d a packet. These increases alone would yield close on £100 millions including an equitable rise in wines.[1] From entertainment duty he required £10 millions: the precise details would be settled in consultation with the entertainment industry. The estimated total revenue would top the £2,900 millions required by a margin of nearly £10 millions, and this figure was a triumphant 56 per cent of the total of £5,156 millions[2] needing domestic finance as opposed to 48 per cent in 1941 and 52 per cent in 1942.

Greenwood[3] opened the post-Budget comments. In a brief speech

---

[1] The yield on this would be only £1 million.
[2] That is, £5,756 millions less overseas disinvestment of £600 millions.
[3] H. 12/4/1943, Cols 983/986.

he disclaimed a good deal of the Chancellor's elaborate calculations: 'Today goods and services matter more than anything else.' In general, however, he admitted that it was difficult to take any serious objections to what the Chancellor called 'optional expenditure', although he professed to finding a certain class distinction in the raising of £33 millions from beer, and only £10 millions from wines and spirits.

The 'minnows of finance', as Muff[1] called them, were now given their chance, although not all would have subscribed to the description. For instance, there was an excellent summary by Holmes.[2] In four Budgets, he concluded, the Chancellor had pursued a definite policy: he had borrowed half the domestic revenue needed and raised half; he had 'put the burdens on the broadest backs'; he had taxed optional article sat the heaviest rates; and he had kept the cost of living down. Thomas's[3] somewhat abstruse analysis went further: he argued the general proposition that as taxation must descend to the lower ranges of income it could only do so through the medium of indirect taxation.

Gallacher[4] saw the proposition too and attacked it with his usual naïve extremism. Beer and tobacco were needed by the workers as compensation for their mechanical toil in wretched conditions: 'And until every penny is taken from those who can pay it and still have sufficient left over to live on, the Chancellor has no right to levy taxes on the poor.' Tinker[5] also protested against the increases in indirect taxes and thought that there should be compensating legislation to cover the hardship caused to pensioners particularly. In fact a number of comments in the debate, for instance those of Adams,[6] reflected the feeling that social security was now becoming a matter almost of first priority and were doubtless a direct result of the Beveridge Report of the previous February.

Press comment on the basic principle of the Budget, that is the raising of some £100 millions from increases in indirect taxation, was almost universally favourable. The *Manchester Guardian*[7] summed it up as very much the mixture as before, but a stiffer dose. It found the Chancellor's claim to have kept down the cost of living

[1] H. 12/4/1943, Col. 1024.
[2] H. 12/4/1943, Cols 998/1002.
[3] H. 12/4/1943, Cols 1013/1020.
[4] H. 12/4/1943, Cols 993/998.
[5] H. 12/4/1943, Cols 109/1013.
[6] H. 12/4/1943, Cols 1005/1009.
[7] 13/4/1943. Leader.

fully justified and gained encouragement from definite indications that he was looking towards the future. *The Times*[1] also approved of taxing the consumer, and praised the Chancellor for not having listened to 'the blandishments of those who would have had him leave taxation where it was'. The only surprise was the comparative smallness of the gap—it had been estimated as being of the order of some £200 to £300 millions. This may have accounted in part for the generally good reception of the proposals; once their scale was known, tobacco and brewery shares were firmer, as were equities on the news of the terminal loss suggestions and discussions.

The weekly journals, which took their tone to a certain extent from the later course of the debate, were equally complimentary. The *Spectator*[2] called it a 'total war Budget': and although there were no surprises, there were equally no complaints. The whole attitude of the Government and the public to budgetary policy was in marked contrast to that in World War I. *The Economist*[3] labelled it the largest and least controversial of all the war Budgets to date and evidence of the massive achievement of British war finance.

It was quite clear from the reaction of the Lobbies and the Press that the measures proposed and the motives behind them had secured a general acceptance and a general welcome. The effect of this on the tenor of the debates was inevitably to make them wider-ranging and sometimes almost speculative, subject to the Speaker's tolerance. Pethick-Lawrence's opening speech was a good example of this, on the first of the two days' customary discussion.

He[4] began by emphasizing a point which he felt was often overlooked, that 'our ingoings from Lease-Lend were no greater than our contributions to our allies'. He wondered, however, whether the Chancellor had underestimated global expenditure, and whether his £100 millions increase was enough, it had been £750 millions in 1942. But whatever the question, he must give qualified approval to the Chancellor's decision to derive the whole of this increase from indirect taxation, even though it was for the second year in succession. 'Not guilty,' was his verdict, 'but don't do it again.' He fully approved, however, his courage in making the concessions on income tax allowances and on converting purchase tax effectively to a selective tax on unnecessary expenditure, while producing an

[1] 13/4/1943, Leader.   [2] 17/4/1943.   [3] 17/4/1943.
[4] H. 13/4/1943, Cols 1082/1093.

over-all addition to the tax burden. Finally he praised the White Paper which had an important bearing on the problems of post-war economy. There should be no financial obstacle to full employment and technical efficiency would increase productivity. 'A kingdom of well-being,' he concluded, 'is within our grasp.'

This speech covered most of the points which were to arise over the next two days, especially the one point of criticism that the deduction scheme for Schedule E needed amendment. The United States had, it was claimed, a 'Pay as You Go' system: it should be possible for this country to produce something similar. Other speakers took up the same theme. Bennett[1] claimed that the whole system should be simplified. Henderson[2] and Jewson,[3] one speaking immediately after the other, both stressed the need for equating the deductions with current earnings; and Kirkwood[4] gave a practical example of how the present system adversely affected shipbuilders who had tax on summer rates and hours deducted from winter earnings which were conditioned by weather and the blackout.

Pethick-Lawrence, however, had not mentioned E.P.T., which was the King Charles' head of the Right just as 'the working man's income tax' was that of the Left. The complaints were more general than specific. White[5] thought that insufficient attention was being paid to the indirect and long-term effects of E.P.T. Schuster[6] followed this up by suggesting that there should be an enquiry into the whole effect of the taxation system on the national economy. Jewson[7] repeated the complaints of the incidence of E.P.T. on new businesses with a meagre standard, and Gibson[8] reported that 'businessmen on the whole throughout the country at the present time do not regard those credits of 20 per cent (the E.P.T. post-war refunds) as being real but rather mythical'.

The complaints against the deduction scheme and E.P.T. were in some ways a carry-over from 1942, and did not add anything to the arguments deployed then, apart from the reinforcement of a year's further experience. The agitation in favour of 'the pensioner's pipe' was also a revival of the 1942 campaign; as Gridley,[9] amongst others, argued, tobacco taxation, at this intensity, was clearly in-

[1] H. 13/4/1943, Cols 1120/1123. [2] H. 13/4/1943, Cols 1144/1148.
[3] H. 13/4/1943, Cols 1145/1151. [4] H. 13/4/1943, Cols 1114/1120.
[5] H. 13/4/1943, Cols 1107/1114. [6] H. 13/4/1943, Cols 1129/1133.
[7] H. 13/4/1943, Cols 1148/1151 (see also Bennett, Cols 1120/1123).
[8] H. 13/4/1943, Cols 1155/1160. [9] H. 13/4/1943, Cols 1133/1137.

equitable in the way it penalized the mid-income groups and especially the pensioners.

Pethick-Lawrence had ended his speech with a series of references
to the post-war world, and although these references seem strangely
premature they triggered off further speculation during the first
day. Loftus[1] thought the country should not be too optimistic about
a high standard of living after the war: if Europe was impoverished
the victors would have to make sacrifices to help the European standard of living. Bennett[2] argued that unemployment had been ban-
ished because there was virtually only one customer—'we are living
in an Eldorado'. But when the war ended the Government would no
longer be content to play the fairy godmother. Hammersley[3]
drew Committee's attention to the plight of concentrated companies
who were losing both trade and technical progress; a melancholy
instance of this was the Lancashire cotton trade.

When Assheton, the new Financial Secretary to the Treasury,
rose to reply, he had very few specific points to which a considered
reply was needed. Ignoring the suggestions for a capital gains
tax[4] and for a levy directed against teetotallers and non-smokers
(although it was not clear how this would operate),[5] his first response
referred to the weight of direct taxation which was still 59 per cent
against 41 per cent indirect, despite the current increases. He was
still carefully considering the deduction scheme, and E.P.T. was also
under constant review. He thought the old-age pensioners were taken
care of by supplementary pensions at a cost of £43 millions and the
stabilization of the cost of living. He could not overstress the importance of saving, and if Sir Patrick Hannon wished to quote
against him Polonius's 'Neither a borrower nor a lender be', he
would beg to retort that Polonius was a Lord Chamberlain not a
Chancellor of the Exchequer.

The second day's debate suffered to an extent by not having so
definitive an opening as the first day's: in fact it opened with comments by Crookshank in an unfamiliar role[6] as Postmaster-General
explaining the changes in Post Office charges which were meant to

[1] H. 13/4/1943, Cols 1099/1103.   [2] H. 13/4/1943, Cols 1120/1123.
[3] H. 13/4/1943, Cols 1163/1165.
[4] H. 13/4/1943, Cols 1137/1144 (Woodburn).
[5] H. 13/4/1943, Cols 1160/1163 (Green).
[6] He had of course been Financial Secretary to the Treasury for the past three
years.

save manpower in the service. On the other hand there were four speeches, each very different in content and delivery, which would have graced any debate.

Complaints from the Right were mainly on the incidence of E.P.T.; Albery,[1] for instance, quite correctly pointed out that the effect of the tax was to penalize the small thriving company as against the long-established concern with a large capital and a moderate increase in turnover only. But surtax on private limited companies[2] was raised as a theoretical issue now that such companies were beginning to accumulate cash reserves[3] in view of the restrictions on capital expenditure. And, possibly one of the most important issues for industry, Edwards[4] put in a strong plea for what he called 'an adequate allowance for replenishing plant'.[5]

The Left was mainly concerned, as it had been on the previous day, with the plight of the pensioner and, to a lesser extent, with the deduction scheme. There was little new to be said on the former theme and one speaker, Tom Brown,[6] in arguing that 'this House, through the medium of the Treasury, conceded 2s 6d a week extra in supplementary pensions in 1940, yet the two Budgets we have had since have taken away that amount', was pulled up by the Deputy Chairman for straying too far from the subject of the debate.[7] There was nothing new said by the two speakers[8] on the Schedule E deduction scheme, but the mounting weight of these criticisms was causing the utmost uneasiness to the Chancellor and his official, and unofficial, advisers. Something would have to be done.

These somewhat run-of-the-mill comments were soon enlivened by a speech from Stokes.[9] He began quietly enough by stressing the importance of revising the deduction scheme, and on the proposals themselves he commented 'that a Budget so universally commended must be bad', its only virtue being that it did make the working man realize who ultimately paid the taxes. This at best

---

[1] H. 14/4/1943, Cols 1258/1264.   [2] In fact this power was rarely used.
[3] H. 14/4/1943, Cols 1251/1256 (Higgs).
[4] H. 14/4/1943, Cols 1310/1316.
[5] Increased rates of wear and tear had been constantly urged in Parliament from the time they were first introduced in 1878 (see the various references in B. E. V. Sabine, *A History of Income Tax*. Loftus had also raised the issue, H. 13/4/1943, Cols 1099/1103.
[6] H. 14/4/1943, Cols 1264/1275.   [7] H. 14/4/1943, Col. 1267.
[8] H. 14/4/1943, Cols 1278/1280 (Guest) and Cols 1293/1297 (Ritson).
[9] H. 14/4/1943, Cols 1280/1291.

somewhat negative virtue was completely outweighed by the failure
to consider old-age pensioners, the unnecessary concessions to firms
concerned with wasting assets, the failure to curb the joint-stock
banks' profits out of interest, and the lack of a tax on site values.

His flamboyant phraseology and reckless enthusiasm were followed by two contributions in quieter vein from Wilmot and Wardlaw-Milne. The former[1] concerned himself mainly with income tax.
He appreciated the very real concessions which had been made over
dependent relative and housekeeper allowances, but there were still
hard cases which had not been touched. He then passed to the
deduction scheme, the anomalies of which he stressed by examples
more effectively than any other speaker. If Canada[2] and the United
States had solved the problem of current tax from current wages,
this country should be able to do the same.

Wardlaw-Milne[3] followed at once. He was equally critical of
the deduction scheme and wished to associate himself completely
with the previous speaker's remarks. He thought the Chancellor's
general policy, the heavy taxation of unnecessary luxuries, was
obviously sound, but he was emphatic on the point that more consideration must be given to industry if after the war there was to
be increased production and increased prosperity.

Hogg[4] provided a thoughtful postscript to the trends of the two
days' discussion, or, as he put it, his own 'modest violets' to the
Chancellor's bouquets 'sufficient to satisfy a prima donna'. The
country had reached a transitional stage in Budget history: the purpose of taxation was altering; it was now becoming an instrument
of national policy for the redistribution of the national income; and
conceptions of national expenditure were changing as the poor bore
a heavier burden of taxation. Speeches such as that of Kirkwood[5]
'were monuments of a gallant and glorious past. He goes on making
the same old speeches as if the rich and powerful remained unassailed
in their original stronghold. The revolution is taking place and we
cannot stop it.'

Grenfell,[6] in his lead-in to the Chancellor's summary, was especially concerned with the dangers of economic and fiscal dislocation

---

[1] H. 14/4/1943, Cols 1300/1306.   [2] *The Times* 16/3/1943.
[3] H. 14/4/1943, Cols 1306/1310.   [4] H. 14/4/1943, Cols 1320/1324.
[5] H. 13/4/1943, Cols 1114/1120 and p. 231.
[6] H. 14/4/1943, Cols 1324/1334.

after the war: any abnormalities, especially a rise in unemployment, would, he maintained, lead straight to a budgetary crisis. The Chancellor,[1] however, was undismayed. He began with a reply to Pethick-Lawrence's charge of under-budgeting, pointing out that Canada's contribution and war damage payments had been excluded.[2] He then gave a frank explanation of why he felt he had been bound to turn to indirect taxation again. In the highest ranges the State only left the taxpayer with 6d out of every 20s 0d earned. Direct taxation started as low as £2 6s. 0d. per week for the single man. The yield from a confiscatory rate of tax on all incomes over £2,000 would only be £30 millions, so that the only way to raise the £100 millions required would have been to pare allowances down even more finely. To give homely illustrations, the increases in indirect taxation could be avoided by anyone on whom they pressed hard, by cutting out two cigarettes a day from a consumption of fifteen, one pipeful in six, and half a pint of beer weekly from an intake of one daily. Apart from these official statistics, he could only repeat that he had helped the old by supplementary pensions and the curb on cost of living. He could assure Committee that he was still considering deduction schemes as a matter of priority and that the incidence of E.P.T. was under equally close surveillance. But he could give a categoric assurance that the Government regarded post-war refund as a definite commitment.

When the Resolutions were reported on the 21st April there was the inevitable and calculable opposition to those dealing with indirect taxation, from Tinker[3] who opposed the increase on the workers' pint, to Harvey[4] who thought that the rise in entertainment tax would penalize the amateur actor 'exercising some of the finest faculties of their minds'. The Chancellor waited until the final comments and replied almost playfully to Granville's speech since he had had 'a regular field day' covering the whole range of indirect taxation in his criticisms, but 'if I followed his advice he would leave me very little out of my Budget'. There was a case for not increasing the rates on any commodity which a Member cared to mention, but, as with entertainment tax, 'it is not of a very large order when you divide it up among the various undertakings'.

The Second Reading represents the middle stage of any Budget

[1] H. 14/5/1943, Cols 1334/1343.   [2] H. 14/5/1943, Cols 1335/1336.
[3] H. 21/5/1943, Col. 1740.   [4] H. 21/5/1943, Col. 1744.

discussions and is traditionally when the Speaker allows the widest latitude in debate. He suggested on this occasion[1] that there should be 'a general discussion for the next two hours or so . . . and then Hon. Members wishing to speak (on any of the Amendments) might be able to do so'.

The Chancellor[2] opened by claiming there had been general acceptance of his indirect taxation proposals which, he reminded the House, 'were part and parcel of the wider policy of the Government on the economic problems raised by the war', one of the most important of which was to keep the post-war service of the National Debt as low as possible. The omens were favourable since, although the Debt was up nearly 100 per cent, service stood at a 75 per cent increase only. He continued with comments on the various outstanding clauses and ended with some detailed observations on two post-war problems, the taxation of profits ploughed back and the task of capital re-equipment.

Pethick-Lawrence,[3] representing Labour opinion, drew a moral from rationing. This had produced an equitable distribution of necessaries in which coupons were almost as important as cash. But would that still hold good after the war? Admittedly the balance between direct and indirect taxation had been maintained but it must always be remembered that the latter was regressive. Any further taxation required must be direct; possibly the surtax range could be extended downwards; and reduction of indirect taxation must be given first priority after the war. Davies,[4] for the Liberals, took as his theme the subtle revolution which had transformed the Budget speech from an executive instrument to a summary of the national position; it could after the war be used to control booms and slumps.

The House had now managed to escape from complaints about the deduction scheme which had been haunting its debates up to April 21st,[5] and its attention was diverted to two very different themes. The first was industry after the war. Benson,[6] considering the melancholy history of industrial under-investment between the wars, was in favour of a differential tax treatment for reserves

[1] H. 18/5/1943, Cols 310/311.   [2] H. 18/5/1943, Cols 970/977.
[3] H. 18/5/1943, Cols 977/982.   [4] H. 18/5/1943, Cols 982/987.
[5] Cf. H. 21/4/1943, Cols 1769/1770 (Price).
[6] H. 18/5/1943, Cols 1005/1011.

but only if they were all put into plant and factories; he was also concerned to limit depreciation to, say, 80 per cent of the cost of assets to prevent them being kept too long. Summers[1] added the point that some further allowance should be given for the increase in replacement costs. Schuster[2] claimed the progress of modernization was being hampered by the tax system: the commercial profit and the profit for taxation were not the same; and there was a case for a different tax for industry.[3] He put forward the additional propositions that there should be tax relief for expenditure on research and development, that the obsolescence allowance should not be dependent on replacement of the asset and that there should be a greater allowance for depreciation on industrial buildings.[4]

The industrial lobby was followed by the five protagonists of land values taxation, Tinker,[5] Silkin,[6] Brooks,[7] Hall[8] and Stokes;[9] their arguments were probably best summed up by the last-named, who concluded his usual polemics by condemning 'the fallacy of taxation which penalized effort and ignored un-worked-for accretions'.

Assheton[10] professed to finding difficulty in replying to such a wide-ranging debate. But in fact he lighted on the two major talking points deftly enough. Questions of wear and tear allowances and undistributed profits were being investigated both by the Treasury in conjunction with the Board of Trade and the Board of Inland Revenue; this mention of the other bodies besides the Inland Revenue was in direct reply to Benson, who had complained of investigations being carried out in camera by a Department which should be the servant not the master of the House.[11] The taxation of land values must await full consideration of the findings of the Uthwatt Report: this was thought by Silverman[12] to be a somewhat cavalier reply as the Report in question was, as Stokes put it, 'an absolute sop'.

[1] H. 18/5/1943, Cols 1011/1017. [2] H. 18/5/1943, Cols 1022/1030.
[3] Not to be realized until F.A. 1965.
[4] The only relief available for industrial buildings was the so-called 'Mills, Factories Allowance' (S. 15, F.A. 1937) of the difference between the gross and the net rating assessment.
[5] H. 18/5/1943, Cols 1031/1034. [6] H. 18/5/1943, Cols 1034/1039.
[7] H. 18/5/1943, Cols 1049/1052. [8] H. 18/5/1943, Cols 1046/1049.
[9] H. 18/5/1943, Cols 1052/1061. [10] H. 18/5/1943, Cols 1061/1070.
[11] H. 18/5/1943, Col. 1055. [12] H. 18/5/1943, Cols 1070/1071.

In general, however, the Financial Secretary had covered a number of questions which left a reasonably uncluttered programme for the coming Committee stage.

For there was no burking the fact that however many Amendments were to be proposed at the Committee stage, they only provided an artificial stimulus to discussing a Bill, the principles behind which the House had virtually passed judgment on. There was very little support for any of the Amendments proposed on indirect taxation[1] which meant a resumption of the controversy over the current deduction scheme and the apparently successful American procedure. The Chancellor was not too sure of this but, possibly to his relief, he was interrupted by the Deputy Chairman, since the discussion of the actions of other Chambers in other countries was not permitted.

Amendments to allowances raised the usual crop of hard cases, and although all the amendments were withdrawn they served the useful function of the ventilation of grievances which had in the past led to later revisions of the law. This was normal procedure. More interesting were the debates on back-service superannuation payments which were to be spread[2] to prevent their incidence in wholly E.P.T. periods and on tax avoidance[3] caused by the disposal of a company's stock at under value.[4] This aroused the usual Parliamentary unease about catching the innocent and the dangers in giving the Commissioners 'Star Chamber powers: certainly inquisitorial powers'.[5]

But the most entertaining argument, and the longest, arose on the following day[6] over the taxation of Easter offerings and a proposal that they should be free of tax up to £50. Heat is usually generated in religious issues and the point was easily comprehensible. Most of the speakers were in favour, and it was hoped that the argument that the offerings attached to a personality (the Rev. A. D. Light as opposed to the Rev. O. Howe Boring)[7] would appeal to the

---

[1] H. 2/6/1943. [2] S.23, F.A. 1943. [3] S. 24, F.A. 1943.

[4] In its simplest form, this consisted of selling the shares in, say, a whisky company where the stock was valued on pre-war manufacturing cost basis at an amount which represented the actual selling price of the whisky—this might be twenty times the pre-war value. The profit on the sale of the shares was, of course, a capital profit. The purchaser of the shares would have a stock of whisky at market price or a little below and if he were also a whisky dealer he would naturally hold on for a rising market and eventually take his profit as well.

[5] H. 2/6/1943, Col. 305 (Thomas). [6] H. 3/6/1943, Cols 389/452.

[3] The proposer's contrast, H. 3/6/7943, Col. 391.

Chancellor as a good Wesleyan. Kingsley Wood, however, took his firm stand on the deciding factor in the tax case[1] that the gift was received by virtue of the office and, when it was pressed to a division, it was defeated, as Higgs[2] bitterly forecast, 'by the Members in the smoking room who are not familiar with the problem'. After these ecclesiastical disputations it was a relief to turn to the technical Amendments on E.P.T. which ended the debate, none of which was pressed to a division.

The phrase used by most of the Third Reading speakers on the Bill's progress was 'a smooth passage', plainly the result of its basically non-controversial nature. The magnitude of the tax burdens, the pressure of the high rates and the over-all fairness of the incidence were all duly recognized; and Members[3] fully appreciated that when taxation was at a low level, further revenue could always be secured by raising the rates, but when the rates were high revenue could only be raised by increases in wages and more profitable industry. This was why increasing pressure was building up for creating a fiscal policy which would benefit the country's wages and industrial structure.

But the specific topic of main interest was avoidance stimulated by Clause 22[4] on the sale of stock below cost which was amended on recommittal.[5] Some Members took the highly moral tone of contrasting those who avoided their rightful obligations with those who were risking their lives.[6] Some objected to the element of retrospection and pleaded the right of the taxpayer to minimize his tax bill.[7] Others thought the whole policy of taxation should be recast as far as avoidance was concerned.[8] The policy should not be to give the Board of Inland Revenue wider powers but to use the phrase 'fictitious and artificial transactions'[9] in combating avoidance schemes, a term definable by law.

The Chancellor,[10] in his final reply, also devoted the greater part of his remarks to avoidance. After hinting that a revised deduction scheme would be ready, he hoped, in early autumn, he went on to

[1] Blakiston v. Cooper.   [2] H. 3/6/1943, Col. 406.
[3] Cf. Schuster, H. 7/7/1943, Cols 2131/2135.
[4] See p. 325 and footnote 4; and F. A. 1943, S. 24.   [5] H. 29/6/1943.
[6] Cf. Collindridge, H. 7/7/1943, Col. 2160.
[7] Cf. Thomas, H. 7/7/1943, Cols 2154/2156.
[8] Benson, H. 7/7/1943, Cols 2162/2166.   [9] From F.A. 1927.
[10] H. 7/7/1943.

discuss 'those who seek to avoid contributing their fair share to the cost of this war. . . . It is true that the methods which are adopted may be within the letter of the law, but I suggest to the House that where they are plainly directed to defeat the purpose of the law, the law must be protected.' And on the point of retrospection he had already given adequate warning in the discussions on Section 35, Finance Act 1941.[1] The Bill was in the best interests of the country as a whole, but there could yet be no talk of remissions—no one could tell what lay ahead.

For the ever-present problem and real phenomenon of the Budget was providing for expenditure of nearly £16 millions daily. Of this sum about one-half was raised from taxes and the other half borrowed. The make-up of the £8 millions from taxes was £3·5 millions from income tax and surtax, £1·333 millions from E.P.T./N.D.C. and £·25 million from death duties; indirect taxes yielded £1 million from tobacco, £·75 million from alcohol, £·25 million from purchase tax, and miscellaneous items such as entertainment and motor vehicles £·5 million. The £8 millions borrowed comprised £1·75 millions overseas disinvestment,[2] £1·25 millions from credit balances of official funds, £·5 million depreciation unspent, and £4·5 millions private savings and undistributed profits.

In view of this, the Chancellor had done remarkably well to contain his increased demands to £100 millions plus, and the weapon of increased indirect taxation had been forced upon him because, as in 1942, he dared not increase direct taxation with an inequitable deduction scheme arousing constant complaints. In addition, any statesman would have to take serious account of the political implications of the increased number of income tax payers.

Other particular issues raised were the adequacy of the whole scheme of depreciation allowances, a long-standing complaint now being widely canvassed again, and the prevalence of both avoidance and evasion. Fortunately, the canard that the post-war repayments were of questionable validity had been finally resolved, although there were a few lingering doubts.[3]

[1] H. 1/7/1941, Col. 1282. The section dealt with transactions designed to avoid E.P.T.

[2] Sales of foreign investments and increase in overseas debts.

[3] See H. 7/7/1943, Col. 2184 (Levy), about their inclusion in balance-sheet assets. In addition there is the story of the taxpayer receiving a Post-war Credit Certificate which he mistook for a Demand Note and promptly paid.

There was, however, one curious feature of the various stages of the Budget for which there was no single explanation. Throughout its progress, the largest Budget in British fiscal history, attendances were small: there was only a handful of Members present, for example, when Votes of Credit totalling many thousands of millions were passed although, admittedly, there were at least fifty Members anxious to express their opinions on the taxability of Easter offerings.[1] Some Members were conscious of this: indeed Davies[2] professed to find a change in Parliamentary procedure creeping in and the power of the House being whittled down because of the dichotomy developing between the Chancellor as Chancellor, and the Chancellor as the spokesman of his Treasury advisers. This distinction Kingsley Wood indignantly denied; indeed he interrupted the speech to do so, an unusual practice for him.[3]

But there was one signal failure which rankled, and that was the failure to produce a deduction scheme on the current basis. There had been delay in starting the deductions due in January 1942, owing to the continued expansion in the number of wage-earners and bottle-necks in the supply of forms and stationery. The staff associations of the Inland Revenue had themselves produced revised schemes which the Chancellor had taken somewhat amiss,[4] although they were examined seriously by both the Trades Union Congress and the United States taxation authorities. Parliament was fully alive to the problem, and the techniques of tax deductions became required reading for the leader writers of *The Times* and the *Manchester Guardian*, the fiscal experts of the *New Statesman* and *The Economist*.

Kingsley Wood was, in fact, in a difficult position. 'What I need,' he had declared at the outset of his 1942 Budget, 'is cash, and cash out of current income.' He was the Member for an industrial constituency and he always thought it possible that complaints were being exaggerated, since he personally had received none. Certainly it was true that while wages generally were rising, the difficulties caused by the six months' time-lag were only marked in seasonal jobs. The yield of income tax was now around the £1,000 millions mark: every penny of revenue was used in the struggle against fascism, and he could be excused for not wanting to change

[1] H. 238/9. [2] H. 7/7/1943, Cols 2139/2142.
[3] H. 7/7/1943, Cols 2141/2142. [4] H. 9/6/1942.

in wartime a system which was intelligible and which had the merit of working. The most important concession he made, however, was a clear indication that he was at all times prepared to consider the matter afresh.

He returned to the theme in his 1943 Budget: the admission that 'a current-earnings basis (for tax deductions) would not be ruled out of his deliberations' was a broad hint of the intense activity which had taken place behind the scenes, the basic spur now being the potential collection troubles when incomes began to fall at the end of the war. By July 19th the Chancellor had put a scheme forward to the Ministers most directly concerned, a few days in fact before the 1943 Finance Act became law. The War Cabinet was informed and consultations with the employers' and workers' organizations took place. A White Paper and an appropriate Bill were drafted to launch what was called the joint brain-child of Sir Cornelius Grigg, the Chairman, and Paul Chambers, the Secretary of the Board. An arranged Parliamentary question was put down for September 21st, but in the early hours of that same morning Kingsley Wood, who was looking forward to announcing that technical difficulties had at last been overcome, collapsed and died.

He had been a successful Chancellor, and his success had come not from any inherent financial skill, but because he was willing to hear advice, to judge its merits and to act upon it. His appreciation of the realities of war finance were unsurpassed by the financial ministers of any of the belligerent countries. He had the courage to apply drastic remedies and to rise above any partisan view of his office. His speeches were often peculiarly drab in tone and streaked with commonplace, but each point was decisively and unequivocally made. It may be that he was fortunate in his fiscal advisers, but he had the modesty and good sense to choose them.

At first it was intended that the new system should apply to weekly wage-earners only; then in spite of the opposition of the new Chancellor, Sir John Anderson, who had once been Chairman of the Board of Inland Revenue,[1] it was extended to all incomes under £600. Finally all Schedule E taxpayers were included. This last announcement was made on the Third Reading of the Income Tax (Employments) Act 1943, but separate legislation was required in the Income Tax (Offices and Employments) Act 1944. The

[1] From 1919–1922.

scheme was put into effect on April 6, 1944, not without a certain amount of anxiety about the element of 'forgiveness' which was, as Sayers pointed out, largely illusory, its true nature being explained to the Chancellor by Keynes[1] and in any case the post-war credit cancellation for 1943–1944 took care of about half of it.

There had been many schemes for putting deductions on a current year basis which had all been considered during the long months of discussion. The original feature of the scheme finally adopted was the cumulative principle operated by means of tax tables which, in the case of a monthly wage-earner, has the effect of dividing a tax-payer's allowances into twelve equal portions. One portion is set against the first month's wage and tax on the difference deducted; for the second month the process is repeated with two portions and two months' wages. The tax to be deducted will now be the amount by which the second total of tax on two months' wages exceeded the first. Thus, whatever the fluctuations in wages may be, the cumulative principle ensures that at any time the tax deducted is in step with the wages paid.

It was 'no mean feat', as the Chancellor said, to introduce such a scheme, involving some sixteen million people, in wartime. For instance, the preparation and printing of forms and tables almost monopolized the output of the printing trade for many months. Both employers and employees had to be taught what to do. There was press and radio publicity; there was a threepenny guide of which four-and-a-half million copies were sold. But the major part of educating the public was done by the Revenue staff itself who visited factories, talked to workers and management, held meetings and answered questions. It was an example of service to taxpayers, the goodwill from which still survives.

[1] Sayers *Financial Policy 1939–1945*, pp. 104/106.

Chapter XII
The Finance Bill 1944

THE ANDERSON SHELTER

Time Table

Financial Statement		April 25, 1944
Budget Proposals		
	1st Day	25
	2nd Day	26
	3rd Day	27
Budget Resolutions		
	Reported	May 2
Finance Bill		
	1st Reading	2
	2nd Reading	23
Committee		
	1st Day	June 14
	2nd Day	15
	As amended	28
	Third Reading	30
Royal Assent		July 13

1944 had opened far more auspiciously than had 1943. The North African Campaign had gone well; the Battle of the Atlantic, with the help of long-range aircraft operating from the Azores and a wealth of American destroyers, was being won; night and day bombing of Germany continued to make encouraging if misleading headlines. Above all, despite diversions in Italy and Roosevelt's occasionally somewhat cavalier treatment of Churchill, the long-awaited

Second Front, under the code-name of Overlord, had been finally resolved upon and was in active course of preparation.

The new Chancellor of the Exchequer, Sir John Anderson, who had been Lord President of the Council, and who still retained his direction of the manpower Budget, was remarkable for an Olympian detachment which had earned him the sobriquet of 'Jehovah'. Perhaps his reputation was responsible for the meagre attendance when he rose to present his first Budget[1] on April 25, 1944; there were tracts of red leather appealing to be occupied; the Prime Minister was absent; but to do the new Minister justice there was a full House before the close.

He plunged, almost without preamble, into the customary review of the previous year. Estimated expenditure, towards which there had been a £4,900 millions Vote of Credit, had been set at £5,756 millions for 1943/1944. Overseas disinvestment was to cover £600 millions of this, leaving a balance of £5,156 millions, of which £2,907 millions should have been the revenue yield, and the balance, £2,249 millions, would be sought in loans. In the event there was a better showing than expected.

For the 1943/1944 revenue had excelled itself. Income tax and other duties exhibited a £5 millions surplus; Customs and Excise had an outstanding surplus of £67 millions showing 'an unexpected and remarkable resilience'; for example, the beer duty produced £18 millions over the estimate and the produce of the oil duties was £24 millions up, a reflection of the massive consumption by the services. Miscellaneous revenue was higher because of the inclusion of premiums and contributions under the War Damage Acts. The total revenue was £3,039 millions, a surplus of £131 millions over the estimate of £2,907 millions; the excess of expenditure over revenue, excluding the £600 millions disinvestment at £2,760 millions, was £89 millions less than the estimate.

With regard to borrowing, the other leg of revenue, after allowing for certain capital receipts, the net total was £2,750 millions, £54 millions less than in the previous year. It was difficult to evaluate the success of the borrowing policy currently since current figures were not available, but it was clear from the White Paper[2] that loans had been covered by overseas disinvestment, by personal and impersonal savings and by the sums available for investment in the hands

[1] H. 25/4/1944, Cols 650/687.   [2] Cmd. 6520.

of the public and the various official funds. He noted with satisfaction the growth in longer-term borrowing and the rise in small savings. And, since he had mentioned the White Paper, he would like to emphasize that he looked upon it as no mere appendix to the Budget statement. 'For the purpose of a policy of full employment,' his credo ran, 'it will be necessary, year by year, to bring under review the income and expenditure, not only of the Exchequer but of the country as a whole, and not only its income but its capital expenditure and its savings.'[1]

Minor taxation proposals were next disposed of. There was a pat on the back for the way Pay As You Earn was operating, a brief reference to the increased sugar quota and a tribute to A. P. Herbert for his campaign to spread authors' royalties; Members would see a provision in the Bill for this. He had also been considering how the balance between duties from petrol and from motor vehicles themselves should be proportioned, and he would welcome representations on the subject. Finally, those relics of a statelier past, armorial bearings duty and carriage licence duty, were to be abolished.

The Chancellor now switched to what he termed 'the background to domestic finance', beginning with a tribute to Kingsley Wood's 'high qualities of heart and mind'. The foundations of his policy had been twofold: first to cover by taxation as much of current expenditure as possible to lessen the future burden of debt and to mop up purchasing power, and secondly to maintain the controls over the loan market so that the Government could borrow at a low and steady interest rate. The latter had certainly been achieved; proof of the former could be found in Table II of the White Paper which showed that although incomes in 1943 were £600 millions above 1942, a greater sum had been drained off by savings of £221 millions and £385 millions additional taxation paid. The 'faithful public' had in fact reduced the percentage of personal income spent on consumption goods from 76 per cent in 1938, to 58 per cent in 1942, and to a mere 53 per cent currently.

But even so he would have to look at the cost-of-living subsidies which, along with rationing, had kept a reasonable stability in household expenses; for 'I cannot claim the position in this field is so satisfactory that I need do no more than leave well alone'. He was

[1] H. 25/4/1944, Col. 653.

not happy, statistically, about the present trend of events, especially the increase in subsidies which had increased from £70 millions in 1940, to £140 millions in 1941 to £190 millions in 1943, and without which the cost of living would have risen a good 50 per cent above its pre-war level. 'I am afraid,' he was forced to add, 'we can no longer regard a cost-of-living figure of 25 to 30 per cent above pre-war as sacrosanct.'

For his predecessor had made it abundantly clear that a steady wage-level was part and parcel of the stabilization policy: if wages rose this policy might have to be abandoned.[1] Now wages had risen 40 per cent above pre-war and 'the purpose of stabilization would be stultified if the Government were to continue pouring out subsidies to keep the cost of living down without regard to the current level of wages and costs'. He would be failing in his duty if he did not issue a warning that both wages and industrial overheads must be pegged; he should also mention the growing cost of imports and the danger of creating a gap between world and domestic prices.

It was his firm intention to continue Kingsley Wood's policy, but the co-operation of all sections of the country was needed. The cost of living must be allowed to float where increases in wages had raised the actual cost of vital commodities, as in the case of coal. stabilization would be artificial, and such increases should be reflected in the cost of living in the natural way. He proposed that the increase over the pre-war level should be of the order of 30 to 35 per cent in place of the previous 25 to 30 per cent, which would only offset a quarter of the increase in wage rates.

As for external finances and the balance of payments, the problems arising were becoming increasingly important as the war drew to a close. It was true the country was receiving aid from the United States and Canada; but this was balanced, and more than balanced, by the aid from this country to other Allies. Britain had sold assets abroad worth £1,000 millions; overseas debts were twice that figure; the pontifical summary was, 'I sometimes detect indications of a temper in the country and in the House which does not pay due regard to these sombre facts.'

He was prepared to hammer these facts home. World War I had seriously harmed the country's export trade and its position as a

[1] Cf. Kingsley Wood, H. 7/4/1941.

creditor nation. World War II had dealt even graver blows in these two sectors. The key must be exporting. 'But,' as he said, 'the Government cannot create an export trade.' What it could and would do was to promote the conditions in which an export trade could flourish. The burdens in industry would be heavy, but the country had massive production potential. Provided peace could inspire the same drive as war, and the error of snatching quick gains instead of a steady build-up of goodwill could be avoided, a full share of what promised to be a heavy post-war demand was a fair expectation.

Turning therefore to the taxation of industry, he had reviewed the incidence of E.P.T. with some care and the main criticisms added up basically to criticism of the rate. No concessions could be made in that direction, but he was proposing to increase the profits standard by £1,000; to some extent it was a token gesture, but it would benefit 30,000 small traders, 10,000 of whom would now be exempt. The cost would be £12·5 millions.

Even after the war taxation would be high for some time to come; heavy borrowing would continue and the need for saving. But taxation had a contribution to make to industrial reconstruction, and here the Chancellor acknowledged his debt to the studies initiated by Sir Kingsley Wood on the taxation of reserves and increased wear and tear allowances for all types of capital expenditure. There would be no relief for reserves, but there would be greater relief for industrial re-equipment. The scheme he was outlining could not be put into operation until peacetime but, briefly, it involved granting an initial allowance of 20 per cent for new plant and machinery, and of 10 per cent for new industrial buildings; for the first time they were to attract an annual allowance of 2 per cent which was to apply to all industrial buildings less than fifty years old. Similar allowances were to be made for capital expenditure on agriculture and in the extractive industries. Patent rights, too, were to come within the ambit of capital allowances, being regarded as income to the seller and capital expenditure to the buyer, on which capital allowances would be due.

But as important as capital expenditure generally or costs of patents was research expenditure; there was a strong case for modifying the current treatment[1] for taxation purposes, as all the

[1] Briefly this was to allow all payments to central research bodies approved by

evidence seemed to show that this country was falling behind other countries in the field of experimentation. The Board of Inland Revenue had tackled the problem with a sense of reality and he was now proposing that capital expenditure on research should be allowed over five years, or the life of the asset if shorter; that ordinary expenditure should be allowed as incurred; and that all contributions to central research bodies approved by the D.S.I.R. should be allowed. He also mentioned that he had the oil duties under review since a good deal of research was taking place in that line also, especially in the realm of plastics.

The Chancellor was nearing the end of his speech, and he turned reluctantly from the shining prospects of the future to the harsh realities of a war-weary country. His statistical summary was almost perfunctory. He thought estimating the national needs was more difficult than at any time during the war, but his four components of a total of £5,937 millions were a Debt Charge provision of £420 millions, £55 millions up on last year to take care of growth, £16 millions, as last year, for other Consolidated Fund services, £501 millions for the ordinary Civil Vote, swollen by an additional £37 millions for welfare, and a massive £5,000 millions Vote of Credit.[1]

He was anticipating £2,000 millions from Inland Revenue duties, an increase of £122 millions, of which £116 millions would be from income tax, £500 millions from E.P.T., as last year, a slight increase in Customs and Excise, if troops left the country, to £1,038 millions, and other items, again as last year, £64 millions. The total was £3,102 millions leaving a 'gap' of £2,835 millions.

There were four main sources of borrowing to fill this. Overseas disinvestment should produce £650 millions; extra-budgetary funds he put at £300 millions; £225 millions was expected from impersonal savings; and he was hoping for £1,550 millions from personal savings. This totalled £2,725 millions, leaving a residue of £110 millions required for domestic finance which he considered 'a very moderate and satisfactory figure'.

---

the D.S.I.R. unless earmarked for a specifically capital scheme, and to make the usual distinction between capital and revenue for a company's own research expenditure.

[1] £4,900 millions had been the previous year's estimate against expenditure of £4,950 millions.

In conclusion, Sir John Anderson made three points: the prospective deficit was the same as that which his predecessor had thought right to accept last year; the revenue from taxation was 52 per cent of total expenditure, a higher proportion than at any time; and he was convinced it was within the capacity of the country to finance the deficit from savings and other sources of a non-inflationary character.

The immediate reaction of the House was almost wholly favourable. Greenwood[1] praised the lucidity and brevity of the speech: it was unique in its width of scope, and while it dangled a prospective carrot before the nose of industry the value of labour would be increased in parallel with improved industrial efficiency. There was equally general approval for the forward-looking nature of the proposals and the emphasis on exports,[2] probably best summed up by King-Hall:[3] the Chancellor's approach he found essentially non-party and non-emotional; the country had to be efficient and had to export; and he saw in the proposals the foundation of a long-term economic policy.

Labour opinion was on the whole with Greenwood, but there was an increasing emphasis on the necessity of co-operation between employers and employees and on the argument that the 'economy of high wages'[4] was not necessarily a dangerous economic doctrine. Sexton[5] was more moderate in considering the proposals a bridge-head that the Government was setting up to pass over from war to peace and full employment, but Tinker was dubious.[6] Cutting the subsidies to allow the cost of living to rise would lead to demand for higher wages: 'He [the Chancellor] must not back up private enterprise to enable it to retain its hold on the community.'

The reaction of the Press clearly illustrated the three salient features of the Budget. The popular dailies seized upon its most satisfactory proposal from the standpoint of the ordinary citizen, the plain fact that happily there was to be no increase in taxation. It was, as the Chancellor put it, precisely the mixture as before with no change in dosage.

The Times[7] and the *Manchester Guardian*[7] were almost rhapsodic

---

[1] H. 25/4/1944, Cols 687/690.   [2] H. 25/4/1944, Cols 690/693 (Harris).
[3] H. 25/4/1944, Cols 712/715.   [4] H. 25/4/1944, Cols 709/712 (Logan).
[5] H. 25/4/1944, Cols 725/726.   [6] H. 25/4/1944, Cols 726/730.
[7] 26/4/1944.

in their admiration. *The Times* hailed the Budget as 'all or almost all that the occasion called for' and singled out the Chancellor's 'candour, courage and realism' in a speech of 'lucidity and discrimination'. The emphasis was now on the second element of the Budget in its forward-looking aspect of promoting industrial recovery through a revised scheme of capital allowances for plant, buildings, patents and scientific research. The *Manchester Guardian* thought the Budget 'would stand out in British history' because it was 'the most constructive of all the war series' in its calculated encouragement to industry, not forgetting the extension of the E.P.T. standards which took a good number of small private businesses out of liability.

The Economist,[1] as usual, went for analysis in depth. On the whole it approved the Chancellor's proposal to keep taxation at the same level as before and to allow the increase in yield to flow from increased income and consumption. It favoured the proposed pattern of capital allowances for industry, with minor reservations, and in fact included an article early in the following month[2] dealing exclusively with taxation on industry. But it also underlined the possible dangers from deliberately allowing the cost of living to rise even though nothing like proportionate to increases in wages. This was calculated to upset labour relations, a point the *Manchester Guardian* had tentatively made already. The *New Statesman*[3] regarded the proposed revision of subsidies as the most significant, indeed almost sinister, feature of the Budget. It pointed out that many Labour Members were 'most disgusted'. But whichever facet of Budget policy was high-lighted, there was general agreement that hopes of an early lifting of the wartime tax burden were doomed to disappointment.

The regulation two days' debate took place on the eve of the most intense war effort by either side; but the House only heard occasional muted references to the current military build-up. Almost as if by tacit agreement attention was concentrated on the immediate matters in hand.

Pethick-Lawrence[4] was the first to deal formally with the Budget proposals. He had been impressed by the Chancellor's emphasis on the post-war development of the country generally—in particular he had four observations to make. He questioned the wisdom of letting the cost of living rise, for although commodity prices had

[1] 29/4/1944.   [2] 6/5/1944.   [3] 29/4/1944.   [4] H. 26/4/1944, Cols 795/803.

been pegged, retail prices were till soaring, with consequent dangers of an inflationary spiral; he thought more weight should have been given to maintaining the exchange rate when dealing with export prospects; and while no change was probably the soundest fiscal policy, the revised capital allowance plans could only be given a conditional welcome—however much they might be 'a distinct benefit to private enterprise in this country', they took no account of the immediate interests of the workers.

Those two veterans of economic debate, Wardlaw-Milne and Schuster, developed a more orthodox and conservative attitude. The former[1] was wholly in favour of the taxation proposals for industry, with the rider that the rate of E.P.T. must be reduced. But his real divergence from Pethick-Lawrence came in his categoric agreement with the Chancellor that keeping price levels down while allowing wages to slide upwards would be disastrous. Schuster[2] was in complete accord. There would be no hardship from the limited increases in living cost to workers if they developed their highest earning potential: wages and price, he maintained, were not as important as wages and production. Simmons,[3] following the same line, reinforced Wardlaw-Milne's plea for reduced E.P.T. rates. He had done a statistical exercise in his constituency and the smaller firms, he found, on which the health of industry so largely depended, were hit hard by the undercapitalization resulting from the drain of E.P.T. payments.

By mid-debate, however, Members were becoming more critical. Douglas,[4] in the light of the mechanics of P.A.Y.E., concluded that the Chancellor had been forced into the position of retaining the direct taxation rates. To increase indirect taxation would have been unfair: a standstill, therefore, was inevitable. He also argued that the grant of heavy initial allowances in the early days of peace would be a serious debit to the Exchequer which the general body of taxpayers would have to finance. Henderson[5] and Benson[6] inevitably seized on the cost of living thaw. Whether to abandon the stabilization policy was, the former said, 'the most grave question' before the House:[7] the latter went further in claiming that the

---

[1] H. 26/4/1944, Cols 803/810.   [2] H. 26/4/1944, Cols 810/816.
[3] H. 26/4/1944, Cols 816/822.   [4] H. 26/4/1944, Cols 822/828.
[5] H. 26/4/1944, Cols 828/833.   [6] H. 26/4/1944, Cols 840/845.
[7] It is interesting to note that one of his suggested remedies was a national loan financed by premium bonds.

Chancellor was out of touch with the feeling of Committee in allowing the cost-of-living figures to rise; the result will be an increase in the cost structure. As for initial allowances, he made the point that they were not so generous a concession as imagined; they merely accelerated the rate of writing off in the early stage of an asset's life, and the allowances due in later years would be correspondingly lower. Lawson,[1] in the same vein, deprecated the suggestion that wages had gone up so much that the Chancellor was excused allowing costs to rise as well, a course which Woods[2] confessed made him feel most apprehensive.

If unfreezing the cost of living was anathema to the left, the pressure of taxation was equally obnoxious to the Right. Sanderson,[3] developing Wardlaw-Milne's point that the rate of E.P.T. should be reduced, felt that the incidence of direct taxation generally should be reviewed, not merely the capital allowance system for industry. Taxation 'had nearly reached saturation point'; and for once this traditional rallying-cry of *laissez-faire* was not very far from the truth.

This somewhat bi-partisan atmosphere was redeemed by the last two speakers of the day. Boothby[4] took his usual wide sweep. Basing his thesis on the argument that the economic crises between the wars arose from a failure in distribution, not in production, he maintained that the object of trade should not be the piling up of export surpluses which led to an unbalanced debt structure and a stagnating economy—rather the aim should be world-wide co-operation to expand commerce. He did not find the increase in the National Debt of alarming significance: far more important was the production of more food, the intelligent location of industry (and here there was a prescient forecast of the dangers inherent in the 'fantastic growth of London'). Summarizing, still in general terms, he thought capital and current expenditure should be segregated after the war and the latter only financed by taxation.

The Financial Secretary,[5] in winding up, filed the customary claim of general approval for his master's voice. He gave punctilious and detailed replies to the points raised by individual Members, including a careful explanation of the cost-of-living index. The posi-

[1] H. 26/4/1944, Cols 851/856. [2] H. 26/4/1944, Cols 865/867.
[3] H. 26/4/1944, Cols 845/851. [4] H. 26/4/1944, Cols 867/875.
[5] H. 26/4/1944, Cols 875/884.

tion had been that if one commodity increased in price another would have its subsidy increased to counter-balance. Now, to a limited extent only, in the case of a commodity price increase, there would be no corresponding subsidy increase. In general he found it necessary to remind Members that the country was still at war and that replacement of capital equipment and reduction of taxation could not yet be envisaged as a practical proposition—the times still called for sacrifices from all sections of the community. Nor would the end of the war bring summary relief: the country would have to ask itself whether current consumption on a scale the majority would like to have it, as well as the maintenance of capital investment in industry, could be satisfied without creating a scarcity value for both labour and materials; and it must realize the imperative need of keeping equipment up to date and be prepared to choose for a time between a desirable standard of consumer goods and the vital plans for new development.

The pattern of the second day's debate was rather more discursive than the first day's, and the Chairman allowed a good deal more latitude to Members in deciding what was relevant; this was understandable when the proposals themselves had far wider political than fiscal implications.

The first five speeches opened up the main lines of discussion which were to be developed during the day's session. Woodburn,[1] commenting that no one had expected any change, saw potential danger in inflation and unpegging the cost of living. The Chancellor intervened to suggest the amendment of 'repegging'. The capital allowance proposals were welcomed if properly used and not made the basis for speculative profits. The orthodox right-wing view, as propounded by Bennett,[2] was grateful to the Chancellor for a new line of approach but still deplored the drain of E.P.T. payments. An ingenious suggestion was to form a national reserve from the E.P.T. post-war refunds 'to help the unfortunates'.

Edwards,[3] however, thought the inequity of E.P.T. arose in the cases of companies who had a good profits standard through trading with the enemy before 1939: it was still possible for people to make fortunes, and only a post-war levy on increased wealth could counter this. But to his panacea of productivity and a minimum

[1] H. 27/4/1944, Cols 950/960.   [2] H. 27/4/1944, Cols 960/966.
[3] H. 27/4/1944, Cols 968/974.

standard of living, Reed[1] replied that the export angle had been overlooked, and that the Chancellor was right in treating finance as a vital factor in promoting industrial efforts. Eccles[2] agreed but stressed the difficulty of exporting and of securing the necessary re-equipment to support an export drive. He feared the demand for consumers' goods after the war would encroach on the capital needed for industrial investment and that there would be a 'scramble for resources'.

Both Left and Right were moving uneasily towards an unspoken question, that of the nature of post-war controls. Eccles had pointed out at the beginning of his remarks that the Treasury was anxious to co-ordinate the whole field of economic planning; it was in a position to do so and had the requisite experience and ability. But this was not a policy which would commend itself to those who wished to synchronize an armistice with a return to *laissez-faire*.

Any further speculation on this point, however, was abruptly broken up by a typical Gallacher[3] speeech with the faithful Kirk-wood acting as a Greek chorus. The freeing of the cost of living 'will have very evil consequences amongst the masses of the workers of this country upon whom so much depends'. The question of wages and prices was not something for the future but for now. The Chancellor was speaking as a confirmed Tory; the wages of workers were always compared with the pay of the Forces, never with profits. ('Shame!' from Mr Kirkwood). The desire was 'to cut down the standard of the working-class' while the rich were amassing 'millions of pounds'. ('They are all robbers' from Mr Kirkwood). Eventually the Chairman mildly suggested the speakers should get back to the Budget proposals.

There were a number of desultory comments before the tempo of the debate picked up again. Griffiths's[4] speech contained faint echoes of Gallacher in suggesting that the threat to wages had 'unsettled thousands of workers' and leading trade unionists. But then it was interesting to see the tentative approach again to the nature and extent of Government economic intervention in peacetime. Loftus[5] stressed the need for control of imports after the war, and along with this his three essentials for a post-war financial policy were a stable

[1] H. 27/4/1944, Cols 974/977. [2] H. 27/4/1944, Cols 977/983.
[3] H. 27/4/1944, Cols 983/989. [4] H. 27/4/1944, Cols 998/1009.
[5] H. 27/4/1944, Cols 1009/1014.

price level, a flexible foreign exchange rate and a cheap money policy. Mander[1] emphasized the need for a minimum wage rate, while Molson[2] professed to find that the Budget was already the instrument of a planned economy.

Anderson,[3] in his winding-up speech, stuck firmly to his brief. After admitting modestly that 'I do not know that I am very good in picking up points', he proceeded to deal swiftly and effectively with the major points in a score or so of speeches. He dwelt longest, however, on taxation and price stabilization. Regarding the former, he could promise no further concessions on E.P.T. apart from the minor relaxations proposed. On his capital allowance innovations, he must draw the attention of the House to the effect of the initial allowance which was not merely an accelerator of the annual allowance, but provided a substantial relief recurring all the time as plant was scrapped and modernised. Price stabilization, he remarked, was the one feature of the Budget which had been criticized in some measure. A price spiral was far from his thoughts, but, as he graphically put it, no more than 'a slow and reluctant movement of prices dragged up after wages but still left far behind'. It must be clear to the House that to allow prices to get too much out of step with wages was simply storing up trouble for the future. Finally, he insisted on replying to a reproof more implied than overt, that he had neglected the human factor: his critics should bear in mind that he was introducing not a Supply but a Finance Bill.

He made the same reply on the Report stage to a group of Members[4] who put in a plea for the plight of the rentier class now the cost of living was being allowed to rise; at least single allowance might be increased to £100. The simple answer[5] was that rates were high and allowances low, and this combination was bound to hit heavily at peoople of all classes. In general, for administrative reasons, it was impossible to introduce too much variation.[6]

An interesting technical point was raised by the Attorney-General which amounted to a confession that Section 35 of the 1941

---

[1] H. 27/4/1944, Cols 1018/1021. [2] H. 27/4/1944, Cols 1021/1025.
[3] H. 27/4/1944, Cols 1035/1042. [4] H. 2/5/1944, Cols 1223/1229.
[5] H. 2/5/1944, Cols 1233/1235.

[6] A greater inequity arose from the smaller allowances for married men and children which narrowed the gap between those with family responsibilities and the single, of £500. A single man would be left with £344, a married man with one child £424.

Finance Act had not worked. This Section had tried to stop E.P.T. avoidance schemes by cancelling any advantage if the main (a qualification inserted at Committee stage) purpose was the reduction or avoidance of E.P.T.[1] Taxpayers were able to plead 'We did not think about E.P.T. and there is some other reason.'[2] The amendment suggested was to substitute 'one of the main purposes'. Benson,[3] as near as makes no difference, was able to say 'I told you so', remarking: 'This is the second time the Government has fallen down on the question of main purpose.'[4] But the Right was uneasy: the Government would clearly have more explaining to do.

The Second Reading was opened by Assheton[5] in a brisk and definitive speech. Deftly he explained the official case for the various clauses and the House paid him the compliment of listening in attentive silence. But his expertise faltered when he tried to gloss over Clause 32, the Amendment to Section 35, Finance Act 1941, which had been raised by the Attorney-General. Members raised the contemporary letter[6] in *The Times*, which had put forward cogent objections to the suggested rephrasing so that the Financial Secretary was forced into a more elaborate defence than he had planned. He pointed out that the proposed legislation did not empower the Commissioners to presume tax avoidance as a main purpose except where the main benefit of the transaction was a reduction in the tax. The onus would now be placed firmly on the taxpayer to show he had some other main purpose. This somewhat legalistic argument was reinforced by recalling to the House the fact that Kingsley Wood had said he might have to some back to them if the legislation did not serve his purpose:[7] 'My Right Hon. Friend, the present Chancellor, feels he is in that position now.'

Pethick-Lawrence,[8] in a thoughtful and instructive speech, agreed that the main lines of the proposals, apart from Clause 32, would be uncontroversial. His major theme therefore was the future prospects of the country's financial position. He wondered whether the Chancellor was fully prepared for the end of the war, whether the lessons of the shortages and prices after 1918 had been learned and whether the dangers of inflation with pent-up purchasing power,

---

[1] See p. 197.   [2] H. 2/5/1944, Col. 1243.   [3] H. 2/5/1944, Col. 1244.
[4] See p. 78 *et seq.* regarding the transfer of assets abroad.
[5] H. 23/5/1944, Col. 595.   [6] May 23, 1944.   [7] See p. 200.
[8] H. 23/5/1944, Cols 605/614.

I

and hoarding, had been appreciated. He could foresee no fall in taxation for at least the next twelve months. Admittedly purely defensive expenditure was falling now the threat of invasion had been removed, but munitions expenditure would stay at the same level until Japan was beaten, and he looked for increased expenditure on such welfare items as pensions and housing. All turned on the country's productive power.

Schuster[1] seized the chance of adapting this summary to his own particular contentions which were that for industry to be prosperous taxation must be less restrictive. He and an all-party group in the previous year had set down a motion for the rejection of the Finance Bill on the broad ground that 'the existing system for taxing indus- trial profits might weaken the financial structure of British industry and discourage its healthy development'. He welcomed the pro- posed revision of capital allowances but claimed it did not go far enough. There should be an allowance for non-industrial buildings; the 'over-price element' in replacement had not been legislated for; no account was taken of the fact that plant must be improved as well as simply replaced; and there should be tax relief for profits ploughed back. In fact he not only looked the Chancellor's gift horse in the mouth, he kicked it in the teeth. In this exercise he was joined by Hammersley,[2] who thought that there was a case for introducing the new allowances now and for giving a depreciation allowance in advance for the 'over-price element'.

The taxation of land values attracted support from Leslie;[3] it was necesary to have control over land for post-war planning. Stokes[4] was much more vehement and more verbose in claiming that this procedure would prove a fiscal panacea quite apart from the equitable considerations.

Clause 32 was attacked more in sorrow than in anger. Williams[5] thought 'it was carrying the doctrine of the State really further than I like'. Hely-Hutchinson's[6] opinion was that 'The officials are taking the easiest course. They are asking for more powers than we would normally give them because they would find it so terribly difficult to catch tax-dodgers if we did not.' The situation was the direct result of high taxation and especially 100 per cent E.P.T.:

[1] H. 23/5/1944, Cols 619/628. [2] H. 23/5/1944, Cols 664/671.
[3] H. 23/5/1944, Cols 634/636. [4] H. 23/5/1944, Cols 654/663.
[5] H. 23/5/1944, Cols 639/647. [6] H. 23/5/1944, Cols 650/654.

contemporary warnings when the rate was first imposed had passed unheeded.

Anderson,[1] as was his practice, had been present throughout the debate despite the unusual move of allowing the Financial Secretary to open it. He could give a complete assurance that the Treasury were fully prepared to deal with post-war transitional problems, although in his view economic problems would be related more to distributive than productive efficiency. He thanked those who had spoken on motor car taxation[2] and the need for double taxation agreements with other nations[3]—both these matters were being actively considered by his advisers, and in reply to an interjection by Stokes, land values were also being studied by the Government and their views would be put before the House 'at the earliest possible date'. Tax relief for reserves again got a specific turn-down, but he was now in a position to promise the new capital allowances legislation before the next Finance Bill. Clause 32, he remarked drily, was, he had gathered, 'the only part of the Bill which might be regarded to any considerable extent as controversial'. It would be fully discussed at Committee stage, but he would permit himself the observation that it would separate the sheep from the goats. Finally, there was hope for tax mitigation, but that would not come, as far as he could judge, in the immediate future.

The Committee stage began quietly: there was general acceptance until Clause 25 which dealt with simplification of procedure. This was the clause the discussion of which the Financial Secretary had postponed, much to the amusement of the House, on the grounds that it was a complex matter. Benson[4] complained that the City Commissioners refused to give up the right of appointing assessors, a sinecure office which provided jobs for the boys. Anderson parried by noting the position but said it was not high on his list of priorities.

There was also considerable discussion on the two following clauses which dealt with the proposed allowances for scientific research expenditure. The House was treated to the unusual sight of an alliance between Schuster and Benson requesting clarification of the appointed day and the nature of the required expenditure.

[1] H. 23/5/1944, Cols 686/692.
[2] E.g. H. 23/5/1944, Cols 614/619 (Robertson).
[3] E.g. H. 23/5/1944, Cols 681/686 (Gridley).
[4] H. 14/6/1944, Col. 2000.

In reply to these and other points Anderson explained that there was still the difficulty of correlating the forthcoming legislation with the Sections relating to E.P.T.; he could however give an assurance now that residual relevant expenditure would be treated as having been incurred on the appointed day. But it must be directly related to research: he was having no truck with a 'directly or indirectly related' proposal or with the suggestion that the clauses should be made applicable to professions.

But as anticipated the clash came over Clause 32. Section 35 of the 1941 Finance Act had directed that the Commissioners could nullify the tax advantage of a transaction where they considered that advantage to be the 'main purpose' of the transaction in question. The word 'main' had been inserted at Committee stage after considerable pressure; and when accepting the amendment Kingsley Wood had said he might appeal to the House if the Section failed to have the desired effect,[1] a warning reinforced by the Financial Secretary[2] who threatened amending retrospective legislation. By 1943 hundreds of cases[3] had come before the Special Commissioners, the body which heard appeals against directions; of these 70 per cent[4] related to increasing the number of directors to obtain a further minimum standard for each director so appointed, the balance related to buying companies to secure an extra £1,000 standard. The Crown had lost about half the cases taken before the Special Commissioners.[5] Appellants could so easily argue that a young son was being made a director for experience and nothing was further from their thoughts than avoidance of E.P.T. The deeming of main benefit to be main purpose in the new clause was intended to restore the position before the addition of 'main' in the original Section.

The debate, which lasted three hours, ran the gamut of fiscal morality and was made a general debate instead of one on specific amendments. The early speakers, Craven-Ellis, Levy and Lewis,[6] thought the original Section adequate. They disliked the element of retrospection; they felt the flaw, if it existed, should have been dis-

---

[1] H. 1/7/1941, Col. 1277.   [2] H. 1/7/1941, Col. 1280.
[3] The Solicitor-General quoted a figure of 1,400, H. 14/6/1944, Col. 2050.
[4] H. 14/6/1944, Col. 2050.
[5] H. 14/6/1944, Cols 2056/2057 (Solicitor-General).
[6] H. 14/6/1944, Cols 2038/2044.

covered before the lapse of three years and, finally, that the Chancellor had not been well advised by his Law Officers.

The opinion and feeling of the House was almost totally against these views. Discounting the inevitable ejaculations by Kirkwood and Gallacher of 'Tax rackets!' and 'Criminals!', there had been ample warning that remedial legislation would be retrospective; the time lag arose from the simple fact that the size of the problem could only now be measured as cases came on to the Special Commissioners' lists; and no blame could be attached to the Law Officers. As Benson[1] took some pleasure in pointing out, 'It was an amendment forced on the Chancellor by his party which had originally weakened the clause.'

It was Hogg[2] who tried to put a less material gloss on the case for opposing the revised clause. He agreed that the retrospection argument did not apply here, but he must point out in general that 'retrospective legislation is tyrannical and bad', and while Levy[3] had gone too far in contending that what is legal should be allowed, even in wartime, he wanted to propose a compromise which, by not imputing motive, might protect innocent parties. Benson's[4] reply brought the debate down from the subtleties of dealing with problems of intent: the Special Commissioners were in some need of a clear definition since they appeared, from their decisions, to be 'a group of elderly maiden ladies who have been kept unspotted from the world'. The plain fact was that the maximum effect of the clause could be no more than to deprive people who did not seek to gain a tax advantage of the tax advantage for which they did not ask.

The second day of the Committee stage was something of an anticlimax, with the familiar series of humanitarian appeals ranging from relief for school fees to travelling expenses for the blind, none of which was adopted. Chancellors of whatever party had always insisted on two main criteria for allowances: they should not be given simply because of the meritorious nature of the expenditure, and they should be based on a flat rate. But it was not possible to use taxation legislation, direct or indirect, as a means of levelling out all the sad inequalities in human nature, human cares and human circumstances.

The amended Bill gained general acceptance. Even the heat

---

[1] H. 14/6/1944, Col. 2045.
[2] H. 14/6/1944, Cols 2046/2049.
[3] See p. 358.
[4] H. 14/6/1944, Col. 2073.

generated by Clause 32 (now Clause 33) had died away possibly because, to the annoyance of Benson,[1] its targets had been narrowed to transactions in shares and changes in directorates.[2] It was, as the Chancellor put it, a practical solution to a practical problem and would prevent some legitimate expenditure being trapped.[3]

Most Chancellors regard the Third Reading as the most enjoyable stage in piloting a Bill to the Statute Book, and Anderson was no

---

[1] H. 28/6/1944, Col. 741.

[2] The full text of the revised section was:

Tax Avoidance

33. (1) Section thirty-five of the Finance Act 1941 (which relates to transactions designed to avoid liability to excess profits tax) shall have effect, and shall, subject to the provisions of this section, be deemed always to have had effect, as amended by the subsequent provisions of this section.

(2) In sub-section (1) of the said section, for the words 'the main purpose for which any transaction or transactions was or were effected' there shall be substituted the words 'the main purpose or one of the main purposes for which any transaction or transactions was or were effected', and in subsection (3) of the said section, for the words 'on the gound that the main purpose of the transaction or transactions was not the avoidance or reduction of liability to tax' there shall be substituted the words 'on the ground that the avoidance or reduction of liability to tax was not the main purpose or one of the main purposes of the transaction or transactions'.

(3) If it appears in the case of any transaction or transactions being a transaction which involves, or transactions one or more of which involve:

   (a) the transfer or acquisition of shares in a company; or,

   (b) a change or changes in the person or persons carrying on a trade or business or part of a trade or business

that, having regard to the provisions of the law relating to excess profits tax, other than the said section thirty-five and this section, which were in force at the time when the transaction or transactions was or were effected, the main benefit which might have been expected to accrue from the transaction or transactions during the currency of excess profits tax was avoidance or reduction of liability to the tax, the avoidance or reduction of liability to excess profits tax shall be deemed for the purposes of the said section thirty-five to have been the main purpose or one of the main purposes of the transaction or transactions.

(4) A direction under the said section thirty-five as amended by this section may be given notwithstanding that a direction has been given under that section before the passing of this Act in relation to the transaction or transactions in question or some of them.

Provided that in any case where a direction so given has, before the twenty-fifth day of April, nineteen hundred and forty-four, been cancelled or varied on appeal by the Special Commissioners, no direction given by virtue of this section in relation to the transaction or transactions in question shall affect any chargeable accounting periods ending before the first day of April, nineteen hundred and forty-four.

[3] H. 28/6/1944, Col. 750.

exception.[1] He had already covered most of the criticisms and could afford to ignore Benson's[2] last shot that his proposals on capital allowances were a carrot to spur industry out of its timidity and lethargy. He closed with a point on the burden of internal debt which he thought should be firmly made; it was not a matter of comparative unimportance, as some speakers had claimed, for it meant the continuation of the cramping grip of high taxation.

At first sight the Budget of 1944 seems fairly summarized by the medicinal label of 'the mixture as before' with which its author had modestly tagged it. It was generally expected that the pattern set by Kingsley Wood would be followed. The country had spent £5,800 millions in 1943: it would be difficult to budget for more, and the yield would automatically increase as incomes and profits increased. In fact the national accounts suggested that the stage had now been reached where the curve of Government expenditure was no longer rising faster than the fiscal product. A good half of the spending would still continue to be met out of income apart from the unpredictable quantum of post-war credits. The only possible change might have been heavier taxes on luxury goods. In the event the Budget made history in that during the fifth year of the greatest war mankind had endured, no taxation increases were considered necessary.

But the Budget had a basically dual structure. It not only proposed a well-tried mechanism for raising the sinews of war, but it was also facing the future in its suggestions for revised capital allowances for industry. The Chancellor laid down as a principle of future fiscal policy that the true trading profits were that part of the annual revenue remaining after meeting not only all current commercial costs but, in particular, after deducting an amount equal in value to the proportional value of assets used up in making that profit.

The new capital allowances inevitably met a certain volume of criticism. The initial allowance was decried as being merely an acceleration of the normal annual allowance giving correspondingly lower allowances in later years. It was also urged that some means should be devised to take care of relief for the continuous improvement in plant: simple replacement was not adequate. Thirdly, the rising cost of renewing plant was not fully catered for. The general

[1] H. 30/6/1944, Col. 956.　　[2] H. 30/6/1944, Col. 950.

answer was, of course, that the proposals to be embodied in the Income Tax Act 1945 were the maximum which could then be afforded.

So much was on the surface, but a closer look at the Budget and the Government speeches reveal unsuspected depths. There was substantial tax relief implicit in the new legislation and quite considerable immediate relief in the increased E.P.T. standards for small companies. There was the Treasury-backed revision of the anti-avoidance legislation, most unpopular with the Right. Against this could be balanced the unpegged cost of living, a moderate proposal offsetting only 25 per cent of the wages increase, which roused Labour opposition. And finally the continuation of Kingsley Wood's policy implied the reorganization of the spread of taxable incomes over a much wider spectrum than pre-war, and, as a corollary, the parallel spread of those incomes as a source of savings.

In fact the Budget of 1944 was a classic example in its layout of the new style Budget. The forensic accountancy which was the main content of pre-war Budgets was compressed into comparatively short passages at the opening and closing of the speech. The central themes were now the wide national and international surveys, the sombre facts, the requirements, the prospects, all of which had become the hall-marks of its presentation.

The Budget was justly called non-party and non-emotional,[1] and it was clearly inspired by Anderson's academic sense of equity. But it failed to recognize the war-weariness the nation was feeling and that the Dunkirk spirit was at last beginning to peter out— the reserves of willingness to make sacrifices could not be drawn upon indefinitely. Secondly, the current industrial unrest[2] could well use the excuse of the cost-of-living increases to demand higher wages. This might be thought unfair, but mere economic justification is rarely the deciding factor in wage negotiations. The inescapable answer was the continuing and even reinforcing of the widespread system of controls, but to the Britain of the identity card, the ration book and the licensing schemes, this was hardly a solution which presented immediate attractions or acceptance.

[1] See King-Hall, pp. 342/343.
[2] A. J. P. Taylor, *English History 1914-1945*, p. 566.

Chapter XIII

The End and the Beginning

THE INCOME TAX ACT AND THE FINANCE BILLS (I) AND (II) 1945

Time Table (the Income Tax Act 1945):

Second Reading		March 14, 1945
Committee		
	1st Day	April 27
	2nd Day	May 15
Report		June 4
Third Reading		4
Royal Assent		15

The Income Tax Act of 1945 was a dramatic and significant curtain-raiser to the first Finance Bill of the same year. Its origin was the discussions on the taxation of reserves and possible changes in wear and tear allowances which Sir Kingsley Wood had initiated with the commercial world and the Inland Revenue, and which had been continued with his successor. These had proved so successful that in the 1944 Budget proposals the Chancellor had been able to sketch the outline of the measure he was now proposing in detail and to lay down the general principle that a commercial profit 'should be struck only after making all proper deductions and allowances especially adequate allowances for the amortization of money expended on assets which are used up in the making of the profits'.[1]

His opening speech[2] occupied only twenty-five minutes and was intended to give Members the basic ideas behind the Bill. The em-

[1] H. 25/4/1944, Col. 672.   [2] H. 14/3/1945, Cols 257/264.

phasis was placed on modernization and re-equipment of industry, which was translated into accelerated capital allowances for plant and a writing-off allowance for the first time in respect of industrial buildings. But here the marginal nature of the innovations showed itself, for hotels and offices were excluded. The Chancellor firmly pointed out that it was productive industry he was aiming to help, that the proposals were expensive and costly to the general body of taxpayers and that any general extension would cause administrative difficulties; allowances on plant and machinery were, however, not discriminatory.

So much had been foreshadowed last year. He was now proposing to go further than he had anticipated last April. All plant and machinery bought, whether new or second-hand, would qualify for initial allowance, and instead of an appointed day after the end of the war for commencing these new allowances any expenditure on plant, machinery and new buildings after April 6, 1944, would rank. There were parallel provisions[1] for the extractive industries. As for agriculture, agricultural plant and machinery would be on all fours with industrial, but there would be different treatment for agricultural buildings and works, giving no allowance for old buildings but a ten-year spread of allowance for new. In Part VI he dealt with relief for scientific and industrial research expenditure which was on the same lines as the new arrangements for plant, machinery and buildings, and in Part VII of the Bill he indicated how the interreaction of the new provisions and the exceptional depreciation allowances would be dealt with.

He summarized by claiming that the Bill was 'inspired by the genuine desire of the Government to prepare for and to stimulate that forward surge of productive industrial activity on the part of our people on which the whole of our programme of reconstruction and reform must depend'.

The debate which followed illustrated the hardening of political postures which was now beginning to show itself in the House: Pethick-Lawrence,[2] for instance, in a speech of studied moderation, felt it necessary to mention the party line of extending the field of public ownership while admitting that inadequate wear and tear allowances had been an industrial grievance for many years. Against this was the right-wing attitude that the measures were less an aid to

[1] H. 14/3/1945, Col. 260.   [2] H. 14/3/1945, Cols 264/269.

industry than the removal of a hindrance.[1] There were only two root-and-branch opponents, Cove[2] and Bowles,[3] the former arguing that the post-war problems of poverty, insecurity and unemployment would not be solved by the relief of capital expenditure, and the latter that it was the despairing effort of the Government to make the capitalist system work in the post-war world. But behind this honest partisanship hints of that special pleading, which was to vitiate the Committee stage, were beginning to emerge.

It had been the general expectation of the principal speakers that most of the details would have to await this stage[4] and any necessary explanations of particular clauses be given then. This was an over-optimistic calculation for two reasons. In the first place the Bill comprised seventy clauses and three lengthy schedules—it would have been impossible to consider this mass of material in the allotted time, and in the event forty of the clauses and two of the schedules passed without debate. There were some two hundred proposed amendments affecting the balance of the Bill; the Chancellor's mainly drafting amendments were all agreed; some minor suggestions from the floor, usually relating to phraseology, were also agreed—but there was not a single major change of principle. Secondly, out of the two hundred columns of debate, nearly one-third[5] was devoted to considering the ambit of the term 'industrial building', which, although important, did not in the circumstances merit such a disproportionate expense of time.

Schuster and his supporters fought long and hard for the widening of this clause[6] to shops and hotels. The former, it was argued, were the outlets of the process of production and required modernization, a view shared by Aneurin Bevan from first-hand experience.[7] The latter, although not productive, were certainly productive of foreign exchange. In general, too, the line was not easy to draw between industrial and non-industrial buildings.[8] The official definition did muster some support including that of Cove, who thought it showed 'a lack of virility to depend on foreigners coming to our

---

[1] H. 14/3/1945, Col 269 (Schuster).   [2] H. 14/3/1945, Cols 291/295.
[3] H. 14/3/1945, Cols 312/316.
[4] Cf. Pethick-Lawrence and Anderson, H. 14/3/1945, Col. 267 and Col. 257 respectively.
[5] H. 27/4/1945, Cols 131/193.   [6] Clause 8, later S.8, I.T.A. 1945.
[7] He had once been a butcher's errand boy.
[8] Although it had been done in the Derating Act of 1929.

hotels to benefit foreign exchange'.[1] Anderson was as adamant as he was orthodox: there must be a limit to the concessions which could be made; his proposals were good despite their inevitably limited objective and he was not prepared to jeopardize them.

The failure of this concerted assault took much of the steam out of the debate, so that the Chancellor was able to claim with some conviction, 'I hope the Committee will believe I have tried to look sympathetically on every proposal put forward in connection with this Bill which is essentially a relieving Bill.'[2] In his final summary on the Third Reading[3] he picked up Pethick-Lawrence's phrase that the Bill was a 'modest attempt' to benefit industry with the challenge that it was 'rather an ambitious attempt'. It broke new ground and would be helpful to industry both by its measures and the implication that the Government was sensible of the effect of taxation on productive industry. Perhaps the Chancellor tended not to face squarely the basic weakness of his measures that it was impossible to provide for the full development of British industry by the purely negative mechanism of tax relief. But he had promised the use of discriminating taxation as an instrument of policy, and despite its occasional obscurity and complexity and its limited objective, it was the measure of a professional not a politician.

THE FINANCE BILL (I) 1945

Time Table

Financial Statement	April 14, 1945
Budget Proposals	
1st Day	25
2nd Day	26
Withdrawn	May 29

Less than six weeks after his confident introduction[4] of the Second Reading of the Income Tax Bill of 1945, the Chancellor opened the Financial Statement for 1945.[5] In that short period tremendous

---

[1] H. 27/4/1945, Col. 1196. [2] H. 15/5/1945, Col. 2321.
[3] H. 4/6/1945, Col. 599. [4] H. 16/3/1945
[5] H. 24/4/1945, Cols 692/720.

events were happening in the war zones which heralded the downfall of both Germany and Italy. But there was still the Japanese war, which it was thought would endure for another eighteen months, as well as the transitional problems of turning over both men and manufactures to a peacetime basis. No wonder he asked the Committee 'to recognize the peculiar difficulties of my task on this occasion, and to regard this Budget as one which may possibly have to be superseded before the year is out'.

However that might be, it did not relieve him from the ritual statistical summary. Expenditure in 1944/1945 had for the first time exceeded £6,000 millions, the precise total being £6,063 millions, £126 millions over the estimate. The reason for this was almost wholly due to the Vote of Credit for which the Chancellor had taken £5,000 millions and which, in the event, required £5,125 millions. There were some other variations from the estimates which had been compensated for by corresponding savings.

Happily revenue had also exceeded estimates. The Inland Revenue estimate of £2,000 millions had been exceeded by £29 millions, of which £17 millions was income tax, and £10 millions E.P.T. Customs and Excise, set at £1,038 millions, had produced £1,076 millions, £20 millions of the excess coming from beer duty. Miscellaneous revenue was £66 millions higher than the estimate, partly because receipts from war damage insurances had, as usual, been excluded from the estimate.

The over-all analysis showed that the amount by which expenditure had exceeded revenue was £2,825 millions, or £11 millions less than the Budget estimate. This balance was amply covered by various borrowings:[1] 'but the really significant figure of 1944 is that the proportion of our total expenditure met out of revenue was 53 per cent, a higher proportion than in any previous war year.'[2] It was also significant that private savings were a little less than last year due to some increase in expenditure on personal consumption.[3]

There were now some special matters he wished to refer to before dealing with the general budgetary prospects for the coming year. Hydro-carbon oils[4] used as raw materials for chemical synthesis

[1] See Tables 17 and 19 of the current White Paper, Cmd. 6623.
[2] The average over the five-and-a-half years was 49 per cent. (Total expenditure £27,400 millions; met out of current revenue, £13,300 millions.)
[3] See Tables 21 and 22 of the current White Paper, Cmd. 6623.
[4] This was the result of the Ayre Committee's Report, 11/4/1945.

were to be freed from Customs duty; along with this were some minor Excise modifications of spirit duty and entertainment tax.[1]

Far more important, however, were the proposed changes in motor taxation which had been worked out in consultation with the motor industry, 'particularly as regards the steps by which the new duty is to be graduated. This is a matter on which there is substantial difference of opinion. . . .' The duty was now to be charged by reference to cylinder capacity instead of horse-power,[2] the duty to proceed by steps of one hundred cubic centimetres. He hoped the changes would be of assistance to the industry, but they would not reduce taxation; that could not be conceded at present.

Turning now to direct taxation, the success of the Pay As You Earn scheme should hold pride of place. The magnitude of the task involved in its introduction could be illustrated statistically. About sixteen millions of wage-earners came within its scope, of whom twelve millions would be liable to tax; one million employers were involved in operating the collection mechanism, which had netted no less than £540 millions in the year just concluded, an increase of £100 millions over the previous year.

With regard to E.P.T., although representations about its rate continued, he still held firmly to his conviction that no relaxation was possible while the war in Europe continued. In the case of small businesses however, 'it cannot but have a cramping effect on their growth quite disproportionate to the revenue involved'. Last year the standard had been increased by £1,000; now he was proposing that where the standard was less than £12,000 there should be an addition of one-tenth the amount by which the existing standard fell short of that figure.[3] The cost of this concession would be some £12 millions, about the same sum as the cost of last year's standard increase.

On the question of double taxation, which had been under active discussion for some time, he could report considerable progress. At present only the Dominions afforded relief for income doubly taxed, which was an intolerable burden on trading concerns earning profits abroad. A unilateral approach was possible, but in his view the double charge should be eliminated and he was happy to say that a double taxation agreement had just been concluded with the

---

[1] H. 24/4/1945, Cols 697/698.   [2] S. 5, F.A. (2) 1945.
[3] Precisely similar to the abatement for N.D.C.

United States; in brief, the procedure was to credit the foreign tax against the home tax; and it was proposed to cover double taxation arising in the field of estate duty also.

He must now turn to another matter which he thought 'our main immediate cause for anxiety', the amount of overseas war expenditure. Apart from what had been spent in Europe and the Americas, from 1942 to 1944 £1,989 millions was the total expenditure in Asia and Africa; the country's total disinvestment throughout the world amounted, strangely enough, to an almost identical figure; and although the physical resources of the Empire had been pooled throughout the war and Mutual Aid from this country had been more than matched by Lease-Lend, total liability to overseas creditors now exceeded £3,000 millions. 'The total is likely to reach at least £4,000 millions before we are finished, and this liability takes no account of the assets we have sold.'

He obviously could not now discuss settling this problem into which other factors and other nations entered. But clearly for some years after the war there must be a very heavy deficit on current account in the balance of payments. How large that indebtedness became and how long it lasted depended on the sense of urgency which was brought to expanding exports and on how far the country would be willing to enforce a strict economy in external cash expenditure.

The Chancellor now dealt with the new and expanded White Paper[1] which sought to measure the national income and to show how that income had been spent. It was the duty of Members to watch the broad tendencies which showed themselves, but especially it would be necessary to have what he called 'a continuous census of production'. He concluded his side-ranging survey of external debts and the domestic economy by suggesting gently that while the Budget should provoke 'lively discussion and controversy', argument 'should be checked by the recognition of indisputable and objective facts'.

Two perennial points now required mention before he could consider his immediate budgetary prospects. He did not wish to underemphasize the weight of the internal debt, but its burden was mitigated by an average rate of interest which had fallen from 3·1 per

[1] Cmd. 6623.

cent in 1938 to the current 2·3 per cent. Secondly, he was still taking his stand on a firm refusal to offset increases in cost automatically by corresponding subsidies, although his aim was to prevent the cost of living rising above 135 per cent of the pre-war figure. His credo was simply put.[1] 'A stable price level will be compatible with a slow and steady increase of wages if that increase corresponds with an increase of efficiency of output. Disciplined and orderly progress in the determination of wage rates should be recognized as the prime interest of the wage-earning class as well as of the community as a whole; it is the level of efficiency wages which determines the purchasing power of money.'

A bare six columns only remained in which to compress his estimates based on evidence he could only regard as 'slender'—all depended on when the war in Europe ended. The Debt charge he put up by £50 millions to £465 millions; other Consolidated Fund Services would require £19 millions. Civil Supply Votes he proposed to increase by £68 millions to £581 millions to take care of additional welfare and educational expenditure. The provision for Votes of Credit was the most uncertain: he was suggesting the 'very round sum' of £4,500 millions from the computations of the spending departments. The grand total was £500 millions below the 1944/1945 total at £5,565 millions.

Revenue estimates were somewhat more evidential. Income tax should produce £1,350 millions, a rise of £33 millions, but E.P.T. he put £10 millions lower at £500 millions to compensate for the increased standards in 1944. The remaining Inland Revenue duties should have an out-turn of £215 millions, £13 millions above the previous year. Customs and Excise yields, however, were more difficult to forecast in the current wild swing of events. Tobacco and beer were running at a figure which would yield respectively £400 millions and £300 millions in duty—these estimates he had adopted. Other duties, such as oil, would bring the total up to £1,130 millions, £54 millions in excess of the previous year's receipts. Finally other heads of revenue he set at £70 millions, giving a grand total of £3,265 millions.[2] The amount for which borrowing powers would be

---

[1] H. 24/4/1945, Col. 716.
[2] Inland Revenue   £2,065 millions
     Customs and Excise   £1,130
     Other Heads   £70

needed was therefore £2,300 millions,[1] some £525 millions less than the figure last year.

But this considerable easing of the position did not mean any relaxation in the drive for all possible economies. The total cost of normal peacetime services and the new developments in policy which the Government had promised made it essential that the burden of taxation should not be increased by any unnecessary expenditure. In the present state of flux he was not in a position to estimate the sources of borrowing, but one fact was clear: the greatest restraint would have to be maintained in personal budgets and the need for savings was as paramount as ever.

There would be no major increase or decrease in taxation, and there were two main reasons for this. It would be 'highly dangerous' to increase the pressure of purchasing power on the market before there could be any corresponding increase of supplies. Secondly, although he could forecast a drop in war expenditure, 'the major reductions in taxation must be made as part of the comprehensive review of the probable course of post-war expenditure and of our system of taxation as a whole in relation to it. . . . Only so can justice be done all round.'[2]

In conclusion he must emphasize that the current readiness to accept the pressure of war taxation should not induce a psychology of readiness to maintain that pressure in peace, and that even 'such an ex-officio prophet as a Chancellor of the Exchequer' could not at this juncture draw any practical conclusions. It was, as he had said at the outset, an interim Budget. He had spoken for less than an hour and a half, and it was to be the last Budget opening before the fall of Germany.

It was a mark-time Budget opened in an unavoidably tentative speech which the Chancellor read from his M.S.S. throughout and which he had couched in his Latinized English, for he seemed to boggle at plain Anglo-Saxon. Nor was its impact helped by his orotund delivery, and the departure of the War Cabinet from a not very crowded House before the end. Lord Keynes, however, was in

---

[1]   £5,565 millions (p. 272)
  Less £3,265
        _____
        £2,300

[2] H. 24/4/1945, Cols 721/722.

the gallery, and perhaps that austere figure could afford some consolation.

It was hardly surprising then, after such an introduction, that the debate itself should have been somewhat desultory; quite apart from the fact that the immediate post-Budget discussions had, over the period, developed into a field-day for the back-benchers and for the ventilation of general principles. At times the principles became a little too general, at which the Speaker would find it necessary to remind the House that Members' contributions must relate to the collecting or borrowing of money.

There were of course some familiar and recurrent themes, chief among which on the Conservative side was a renewed attack against E.P.T., the basic complaints being that the rate was too high,[1] that it had a deterrent effect on the small business,[2] and that it prevented the building up of reserves.[3] There was support from outside the House: 'Of all the taxes on businesses,' wrote *The Times*,[4] 'which impede development, encourage carelessness and create widespread injustice between one business and another, 100 per cent E.P.T. is by common consent unrivalled. So long as it exists no growing business can finance its development, and in the case of a large proportion of business enterprises . . . it is a standing encouragement to wasteful administration and expenditure.' Combined with these specific complaints were criticisms of the rates of income tax,[5] the operation of Pay As You Earn,[6] although Leslie[7] argued the average worker did not object to it, and its pressure on the fixed-income groups from pensioners to the retired members of the middle-class,[8] whose incomes had not increased on account of the war.

But behind the natural reaction to the burden of taxation when the war was nearing its end lurked the spectre or saving grace of a controlled economy, depending on the side of the House from which the coming transitional problems were viewed. Greenwood[9] had been quite specific: 'Nobody likes being controlled if they can avoid it,

[1] H. 24/4/1945, Cols 762/764 (Procter).
[2] H. 24/4/1945, Cols 743/746 (Kendall).
[3] H. 24/4/1945, Cols 777/780 (Allen).   [4] 23/4/1945.
[5] H. 24/4/1945, Cols 702/764 (Procter).
[6] H. 24/4/1945, Cols 772/777 (Wootton-Davies).
[7] H. 24/4/1945, Cols 780/782.
[8] H. 24/4/1945, Cols 782/787 (Nicholson and Tinker).
[9] H. 24/4/1945, Cols 728/732.

but it is quite clear, whatever may be the broad future of this country on a long-term policy, during the transition period there must be an orderly direction of our national resources to those objects which are of the greatest social service.' King-Hall,[1] as an uncommitted Member, could agree that control of expenditure was desirable. Tasker,[2] however, felt that control implied an increase in executive and bureaucratic power and a corresponding diminution in the authority of Parliament.

To do him justice, Anderson had covered the complaint of the pressure of E.P.T. on the smaller concern as far as he felt able;[3] but on the question of control, he was not prepared to go further at the present than his admonitions on savings and personal consumption whatever plans he and the Treasury might have under wraps.

Gallacher,[4] however, exhibited a fine contempt for both taxation revision and controls. He was convinced that if the Chancellor 'and his gang are returned there would be a hand-out in the form of reduced taxation'. Equally, control of spending and increase in investment he dismissed as 'a capitalist ramp'. The vaunted 'good housekeeping'[5] of the pre-war years was a myth: it consisted of 'wasting unearned money while masses of the people in the country were starving'. An adequate standard of living was the real target, not the export trade. In all, it was Gallacher's usual mixture of muddled Marxism and honest humanity.

The Press, without exception, took its cue from the tone of the debate; it was an interim Budget which went some distance in unfolding what might well become a master-plan for post-war Britain. The *New Statesman*[6] found little in the speech to attract attention; and it was true that particular details remained unchanged. But, as *The Times*[7] pointed out, the Chancellor's general review was far from negative and made it clear that there would very likely be the opportunity for considerable cuts in taxation later in the year —indeed, so much had been patently hinted at. This was the line, too, which was broadly taken by *The Economist*.[8]

The comments of the *Spectator*[9] and of the *Manchester Guardian*[10] also ran parallel. The former went so far as to call it a 'hopeful bud-

---

[1] H. 24/4/1945, Cols 755/759. [2] H. 24/4/1945, Cols 735/740.
[3] See p. 270. [4] H. 24/4/1945, Cols 764/772.
[5] The phrase was Anderson's. [6] 28/4/1945. [7] 25/4/1945.
[8] 28/4/1945. [9] 27/4/1945. [10] 25/4/1945.

get' and agreed to an extent with the *New Statesman* that if the excitement of a Budget speech is measured by the new burdens imposed or the old burdens lifted, it was unexciting. From other points of view, however, it was instructive and impressive in its exposition of war expenditure and transitional problems. The latter, approving the argument that it was too early to begin the task of reconstruction, stressed the importance of the Chancellor's warnings that 'free expenditure' would be out back ruthlessly and that continued discipline in spending was needed. Judging from the financial columns of both the dailies and the weeklies, the Budget was well received by the City, with understandable reservations.

If the immediate-post-Budget debate was the chance for the amateurs, the first full day's debate invariably brought out the professionals. But even their speeches were somewhat tentative and inconsequential. Perhaps it was because, as the Chancellor himself admitted, in a burst of candour, 'there was very little to criticize in the Budget because there was in fact very little in the Budget itself'.[1] This meant comments on the general financial situation which could only be, basically, reasons for suspending final judgment which was the line Anderson himself had been forced to take with much more information at his disposal. In addition the House was never anything like full and the Chancellor could not always be present, two factors which made neither for cogency nor inspiration.

Pethick-Lawrence,[2] as usual, set a reasoned Labour tone. It was a good pedestrian Budget, and considering the work of the infantry during the war this comment was not necessarily disparaging. He broadly approved of the E.P.T. concessions, the Double Taxation Agreement and the revised scheme for motor duties. The big danger was, as he saw it, an undue inflation of purchasing power despite a prospective fall in wages through reduced overtime. He was asking the Chancellor to examine the whole incidence of income tax, now it extended so far down the wage-earning scale, since its weight was causing a 'diminution of enterprise' both in workers and employers.

The problem of revising the whole direct taxation system was to prove the major theme of the day, cropping up to a greater or lesser extent in most of the contributions to the debate. Sometimes it was a simple plea, from the Right usually, for the reduction or abolition of

[1] H. 26/4/1945, Col. C. 1094.   [2] H. 25/4/1945, Cols 846/855.

E.P.T.[1] or taxation generally,[1] but in three major interventions it went far beyond mere rate revisions.

Wardlaw-Milne,[2] for example, called for a relaxation in E.P.T. and taxation generally, although he combined this with a warning of the dangers of increased spending power and the need for planning. Schuster[3] was in full agreement with the thesis that current rates of taxation restricted productive enterprise and wanted 'a comprehensive independent review' of fiscal influences on the national economy. With the need for exports and limitation of expenditure must go an increase in productive efficiency initiated by the present system. Benson[4] was a strange bedfellow for these two apostles of enlightened right-wing economics; but while considering the prospect of any serious reduction in taxation in the present circumstances remote, he was still gravely concerned with the pressure of high taxation. The system was admittedly efficient 'but it cannot be said to cause the minimum of economic damage'. It affected incentives, as other speakers had said; but he wished to emphasize its effect on industrial reserves, where he would be prepared to advocate a differential rate, although this violated the canons of fiscal equity. The true solution would be a 'drastic and fundamental examination of the income tax system', by means of a Royal Commission. Its purview should be not merely what he called 'the internal logic' of direct taxation but its effect on the whole economic structure of the country. This proposal was endorsed by Loftus,[5] a self-confessed missionary for fiscal and monetary reform.

But Anderson was not without his critics, the most vocal being Stokes.[6] Starting from the thesis that greater industrial efficiency should bring greater rewards to individual workers, he found the Chancellor's speech overpraised. The House was becoming 'a sort of fan's paradise' which was quite unjustified, as the Budget 'was written out for him by his scribes in the Department' and was essentially 'a rather subtle attack on both the wages and savings of the worker'. The Government was allowing the Banks 'to create money in debt and pay interest on it'; it was mulcting the employers of the

[1] Cf. Morgan, H. 25/4/1945, Cols 897/898, or Henderson, H. 25/4/1945, Cols 892/897. But both Pethick-Lawrence (see p. 380) and W. J. Brown (see p. 383) advocated a reduction of E.P.T.
[2] H. 25/4/1945, Cols 862/869.   [3] H. 25/4/1945, Cols 877/886.
[4] H. 25/4/1945, Cols 898/904.   [5] H. 25/4/1945, Cols 911/919.
[6] H. 25/4/1945, Cols 869/878.

collection costs of Pay As You Earn, but worst of all it was over-looking the panacea for all fiscal problems, the taxation of land values, which 'would tackle wealth at the source'.

Brown[1] proposed to apply three tests to the Budget. Were the methods proposed the best way of raising the required revenue? Here he thought an answer should be given to the case made out by Stokes. Did the Budget effect social justice as between one class and another? Here the plight of the old-age pensioners was sufficient indictment: if their pensions could not be increased, at least the severity of the taxation levied on them should be mitigated. The third test was one of economic validity, and since post-war Britain would be immediately a capitalist country he thought, much though it went against the grain, that taxation remissions, when they came, should be of E.P.T. not income tax.

Peake,[2] the Financial Secretary to the Treasury, in summing up the first day's debate, could fairly 'doubt if there has ever been a Budget which has been the subject of less controversy than this'. He was surprised at the few references to the change from a creditor to a debtor nation, but apart from that he was in general agreement with the tenor of most speeches that controls should be maintained, that the rate of saving must be continued for capital re-equipment and maintenance, for the export markets and for the reconstruction of war damage. He too felt 'it is essential before very long to achieve a reduction in taxation'. But remission must be comprehensive not individual and 'conditional upon the maintenance of personal savings at a high level'. It was a somewhat bland speech and Stokes was heard to complain bitterly that 'it did not deal with a single point made by Hon. Members'.[3]

The second full day's debate was more desultory by far than the first day's, although it was opened by an eminently reasonable speech from Bennett.[4] He certainly would not class the Budget psoposals as barren; double taxation relief had great significance especially for the future; equally important was the E.P.T. concession to the small business. He still had reservations, however, about the validity of post-war refunds. Unlike Plugge,[5] who had advocated a motor tax based on petrol consumption, he approved the protec-

[1] H. 25/4/1945, Cols 928/933.   [2] H. 25/4/1945, Cols 933/1011.
[3] H. 26/4/1945, Col. 1011.   [4] H. 26/4/1945, Cols 1011/1016.
[5] H. 25/4/1945, Cols 904/911.

tion which the proposed system would give against foreign cars—although admittedly it would give no real impetus to car production. The majority of the subsequent speeches, of which there were fourteen, continued to stress some aspect of direct taxation. They ranged from MacLaren's[1] general denunciation of the current system which was 'detrimental to the progress of the community', and his particular condemnation of 'your Pay As You Earn nonsense' as leading to a taxpayers' revolt, to Hannon's[2] measured praise of the Chancellor. 'He [the Chancellor] was more complete and more logical, conveying more the spirit of his own personal competence than I have ever known a Chancellor to be.' Between these two extremes fell Stephen's[3] plea for people of small incomes, which was echoed by Price[4] who combined it with a rider that taxation must be used 'as it should be' for redistributing the national income. Galbraith[5] argued that if industry and trade were to be got going at the earliest possible opportunity, E.P.T. and purchase tax must be reduced, then indirect taxation—there was no room for income tax remissions for some time to come. It was Sanderson,[6] however, who stated most unequivocally the classic Conservative doctrine that the whole policy of post-war taxation should be directed to providing economic incentives. Indirect taxation should remain high; income tax and E.P.T., which were economic disincentives, must be reduced.

It was possible for the Conservative interest to justify its arguments for reducing direct taxation on the comparatively lofty grounds that such a course would promote the industrial revival so vital for the post-war period; indeed, as far as E.P.T. was concerned, there was Labour support. But party strife, so long hidden beneath the cloak of coalition, was beginning to emerge. Admittedly White,[7] for the Liberals, indulged in academic protest only. He gave the Chancellor credit for his 'good intentions' and praised his excellent record in management of interest rates and, possibly with a touch of irony, his contribution towards the redistribution of the national income. He recognized the 'serious difficulty' of the extent of sterling indebtedness and the significance of double taxation arrangements

---

[1] H. 26/4/1945, Cols 1048/1057.
[2] H. 26/4/1945, Cols 1057/1062.
[3] H. 26/4/1945, Cols 1062/1065.
[4] H. 26/4/1945, Cols 1070/1074.
[5] H. 26/4/1945, Cols 1074/1076.
[6] H. 26/4/1945, Cols 1066/1070.
[7] H. 26/4/1945, Cols 1030/1037.

in this connection. But he thought purchase tax should have been revised even at the risk of increased consumption; he regarded the omission of details of the country's capital assets from the White Paper as a serious deficiency; and he argued there should be a defined policy towards subsidies, not simply the current, casual *ad hoc* arrangements.

But some of the left-of-centre Labour Members staked their claim boldly on thinly veiled political speeches. Cove[1] very much doubted whether there would be the same productive effort for peace as for war; a new Jerusalem would not easily be come by; and while he accepted the need for technical efficiency, 'of equal importance is the position of the common people'. Mack[2] was even more forthright. 'The Budget is a class Budget. It is weighted against the poorer elements of the community.' He was especially concerned about the plight of pensioners and the lowly-paid workers. Everyone was in the same boat during the war, but it was the toilers at the benches who had done the rowing. The real debating speech, however, was Shinwell's.[3] He made telling play with the contradictions in the Chancellor's public pronouncements on prosperity, with Lord Woolton's optimistic forecasts, and he contrasted the Financial Secretary's statement on the retention of controls with the opinion of the London Chamber of Commerce, a Tory stronghold which was all for their removal. He moderated his remarks when discussing the national economy to comparative orthodoxy, especially on the subject of taxation where he took the enlightened line that E.P.T., but not personal taxation, should be reduced. On the vexed question of coal and transport, however, he was adamant; the State must step in and take them over—there was no half-way house.

Anderson[4] permitted himself a brief pleasantry when he rose to wind up. He had, he remarked, listened to a great many arguments, some mutually destructive. The inference was that he did not propose to answer these. For the rest, he devoted his usual meticulous and scrupulous attention to dealing with the main points raised one by one.

In the first place he had, he assured the House, every intention of promoting, as soon as possible, a comprehensive review of every aspect of the tax structure, and 'while I do not maintain for one

[1] H. 26/4/1945, Cols 1039/1044.   [2] H. 26/4/1945, Cols 1076/1080.
[3] H. 26/4/1945, Cols 1016/1030.   [4] H. 26/4/1945, Cols 1080/1095.

moment that the tax does not, in individual cases, encroach upon the amount available on a reasonable view, for the purchase of the necessaries of life, with a little margin, I think on the whole we can, without doing violence to our consciences, wait until that review is possible'. He again repeated that E.P.T. post-war refunds could be used both for industrial development and for covering overdrafts which had been taken up for that purpose. But he tended to skate over the proposed taxation of land values with a facile 'Land is changing hands all the time, on a rising market, at increasing rates, and unless you are going to do very grave injustice you cannot suddenly pounce selectively on that class of property.'

The second major point was the cost of living which was still being regulated by subsidies; both he and his advisers were carefully watching for inflation and were checking any over-release of purchasing power. He would never support control for the sake of controls, but in those spheres he had mentioned, and in rationing generally, controls would obviously have to be maintained.

Stemming from this, and in reply to Shinwell, he thought that there was 'every sort of compromise possible' between undiluted private enterprise and full State control, or, as he put it, 'You may leave a thing to private enterprise, and at the same time reserve certain powers to the State'. On the general financial situation, as he had outlined it, he thought there was a great measure of general agreement: 'it is really very desirable that we should try to find common ground in these matters'. But the final, and most melancholy, comment should come from Pethick-Lawrence. 'This is the last time, ' he said, 'when we shall be talking with one another instead of at one another'.[1]

For the evening before, the lantern light over Big Ben which normally showed the House was in session had been lit as a sign the war in Europe was over, after being extinguished 'for five years, seven months and twenty-three days'. The German army surrendered in May and, following the Whitsuntide meeting of the Labour Party Conference, Attlee wrote to Churchill urging an October election. Churchill promptly resigned and formed a caretaker Government which held office until June 15th. The net result of these political manoeuvrings from the standpoint of the Budget was the withdrawal of the original Finance Bill for 1945 on May 29th.[2] A second

[1] H. 25/4/1945, Col. 853.   [2] H. 29/5/1945, Col. 174.

Bill,[1] introduced as the Finance (No. 2) Bill and printed accordingly, was enacted within a few days and became the Finance Act, 1945. It had seven clauses only, covering rates of direct and indirect tax, preserving the E.P.T. amendment to standard profits and making the statutory provisions for the National Debt service. But the original Bill[2] had not exercised the talents of the Parliamentary draughtsmen in vain, for a good deal of it was resurrected in the autumn of 1945 and incorporated in the Finance (No. 2) Act, 1945.[3] By then the political scene in Britain had changed completely, and the brave new world of finance was to be ushered in not by Anderson but by Dalton.

There were two curious pieces of irony relating to Anderson's abortive Budget of 1945, a Budget which turned out to be his last. The first was that all the pre-Budget statistics of revenue and expenditure indicated very close planning and estimating; and, as the Chancellor hinted more then once in his opening speech, the continuation of the war, to which the fiscal system had been geared for five years and more, posed fewer problems then the prospective outbreak of peace, however welcome. The imponderables of the end of the war made the Budget a particularly frustrating exercise, quite apart from the ultimate withdrawal.

But the efforts which Anderson and the Treasury had put into the Budget were not wholly wasted. The Budget speech itself was a pattern for many a future opening in its wide survey of the economic scene, which yet was infused and guided by the salient statistics and trends of the current economic pattern. It was a pioneering speech, too, in its brave attempt to indicate a blueprint for the coming year in spite of so many immediately unknown factors.

Secondly, the increased standards for small businesses[4] was incorporated in truncated Finance Act of 1945[5] passed by the caretaker Government. This went nothing like as far in the way of general relief from E.P.T. as many of the speakers in the debates, both Conservative and Labour, had requested, but it was at least a pledge of better things to come in the anticipated autumn Budget.

But most important, possibly, in the way of setting a precedent and of providing practical benefit to the reviving export trade, was the Double Taxation Agreement with the United States. The existence of double taxation arose quite simply from the fact that few countries were altruistic enough to confine the purview of their

[1] Bill 61. [2] Bill 49. [3] Bill 28. [4] See p. 270. [5] S.5, F.A. 1945.

taxation either to the income arising within their territory whatever the domicile of its owner, or alternatively to income received by their own residents regardless of its source. Obviously the conclusion of such an agreement ensuring that profits and income were not doubly taxed was of immense advantage to Britain in fighting to restore traditional export markets and in acquiring new ones.

As far as indirect taxation was concerned, the most important proposal was in the field of motor taxation where a new basis of cubic capacity of cylinders had been put forward. Anderson had tried to reach a compromise between the various conflicting interests in the motor-car industry with the familiar result that he had succeeded in satisfying no one section completely. In fact the legislation was not finalized until Finance (No. 2) Act 1945. But Section 5 of that Act repeated word for word the draft Clause 12 of the original Bill of April 1945. The net result of the legislation was to make the British motor industry something of a hothouse plant, sheltered from the winds of Continental and American competition and suffering to an extent from in-breeding.

Looking again, however, at the over-all position presented by the Chancellor, four projected stages of recovery can be distinguished. Until the end of the war in Europe, a strict limitation on income and expenditure must be maintained, and it would be necessary to begin to think less and less of lavish State expenditure regardless of cost, and more and more of economy under Treasury control. Then when the war in the Far East was over, a start could be made on actually pruning expenditure and injecting into the economy gradually increasing shots of purchasing power; manpower would have to be directed to productive tasks; and above all the same sense of urgency which had prevailed in wartime must be fostered in peace. After, say, a five-year period release of purchasing power might be accelerated, subject to the overriding demands of housing, defence and re-equipment. Finally, when reorganization was seen to be truly under way, the economy could be allowed to expand with a progressive slackening of controls.

It is easy to accuse Anderson of over-simplification, and clearly the orderly sequence of events which he envisaged depended a great deal on the full restoration of international trade and was not susceptible to unilateral planning only. Then again, although an academic rather than a political exercise in crystal-gazing, it had nothing of the hopes of progress toward a less class-ridden society which inspired the Opposition benches. But for all that it was an attempt to plan, to organize, to control far different from the chaotic free-for-all which had distinguished the years after 1918.

As suggested, ironically enough Anderson would have had an easier task to prepare a further wartime Budget than a potential peacetime one. The second piece of irony was the fact that a radical reduction in E.P.T. rates, so long the Sangrail of the Conservative industrial and commercial interest in the House, should have been legislated for in Finance (No. 2) Act, 1945, Section 27,[1] by the first Labour Chancellor of the Exchequer since Snowden.

[1] By which the rate was amended to 60 per cent.

Chapter XIV

Restrospect and Prospect

The period from 1933 to 1945 saw more radical changes in taxation, particularly in direct taxation, and in budgetary policy and format generally, than any other dozen or so consecutive years in British fiscal history. Chamberlain's first four Budgets were pitched in a minor key but played a vital, if unspectacular part in the limited recovery of 1933 to 1936 by a delicate combination of inflatory and deflatory measures. His last three Budgets were inevitably circumscribed by mounting armaments expenditure, a handicap which intensified under Simon; but even when war broke out the level of taxation rose in an alarmingly slow curve. It was left to Kingsley Wood and his advisers from 1941 onwards to put taxation on a war basis; Anderson, his successor, completed the transformation of the Budget from a bookkeeping statement of income and expenditure to its use as a cardinal instrument of State policy.

Direct taxation holds pride of place in the catalogue of change. For, although there was no basic alteration of principles apart from the grafting on of N.D.C./E.P.T. which were new taxes altogether, the rejigging to meet the demands of war was so drastic that the total yield rose from £484 millions in 1938 to £2,054 millions in 1945, the major ingredient of which was income tax, with surtax producing £371 millions in 1938 and £1,426 millions in 1945. The scaling down of allowances and increase in rates which helped to accomplish this were not, of course, a steady process over the whole period. In Chamberlain's third and fourth Budgets he had been able to relieve industry by reducing the standard rate in 1934 and then to give the smaller taxpayer his turn by increasing allowances in 1935.[1]

---

[1] See Appendix A.

From then onwards allowances declined while rates ascended to a plateau in 1941, where they stayed until 1945.

Surtax rates were hoisted from a maximum of 7s 6d on incomes of £50,001 upwards in 1937/1938 to the almost confiscatory level of 9s 6d on incomes of £30,001 upwards in 1938/1939; for the rest of the war period the total income figure was amended to £20,001 and upwards.[1] Strangely enough an enabling clause in 1939 to allow the Chancellor to drop the surtax limit to £1,500 was never implemented, partly for administrative reasons and partly because, with a standard rate of 10s 0d in the pound, incomes between £1,500 and £2,000 were mulcted enough.

A second factor in producing these massive aggregations of tax had been the changes in legislation which brought additional profits within the scope of the taxing Acts. A liability to tax under Schedule D was imposed on rents under short leases on the difference between a notional Schedule A assessment based on the rent and the existing Schedule A assessment, or, as it came to be called, an 'excess rent' assessment was raised to cover such cases. Farmers, to some extent because of their inability, or possibly disinclination, to keep accounts had been assessed on a nominal basis or on actual if less, thus enjoying the best of both worlds. Now they were placed within the ambit of Schedule D in two stages; in 1941 those who occupied land of over £300 in value were so included, and in 1942 those whose lands were over an annual value of £100.[2]

From the outset of the war, however, there had always been a measure of relief from income tax, including surtax, to any individual whose actual earned income for the current year had, owing to circumstances connected with the war, fallen substantially short of his earned income as assessed, normally on the amount of the preceding year's income. This relief, continued annually, was a specific wartime measure. But despite the need for cash, 'and cash out of current income', as Kingsley Wood put it, there were some other small legislative concessions which also acted as a lubricant to the high-geared tax machine. An allowance was given for additional travelling expenses incurred through a wartime change in circumstances to cater for employees who, through bombing, perhaps or

[1] See Appendix B.
[2] The process was completed in 1948 when all farming came under Schedule D.

direction, had further expense to bear out of net income. Since Forces' travelling was always paid for, it was only fair to extend the same consideration to lowly-paid workers especially. It was pressure from the House, too, which had induced Kingsley Wood to accept a wider definition of housekeeper allowance, and to raise the amount of the dependent relative allowance from £25 to the amount of the house-keeper allowance, £50. A further concession, originating this time in the Trade Union Congress, was the uplifting of wife's earned income allowance from £45 to £80 in 1942. This served the dual purpose of attracting married women into employment and, at most income levels which mattered, removing the obloquy of the Revenue con-niving at the offer of a premium for living in sin.

Finally, there was the general relief afforded by the Post-War Credit system which softened the blow of the reduced allowances brought in by the Finance Act 1941. This had provided that for every year of assessment during which the reductions in earned income allowance, age allowance, personal allowances and the exemption limit should be in force, the extra tax ultimately borne by any indivi-dual should be recorded annually and notified to him for eventual repayment.

It would not have been possible to cope with both the augmenta-tion of rates and numbers of taxpayers without a certain stream-lining of the administration. Collectors, for instance, in England and Wales, excluding the City of London, had only been appointed by the Board of Inland Revenue since 1931. Now, amongst other provisions for simplifying the machinery for the assessment and col-lection of tax in the Finance Act 1942, was the vesting of the right to appoint all collectors in Scotland and Northern Ireland in the Board, and in 1945, to the delight of Benson who had always advocated this step, the City of London was assimilated to the rest of Great Britain.

A further improvement in collection procedure was the institution, late in 1941, of the Tax Reserve Certificate, an idea which was bor-rowed from the United States. Most individuals, firms and com-panies whose taxation liabilities were likely to be heavy would re-serve for their payment by earmarking certain bank deposits or by purchasing Treasury Bills. The former procedure caused an alarming distortion in bank deposits early in the year when a good deal of tax was normally paid, and the latter's low rate of discount and administrative inconvenience were not attractive. There was, of course, a discount scheme in operation for Schedule D tax, but even at 2½ per cent this had never proved popular. The Tax Reserve Certificate was issued by the Bank of England in units of £25 and upwards; larger units could be divided upon payment of tax. Their maximum life was two years and, their most attractive feature, the interest which was calculated up to the time when the tax is deemed to be due, was made free of tax. The scheme worked well from the outset and successfully tapped the cash which had been reserved between accrual and liquidation of tax liability. It was the Finance Act 1942 which exempted the interest from income tax as from 1941/1942 and, incidentally, repealed as from 1942/1943 the provision allowing discount on the prepayment of tax under Schedule D.

The outstanding administrative innovation of the period again basically in collection procedure, was Pay As You Earn. The idea of paying wages and salaries net of income tax was not, of course, a new one. The Civil Service itself had always operated such a scheme, but an attempt by the Board to extend the principle to weekly wage earners had been turned down by the Courts as long ago as 1864. A similar bold experiment had been suggested in World War I but Trade Union hostility had frustrated its adoption. A variation of the deduction principle had been a scheme for the weekly payment of tax by stamps in Snowden's crisis Budget of 1931, but this was neither popular nor successful and the Board, understandably, was reluctant to promote any extension of it despite the mounting number of taxpayers netted from decreased allowances and increased wages.

The interim solution for the difficulties of collection increasingly felt by both Revenue and taxpayers was the formal grant to the Board in 1940 of 'the power to make regulations for the assessment and collection of tax chargeable under Schedule E and, in particular, for requiring employers to deduct tax so chargeable from remuneration paid to their employees and to account to the Revenue for the tax'. The new system was a curious amalgam of the old yearly and half-yearly assessment procedure and the principle of deduction of tax at source. The basis of assessment remained the same, a previous year or previous half-year basis, the ascertained liabilities being deducted from wages on a monthly or weekly basis, as paid,

This procedure was successfully introduced for 1941/1942 but there were complaints about the delays in starting the 1942 deductions, and when Kingsley Wood opened his 1942 Budget he admitted the inequity arising when, say, the Clyde shipbuilders were having the tax on their earnings in the long light summer months deducted from wages restricted by bad weather and blackout in winter. The compromise of a minimum wage was suggested before finally, the cumulative system was tested and approved, and the whole revised system was applied to the body of wage and salary earners now totalling sixteen millions from April 5, 1944.

So, although Pay As You Earn was a vital change in the mechanics of tax collection, it was not an overnight revolution, a sudden *coup de fisc*, so to speak, since it had a long and respectable lineage, stretching back some eighty years. In addition, the patchwork system of a previous year's or previous half-year's deductions from current earnings prevailed until the last eighteen months or so of the war, and it was this system which accounted largely for the massive upsurge in Schedule E receipts. Pay As You Earn, as it is now known and operated, did make a very important contribution to the battle against inflation by immediate and related deductions from wages as paid weekly or monthly. But the full weight of that contribution was perhaps delayed longer than it should have been.

The adjustment of rates and allowances, and improvements in collection, were the two well-proved methods of increasing tax yield and efficiency. A third factor was the imposition of new taxes. Income tax itself had started as a war tax; it was renewed as a national emergency tax in 1842; and when it became an accepted part of the fiscal system, additional taxes had to be imposed in times of crisis such as the Excess Profits Duty of 1914 to 1918 or the Corporation Profits Tax of the period immediately after World War I. So when, following his all-too-short period of fiscal relaxation, Chamberlain was forced to retrench, the first sign was a new tax bearing the ominous title of National Defence Contribution.

Chamberlain's idea had been to tax not profits as such, but their rate of expansion, and the rate of charge was to vary according to the percentage of growth. A minimum return of 6 per cent on capital was exempt; between 6 per cent and 10 per cent the expansion was charged at 20 per cent, with higher percentages of growth being taxed up to a maximum of $33\frac{1}{3}$ per cent. He admitted he could not expect Members to grasp it at first hearing, which was hardly sur-

K

prising as there were further complications including the preparation of capital details. It was 'our old friend, E.P.D., resurrected from the grave and given new clothes', said one M.P.

Chamberlain's motives, the raising of additional revenue and the prevention of profiteering, were impeccable, but the results were a near disaster, including a slump on the Stock Exchange, an unholy alliance between Keynes and the City and even a flash of international monetary unrest. The Opposition, with some exceptions, approved the principle of the tax, but the very day he kissed hands as Prime Minister after Baldwin's retirement, his party begged him to drop the tax, which he did provided there was an acceptable alternative with a yield of £25 millions.

This was National Defence Contribution, Mark II,[1] levied on the profits of corporate and similar bodies, from April 1, 1937. The starting point of the computation was the income tax profit. This was adjusted by adding the net annual value of premises owned and occupied for the trade, investment income not received from bodies corporate liable to N.D.C., and excess directors' remuneration where the company was director controlled. A deduction was allowed for annual charges from which tax was legally deductible, and wear-and-tear allowances for the accounting period. The resulting figure was taxed at 5 per cent, the duty being allowed as a deduction against the Case I, Schedule D assessment. The first full year of the Contribution was the promised £25 millions, less about £200,000, and the yield showed a gradual rise, apart from one trough in 1941/1942, to £33·5 millions by the end of the war.

But clearly, to use its own nomenclature, while such a tax could usefully contribute towards a slow build-up of expenditure on arms, it was not a war profits tax either in yield or intention. Nor was the abortive Armaments Profits Duty, imposed by the 1939 Finance Act, at the rate of 60 per cent on excess profits arising from armaments contracts in any armament business, which was repealed before any assessments thereto had been made. But Excess Profits Tax, based to an extent on the old Excess Profits Duty of World War I, became one of the main sources of tax revenue from 1939 to 1945. E.P.T., however, was considerably the more elaborate than its predecessor: attempts were made to legislate for all types of case leading to a much greater complexity of law and a greater rigidity of admini-

[1] It was the ancestor of the profits tax of ten years hence.

stration. The avowed aim was to make the tax not only a weapon of heavier calibre than its predecessor, but of greater accuracy also.

At 60 per cent, the projected Armaments Profits Duty rate, such a tax was penal enough; at 100 per cent the danger to the accumulation of industrial reserves was manifest, and this was the main burden of complaints against the tax even from the Labour side when towards the end of the war the need for a trade revival and competitive exports was under consideration. Its confiscatory nature was appreciated early in its life and the impact softened by such concessions as exceptional depreciation allowances for war purposes buildings and plant, the treatment of borrowed money as capital, deductions for repairs deferred owing to the war and consideration for terminal expenses. There were also favourable alterations both in the profits standards as applied to concerns dealing in wasting assets and in the minimum standard which mainly affected small companies and firms.

The most important abatement of the 100 per cent rate, however, was announced by Kingsley Wood in 1941. E.P.T. was directed primarily against taking the profit out of war: 'but it is quite another thing to tax a business in such a way that it is worse off at the end of the war than at the beginning'. 20 per cent therefore of all E.P.T. paid at 100 per cent less income tax would be repaid as a post-war refund for expenditure on reconstruction, and although the promise was made as categoric as possible it was treated at first with a good deal of scepticism and did not immediately appear on balance sheets as an actually ascertained reserve. It was only towards the very end of the war that industrialists began to realize how important these balances would prove to be in financing post-war capital expansion.

It is a fiscal axiom that high rates of tax attract both avoidance and evasion in direct proportion to the steepness of those rates. The defence of the Government against those techniques in the twenties and early thirties consisted mainly of a continuous lookout for the exploitation of loopholes in taxing statutes and promoting suitable controlling legislation as soon as possible; although, as a contemporary law officer remarked, 'The way of the man who tries to stop up the holes of the tax evader without hitting the innocent is extraordinarily difficult.' In general, avoidance had remained an art rather than become an industry.

But in the period under review there was hardly a Finance Act which did not contain, to a greater or lesser degree, anti-avoidance sections. In 1936 there was legislation against transfers of income abroad, and the twin abuses of 'one-man companies' and educational trusts. The following year saw the first of a long line of measures against 'bond-washing'. This flood of protective statute reached its height in the 1938 Budget with its proposals on settlements, the valuation of trading stock on cessation and the restrictions on transferring income abroad. The period also saw measures to cope with avoidance of estate duty as well as of income tax and surtax.

Within two years of the outbreak of war, taxation had reached unprecedented heights. But even the restraining influence of patriotism could not stifle the activities of the avoidance merchants who resented the bulk of their profits being confiscated at an immediate E.P.T. rate of 100 per cent; and anti-avoidance legislation, when it tried to get away from the correction of specific abuses and turn its attention to more general escape mechanisms, was not notably successful. For example, the E.P.T. provisions contained an early prohibition on transactions which artificially reduced profits and on the deduction of any expenses in excess of those reasonable and necessary, including remuneration. Clearly, however, a good case could almost always be made out for substantial salary increases and only the most flagrant cases could be successfully challenged. Then of course there was the notorious addition of the word 'main' before 'purpose' in dealing with avoidance transactions which had eventually to be amended by retrospective legislation.

There remained the alternative of evasion, either in a minor way through inflated, almost undetectible, expenses, through to the fraudulent omission from books of account of receipts, or the inclusion of charges not in fact incurred. The acquiring of illegal profits through black-market activities was a further inducement to concealment. It was the danger of increases in this sphere which produced the 1942 legislation which strengthened the technical powers of the Revenue against the deliberate evader.

The problems of avoidance never really became a party issue. It is true that in 1936 the Opposition did not consider the anti-avoidance legislation went far enough, while the Government, on its side, professed to find some virtue in educational trusts. It is true that the admission of the adjective 'main' was a tactical error in trying to draft the appropriate avoidance legislation, as the Opposition gleefully pointed out. But in general, although the House never showed sympathy with the out-and-out avoider, it sometimes inevitably found itself in an ambivalent position. There were frequent complaints throughout the period of difficult and apparently obscure legislation, but complex laws are unavoidable when the schemes to be neutralized were equally tortuous. On the other hand, Parliament had always set its face resolutely against any statutory powers of a general character, not merely on account of the difficulty in framing the appropriate clause but because of the ever-present fear of granting too much power to the executive.

It was never possible to arrive at any firm figures, or even any reliable estimate, of duty saved by this mass of legislation and expense of Parliamentary time; this, however, is less important than the fact that the first casualty in avoidance schemes is public trust in fiscal justice and public confidence in fiscal equity. And it was without doubt the confiscatory nature of the rates of tax levied on industry and the constant temptation to avoidance, quite apart from the erosion of old reserves and the failure to build up new, which led to the over-all mitigation proposed by the revised capital allowance system of the 1945 Income Tax Act.

But direct taxation was only one weapon in the battle for current revenue and the struggle against inflation; indirect taxation[1] played a rôle which, although not so important, and certainly not as spectacular, was equally indispensable. The rise of indirect taxation to its climax was a more gradual process than that of direct taxation. But towards the end of the war it was the only fiscal sector where expansion could still be justified both for practical and psychological reasons.

Chamberlain had not been greatly concerned with indirect taxation. His main ambition, as he so often declared, was the restoration, as soon as possible, of the salary scales and direct taxation rates and allowances existing before the savage economies forced on, and enforced by, Philip Snowden. He did, however, import this ambition into the field of indirect taxation by taking a penny a pint off beer in 1933 which accounted for five-sixths of his disposable surplus,

---

[1] Some economists object to the traditional distinction between direct and indirect taxation. Mrs U. K. Hicks, for example, does not find it 'economically meaningful'; but it was the normal and accepted terminology in the period and is readily intelligible.

although the reason was partly that, despite increases in duty, yield had fallen. His gamble was justified and the fall for which he had budgeted was modified considerably by increased consumption.

Apart from two increases in oil duty, the first of which, in 1935, was designed to level up the variation in duty between diesel oil and petrol, Chamberlain's principal victim, when indirect taxation began its slow climb under threat of war, was tea. There were two increases, each of twopence on the pound, in 1936 and 1938. These sparked off in both years the customary, almost ritualistic complaints from the Opposition, of class legislation and pressure on the poorest section of the community, and, of course, in conjunction with the decrease in beer duty, from Lady Astor. Tea duty might well be 'the plaything of every Chancellor', but the two adjustments only increased the average household's expenditure by well under two shillings annually. The fact was that Chamberlain did not feel as obliged to rectify the Snowden increases in indirect taxation, which had been of the order of £24 millions, since the cost of living was falling. In addition, it is more than likely that the stepping up of indirect taxation might have been heavy enough to justify full-scale Opposition attacks had not the general increase in consumption of dutiable subjects, reflected in the continuous rise in Customs and Excise receipts over estimates, kept rates at their comparatively modest level.

In the last Budget before the outbreak of war in 1939, indirect taxation was again called upon to take the strain. Fearing that an increase in the standard rate would act as a depressant on industry, already suffering from the new National Defence Contribution, Simon clapped two shillings further on a pound of tobacco, roughly a penny on a packet of cigarettes, 2s 4d a hundredweight on sugar, as well as ten shillings on the road fund tax, thus doubling the amount of the decrease which Chamberlain had been able to afford in 1934. These increases, however, assailed from both sides of the House as being inadequate, were admitted to be so when the sirens first sounded and there were immediate increases of a penny a pint on beer, 1s 2d on a bottle of whisky, a penny a packet on cigarettes, a penny a pound on sugar and corresponding amounts on the various classes of wines, in the second Budget of 1939.

This trend continued in 1940 when the two Budgets for that year increased the duties on wines, put a further twopence a pint on beer,

1s 9d a bottle on whisky, threepence a packet on cigarettes, and dealt also with matches, the cinema and the theatre. The primary motive was, of course, the raising of revenue. But the philosophy backing the policy was that no citizen should resent paying tax on his luxuries or his indulgences especially in time of war when the stabilization policy was all-important. There were, too, the plain economic motives that as far as tobacco was concerned, the current supply position demanded a 15 per cent reduction; and as for beer, queues when supplies arrived at public houses and its consumption of sugar and grain justified the increased contributions.

The duties were allowed to settle down in 1941, but there was a fresh round in 1942 which doubled the entertainment tax for both the cinema and the theatre, put twopence a pint on beer, 4s 8d on a bottle of whisky and sevenpence a packet on cigarettes. But when even these fierce increases came to be reviewed it was found that they had not affected consumption as much as expected. There was a final round of increases, therefore, in 1943 with the usual penny a pint on beer, 2s 4d a bottle on whisky, further duties on wines, fourpence a packet on cigarettes and amendments to entertainment tax to bring the yield to £10 millions. This resilience of Customs and Excise receipts was vital to the revenue when direct taxation had been pushed to its limits. The 'no change' Budget of 1944 was a triumphant vindication of indirect taxation, producing a massive surplus of £67 millions; and these rates remained in the pre-Armistice proposals of 1945.

The limits of indirect taxation may well have been reached also, for the results of the steady increases in rates over the years were that the duty on beer was now 7·4 pence per pint, on a bottle of whisky 18·35 shillings, on wine up to five shillings a bottle and on a packet of twenty cigarettes 1s 9d. In terms of total duty the Chancellor in 1945 could reckon on a round £400 millions from tobacco and £300 millions from alcohol.

From a fiscal point of view the two most significant features of indirect taxation during the period were, first, its remarkable and consistent buoyancy and, secondly, the fact that the Chancellors never felt the need to resort to 'frill' or 'fancy' taxes. Indeed these two features might well be labelled cause and effect, since the Revenue's best payers, tobacco and alcohol, invariably attained or exceeded expectations; but they made for a rather humdrum period, as there was no inducement to experiment. Every Chancellor is familiar with the lunatic fringe of suggestions for new taxes, and no Chancellor wants to be burdened with a 'pannier of trifles' which could well have resulted if the Revenue had adopted such proposed taxes as those on cats, bicycles, and restaurant meals, to name only three of the more reasonable but which had neither prospective yield nor administrative convenience to recommend them. Some valuable ideas in this field were, however, overlooked—notably a betting tax, the brain-child of A. P. Herbert, which could well have produced a self-policing £20 millions and which eventually found a place in the country's fiscal armoury.

But there was one outstanding innovation in the sphere of indirect taxation, parallel to the introduction of Excess Profits Tax into the field of direct taxation, namely purchase tax. This levy joined the tax structure in 1940, although its outlines had been sketched out twelve months before. It was a sort of fiscal Morton's fork in that it was designed both for raising revenue and restricting consumption, and to the extent that it succeeded in attaining the one objective, it failed in the other; fortunately, as far as Kingsley Wood was concerned, either result was equally satisfactory.

Originally it had imposed two rates of tax, but in 1942 a third rate of 66⅔ per cent was brought in which was to be applied to luxury goods; this increase was tied in with the new utility range of goods which were to be free of tax and formed part of the campaign to keep the price index stable. Further concessions to the utility range, such as furniture for bombed-out families, black-out material and certain soft furnishings, forced the rate on luxury goods to 100 per cent in 1943. From then until the end of the war the tax remained virtually unchanged.

Purchase tax was an undoubted success on both its fronts. But again, like Excess Profits Tax, its rates encouraged evasion, and, with rationing, was a powerful stimulus to black-market activities. On the whole, however, it proved its worth; it was reviewed very carefully towards the end of the war and, from the fact that Anderson did not mention purchase tax in his final 1945 Budget speech, there was clearly a tacit assumption that it was losing the label of a wartime, temporary, weapon and gaining grudging approval as a permanent fiscal measure.

There had been a certain shift in the interaction between direct and indirect taxation and the high proportion of the former to the latter which had been a Victorian fiscal canon and which in 1918 had been of the order of four to one, was, at the opening of the period, almost evenly balanced. This trend was the most usual target of general criticism by the Labour Opposition in successive Budget debates; it was an axiom of the party's fiscal policy that direct taxation should be preferred to indirect taxation. The adoption of Protection by the National Government had been a considerable factor in the levelling process, but this would, in some degree, be balanced by the poorer classes enjoying a greater amount of social services than they paid in taxation.

The increases in direct taxation, however, resulting from mounting arms expenditure, began a gradual reversal of the process, and by 1938 direct taxation was 52 per cent of total revenue. For the next four years the increases in both categories of taxation kept roughly in step, direct rising by 177 per cent and indirect by 145 per cent over 1939. From then on the proportion of direct taxation steadily rose to 63 per cent of total revenue in 1945. This widening of the gap again explains why the fiercely regressive purchase tax and the complete dependence in the latter years of the war on indirect taxation for the increased revenue needed, only roused a mainly token resistance from Labour.

Just as the staples of indirect taxation, tobacco and alcohol, by the resilience of their yield made experiments in this field unnecessary, so the titans of direct taxation, income tax and Excess Profits Tax, did the same service in their sphere. There had of course been the abortive tax on land values of 1931 which had been repealed owing to difficulties of valuation. But apart from this ill-fated piece of legislation, the Budget debates had thrown up various suggestions for the taxation of capital growth, a policy which appeared to be endorsed by the Government in 1939 but which again was quietly shelved on the grounds of administrative inconvenience, since it involved an annual computation of chargeable wealth. A true capital gains tax was never in fact proposed, and tentative ideas bordering on this conception were more often than not put forward by fiscal eccentrics whose views commanded more diversion than respect. In many ways this was a pity since a capital gains tax, although it might not have produced much in the way of current revenue, could well have been passed as a crisis measure, would not have been stigmatized as class legislation, and would certainly have proved its worth during the spate of property dealing in the fifties.

Taxation was the essence of budgetary policy, and it was taxation in all its aspects which occupied the major part of any Budget debate. But the colossal Government expenditure of the war years could not be met from current revenue; and each Chancellor's opening speech made a point of giving the proportion of the total requirements attributable to taxation and borrowing respectively, and showing, with some pride, how the contribution of the former had increased progressively over the period.

Virtually the whole of the gap between taxation and estimated requirements was met from domestic loans of all types; the Chancellors all made full allowance for and grateful acknowledgment of Lease-Lend and gifts from Colonies and Dominions, but these latter sources were balanced almost exactly by counter-expenditure met by this country in war sectors abroad.

To appropriate practically the whole of the savings of the private sector the Government employed a complete range of controls, inducements and mechanisms. In the first category were the restrictions on individual spending and industrial re-equipment, the licence system for the purchase of raw materials, and the restraints imposed by the Capital Issues Committee; in the second category were the general terms offered to the loan market. These, owing to the quiet pursuit of cheap money from 1932 onwards, were established at a fairly steady 3 per cent. In the third category were such schemes as Treasury Bills and Treasury Deposit Receipts, as well as Tax Reserve Certificates.

Not a great deal of these vital operations emerged in much detail in the course of the Budget debates. Indeed, as far as the rate of interest is concerned, the fundamental decision was a carry-over from the cheap money policy of the Chamberlain era, almost automatically. But there was a good deal of discussion in the House of the National Savings movement, where again the security offered usually was on the 3 per cent. level of yield. There was criticism from both the Treasury and Parliament of the movement's misleading propaganda and its expensive publicity and to the extent that some of its dramatic campaigns were inflated by idle money from banks, insurance companies and industry, the results were often abnormal and even discouraging to the small saver. But the day-to-day work of the movement was indispensable in providing a readily available channel for the small individual contribution: 'Wings for Victory' and similar savings spectaculars were notable more for light relief than fiscal benefit. For all that, the ordinary man was saving about a quarter of his net income as contrasted with a pre-war one-twentieth or less.

In managing the difficult and delicate economy with which the country had to support itself in the recovery period from the depression in 1938, and in the succeeding war years, there was little margin for avoidable mistakes or dramatic reversals of fundamental policy. There was a clear continuity in trends both before 1932 and after 1945. This does not mean, however, that the four Chancellors who held office between 1933 and 1945 allowed themselves to be carried along by that insidious current known as 'The Treasury View', that their Budgets clung to the traditional Victorian pattern, or that Parliament had little influence on the final shape of Finance Acts.

In some ways Chamberlain was the most predictable of the four, partly because he had been courageous enough to publicize the target he had set himself. He would continue Snowden's austerity only as long as necessary, while refusing to unbalance. Then he would give relief, first to industry by a standard rate reduction, and then to the general body of taxpayers by upraising allowances. This he had done by 1935. But in 1936, with the mounting defence expenditure, he had to balance further slight increases in allowances with a rise in standard rate and in tea duty. Further minor tax rises the following year were coupled with the unveiling of a new tax, rightly intended to hit the expansion of profits, not profits as such. The National Defence Contribution was Chamberlain's personal responsibility which he only dropped with the greatest reluctance when he became Prime Minister. If he had stayed as Chancellor he might possibly have tried to force its passing through sulky lobbies, and even have succeeded.

For he was also the strongest of the four Chancellors. He combined experience and orthodoxy, and although that mixture is not necessarily a recipe for recovery, in the crisis of confidence which was the basic trouble in the thirties, deficit budgeting could have brought back the nightmare of recession, whatever its apparent justification. His conversion schemes, reducing war interest to £200 millions in 1938 from £300 millions in 1918, and his cheap money policy were totally successful; and when the Opposition failed to find a constructive economic policy, it is unfair to criticize Chamberlain for pursuing a line which was showing at least qualified results.

Simon, his successor, had no specialized knowledge of national finance. His assets were a brilliant legal brain and a temperament well suited to working within the limits of hard financial facts and nice legalistic considerations. His first task was to find an alternative to Chamberlain's original National Defence Contribution, which he did with an impressive display of loyalty and debating ability; and his pre-1939 Budgets were in effect a brave attempt to contain expenditure appropriate to wartime inside the framework of tax increases more relevant to peace.

His wartime Budgets were criticized as being designed to ensure that the country had enough money left to pay indemnities to the victors—a remark more notable for malice than accuracy. Simon's tenure of office, in the bewildering atmosphere of the phony war, saw a further drive against avoidance, legislation to assess excess rents, the beginning of Excess Profits Tax and the proposal of purchase tax. He was himself impatient of the slow build-up to a war economy, and although it was not his nature to show independence or initiative, he laid the foundations of a fiscal system on which Kingsley Wood's success was firmly based.

But even when an accelerated war effort was needed under the twin stimuli of isolation and danger, Kingsley Wood's first Budget, despite 100 per cent Excess Profits Tax and a standard rate of 8s 6d, was still not regarded as confiscatory enough, especially in the lower-wage sector. 1941, however, was the watershed year when the Budget could at last be seen to be performing its correct dual function of raising the taxation required and restricting purchasing power. The consolidating Budget, as Kingsley Wood termed it, was a logical extension of the developing fiscal measures which had preceded it; in addition the whole economic situation was illuminated by the simultaneous publication of the first White Paper on national income and expenditure.

It is impossible to divorce the practice of the Kingsley Wood régime from the theories of Keynes, not as much in relation to particular suggestions such as post-war refund which was a success for industry and a comparative failure for the individual, as in the recasting of Budget mathematics to highlight the gap. In this context the Budget of 1942 is as significant as that of 1941, for in the battle to restrict consumption and prevent inflation the stress in the former was on direct taxation, and in the latter on indirect— the motive for using these contrasting techniques was identical.

Kingsley Wood was one of the few Chancellors who paid tribute to his financial advisers by name. He owed them a great deal; but had there not been, beneath his own prim exterior and common-place phraseology, a ruthless mind and a lawyer's capacity for sifting and weighing evidence, the fiscal revolution which both fostered could not have taken place, with infinite damage to the war effort. In some ways the weakest of the Chancellors, he was, without doubt, the most obviously successful.

Anderson, the fourth of the Chancellors, had an unenviable task. He was not a professional politician and functioned better as a co-ordinator and go-between than a ministerial head. He disliked read-ing the mass of papers which Chamberlain, for instance, had revel-led in, but this detachment and professionalism had one great ad-vantage: he never treated the Budget as a measure from which party capital could or should be made; and this gained him the respect both of the Treasury and of the House, although he was never really at home there.

His greatest achievement was to see beyond the current revenue-raising difficulties, which were twofold; the switch from direct taxa-tion, commonly assumed to have reached its limit, to indirect taxa-tion and the scaling down of subsidies, to the essence of the problem, namely the need for selective encouragement to industry in general and export industry in particular. This was the origin of the revised capital allowance scheme which tackled high rates of taxation from the standpoint of economic incentive by granting increased relief for modernization and re-equipment.

The Budgets were reflections of the Chancellors who opened them. Chamberlain's were orthodox profit and loss accounts, the product of an accountant-politician. Simon's were cast in the conventional mould but were drafted by a lawyer who had accepted a brief for their defence. Kingsley Wood altered and simplified the form of presentation entirely, a process continued and perfected by Anderson in, for instance, the Budget of 1944, where the statistics occupied a comparatively short space in the introductory speech.

But however dramatic the changes in taxation and the method of its presentation, Parliament continued to play its traditional rôle of watchdog, critic and keeper of the national conscience. It was Parliamentary pressure which forced the withdrawal of Chamberlain's National Defence Contribution. It was Parliament's conception of fiscal morality which supported the long line of anti-avoidance sections, although the inexorable pattern of avoidance schemes, nullified by anti-avoidance legislation followed by further refinements of avoidance, continued on. Yet Parliament was flexible enough to entertain second thoughts, notably over Excess Profits Tax and anti-avoidance proposals where it actually sanctioned retrospective legislation. But in general it remained the guardian of the principles behind the legislation that tax law should be specific so that the executive would not be given general powers and that individual privacy should be respected—it was fear of trespassing on this tradition which accounted for much of the original hostility to Pay As You Earn. Members did complain that when the Chancellor produces a Budget, it is set, and a minority on Committee can do practically nothing more to it. But this was far from true: Parliamentary criticisms were taken very seriously and often, although admittedly in a possibly modified form, found their way eventually into the statute book. Criticisms could be on a party basis even during the coalition period, but equally often they had the merit of strict impartiality.

In considering the over-all result of the fiscal legislation from 1932 to 1945 the broad strands are not difficult to detect. There was the extension of income tax far down the social scale giving it a far greater social impact, and its mounting complexity caused by equitable considerations. There was the increase in avoidance due to the high rates of direct and indirect taxation, the effect of the former being to stimulate interest in and eventually to create sustained pressure for the revision of the capital allowance system. There was the advent of Pay As You Earn which would make any future radical change of tax rates or mechanisms subject to grave administrative difficulties. There was the failure to take advantage of an opportunity of introducing a capital gains tax or a betting levy. And over-all there was the incalculable and ever-present danger of disincentive both for the individual and industry, modified in this period by the conflicting claims of patriotism.

Each generation is convinced that its trials and difficulties are unprecedented, and one of the few constants in history is the recurrent crisis. The economic crisis of 1932 to 1939, and the military crisis of 1939 to 1945 were all-pervasive in their effects. The importance of the Budget debates is to see how far the Chancellor and his advisers read the economic auguries aright and how far the average Member understood the basic economic trends of the period—for both are a guide to the thinking of the common man upon whose consent rests finally the validity of a fiscal policy and the steady inflow of revenue. The problem of communication increased as legislation became more complicated; but in wartime the issues are clear and unmistakable, so that the philosophy of taxation resolves itself into an inspired pragmatism. In peace the issues tend to be blurred by party prejudices and theoretical experiments. It is in the nature of taxation that its victories are more easily achieved in war than in peace.

APPENDIX A

Rates of Income Tax and Allowances 1932/1933–1944/1945

Year	S.R.	R.R. On first	R.R. at	E.I.R. Fraction	E.I.R. Max.	A.A.	W.E.I.R. (Max.)	Exempt	P.A. A.S.	P.A. A.M.	C.A. First	C.A. Others	H.K.	D.R.	L.A.
1932/3	5s 0d	175	2s 6d	$\frac{1}{5}$	300	$\frac{1}{5}$	45	100	100	150	50	40	50	25	Per S.32 F.A. 1918
1933/4	5s 0d	175	2s 6d	$\frac{1}{5}$	300	$\frac{1}{5}$	45	100	100	150	50	40	50	25	,,
1934/5	4s 6d	175	2s 3d	$\frac{1}{5}$	300	$\frac{1}{5}$	45	100	100	150	50	40	50	25	,,
1935/6	4s 6d	135	1s 6d	$\frac{1}{5}$	300	$\frac{1}{5}$	45	125	100	170	50	50	50	25	,,
1936/7	4s 9d	135	1s 7d	$\frac{1}{5}$	300	$\frac{1}{5}$	45	125	100	180	60	60	50	25	,,
1937/8	5s 0d	135	1s 8d	$\frac{1}{5}$	300	$\frac{1}{5}$	45	125	100	180	60	60	50	25	,,
1938/9	5s 6d	135	1s 8d	$\frac{1}{5}$	300	$\frac{1}{5}$	45	125	100	180	60	60	50	25	,,
1939/40	7s 0d	135	2s 4d	$\frac{1}{5}$	300	$\frac{1}{5}$	45	125	100	180	60	60	50	25	,,
1940/41	8s 6d	165	5s 0d	$\frac{1}{6}$	250	$\frac{1}{6}$	45	120	100	170	50	50	50	25	,,
1941/42	10s 0d	165	6s 6d	$\frac{1}{10}$	150	$\frac{1}{10}$	80	110	80	140	50	50	50	25	,,
1942/43	10s 0d	165	6s 6d	$\frac{1}{10}$	150	$\frac{1}{10}$	80	110	80	140	50	50	50	25	,,
1943/4	10s 0d	165	6s 6d	$\frac{1}{10}$	150	$\frac{1}{10}$	80	110	80	140	50	50	50	50	,,
1944/5	10s 0d	165	6s 6d	$\frac{1}{10}$	150	$\frac{1}{10}$	80	110	80	140	50	50	50	50	,,

APPENDIX B

Wartime Rates of Surtax

Income Range	On the Last	Rate	Total S.T. payable on	
£	£		£	£
2,001–2,500	500	2s 0d	2,500	50
2,501–3,000	500	2s 3d	3,000	106 5
3,001–4,000	1,000	3s 3d	4,000	268 15
4,001–5,000	1,000	4s 3d	2,000	481 5
5,001–6,000	1,000	5s 0d	6,000	731 5
6,001–8,000	2,000	5s 9d	8,000	1,306 5
8,001–10,000	2,000	7s 0d	10,000	2,006 5
10,001–15,000	5,000	8s 3d	15,000	4,068 15
15,001–20,000	5,000	9s 0d	20,000	6,318 15
20,001 onwards	—	9s 6d	—	—

APPENDIX C

Summary of Expenditure and Revenue

Year	£ millions estimated expenditure	£ millions estimated Revenue	£ millions Yield of Tax Changes	Notes
1933	697	713	−14[1]	[1] Mainly beer duty
1934	698	727	−24[2]	[2] Reduction in Standard Rate
1935	730	736[3]	−10	[3] Excluding Road Fund surplus
1936	798	793[4]	16	[4]Excluding Road Fund surplus
1937	863	848	15	Introduction of N.D.C.
1938	944	914	30	
1939 (i)	942	918	24	
1939 (ii)	1,993[5]	882	227	[5] Including £512 millions Defence Loans Act
1940 (i)	2,667	1,133	128	
1940 (ii)	3,467[6]	1,234	239	[6] The Vote of Credit was increased by £800 million
1941	4,207	1,636	252	
1942	5,286	2,469	146	
1943	5,756	2,805	103	
1944	5,937	3,098	−8	
1945	5,565	3,265	−11	

APPENDIX D

Indirect Taxation

Year	Beer	Tobacco	(i) *Wine and* (ii) *Spirits*	Sugar	Oil	*Purchase* Tax	Miscellaneous
1933	—1d per pint		6s on British wines		+1d per gallon		Heavy goods vehicles
1934							—5s per h.p. on cars
1935					+7d per gallon		—6d on entertainment tax
1936							2d per lb on tea
1937							
1938					To bring in £5 million		2d per lb on tea
1939 (i)		2s per lb		2s 4d per cwt			On cars 10s per h.p.
1939 (ii)	+1d per pint	2s per lb	(i) 8d to 1s 4d per bott. (ii) 1s 2d per bott.	9s 4d per cwt			
1940 (i)	+1d per pint	4s per lb	(ii) 1s 9d per bott.				G.P.O. charges up Matches and lighters
1940 (ii)	+1d per pint	2s per lb	(i) 4d to 8d per bott.			Rates at 16·⅔% & 33%	Increases in entertainment tax
1941							Repeal of medicine stamp duty
1942	2d per pint	10s per lb	(i) 1s to 2s per bott. (ii) 4s 8d per bott.			Some rates now 66·⅔%	Doubling of entertainment Tax
1943	1d per pint	6s per lb	(i) 6d to 1s per bott. (ii) 2s 4d per bott.			Some rates now 100%	Increase in entertainment tax
1944	Minor changes only						
1945	Minor changes only						

Bibliography

AMERY, L. S., *My Political Life* Vol. III, Hutchinson, London, 1955.

ARNDT, H. W., *Economic Lessons of the Nineteen Thirties*, Cass, London, 1963.

BEER, S. H., *Treasury Control*, Oxford, London, 1956.

CALDER, A., *The People's War*, Cape, London, 1969.

ELLETSON, D. H., *The Chamberlains*, Murray, London, 1966.

FEILING, G. K., *A History of England*, Macmillan, London, 1950.

FEILING, G. K., *Neville Chamberlain*, Macmillan, London, 1946.

GRIFFITH, W., *A Hundred Years: the Board of Inland Revenue 1849–1949*, Somerset House, London, 1949.

HARROD, R. F., *John Maynard Keynes*, Macmillan, London, 1951.

HARROD, R. F., *The British Economy*, McGraw Hill, London, 1963.

HICKS, J. R., HICKS, U. K. & ROSTAS, L., *The Taxation of War Wealth*, Clarendon, Oxford, 1942.

HICKS, U. K., *The Finance of British Government 1920–1936*, O.U.P., London, 1938.

HICKS, U. K., *British Public Finance*, O.U.P., London, 1958.

KEYNES, J. M., *How to Pay for the War*, Macmillan, London, 1940.

MACLEOD, I., *Neville Chamberlain*, Muller, London, 1961.

MARTIN, K., *Editor*, Hutchinson, London, 1968.

MORTON, W. A., *British Finance 1930–1940*, University of Wisconsin Press, London, 1943.

MOULT, F. G., *The Economic Consequences of E.P.T.*, Regent Press, London, 1942.

MOWAT, C. L., *Britain Between the Wars*, Methuen, London, 1955.

MUGGERIDGE, M., *The Thirties*, Collins, London, 1940.

PREST, A. R., *Public Finance*, Weidenfeld & Nicolson, London, 1967.

POLLARD, S., *The Development of the British Economy*, Arnold, London, 1962.

RADICE, E. A., *Savings in Great Britain*, Clarendon, Oxford, 1939.

RICHARDSON, H. W., *Economic Recovery in Britain 1932–1939*, Weidenfeld & Nicolson, London, 1967.

SABINE, B. E. V., *History of Income Tax*, Allen & Unwin, London, 1966.

SAYERS, R. S., *Financial Policy 1939–1945*, H.S.W.W., London, 1956.

SEAMAN, L. C. B., *Post-Victorian Britain*, Methuen, London, 1966.

SIMON, VISCOUNT, *Retrospect*, Hutchinson, London, 1952.

STONE, R. AND MEADE, J. E., *National Income and Expenditure*, Bowes and Bowes, London, 1944.

TAYLOR, A. J. P., *English History 1914–1945*, Clarendon, Oxford, 1965.

THOMSON, D., *England in the Twentieth Century*, Cape, London, 1962.

TITMUSS, R. M., *Income Distribution & Social Change*, Allen & Unwin, London, 1962.

WHEELER-BENNETT, SIR J. W., *John Anderson*, Macmillan, London, 1962.

WILLIAMS, A., *Public Finance and Budgetary Policy*, Allen & Unwin, London, 1962.

WISEMAN, J. and PEACOCK, A. T., *The Growth of Public Expenditure in the U.K.*, Oxford, London, 1961.

This bibliography is by no means exhaustive. There may be twice as many books from which a half-remembered turn of phrase or the stimulus of an idea have been incorporated but which have not been specifically mentioned. This is always the way with contemporary or near-contemporary history and it is hoped this general acknowledgment will be some apology to anyone the title of whose work is missing.

There are four authors who should be mentioned specifically, H. W. Richardson whose research on the period 1932–39 is indispensable, R. S. Sayers whose financial judgments are an infallible guide through the 1939–45 maze, A. J. P. Taylor, for his illuminating general opinions and S. Pollard for his equally helpful economic comments.

ORIGINAL SOURCES

Government Publications

Hansard: Budget Debates, etc.
Reports of the Commissioners of Inland Revenue from 1933 to 1945.
The Income Tax and Finance Acts from 1933 to 1945.
The Report of the Income Tax Codification Committee (Cmnd. 5131).
The Report of the Tucker Committee (Cmnd. 8189).
The First and Second Radcliffe Committees Reports (Cmnd. 8761, 9105, 9474).
(These last two Reports are, of course, outside the period but include significant historical surveys).

Newspapers

The daily newspapers mainly quoted have been *The Times* and the *Manchester Guardian*. Others have been used, but mainly for background. The *Financial Times* has been an invaluable source of reference.

Political Periodicals

The *Economist* is the obvious first choice for authoritative comment and the occasional fiscal hobby-horse. The *New Statesman* and the *Spectator* have provided useful and stimulating counterweights.

Technical Periodicals

The three on which reliance has mostly been placed are the *Accountant, Taxation,* and the *British Tax Review.* Each one is invariably accurate, clear and independent. Some articles of the last-named are more theoretical and academic than those of the first two which are naturally more practical. All three, however, have a markedly professional pride and expertise.

Index

L

NOTE: To prevent the index from being overloaded, speakers who are only mentioned once and side-events mentioned merely for historical continuity have not been referenced.

GEORGE ALLEN & UNWIN LTD

Head office:
40 Museum Street, London, W.C.1
Telephone: 01-405 8577

Sales, Distribution and Accounts Departments
Park Lane, Hemel Hempstead, Herts.
Telephone: 0442 3244

Athens: 7 Stadiou Street, Athens 125
Auckland: P.O. Box 36013, Northcote, Auckland 9
Barbados: P.O. Box 222, Bridgetown
Beirut: Deeb Building, Jeanne d'Arc Street
Bombay: 103/5 Fort Street, Bombay 1
Calcutta: 285J Bepin Behari Ganguli Street, Calcutta 12
South Africa: P.O. Box 2314 Joubert Park, Johannesburg
Dacca: Alico Building, 18 Motljheel, Dacca 2
Delhi: 1/18B Asaf Ali Road, New Delhi 1
Hong Kong: 105 Wing on Mansion, 26 Hankow Road, Kowloon
Ibadan: P.O. Box 62
Karachi: Karachi Chambers, McLeod Road
Lahore: 22 Falettis' Hotel, Egerton Road
Madras: 2/18 Mount Road, Madras 2
Manila: P.O. Box 157, Quezon City D-502
Mexico: Liberia Britanica, S.A. Separio Rendon 125 Mexico 4DF
Nairobi: P.O. Box 30583
Rio de Janeiro: Caixa Postal 2537-Zc-00
Singapore: 36c Prinsep Street, Singapore 7
Sydney, N.S.W.: Bradbury House, 55 York Street
Tokyo: C.P.O. Box 1728, Tokyo 100-91
Toronto: 145 Adelaide Street West, Toronto 1

Export Performance and the Pressure of Demand
A Study of Firms
R. A. COOPER, K. HARTLEY, C. R. M. HARVEY

Export Performance and the Pressure of Demand arose out of an interest in the hypothesis that high or rising home demand is in some way 'bad' for exports and that low or falling home demand is 'good'. The validity of this hypothesis has some important implications for government economic policy in relation to the United Kingdom balance of payments. For it suggests that government deflationary measures applied at a time of boom will benefit the balance of payments not only by reducing imports but also by improving firms' export performances.

The present pilot study covers a fairly small number of industries and is based upon statistical data from firms and interviews with senior management. It gives, for the first time, an indication of the wide differences between firms and between industries in the way their exports and export policies respond to varying home market situations, and it points to the factors which really affect the behaviour of different firms, in this export field. As usual, the close-up picture shows that the influences involved are far more complex than overall generalizations have suggested.

The industries studied are the U.K. pottery industry, the motor-cycle and pedal cycle industries, the office machinery manufacturers and the manufacturers of domestic electrical appliances.

Public Finance and Budgetary Policy
ALAN WILLIAMS

This is a book which will appeal to all who are interested in the principles underlying modern budgetary policy. Although intended primarily for second and third year undergraduates, it is equally accessible to anyone with an elementary knowledge of the methods of economic analysis. It is a careful exposition of modern ideas not only on the traditional subject matter of courses on public finance, but also on their relevance to, and implications for, the major issues of controversy in post-war economic policy.

The author has integrated into one coherent analytical framework the many important contributions to our knowledge of these matters that have been made in recent years, hitherto available only in articles scattered through the journals. This synthesis itself leads to a new appreciation of the ramifications of budgetary policy, and makes possible a more sophisticated and discriminating appraisal of its effectiveness.